Alexander Boyd

THE SOVIET AIR FORCE

SINCE 1918

STEIN AND DAY / *Publishers* / New York

Dedicated to my father

First published in the United States of America, 1977
Copyright © 1977 by Alexander Boyd
All rights reserved
Printed in the United States of America
Stein and Day/*Publishers*/Scarborough House,
Briarcliff Manor, N.Y. 10510

Library of Congress Cataloging in Publication Data
Boyd, Alexander, 1936-
    The Soviet Air Force since 1918.

    Bibliography
    1. Russia (1923-   U.S.R.R.).   Voenno-
Vozdushnye Sily—History.   I. Title.
UG635.R9B68   358.4'00947   76-56690
ISBN 0-8128-2242-0

Contents

Introduction		ix
Foreword		xiii
1	The Birth of an Air Force	1
2	Commanders of the Winged Army	18
3	Higher! Faster! Further!	35
4	The Fortunes of Soviet Air Strategy	55
5	Stalin's Falcons	74
6	The Falcons Culled	88
7	Barbarossa	108
8	The Air Battle for Moscow	127
9	The New Command	140
10	Directive No. 41	155
11	The Falcons Swarm	167
12	Factories at War	187
13	The Day of the MiG-15	205
14	Continuity & Change in the Soviet Air Forces	218

15	The Soviet Air Forces in the Seventies	231
	Glossary of Abbreviations	239
	Bibliography	246
	Index of Names	254

Maps

1)	The Red Air Force in 1941: Production, Training & Evacuation	125
2)	The Soviet Air Armies: Command Histories & Disposition in October 1943	153
3)	The Soviet Air Force Today: Production & Training Centres	236

Diagrams

a)	Army Composite Air Division — 1940	106
b)	Military District Air Command Structure 1940-41	107
c)	The *Shturmovik* Regiment — late 1941	126
d)	The Soviet Air Command Structure c. 1943	154
e)	Structure of a Soviet Air Army c. 1943	185
f)	The Headquarters Staff of the Army Air Forces c. 1944	186
g)	Layout of Typical Tactical Air Force (FA) Fighter Division	230
h)	The Headquarters Staff of the Soviet Army Air Forces — 1976	237

Introduction

As a contribution to the study of the military establishment of the USSR, this historical survey of the Soviet Air Force draws upon a wide range of material and reference accumulated over the past twenty years by an author who has thereby had access to sources now extremely difficult or impossible to obtain. It was written in the belief that while a considerable body of literature devoted to the Soviet Army exists — notably in Prof. John Erickson's monumental studies — the Air Force has received comparatively little serious attention since the appearance of Asher Lee's 'The Soviet Air Force' in 1950 and the subsequent 'Soviet Air & Rocket Forces' to which he contributed and which he edited in 1958.

The Soviet Air Force has certainly not diminished as a threat over the past two decades and, while its strategic bombers have suffered fluctuating fortunes in their rivalry with the ICBMs of the Strategic Rocket Forces and may only now be receiving renewed attention in the councils of the Kremlin, there can be no doubt that its fundamental role of supporting the Soviet Army in the field has been progressively examined and perfected and that its new role in backing the global presence of the Soviet Navy is being vigorously developed. Over recent years the Soviet Tactical Air Force has been rearming at alarming speed and taking a major part in Warsaw Pact exercises and manoeuvres. The first Soviet aircraft carriers carrying ASW helicopters and STOL fighters are a logical step in the USSR's determination to break free of the Baltic and Black Seas, and NATO naval exercises are now accustomed to the shadowing wings of Soviet ELINT (Electronic Intelligence) aircraft whose bomber counterparts are armed with increasingly efficient anti-shipping missiles. Clearly, the West ignores an awareness of the structure, background and nature of such a potential air adversary at its peril.

In common with any other book on the *Vooruzhyonnye sily SSSR* or Armed Forces of the USSR, this study can only represent the latest state of knowledge. We are reliant almost entirely on what the Russians choose to disclose about themselves and where such disclosures are disparate as they often are or, as again occurs only too frequently, tantalisingly incomplete, an author is responsible for sifting the information he has and for advancing conclusions justifiable in the light of data he accepts as most likely to be accurate. The author of the present book cannot evade such a responsibility and he must, in addition, admit to its effect on the balance of his study since the Russians, irritatingly but understandably, are more inclined to be communicative about their air power and air technology up to 1945 than since. Moreover, as the work was conceived as a history rather than a portrayal of the Soviet Air Force today, it was seen as essential to treat the emergence of Soviet air power in the nineteen-twenties, its rapid growth in the thirties, the effects upon it of Stalin's sweeping purges and its performance in battle against the *Luftwaffe*. It is concerned first and foremost with people and policies and the impact upon them of technological, doctrinal and political change and makes no endeavour to provide comprehensive details of Soviet combat aircraft — there are, in any case, a number of books easily available to the general reader in which this has been accomplished very adequately.

Aircraft are only introduced here for their place in the evolution of Soviet air power, their part in the life and death of air doctrines and their success or failure in maintaining operational and technical impetus. It was far more relevant to this study to give some idea of the contributions to the making of the Red Air Force by such men as Yakov Alksnis and Vasili Khripin who were for many years after their liquidation by Stalin 'unpersons' and about whom biographical information is still scant and uncollated. I have also drawn on the recently more copious and candid memoirs of participants in the Spanish Civil War to assess the repercussions of Soviet air experience there on the Red Air Force as a whole, and brought together and made available in English for the first time new material which sheds light on the havoc wrought by Stalin's 'Great Terror' on the Red Air Force and the Soviet aircraft industry. If there are still gaps in our knowledge — even of this relatively well documented era — the reader may perhaps console himself with the thought that the author no less than he has asked the questions posed by these omissions and would be only too ready to answer them if he could.

Nor is any excuse offered for the amount of space devoted to the Soviet-German War of 1941-45 — the *Velikaya Otechestvennaya Voina*' or 'Great Patriotic War'. Historically, this is the most important conflict in which the Soviet Air Forces have been engaged and although the official *Sovetskie voenno-vozdushnye sily v Velikoi Otechestvennoi Voine* — the 'Soviet Air Forces in the Great Patriotic War' — published by the Soviet Ministry of Defence in 1968 should present under the terms of its title a full and detailed account, it is in fact a drab, stilted and disappointing work with glaring omissions, highly 'political' in tone and entirely lacking the colour and candour to be found in the memoirs of such key participants as Krasovski, Vershinin and Rudenko and the detailed treatments of major air operations afforded by Fyodorov's 'Aviation in the Battle for Moscow', Timokhovich's 'Soviet Aviation in the Battle of Kursk' or the chronicles of the individual air armies. Another fascinating, and I believe a valuable, dimension resides in the detailed studies of their Soviet air opponent made by high-ranking *Luftwaffe* officers on behalf of the United States Air Force Historical Division, since for four eventful years the *Luftwaffe* was in a unique position to view the Red Air Force on intimate if not always dispassionate terms as it went from overwhelming victory to demoralising disintegration. The Soviet aircraft industry during the Great Patriotic War has been given a chapter to itself and, while this may appear over-indulgent in a survey on this scale, it is done with the conviction that a knowledge of the conditions and terms under which it functioned is crucial to our proper understanding of the nature and effectiveness of the Red Air Force it supplied.

Subsequent chapters deal with the great leap forward in the immediate post-war years culminating in the legendary MiG-15 of the Korean War, the debt to German, United States and British aviation technology and the fortunes of the various component air forces and their commands under Stalin and Khrushchov. An examination of the changing equipment and potential of the Tactical, Long-Range, Air Defence and Naval Air Forces and of the policies underlying post-war military aircraft design and production concludes with a postscript on the Soviet Air Force today and in the near future.

The development of the Soviet Strategic Missile Forces, the nurturing of the post-war satellite air forces and the growing presence of Soviet combat aircraft in the world since 1954 when the USSR first offered the MiG-15 for sale to 'friendly' countries would make in themselves fascinating and rewarding studies although they fall outside the confines of the present book.

Lastly, the author would like to acknowledge his great debt to Miss Jean Alexander who has, with unstinting generosity, made otherwise unobtainable material available, and his grateful thanks to Mr. Alexander Vanags-Baginskis for his advice and perceptively constructive observations on drafts of the earlier chapters. His thanks must go as well to the many others who have encouraged or assisted the preparation of this book. As always, the author shoulders entire responsibility for the selection and interpretation of the material supplied to him.

Terminology and Transliteration

A number of Russian terms, for example *zveno* (plural *zven'ya*) and *shturmovik*, have been retained in the text after an initial explanation since their replacement by any arbitrary term in translation would tend to obscure rather than clarify their specific significance. German designations have been used with reference to the *Luftwaffe* where the possibility of confusion with similarly titled Russian air formations was likely to occur.

The transliteration from Cyrillic to Latin characters has followed the generally accepted forms with the following exceptions: Russian E has been transliterated into English as phonetically correct 'Ye' where it begins a word, and Russian Ё as phonetically correct 'Yo'.

Foreword

Officially the Soviet air force traces its origins to a decision of the Bolshevik government, taken on 10 November, 1917 and a mere three days after the seizure of power itself, to set up a Bureau of Commissars of Aviation and Aeronautics (*Byuro komissarov aviatsii i vozdukhoplavaniya*), though the Russian air arm as such has an appreciably longer history.* Within the space of some two months this agency had managed to organise six 'Socialist aviation detachments': I. Ya. Ivanov set up and took command of the '1st Socialist Aviation Detachment', utilising the aeroplanes of what had been the Imperial Army's 12th Army Aviation Detachment. The '2nd Socialist Aviation Detachment' was also formed from the same park, with both detachments playing a part in the early defence of Petrograd. The Imperial legacy, made up of over 1,000 aircraft with almost 600 fit for front-line service, was by no means negligible: indeed, as Mr. Boyd points out, the immediate responsibility of the successor to the Aviation Bureau — the All-Russian Board for the Administration of the Republic's Air Fleet (*Vserossiiskaya Kollegiya po Upravleniyu Vozdushnym Flotom Respubliki*), directed by the pilot and aeronautical engineer K.V. Akashev — was to conserve and reorganise this Imperial force rather than to build an air force in the accepted sense. In September, 1918 the Red Air Fleet (*Krasny Voenno-vozdushny Flot*) mustered 266 aircraft in front-line aviation groups and detachments, with a further 59 damaged or unrepaired machines to hand; the central stores and reserves held 169 aircraft, all in flying condition. These forces came under the operational control of their own Field Administration (*Polevoe Upravlenie*), which came to have its own acronym, *Aviadarm* (*Aviatsiya deistvuyushchei armii*),

---

*See David R. Jones, 'The Birth of the Russian Air Weapon 1909-1914', *Aerospace Historian*, September 1974, pp. 169-171. Also Heinz J. Nowarra and G.R. Duval, *Russian Civil and Military Aircraft 1884-1969*, London 1971 (Fountain Press), pp. 13-32.

as an air operations directorate. Among the more successful strikes carried out by Red air units were those mounted with the astonishing four-engined 'Il'ya Muromets' heavy bombers, the first of its kind in the world and designed by Igor Sikorski, who went on to make an outstanding contribution to the aviation industry in the United States. The 'I.M.' as it was known (and less reverently as 'the flying tramcar' to the factory workers) had a wing-span of 113 feet, a length of 67 feet and with its four 100 h.p. engines* could carry a bomb-load in the order of 3,000 lbs.

Even allowing for the precociousness and brilliant ingenuity of the 'I.M.'s, it seems to be a far cry from the days of hurriedly improvised Red 'Socialist aviation detachments' and the strenuous efforts of *Aviadarm*, the straitened circumstances of the 1920s, the excitements and innovations of the 1930s followed by that ghastly martyrdom inflicted by the *Luftwaffe* in the early days of the 'Great Patriotic War' and the agonising Soviet struggle for recovery in the air and eventual mastery, to the post-war days of advanced jet fighters such as the MiG-15 and so the massive accretion of all types of air strength and capability. The scale of this effort received dramatic illustration recently when Air Chief Marshal Sir Andrew Humphrey (then Chief of the Air Staff, Royal Air Force and now Chief of the Defence Staff) pointed to the annual rate of production of military aircraft in the Soviet Union — no less than 1,800 (more than half of which are high-performance combat machines) and a figure which would suffice to replace the entire front-line strength of the Royal Air Force *once every six months*. The new Soviet strategic bomber, code-named *Backfire*** and sometimes identified as the Tu-26, with its variable-geometry (VG) configuration combines supersonic performance with intercontinental range. As such, and since it is already in squadron service with Soviet Air Force, it has obtruded dramatically on the course of the second stage of the strategic arms limitation talks (SALT-2) between the United States and the Soviet Union. Nor is there much comfort to be derived from the Soviet disclaimer that the *Backfire* is not a true intercontinental bomber lacking the range to make the full round-trip on a strike mission against the United States: this still

---

*'I.M.' Type A utilised French Salmson radial engines developing 150 hp, but these were discarded in favour of the thoroughly reliable Argus 100 hp water-cooled engines driving tractor propellers. On June 17, 1914 a flight was made with two 132 hp engines outboard and two 140 hp engines inboard.

**This, like *Fencer*, *Flogger* and *Foxbat*, is a NATO code-name.

makes the *Backfire* a formidable weapon for use in any of the reaches of the Eurasian land mass, including western Europe and the United Kingdom. An enhanced air threat to the United Kingdom and its air space is also presented by the latest Su-19 (*Fencer-A*) fighter optimised for a long-range interdiction role and carrying an offensive load comparable to modern western aircraft. Improved air-to-air missiles, a variety of air-to-surface missiles and newer cluster and retarded bombs also contribute to increasing the effectiveness of each tactical air sortie. Finally, the 'MiG family' has been enlarged with the introduction of the MiG-23 (*Flogger*) and the MiG-25 (*Foxbat*), though some of the mysteries of the latter aircraft are being laid bare after Lieutenant Belenko landed his *Foxbat* No. 31* at Hakodate air base in Japan.

There is a certain irony in the fact that while the Soviet naval build-up has dominated the headlines — if headlines mean anything at all — the expansion of Soviet air power has slipped by largely unnoticed. Nor is that merely some subjective impression. Recent American re-appraisals of Soviet military expenditure over the past five years or so tend to confirm the fact that the greatest single beneficiary from this much increased expenditure has been the Soviet air force; while the Soviet Navy received an apportionment which remained constant at 18% (in terms of total military expenditure), the Soviet Air Force gained by 3% between 1970-75, its share rising from 17% to 20%. The implications reach far and wide: not only has there been a visible expansion in the means to conduct deep-ranging offensive air operations but the rather more mundane topic of airlift capability commands close attention, since the big new transports — which also fly in their civilian guise with *Aeroflot* — facilitate a speedy build-up in the European theatre and also provide support for air assault throughout the depth of NATO's positions in Europe.

Even on this brief demonstration there is an urgent need to understand the evolution and organisation of the Soviet air force and Soviet concepts of air power. Mr. Boyd's historical survey of the Soviet air force, therefore, could not be more timely. No one can seriously argue that we are blessed with up-to-date, authoritative and

---

*The MiG-25 evidently uses non-standard fuel. The outside of the aircraft is covered with a heat-resistant steel alloy, mainly on the leading edges of the wings and on the forward sections of the fuselage, but its considerable weight impedes acceleration and the highest figure on the Mach meter is 2.8, followed by red danger marks. Heat caused by air resistance reaches 117 degrees Centigrade at 30,000 feet, rising to 334 degrees at speeds higher than Mach 2, and fuel consumption is high. Obviously much more information is to be awaited on this aircraft.

reliable monographic studies of the Soviet air force, either from Soviet or non-Soviet sources. The author makes a very proper acknowledgement of the contribution of the earlier works of Wing Commander Asher Lee, as well as the many excellent handbooks on Soviet aircraft such as Miss Jean Alexander's *Russian Aircraft since 1940* or *The Observer's Soviet Aircraft Directory* compiled by William Green and Gordon Swanborough. Professional aviation journals throughout the world also make a most impressive contribution in this field. All this excellence notwithstanding, it cannot amount to a sustained analysis of Soviet military aviation and the development of air power. What is surprising here, and Mr. Boyd rightly underlines the fact, is the paucity of good Soviet studies; perhaps the most undistinguished example was the history of the Soviet air force during the Great Patriotic War, *Sovetskie Voenno-vozdushnye sily v Velikoi Otechestvennoi voine 1941-1945 gg.*, produced under the general editorship of Air Marshal S.I. Rudenko, in all a work markedly short on fact, analysis and truth. Published in the same year (1968), *Aviatsiya i kosmonavtika SSSR* under the general editorship of Air Marshal S.A. Krasovski added some historical background and a section on Soviet space programmes, but it was still no substantial advance.

Soviet airmen are well represented in the memoir series (*Voennye memuary*) which covers mainly the wartime period, though too often there is a heavily contrived touch to these works, suggesting more often than not the derring-do associated with Biggles. The separate histories of the individual air armies, such as Air Chief Marshal Vershinin's narrative of the 4th Air Army, are but pale public versions of what must have been originally highly classified official compilations, used for battle analysis and operational research purposes; the same can be said for a recent and very indifferent history of the Soviet Naval Air Force*. All this contrasts sharply with the excellent material contained in Soviet journals, not least *Aviatsiya i Kosmonavtika* itself, though let me cite also Colonel V. Myagkov's very professional analysis of wartime experience in employing aviation in the course of ground offensive operations published in a

---

*P.N. Ivanov, *Kryl'ya nad morem*, Moscow, Voenizdat, 1972, 304 pp.

more recent issue of *Voenno-istoricheskii Zhurnal**. V.B. Shavrov's history of Soviet aircraft construction in the Soviet Union up to 1938 is also in a class by itself. We shall return to these disparities in a moment, for they are worth investigating, indeed they are the very crux of the matter.

Mr. Boyd has made extensive and impressive use of these Soviet materials, augmenting them with German sources for the period of the 'Great Patriotic War': the German Air Force Monograph Project (and the associated 'Karlsruhe Collection') managed by the USAF Historical Division and Air University furnishes invaluable data on the air war in the east. There would appear to be no reason for the author to feel that he might have given undue space and prominence to the wartime history of the Soviet air force. On the contrary, here was the crucial test of doctrine, organisation and technical progress, not to mention the performance of the Soviet aviation industry under conditions at once disastrous and dangerous. Here also we see the performance of the men as well as the planes. In a lesson which has not lost its contemporary relevance — and it is certainly not lost upon the present Soviet command — the Soviet air force took terrible punishment at the outset but set about brutally and bloodily learning the lessons of modern air warfare. Centralisation, even super-centralisation became immutably established and while it imposed rigidities, it had also the advantage of facilitating the rapid movement of air resources both to stave off defeat and to exploit success. Much credit for this mode must go to A.A. Novikov, the successful air commander and co-ordinator who first wrenched the Soviet air force out of disaster in 1941 and after 1942 led this increasingly professionalised force to its hard-won, slogging victory; his reward after the war was to be put behind bars by Stalin.

The relevance of Mr. Boyd's historical approach has been underlined at the present juncture by an authority emanating from the Soviet air force itself, namely, Colonel I.V. Timokhovich and his monograph on 'the operating art of the Soviet Air Force during the Great Patriotic War'**: this is a recent work of singular importance,

---

*See Colonel V. Myagkov, 'Boevoe primenenie aviatsii v armeiskoi nastupatel'noi operatsii', *Voenno-istoricheskii Zhurnal*, 1976, No. 7, pp. 20-28. The same journal has carried extensive writing on Long-Range Aviation, Air Defence forces, Military Transport and air support for partisan operations.

**Colonel (Professor and Dr. of Historical Sciences) I.V. Timokhovich, *Operativnoe iskusstvo Sovetskikh VVS v Velikoi Otechestvennoi voine*, Moscow, Voenizdat, 1976, 343 pp. (18,000 copies printed).

which examines Soviet air warfare theories, organisation and operational performance, all against an impressive background of statistical material and prime historical sources. The 'Great Patriotic War' still represents a major stock of operational experience, particularly for a military establishment which has not been committed to large-scale and protracted military action since 1945. Not unexpectedly, Colonel Timokhovich stresses the overriding importance of centralised control of air operations, as well as the significance of sheer numbers: with mass came manoeuvre as Soviet aviation was committed to the support of ground troops, facilitating flexibility and promoting successful surprise. Deception combined with rapid re-grouping led to further success, assisted in turn by extensive use of decoy airfields, strict radio disciplines and constant improvements in technology. The 'air preparation' for offensive operations became increasingly important: the depth of air operations constantly increased, moving from the immediate battle area to the full depth of enemy defences, though the main Soviet air strength was concentrated on the battlefield in a close-support role. In 1941-42 81.3% of all ground-attack and bomber sorties were expended for close tactical support, in 1943 this rose to 91%, in 1944 the figure was 77.8% and in 1945 no less than 87%.*

While stressing the centralised mode and the critical role of the battle for air superiority, Colonel Timokhovich adopts a markedly ambiguous tone in dealing with strategic aviation. Here Mr. Boyd's analysis of Soviet theories of air power and air warfare, including strategic aviation, is as illuminating as it is excellent. His is an important account of the strange fate of the 'strategic air strike forces', whose fortunes have waxed and waned. It would appear that we are presently in a phase when Soviet Long-Range Aviation (ADD) is once more coming to the fore. It is not too fanciful to suggest, as Mr. Boyd does, that the 'I.M.' has indeed cast a long shadow, not merely as a symbol of gigantism but also as a portent of the true potentiality of air power in its full strategic array. It is this amalgam of technology, organisation and doctrine whicch imparts a particular fascination and singular importance to Mr. Boyd's study. Much of the story of the evolution of Soviet air power has been

---

*Timokhovich, *op.cit.*, on 'the general characteristics of air operations in Front offensive operations', pp. 106-155: see also review of Timokhovich by Major-General (Air Force) G. Lavrik, *Voenno-istoricheskii Zhurnal*, 1976, No.8, pp. 109-111.

wrapped either in myth or exaggeration, or else dismissed in simplistic fashion as an unalterable fixation over nothing more than a limited ground-support role. The true position is vastly more complicated and it is perhaps time that we tried to understand it for what it truly is. Brilliant engineering achievement and persistent innovation has long been the hall-mark of Russian and Soviet aeronautical practice. This much cannot be denied. That the Soviet air force can fight in brutal, hard-driving yet increasingly professionalised fashion has been amply demonstrated by the years of the 'Great Patriotic War'. It is all here in Mr. Boyd's book, the machines, the organisation, the politics and the men — and it is upon the men that we should perforce ponder most. Under Air Chief Marshal Pavel Kutakhov's command, begun in 1969, the Soviet air force in its several components (strategic strike, air defence, tactical support and air transport) has steadily diversified itself and developed a growing capability for offensive air operations at an increasing range. There is no great body of evidence which presently suggests imaginative tactical handling or operational originality*, but perhaps Kutakhov has learned a prime lesson from the history of his own service: first acquire the requisite quantity and quality of first-line combat aircraft and then proceed to work on tactical application, unlike the 1930s when exciting theories tended to outstrip the limits of technology and the constraints of Soviet industrial capacity. The blight of sheer obsolescence all too quickly swept upon the Soviet air force; quite the opposite condition prevails at the present.

Mr. Boyd's illumination of the past in Soviet military aviation and his elucidation of current policies point the way to the future. It is one in which Soviet air power can only increase, its offensive capability expand and its political utility grow, not to mention the awesome possibility of it bein applied on the battlefield. The Soviet command does not ignore its own history, whose lessons were bought at a high price in blood and desperate exertion. Then, by the same token, neither should we.

Professor John Erickson
Director of Defence Studies
University of Edinburgh

---

*I would nevertheless exempt the Soviet Naval Air Force from this stricture: see Norman Polmar, 'Soviet Naval Aviation' in 'Second Annual Soviet Aerospace Almanac', *Air Force Magazine*, March, 1976, pp. 69-72.

1 Birth of an Air Force

Although Csarist Russia was considered among the industrially and technically backward nations of the world at the dawn of the twentieth century, it had manufactured its first aircraft by 1910, begun to form its first military air units a year later and entered the First World War with some 250 aircraft. When the Bolsheviks became the new masters of Russia on 7 November 1917 they inherited between two and two and a half thousand aircraft from the Imperial Army and Navy and an aircraft industry that was extensive if still comparatively primitive and technically dependent on Russia's wartime allies, France and Great Britain.

A survey carried out in December 1917 accounted for 579 machines deployed along the Eastern Front confronting the air forces of Germany and Austria-Hungary, a further 237 entrained for the front, 293 in flying schools, about 150 aircraft — mainly flying boats — in service with the Baltic and Black Sea Fleets and 40 to 50 more comprising the 'Flotilla of Flying Ships'. At least 400 other aircraft were held in the five great air parks, formerly the bases of the Imperial Air Force, at Moscow, Vitebsk, Smolensk, Kiev and Odessa; as many as 1,000 were scattered through the length and breadth of the vast Russian Empire, in ports, on railway sidings, in repair shops and awaiting completion in aircraft factories.[1] Three years later these acquisitions barely existed. The aeronautical resources nurtured by Csarist Russia had been expended, lost or neglected in the new regime's battle for survival.

At first the Bolshevik leaders paid little attention to their air force. There were more immediate and pressing demands on their notice and they hoped that the spread of revolutionary anti-militarism would succeed where the Csar's generals had failed. Several at least

---

[1] Shavrov *Istoriya konstruktsii samolyotov v SSSR*

viewed the aeroplane as a borgeois extravagance on the field of battle where a grimly held earthworks, an artillery barrage or a dashing charge of sabres could still decide the day. On 10 November, three days after the Bolshevik coup, a special committee of eight commissars was appointed to report on aviation matters; in essence its task was to supervise the disarming and disbanding of all unreliable units and organise the nucleus of a totally pro-Bolshevik air arm. After less than two months the committee was reformed as The All-Russian Board for the Administration of the Republic's Air Fleet under the chairmanship of K.V. Akashev. Consisting of three airmen and six representatives from aircraft factories, its interests were more industrial than military and its terms of reference lay not in drafting a blueprint for a new air force but in Lenin's instruction, 'to preserve intact all air units and flying schools for the working people'.

Scores of Russian fighters and scouts, many abandoned by the disintegrating armies, were still standing on their airfields along the Eastern Front when Germany renewed her offensive in February 1918 and drove deeply into the Ukraine. Before the humiliating Treaty of Brest-Litovsk had been signed on 3 March, over 500 Russian aircraft had fallen into German hands, aircraft in the main of the latest types and in the most serviceable condition, and of the ninety-one *otryady* or flights only thirty-three were saved. The gravity of this loss was realised as the Interventionalist forces poised themselves along the frontiers of the crumbling Romanov Empire. Naval aircraft were lost at Helsinki and training machines at Baku. Airfields, flying schools, stocks of spares, fuel and materials were seized by French, British and White Russian forces on the Black and White Sea coasts and along the Volga. The fight for survival had begun and it was already clear that without aircraft for reconnaissance and ground attack the Red Army would be severely handicapped. The military parade on May Day 1918 accorded the aeroplane pride of place with the banners and bayonettes of the infantry eclipsed by the red Nieuport 21 fighter scattering leaflets over the crowds on Red Square, and later that day Lenin attended a flying display given by pilots of the Moscow Flying School at Khodinka. On 24 May the All-Russian Air Board was replaced by *Glavvozdukhoflot*, the new Chief Directorate of the Workers and Peasants Red Military Air Fleet (GU — RKKVVF) with Akashev at its head.

Birth of an Air Force

Twelve aircraft were sent north to oppose the British and French landings at Murmansk in the spring of 1918 and in August thirty flew east to shower pamphlets on the heads of the Czech Legion and the White armies moving west from Samara (later Kuibyshev). Forty were despatched to Csaritsyn (later Stalingrad) to support the Fifth Red Army holding the Don. As the threats multiplied and the demands for air support increased, the work of the GU—RKKVVF was supplemented by the *Polevoe upravlenie aviatsii i vozdukhoplavaniya*, the Operational Air Directorate (*Aviadarm*) under A.V. Sergeev, a member of the former All-Russian Air Board, which was directly responsible to Trotsky's Revolutionary Military Council, the *Revvoensovet*,[2] for air support to the Red Army in the field. *Aviadarm* was only able to provide 315 aircraft with a reserve of 169 in flying schools and air parks when it was formed in September 1918. Not only were *Aviadarm*'s aircraft few in number, they were of diverse and often obsolescent types for which spares were frequently in short supply. They consisted largely of French Nieuports and Farmans of various marks built under licence which had constituted some 70% of the Imperial Air Force with smaller numbers of Morane, Spad and Caudron machines, some British aircraft — notably Sopwiths,[3] a few captured German and a smattering of Russian types, the latter primarily Lebed, Anatra and Sikorski designs. As in the Imperial Air Force the basic formation was the flight (*otryad*) nominally comprising six machines. More often than not the Red air flight was under strength and made up of a variety of types; the 5th Reconnaissance Flight formed at Tambov in 1918 on the basis of the former 34th Army Corps Flight was equipped with one Sopwith, two Nieuport 17 and two Nieuport 23 machines and can be taken as typical of its time.

Despite the urgency of the situation, air units were carefully conserved and only committed with the sanction of the *Revvoensovet*.

---

[2]The *Revvoensovet* was formed in September 1918 under Leon Trotski to direct the operations of the Red Army. After the Civil War it contained the heads of arms and services with its chairmanship representing virtual control of the Red Army itself. Frunze replaced Trotski as chairman of the *Revvoensovet* in January 1925 and was himself succeeded by Voroshilov after his death that October.

[3]Production of the Sopwith 1½ Strutter had been started at the Lebedev factory outside Petrograd in 1917 but a shortage of engines had confined production to 140 examples by the end of the year. About 300 were later built between 1918 and 1923 at the *Dux* factory (GAZ No. 1) in Moscow, making it one of the most important aircraft in the early days of the Red Air Force.

Petrol too was in short supply after the loss of the Caucasian oil fields and the supply of lubricants, ammunition and spare parts was faltering and uncertain. By 1919, however, the Red Air Fleet was flexing its wings and ready for action on a more adventurous scale. Seventeen flights totalling about a hundred aircraft were committed against Admiral Kolchak's White forces in the east and 87 machines were available to assist in halting General Yudenich's offensive against Petrograd. The autumn saw the largest Red air concentrations so far in the Civil War with almost 200 aircraft supporting the Red Army against General Denikin in the south, but in spite of these resources every available machine and pilot — including the instructors and trainees of the Moscow Flying School — had to be thrown into battle in October when Denikin's forward units reached Oryol.

By the middle of July 1920 I.A. Buob, then Deputy Head of *Aviadarm* under Sergeev, was able to concentrate the impressive total of fifty-one flights with 210 aircraft to back Tukhachevski's drive on Warsaw. In fact the Red Air Fleet did not contribute significantly to Red Army operations in the Soviet-Polish conflict. The scale and speed of the campaign with its surging cavalry armies revealed the limited scope of its organisational flexibility, with repair and maintenance almost entirely reliant on special trains serving as mobile bases and carrying fuel and spares. In short, the effectiveness of the Red Air Fleet depended heavily on the presence of the railway. Air operations against the remnants of Vrangel's White forces as they were driven back through southern Russia and expelled from the Crimea in the late autumn of 1920 were more successful. Here an outstanding contribution was made by the remaining *Il'ya Muromets* four-engined bombers designed by Igor Sikorski and built at the Russo-Baltic Carriage Works in Petrograd for the famous 'Flotilla of Flying Ships' formed in 1915.[4] The *Il'ya Muromets* bombers were

---

[4] The *Eskadra vozdushnykh korablei* or 'Flotilla of Flying Ships' enjoyed a conspicuously successful career on the Eastern Front flying the world's first four-engined bombers. Many were destroyed at their Vinnitsa base in 1918 during the German offensive, but a number were flown out on the initiative of Colonel Bashko who subsequently commanded the Heavy Aviation Flotilla after eleven *Il'ya Muromets* bombers had been renovated at Sarapul. These machines saw action in various phases of the Civil War and were only retired from service in 1922. Bashko, a Latvian, returned to his native country in the early nineteen-twenties and was Commander of the Latvian Air Force when the USSR occupied Latvia in June 1940, disappearing soon afterwards in the Soviet purge of the Latvian High Command.

particularly effective in dispersing cavalry and in attacks against armoured trains, supply depôts, rail junctions and airfields, and their mere appearance overhead was often enough to induce panic with abandoned guns and stampeding horses. They were so successful that a replacement was requested by the *Revvoensovet* as a top priority and a Special Committee for Heavy Aviation (*Komta*) headed by Nikolai Zhukovski and Andrei Tupolev was formed with the express purpose of producing a new multi-engined bomber for the Red Army. Ambitious plans for thirty *otryady* of these bombers were frustrated by the failure of the *Komta's* design, a twin-engined triplane completed in 1922, but the legend of the '*Muromets*' continued to haunt the imagination of the Red Army Command and did much to spur on the development of the first Soviet heavy bombers.

In spite of the *Komta's* failure, Zhukovski contributed more than anyone else to the technical foundations of the new Red Air Fleet during the Civil War period. Born in 1847, Nikolai Yegorovich Zhukovski lectured in Mechanical Engineering at Moscow University in the eighteen-nineties where he published a series of papers on the theory of flight. He later taught at the Moscow Higher Technical College (MVTU) where in an atmosphere more sympathetic to a speculative science he set up an aerodynamic laboratory and was provided with more elaborate research facilities by a wealthy amateur, Ryabushinski, including a wind-tunnel constructed on Ryabushinski's Kuchino estate. News of the Wright brothers' successful flight created an extensive surge of interest in aviation in Russia and Zhukovski started an aeronautical study circle at MVTU composed of student enthusiasts, many of whom were destined to become leading figures in the history of Soviet aircraft design and including Andrei Tupolev, Aleksandr Arkhangel'ski, Boris Yur'yev — a pioneer in the development of rotating-wing aircraft — and the aerodynamicist Vladimir Vetchinkin. When Zhukovski died in 1921 he had helped to lay the foundations of the Central Aero & Hydrodynamics Institute (TsAGI), the Air Force Engineering Academy which later bore his name and the Air Force Scientific-Test Institute (NII-VVS). His title, 'the Father of Russian Aviation' is, therefore, far from being an exaggeration.

The end of the Civil War obviated the need for the dual command exercised over the Red Air Fleet since September 1918 and in February 1921 *Aviadarm* was abolished, its former head, Sergeev, replacing Akashev as Head of GU-RKKVVF until March 1923

Soviet Air Force

when he was dismissed in favour of A.P. Rozengol'ts[5]. The Red Air Fleet in the immediate post-Civil War period was reduced to some 300 aircraft, the majority unserviceable and the rest obsolete. No new machines were forthcoming to replace them due to the neglect and damage suffered by the aircraft industry over the previous three years. In 1914 Russia had entered the First World War with five airframe and two aeroengine factories and a workforce of just over 2,100 men; by 1917 she possessed eleven airframe, five aeroengine and two propeller factories with a workforce that had increased almost fivefold. In 1921 only a shadow remained of the industry that had supplied 5,600 aircraft during the course of the First World War[6]. The three largest airframe factories, the *Dux* in Moscow, the Shchetinin in Petrograd and the Anatra in Odessa, had manufactured 1,569, 1,340 and 1,065 aircraft respectively during the war years, mainly Nieuport, Farman and Voisin types built under licence. At peak production in late 1916 and early 1917 Russian factories achieved a monthly output of two hundred and thirty to two hundred and fifty machines supplemented by the shipment of 1,800 aircraft and 4,000 engines by Russia's allies to Murmansk[7]. In comparison with these figures, production during the Civil War was trifling with only 558 airframes and 237 engines manufactured between 1918 and 1920[8].

The nationalisation of aircraft factories was begun towards the close of 1917 and had been largely completed by the end of the following year. Decrees issued by the Council for Labour and Defence and endorsed by Lenin in November 1918 and June 1920 to draft a workforce of 5,500 for the Chief Directorate of Nationalised Aircraft Factories (*Glavkoavia*) had little effect. By the end of 1920, when no new aircraft or engines at all were built, the industry's

---

[5]Details of Sergeev's later career are unknown, but he was the author of 'Strategy and Tactics of the Red Air Fleet' published in 1925.

[6]Shavrov. It should be noted that *Aviatsiya i Kosmonavtika SSSR* claims that the Russian army received 3,150 aircraft of which 2,250 were of Russian manufacture. However, this figure may preclude aircraft supplied to the Imperial Navy, flying schools, air parks and reserve air units.

[7]The Soviets claimed to have seized 139 Sopwith, 44 Nieuport and 31 Farman machines and about 300 engines when Murmansk was evacuated by the Allied expeditionary forces.

[8]Shavrov. *Aviatsiya i Kosmonavtika SSSR* advances slightly higher figures with 669 new aircraft and 270 engines produced and 1,574 aircraft and 1,740 engines overhauled or reconstructed by factories during this period.

Birth of an Air Force

workforce had dwindled to 3,500 and it continued to decline despite the incentives offered to key workers prepared to resume their jobs. Three million gold roubles were allocated in 1921 to regenerate the aircraft industry, followed in August the next year by a further thirty-five million for the purchase of aircraft abroad and the reconstruction of Russian factories. The situation was in fact desperate. In 1922 only forty-three airframes and eight engines were produced and by 1924 manufacture had slumped to only thirteen aircraft supplied. The Red Air Fleet with an overall strength of 322 machines, 36 of these naval, on 1 October 1923 could barely be considered an effective component of the Red Army.

A manufacturing revival had to be made by concentrating on one or two simple and versatile designs suitable for production by an enfeebled and retarded aircraft industry. A general-purpose light bomber and reconnaissance type and a basic trainer were seen as the most immediate requirements for the new air force and British designs were copied as models. The DH.4 had been selected for licence production at the *Dux* factory shortly before the revolution, and the first twenty aircraft with 240 hp Fiat engines were built there in 1920-21. Supplemented by captured examples of the DH.9 and DH.9a and a number of airframes purchased from Britain, the de Havilland reconnaissance bomber was used as the basis for a Soviet adaption fitted at first with a variety of available Italian, German and British engines and later with the licence-built 400 hp American 'Liberty' engine, the M-5[9]. A total of 1,910 landplane versions of the DH.9 development under the Soviet designation R-1[10] were built at State Aviation Factory No. 1. (GAZ No. 1), Moscow, and a further 950 as floatplanes at GAZ No. 10, Taganrog[11]. A series of design

---

[9] Soviet aeroengines were numbered in the 'M' (*Motor*) series until 1944 when this system was replaced by a designator derived from the designer's initials.

[10] Until the introduction of designators derived from designers' names in 1941, Red Air Force machines were denoted by functional letters indicating their type. See Glossary of Abbreviations.

[11] State Aviation Factories (*Gosudarstvennye Aviatsionnye Zavody*) were given numbers during nationalisation, the *Dux* factory becoming GAZ No 1, the Moscow Gnôme-Rhône engine factory GAZ No. 2, the Aircraft Division of the Russo-Baltic Carriage Works in Petrograd GAZ No. 3, the Moscow *Motor* engine plant GAZ No. 4 etc. Certain factory numbers were later changed, often by the addition of twenty to the original number, making GAZ No. 3 into GAZ No. 23 and GAZ No. 4 into GAZ No. 24. This policy was not, however, consistent as GAZ No. 21 built in Nizhni Novgorod (later Gorky) in the early thirties was a new plant and not a renumbering of GAZ No. 1, Moscow. The major airframe and engine factories often had honorary titles as well as their official numbers — GAZ No. 1 being known as the ODVF (later *Osoaviakhim*) factory, GAZ No. 3 as the *Krasny Lyotchik* (Red Airman) and GAZ No. 24 as the *Frunze*.

refinements had been introduced before production came to an end in 1931 and the concept was revived in Polikarpov's R-5 which replaced it. A model for a basic trainer was provided by the fortunate acquisition of a British Avro 504K in northern Russia. The aircraft, which had force-landed in forested country, was dismantled and taken to GAZ No. 1 where drawings were made so that the design could be copied. The recovery and delivery of the Avro were the work of the future aircraft designer Sergei Il'yushin, then serving as a mechanic on an air force support train. Powered by a M-2 rotary engine developing 120 hp, a licence-built copy of a Rhône engine, the Avro was placed in production in 1922 as the U-1, initially at GAZ No. 5, Moscow, and later at GAZ No. 23, Leningrad, where by far the majority of the U-1s were produced. Between 1923 and 1931 737 examples of the U-1 were built, of which 73 were delivered as floatplane trainers under the designation MU-1. The faithful U-1 remained in Red Air Force service until 1932 when the remainder were handed over to *Osoaviakhim* flying schools where they enabled part-time pilots to try out their first bumps and circuits until well into the thirties.

The first Soviet built aircraft had to be supplemented by quantities of machines bought abroad, mainly between 1922 and 1924. Some 500 Fokker fighter and reconnaissance machines were obtained from Holland of which about 200 were D.XI and over fifty D.XIII single-seat fighters — the latter on behalf of the clandestine German air school at Lipetsk — together with an undetermined number of C.IV two-seat reconnaissance machines[12]. Fokker types featured prominently in Red Air Force squadrons throughout the twenties and a number of the D.XI fighters saw action against the Chinese during the border clashes of 1929. GAZ No. 39, Moscow, was responsible for maintenance and renovation work on Fokker aircraft in Russia, installing M-6 — licence built Hispano-Suiza — engines in a number of the D.XI airframes. Plans to produce a Russian fighter based on an amalgam of the D.XI and D.XIII designs for production at GAZ No. 39 were not realised in the form of a viable prototype until 1928 when the concept was already outmoded.

As well as Fokker types, 30 Italian Balilla and 100 British

---

[12]Shavrov. Yakovlev in *50 let sovetskovo samolyotostroeniya* puts the total number of Fokker D.XI fighters purchased by the USSR as high as three hundred.

Martinsyde F.4 fighters were bought with smaller quantities or single examples of other foreign aircraft for evaluation or advanced training. These expensive purchases abroad were necessary but unpopular measures, a drain on Soviet currency resources whose long-term application would delay and frustrate the emergence of Soviet designers and retard the aircraft industry as a whole. There was a particular need for experience in the design and manufacture of all-metal aircraft and it was here that Soviet Russia and Germany as the European outcasts were drawn readily together. Shortly after the signing of the Soviet-German Trade Agreement in May 1921, Junkers staff arrived in Moscow to prepare for the assembly of F.13 all-metal monoplanes at Fili on the western outskirts of the capital[13]. Soon after, under the auspices of the Trade Enterprises Development Company (GEFU) — a cover organisation for the development and manufacture of German armaments in Russia — an agreement was ratified between the Junkers Company at Dessau and the Council of People's Commissars (*Sovnarkom*) and backed by the *Reichswehr* ministry for the production of Junkers aircraft at Fili by German engineers and Russian labour. An annual production of 300 machines was envisaged of which sixty would be for the Red Air Force and a proportion of the remainder for the Lipetsk Air School.

As important to the Russians as the provision of modern aircraft was the German consent to the presence of Russian aircraft engineers who could study the production methods for all-metal aircraft at first hand. Accordingly, the deal also provided for Russian observers from the Central Aero & Hydrodynamics Institute (TsAGI) to be based at Fili. Established in December 1918 under *Sovnarkom's* Scientific-Technical Committee, TsAGI was the successor to Zhukovski's Evaluation and Test Bureau (RIB) set up at the Moscow Higher Technical College in July 1916. RIB had barely settled to its main tasks, the co-ordination and centralisation of a fund of aerodynamic research and reference and endeavours to place the testing of prototype and production aircraft on a systematic footing, before the revolution of March 1917 erupted. Revived a year later as the Flight Laboratory, it became the basis of TsAGI whose small staff of thirty-three was initially headed by Zhukovski. The scope of its work was at first extremely wide, embracing the design of air-sleighs, high-speed

---

[13]Junkers allegedly made the first unofficial overtures to Soviet Russia as early as October 1919 when the pilot of a F.13 which landed near Kovno claimed that he had been authorised by Professor Junkers to discuss the sale of these aircraft to Russia.

boat hulls, airframes, aircraft engines and structural materials, but was later limited with the creation of other specialist research organisations. TsAGI grew to become the Soviet Union's most important centre for aerodynamic research, working in close cooperation with the aircraft industry and with the Air Force Scientific-Research Committee (NTK GU-VVS), headed by Sergei Il'yushin between 1926 and 1933, which formulated the requirements for new types of military aircraft.

The Soviet-German Agreement was also to include the production of Junkers aeroengines at GAZ No. 4 where a small team of Russian engineers — including the future aeroengine designers Arkadi Shvetsov and Aleksandr Mikulin — had already been formed. When this hope failed it was a bitter disappointment to the Russians who were only too keenly aware of their weakness in aeroengine technology. The Junkers machines assembled at Fili included the A.20, F.13, H.21 and H.22. A hundred examples of the Junkers H.21 parasol-wing two-seat reconnaissance bomber were built exclusively for the Red Air Force between 1923 and 1925 and were used in counter-insurgency operations in Central Asia; its unsuccessful single-seat fighter variant, the H.22, was not accepted for service and Junkers position would undoubtedly have been stronger if they had been able to supply the Russians with a good single-seat fighter. The Junkers aircraft were fitted with 185 hp BMW IIIa engines shipped out by *Bayerische Motorenwerke* who later supplied the BMW VI which was licence-built as the M-17 — a twelve-cylinder inline engine which proved its worth and was widely used in Soviet aircraft during the First Five-Year Plan period between 1928 and 1932.

No less acute than the shortage of aircraft was the lack of trained and experienced pilots, observers and mechanics. Only a small proportion of the officers in the Imperial Air Force had decided to throw in their lot with the Bolsheviks, the majority choosing to flee abroad or fly for the White generals. Pilots and observers had to be hastily trained during the Civil War years and sent as soon as possible to the *otryady* at the front where they often arrived with only the most scant knowledge of navigation, bombing and air-gunnery. Flying training suffered too from the posting of instructors to operational units and the loss of seven of Russia's ten flying schools in areas controlled by White or Interventionalist forces. Aspiring cavalrymen found themselves posted to flying schools and emerged with the firm intention of transferring to the cavalry at the first opportunity. Losses were high and replacements difficult to find; machines were frequently grounded because there were no pilots to fly them and the real measure of Red air strength lay in the availability of trained pilots rather than in the number of serviceable aircraft. In late 1918 the Red Air Fleet had only 269 pilots and 59 observers, and only 500 additional pilots had passed through the Moscow and Yegor'evsk flying schools by the end of the Civil War.

Post-war reconstruction was further complicated by the high proportion of army officers posted to air units who remained ignorant or suspicious of the complicated machines and new skills they were expected to master. In 1926 40% of all Red Air Force officers had been transferred from the infantry and standards of technical and tactical expertise were low with a pressing need for in-service courses and for developing the potential of the small percentage of experienced air veterans. Training facilities in the Moscow and Petrograd areas used during the Civil War were expanded. The Moscow Advanced Pilot's School was restarted as the Moscow Air *Tekhnikum* in 1919 with a two-year course for pilots and mechanics, and in September 1920 its technical division was retitled the Institute for Red Air Fleet Engineers with Zhukovski, a lecturer at the Advanced Pilots' School and the *Tekhnikum,* as its first rector. A three-year course was inaugurated, extended to four in 1922 when the institute was renamed the Zhukovski Air Force Engineering Academy. Under the directorship of S.G. Khorkov, head of the academy between 1927 and 1933, it became the Soviet Union's most exclusive air force college and the threshold to key technical and command posts. Its most outstanding early success was in producing a new generation of aircraft designers; Sergei Il'yushin who graduated in 1926, Aleksandr Yakovlev in 1931 and Artyom Mikoyan in 1936 were to become the academy's most illustrious 'old boys'.

It was less successful in producing the urgently needed new cadres of air force commanders, and after a first intake in 1923 for a four-year command course the command faculty closed its doors for two years. Interim air force command courses were held at the Leningrad Military-Theoretical School and, at the highest level, at the Frunze Military Academy until 1929 when the Air Force Academy's command faculty was re-opened and its graduates — Vershinin, Zhigarev, Kamanin, Rudenko, Khudyakov and many others — were destined to form the Red Air Force command élite during the wartime and post-war years. Early in 1933 an operations faculty was opened to provide one-year advanced courses for senior commanders, and the year after the Advanced Tactical Air School was detached from the academy and established at Borisoglebsk, formerly the German-staffed command school, under Pomerantsev. The school's main function was to train *zveno* leaders but special courses in night and bad-weather flying were also held.

The Moscow Flying School at Khodinka airfield had played an important part in training during the Civil War but had suffered heavy losses during the desperate attacks against Mamontov's White cavalry in 1919, and in the immediate post-war years it was able to operate only on a much reduced scale. The Gatchina Military Flying School outside Petrograd, the oldest of its kind in Russia, was taken over by the All-Russian Air Board in February 1918 together with its advanced flying section at Alatyr. Both parts of the school were promptly evacuated, the Gatchina school to Yegor'evsk, south-west of Moscow, and the advanced flying section to Zaraisk. September 1920 saw both parts of the school reunited at Zaraisk as the First Air Force Flying School, leaving only the theoretical department behind as the foundation for the Yegor'evsk Aeronautical Technical College. The school was moved again the same year, this time to Kacha near Sevastopol in the Crimea — the site of an Imperial Air Force school — with a primary training division at nearby Simferopol. Kacha grew in importance with the decision in 1924 to implement a year-round flying training programme to accelerate the supply of pilots and, since weather conditions in central and northern Russia limited flying training to the summer months only, Kacha was able to offer uninterrupted training courses on the U-1 and R-1, later U-2 and R-5, biplanes. Between 1923 and 1940 the Myasnikov Flying School[14] produced 6,260 qualified pilots for the Red Air Force including Heads of GU-VVS Baranov, Alksnis and Smushkevich and future Air Marshals Vershinin, Rudenko, Skripko and Sudets.

Close behind Kacha in importance came the Naval Air School, evacuated from the Baltic to Nizhni Novgorod and finally to Yeisk on the Sea of Azov. Training was carried out on floatplanes and flying boats to supply pilots for the air units of the Baltic and Black Sea Fleets, but the late thirties saw a greater degree of instruction on landplanes as the strategic role of the naval air forces was reshaped.

---

[14]The school received this title in 1925 on the death of the Red Army commander, A.F. Myasnikov. It is now the Kacha Red Banner Air Force College.

Birth of an Air Force

Other important military flying schools were established at Khar'kov, Tambov, Orenburg, Lugansk and Stalingrad[15] and, from January 1919, observers were trained at the Air Observers' School in Petrograd which replaced the Kiev Observers' School founded in 1916. From 1929 training for the Red Air Force was already being conducted through elementary theoretical schools followed by eighteen months flying instruction for army and twelve for navy pilots. The theoretical course itself had a broad educational basis as entrance qualifications were extremely modest and candidates between the ages of eighteen and twenty-five accepted, many of whom had received little or no formal schooling. Army pilots were given an eighteen month course and naval pilots a longer course of two years and six months to include naval training and more advanced navigational tuition. On graduation, the most promising were selected for further advanced tactical and command training, primarily under German tutelage at Borisoglebsk. Junior mechanics were given a two-year course and certain schools combined courses for both pilots and mechanics to allow the pupils' training to be directed according to his aptitude. By the late twenties most applicants for the Air Force schools had undergone preparatory training in the volunteer para-military *Osoaviakhim* organisation, and no account of the Red Air Force's formative years would be complete without reference to *Osoaviakhim*'s creation and development.

Indeed, one of the salient lessons of the Civil War had been the need to accustom the entire Soviet population to accept a vital role in national defence and to educate and stimulate its military and technical awareness. From its earliest days, therefore, the Red Air Fleet was to be provided with a wide basis of popular support in the form of the *Obshchestvo Druzei Vozdushnovo Flota* or Society of Friends of the Air Fleet (ODVF) founded by Trotski in 1923. The society was to promote interest in aviation by arranging air displays, visits to factories and airfields, lectures and exhibitions, while posters with the slogans — 'Workers! Build An Air Fleet!' and 'Proletariat! Take To The Air!' — exhorted everyone to contribute to the purchase of new aircraft. The recalcitrant were admonished with the

[15] The Khar'kov, Tambov and Orenburg Air Schools are now named the Gritsevets, Raskova and Polbin Schools after their famous graduates. Similarly, the Yeisk school is now the Komarov Higher Air Force College in honour of the cosmonaut. Orenburg and Lugansk, renamed Chkalov and Voroshilovgrad under Stalin, have now reverted to their former names.

accusatory — 'What Have You Done For The Red Air Fleet?' and the poet Vladimir Mayakovski lent his prolific talents with the propaganda poem 'The Flying Proletariat'. Everything, in fact, was aimed at identifying the new air force with the industrial worker and ridding it of the image of an ex-Csarist officer arm.

The ODVF popularisation campaign opened with an extensive editorial by Trotski in *Pravda* for 6 March 1923 under the headline, 'The Air Fleet: The Order Of The Day', and the first session of the new organisation's committee was held two days later. ODVF lost no time in making its presence known. Visitors to the First All-Russian Agricultural Exhibition were given joy-rides from the Moscow River on a Junkers F.13, while on a similar machine Boris Velling, Head of the Moscow Flying School, inaugurated the era of Soviet long-distance flights by flying to Tiflis and Tashkent. Membership and donations mounted, reaching a peak during Aviation Week in late June when the first two R-1 biplanes built at GAZ No. 1 and paid for with ODVF funds were handed over to the Red Air Fleet. On 1 June 1924 nineteen brand-new dark-green R-1 biplanes with red stars freshly painted were handed over by Sergei Kamenev, Deputy Chairman of the *Revvoensovet*, to Mikhail Kalinin, Chairman of the Central Executive Committee of Soviets, as the Lenin Squadron — ODVF's tribute to the Thirteenth Party Congress. At the end of its first year of life ODVF had recruited 1,500,000 members and was already publishing its own monthly magazine, *Samolyot* (Aeroplane).

In May 1925 ODVF was merged with the smaller Society of Friends of Chemical Defence to become *Aviakhim*, and two years later with the inclusion of the Defence Support Society it was retitled *Osoaviakhim* with responsibilities now extended to provide pre-training induction courses for Red Army recruits, refresher courses for reservists and elementary education for the civil population. Propaganda for the Red Air Force and fund-raising to buy aircraft remained, however, an important aspect of its activities. In 1925 a special commission to arrange long-distance flights was set up under Sergei Kamenev — a member of ODVF's original praesidium and later a prominent member of *Osoaviakhim*'s central committee — and record flights abroad and at home by such well-known pilots as Moiseev, Mezheraup, Shestakov and Gromov kept aviation in the forefront of popular attention and contributed to Soviet prestige in the world at large.

While funds were still collected to equip new air force squadrons, notably the 'Ultimatum' and 'Our Answer to Chamberlain' during the diplomatic rupture with Britain in 1927, resources were also made available to promote amateur flying and finance the building of gliders and light aircraft. The sporting section of ODVF came under Konstantin Mekhonshin, the *Revvoensovet* member in charge of military training, who approved and backed the formation of an ODVF gliding group under Konstantin Artseulov of the Moscow Flying School and Sergei Il'yushin, then student leader of the Zhukovski Air Academy's glider club. The first glider contests were held at Koktebel (now Planyorskoe) on the south-western coast of the Crimea in November 1923 and Koktebel with its annual glider and sailplane competitions soon became the focus for design and piloting expertise. Gliders were built for flying at Koktebel by such future aircraft designers as Sergei Il'yushin, Aleksandr Yakovlev, Boris Cheranovski, Oleg Antonov, Sergei Korolyov and Vladislav Gribovski, and Andrei Yumashev and Vasili Stepanchonok, two leading test pilots for the next decade, were also keen participants. In the summer of 1925 sixteen Soviet glider pilots took part in the international gliding contests held in Germany and seven Germans paid a return visit to compete with forty Russians in the Third All-Russian Gliding Competitions held at Koktebel that autumn. Most of the home-made gliders brought down by train to Koktebel, their young designers sleeping beside them on the flat-cars, were built by Air Academy students for whom the competitions provided an excellent opportunity to put their talents to the test. When the Ninth All-Union Glider Competitions were held in 1933, sixty-five new gliders were entered and the emphasis was on aerobatic virtuosity and endurance.

Osoaviakhim also inherited ODVF's policy of encouraging and assisting young design engineers. Over the winter of 1924-25 a contest for the design of light aircraft and engines was announced under the slogan 'Stability, Simplicity and Low-Cost: The Three Best Friends to the Air Fleet'. None of the contestants came up with a design suitable for series production, but the building of three machines was financed and the most outstanding, the 'Three Friends', was sent to the 1928 Berlin International Air Salon in company with Tupolev's ANT-3, Polikarpov's U-2 and Kalinin's elliptical-winged K-4. Through the agency of *Osoaviakhim* a number of foreign light aircraft were purchased and made available for study as the enthusiasm for light aircraft design increased, although most young aspirants built single prototypes powered by imported Blackburn, Anzani and Walter engines. *Osoaviakhim*'s leading protegé of the thirties was Aleksandr Yakovlev who designed and built his first light aircraft while still a student at the Air Force Academy using funds collected by children of Moscow's Pioneer youth organisation.

Vadim Shavrov's light amphibians were also built with *Osoaviakhim*'s help and the Sh-2 accepted for production at GAZ No. 23, Leningrad, in 1931. The Sh-2 was still in service with *Aeroflot*'s forestry and fishery services in 1964, a record of longevity only paralleled by Polikarpov's U-2. Oleg Antonov and Vladislav Gribovski were both established as leading sailplane designers by *Osoaviakhim*, Nikolai Kamov received grants to design and construct his first autogyro and Fridrikh Tsander was supported in the design of his second experimental rocket engine intended for installation in Cheranovski's flying-wing glider. In its early years, experimental rocket-motor research received more support from *Osoaviakhim* than from any other source, and but for Tsander's premature death in 1933 the Soviet Union could well have gained an early and invaluable start in the development of rocket-powered flight.

With the expansion of the Red Air Force in the early thirties, much of the onus for recruitment and preliminary training devolved upon *Osoaviakhim* with the provision of a full-time training staff and a grant of fifty thousand million roubles in 1931. The Ninth *Komsomol* Congress held that year pledged itself to the support of *Osoaviakhim* and the Red Air Force with speeches by Iosif Unshlikht and Aleksandr Kosarev, chairmen respectively of the *Osoaviakhim* and *Komsomol* Central Committees, urging young communists to take part in air and parachute training and to study for defence qualifications. Gliding was no longer to be the prerogative of the few but a mass, popular pastime. A new glider school was founded at Tushino, outside Moscow, together with a new factory completed in 1932 to mass-produce Antonov training gliders; parachute towers became familiar landmarks in parks of 'rest and culture' in the larger towns and cities, and Red Air Force flying schools were directed to assist and supervise the setting up of flying clubs and the training of civilian instructors for the anticipated thousands of part-time pilots.

Osoaviakhim membership rose from just under three million in 1927 to eleven million by 1933, but the soaring and impressive statistics were not matched by improvements in training proficiency or increased air force recruitment. Complaints of apathy among young communists were made at the Third Plenum of the *Komsomol* Central Committee in 1932 and repeated the following year when Kosarev again vowed that he would overcome all shortcomings by the *Komsomol* in its support of the Red Air Fleet, but the sheer size of *Osoaviakhim* was now leading to wastage, inefficiency and escalating costs while a veneer of zeal above served to cover mass indifference and superficial conformity below. The day of reckoning was postponed, but in common with the Red Air Force Command and the aviation industry *Osoaviakhim* would experience the displeasure of Stalin before many years had elapsed.

2 Commanders of the Winged Army

By 1924 the Red Air Fleet Command was already being drawn into the campaign to depose Trotski from the chairmanship of the *Revvoensovet* and strip him of his authority over the Red Army — the opening gambits of the power struggle on Lenin's death from which Stalin was soon to emerge victorious. Rozengol'ts, appointed Head of the GU—RKKVVF with Trotski's backing in March 1923, had faced an unenviable task. The Red Air Fleet was run down and ill-equipped after the chaos of Civil War, the aircraft factories under reconstruction had barely started production and relationships with the Junkers firm were swiftly deteriorating. The Fili factory had proved a costly undertaking for Junkers, carried out in the expectation that the firm would be a major source of supply of new aircraft to Soviet Russia. The Russians, on the other hand, saw matters quite differently; they were prepared to buy only the types and quantities suited to their interim plans for military and civil aviation and were more interested in picking German brains.

Aware of the Achilles heel of Soviet aeronautical technology and reluctant to commit themselves to further financial ventures in Russia, Junkers hedged on the issue of setting up aeroengine production. A proposal by the *Reichswehr* that the firm should combine with *Bayerische Motorenwerke*, already supplying the engines for aircraft assembled at Fili, was received coldly by Junkers as undermining their monopoly and bargaining position with the Russians. Rozengol'ts found *Bayerische Motorenwerke* reluctant to act independently when he approached them about a factory in the USSR in June 1924, and by the following year Junkers had finally backed out of any aeroengine provision when the *Reichswehr* ministry refused them further subsidies for the Fili plant.

The developing crisis in the Red Air Fleet was ruthlessly exploited by Frunze in the campaign to discredit Trotski. Proclaiming that the

Red Air Fleet had a vital part to play in any future war and was now in danger of extinction due to mismangement, Frunze succeeded in having Rozengol'ts replaced by his own candidate, Pyotr Ionovich Baranov[1].

The son of a Petersburg worker, Baranov had joined the Bolsheviks in 1912 and taken part in revolutionary propaganda work before being conscripted in 1915. Sentenced to eight years imprisonment for subversive activities within the army by a military court, Baranov was liberated by the March revolution and joined the Red Army the following year where he rose to command the Fourth Ukrainian Workers Army, served as Chief of Staff in southern Russia and held a series of key political appointments. In 1921 he was decorated with the Order of the Red Banner for his part in the suppression of the naval mutiny at Kronshtadt[2] and for the next two years occupied commissar posts in the Red Army in southern Russia and central Asia until his recall to Moscow to take charge of the Red Army's mechanized forces. It is doubtful if Baranov ever occupied this post as he was already being primed to serve as Political Deputy to Rozengol'ts from August 1923 and in the following year replaced him as Head of the Chief Directorate of the Military Air Forces of the Workers' and Peasants' Red Army (GU—VVSRKKA) — the Red Air Fleet's new title — as well as taking over control of the aircraft industry as head of its newly created Chief Directorate (GUAP). These two posts were combined under Baranov until June 1931, the result of Frunze's pledge, 'to examine as speedily as possible extant plans for the development of the air forces and at the same time take measures to establish a national aircraft and aeroengine industry'. In reality, the merger had already been proposed by Trotski in urging that the expansion of military aviation should be planned in close collaboration with the aircraft industry.

Baranov's position was strengthened by the fruits of Rozengol'ts labours and in 1925 264 military aircraft were supplied by Soviet factories, making reliance on Junkers less essential. In fact the

---

[1] Later a diplomat and Commissar for Foreign Trade, A.P. Rozengol'ts was tried with Bukharin, Rykov and the 'Right-Wing Opposition' when he 'confessed' to being implicated in a 'treasonable agreement' between Trotski and the *Reichswehr* in 1923.

[2] The mutiny by sailors of the Baltic Fleet garrisoned at Kronshtadt in March 1921 was suppressed by Tukhachevski's re-formed Seventh Army. Some thirty Red Air Fleet aircraft supported Tukhachevski's storming of the fortress, dropping pamphlets, making spotting flights and bombing and strafing the insurgent batteries and the battleships *Petropavlovsk* and *Sevastopol*.

19

Russians had learned their lessons well from the Germans and were eager to put them into practice. Self-sufficiency in aircraft production had been one of Frunze's most strident slogans. Addressing the Third Congress of Soviets in May 1925 Frunze claimed that although the USSR had purchased over seven hundred aircraft abroad over the previous three years — 'this year we have not bought one, and next year I feel convinced that we shall be fully supplied by the growing output of our own factories'. As later events proved, Frunze was somewhat optimistic in this claim and the necessity to shop abroad continued for several years. The mood of optimism over air matters was, however, in other respects reasonably well founded. Co-operation in air training with the *Reichswehr* was going well to the satisfaction of both parties, and in August 1926 Baranov's expanding responsibilities were shared with the appointment of a Deputy Head of GU-VVS, Yakov Alksnis.

A Latvian, five years Baranov's junior, Yakov (Jekabs) Ivanovich Alksnis was also a Civil War veteran with a spectacular military career behind him. After serving briefly as an ensign before the revolution, Alksnis joined the Red Army in 1919 and had already been promoted to the command of a military district the following year. When the Civil War ended he went on to study at the Frunze Military Academy and then directly to a staff appointment under Unshlikht, Chief of Red Army Supply, who disclosed to him in the spring of 1926 the *Revvoensovet*'s plans for his future.

Although Baranov had learned to fly at Kacha he remained more the able administrator than airman, astute and reserved, while Aksnis complemented him well as he threw himself vigorously into the day-to-day work of the Red Air Force without stinting time or energy. As a German-speaker who had already visited Germany several times on military matters, he was the obvious choice to supervise German-Soviet technical collaboration and training. In 1927 he was sent again to Germany to study aircraft and aeroengine technology, and was back there soon afterwards to negotiate the purchase of Heinkel fighters and flying boats. Aware of Soviet technological backwardness he cultivated ties with foreign air forces and aircraft industries and insisted on the highest levels of technical proficiency the Red Air Force was capable of maintaining. Like Tukhachevski whom he admired and on whom he modelled himself, his outlook was cosmopolitan and he expected and encouraged similar attitudes from those who served under him. At his request the study of foreign languages was introduced into the Air Force Academy's curriculum and technical literature from abroad was made available for circulation in air schools and colleges. He spent the winter of 1930-31 in Paris studying the French aircraft industry, and during the six years when he was Head of GU-VVS numerous visits to air displays, air exhibitions and factories abroad were arranged for senior Air Force commanders and aircraft designers. In 1935 a group of Soviet designers including Yakovlev, Sukhoi and Polikarpov attended the Milan Air Salon where the 1-16 fighter, the Stal'-3 passenger aircraft and the M-34 engine were exhibited and the opportunity was taken to tour Italian aircraft plants. In 1936 Alksnis took a delegation to the Paris Air Salon and round the Blériot, Renault and Potez factories, followed by a trip to the Hendon Air Show and the De Havilland factory at Hatfield.

Acting as chairman of the editorial board of the Red Air Force monthly 'Air Fleet News' (*Vestnik Vozdushnovo Flota*), Alksnis contributed a stream of articles on technical and tactical subjects. In November 1929 he had qualified as a pilot at Kacha and was soon touring every airfield, inspecting, advising and reprimanding whenever he came across signs of slackness or incompetence. In 1932 he put himself through the navigator's course and personally organised and headed the 1936 May Day flypast. The smart, dynamic Latvian with his dark hair *en brosse* and the four diamond symbols of an army commander on his collar was a figure to be respected. His eyes missed nothing and his tongue was sharp; but he set no task he was not prepared to undertake himself and when, as sometimes did happen, his desire for perfection over-stepped his practical knowledge of flying, he was prepared to admit his mistake and apologize — even to the humblest mechanic. An austere but popular commander, no Chief of the Soviet Air Force before or since has left such an imprint on the character of his arm. Ultimately, it was to contribute to the hard-won victory of 1945 — not so much as a legacy of technical sophistication or military success as an underlying spirit of perseverence and determination, a rugged, stubborn refusal to admit that anything could be impossible.

In September 1923 plans had already been drawn up for the reorganisation of the Red Air Force in anticipation of its future expansion. The old flight (*otryad*) of up to six aircraft was replaced by the *zveno* of three machines as the basic unit, and the air group (*aviagruppa*) — a tactical concentration of flights varying in size — by

Soviet Air Force

the new squadron (*eskadrilya*). The new flight of nine machines was to be composed of three *zven'ya*, fighter squadrons to possess three and reconnaissance, light bomber and ground-support squadrons two such flights to give total strengths of twenty-seven and eighteen aircraft respectively. During the mid-twenties these planned squadron sizes were rarely attained, nor was the generous intention of providing twelve spare machines for each service squadron. The new squadrons were developed to consist solely of fighter, bomber or reconnaissance aircraft, and by the end of the decade were normally combined to form a composite air brigade (*aviabrigada*) consisting of between two and four squadrons. A typical composite air brigade of this period might have consisted of two squadrons of Fokker D.XI fighters and a squadron of R-1 reconnaissance bombers — some fifty to seventy aircraft in all. During the latter half of the First Five-Year Plan period a number of air brigades became purely fighter or bomber brigades while certain squadrons, usually for liaison, transport, artillery spotting or reconnaissance remained 'independent' — their subordination being directly to the highest and by-passing intermediate command echelon levels — and some rifle and cavalry corps had special 'independent' flights attached directly to them.

Operational control of the Red Air Force remained firmly in the hands of the Red Army Command and was exercised through the tactical authority of the Military District Commanders[3] with the Head of GU-VVS responsible for training, supply, technical matters and operational readiness via his Military District Air Commander who served as tactical adviser and air deputy to the military district's commander. Initially, each military district of strategic importance had one air brigade under a brigade commander (*kombrig*), but later the vital Leningrad, Moscow, Belorussian and Kiev Military Districts were provided with a number of air brigades, some composite and some of single types. The naval air units of the Baltic

---

[3]The military district (*voenny okrug*) is a defence zone within the USSR. In 1926 there were seven of these — the Moscow, Leningrad, Ukrainian, Belorussian, Volga, North Caucasus and Siberian M.Ds. The Ukrainian M.D. was later divided into the Kiev and Khar'kov M.Ds., and new districts for Central Asia, the Trans-Caucasus, Odessa, Oryol, the Urals and Trans-Baikal created to make fourteen by January 1938. In 1940 the territory acquired from Finland was incorporated into the Leningrad M.D., Latvia, Lithuania and Estonia formed into the Baltic M.D., Eastern Poland absorbed into the Special Western (ex-Belorussian) and Kiev M.Ds, and Bessarabia and Northern Bukovina taken from Rumania into the Special Odessa M.D.

and Black Sea Fleets had been placed under Red Air Fleet control in 1920 and remained administratively subordinate to the Head of GU-VVS until 1935. Naval Air Commanders for the two fleets functioned in parallel with the Army Air Force Commanders in the military districts with Fleet Commanders holding operational control. Many military district air commanders like Ingaunis, Korf and Pavlov — the last two having been twice decorated with the Order of the Red Banner — were the most able and experienced veterans of the Civil War. Almost without exception they were swept away in the purges of the Red Army Command unleashed by Stalin in 1937.

The Chief Directorate of the Red Air Force under Baranov and Alksnis was greatly amplified during the latter half of the twenties as new heads of specialised services were appointed. Among the most important of these posts was that of Assistant (*Pomoshchik*), later Chief of Staff (*Nachal'nik Shtaba*), to the Chief Directorate occupied by Mezhenikov, and the Inspectorate (*Inspektsiya*) headed by Mezheraup until his death in an air crash in September 1931 and then by Korf, ex-Air Commander for the Moscow Military District. In 1928 the Inspectorate was enlarged and a separate Engineering Inspectorate, the foundations of the later Engineering-Technical Service (ITS), added under Khrustalev. Other important appointments were the Heads of the Political Department and Navigational Section — Troyanker and Sterligov — and staff officers in charge of Training and Operational Readiness. By the mid-thirties the heads of these major headquarters departments and sections already carried the titles of Deputy Commander GU-VVS with the rank of Corps Commander (*komkor*).

The nineteen-twenties were also marked by Russo-German collaboration in air training, the Germans obtaining facilities forbidden to them under the terms of the Treaty of Versailles whereby Germany was prohibited from maintaining an air force, carrying out air training and developing and building military aircraft, while the Russians looked for technical assistance and aid with their advanced flying and command training programmes. Shortly after the signing of the Treaty of Rapallo in April 1922 preparations were made for the establishment of a clandestine German flying training base at Lipetsk in central Russia. Here everything was conducted with the utmost secrecy, the Russians undertaking the purchase of Fokker D.XIII fighters on behalf of the Germans, arranging for their transport and delivery and facilitating the entry and departure of German personnel. Lipetsk was staffed at first by some hundred and sixty German flying instructors, officers and ground crew mechanics under the command of Major (Reserve) Stahr with an assortment of aircraft including Fokker D.XIII fighters and smaller numbers of Fokker D.VII, Heinkel He 17 and He 21, Junkers A 20 and F.13, and Albatros L 76 and 78 machines. Summer courses for novices lasted for between four and five months and were supplemented in the autumn by special exercises in which the resident instructors were able to develop their own skills in formation and advanced flying techniques. The Lipetsk school was under way by 1924, and over the next nine years 450 German flying personnel were trained there, of which 120 were fighter pilots. Among these officers were several who were to return to Russia in June 1941 — Dessloch who commanded I *Flak Korps* and later *Luftflotten* 6 and 4, Fiebig, von Richthofen's successor to the command of VIII *Fliegerkorps,* Pflugbeil, Commander of IV *Fliegerkorps* and *Luftflotte* 1 and Plocher, Chief of Staff to V *Fliegerkorps,* later *Luftwaffe* Command East.

Not only did Lipetsk play an invaluable part in training the future *Luftwaffe,* it gave German officers who trained or taught there an insight into the temper and potential of Soviet air power. German staff at Borisoglebsk, two hundred kilometres south-west of Lipetsk, discharged obligations to the Russians by providing command tuition and laid the foundations of the Advanced Tactical Air School established after their departure. Joint manoeuvres and battle training were carried out over the Voronezh range in conjunction with the School of Bombing and Air-Gunnery formerly at Serpukhov.

From 1930 until its closure on Hitler's orders in August 1933, Lipetsk also served as an important test centre for the newest German prototypes, the trials being followed with close interest by representatives from TsAGI and the Air Force Scientific-Test Institute (NII-VVS)[4]. Most of the new German machines were

---

[4]Known as the Scientific-Test Aerodrome (NOA) at Khodinka, Moscow, prior to 1926, NII-VVS was responsible for the evaluation of prototypes on state trials for air force acceptance and for the testing of foreign aircraft when of particular interest or where licence production was contemplated. Its work was subsequently extended to cover the testing of engines and equipment, assistance to experimental design bureaux in the flight tests of prototypes and the direction of conversion and familiarisation programmes when new types were introduced into Red Air Force service. In the thirties NII-VVS moved its headquarters to Monino, just east of Moscow.

tested at Lipetsk, including the Arado Ar 64 and Ar 65 and the Heinkel He 38 and 51 biplane fighters, the He 45 and He 46 reconnaissance biplanes, the He 59 twin-engined biplane, the Junkers W 34 monoplane transport and, of particular interest to the Russians at this time, the Dornier Do P four-engined heavy bomber and the Do F twin-engined medium bomber — the forerunner of the Do 11. The Germans gained little of interest from the Russians, as they had expected, and the Russians were continually suspicious that the Germans might be holding back something from them. On the training side, cordial relations were preserved right up to the end of the Lipetsk venture, and a farewell dinner for the Russian and German officers concluded with toasts of friendship and the playing of the *Deutschlandlied* and the *Internationale*. These ties, encouraged by Tukhachevski and Alksnis, were to be sufficient proof of treason when the *Luftwaffe* and the Red Air Force clashed in the skies of Spain. The few who remained, often released from camps and prisons, proved useful once more in easing the detente with Hitler's Germany after the Non-Aggression Pact of 1939.

The most acceptable Junkers aircraft assembled at Fili had been the F.13 low-wing all-metal monoplane whose versatility accorded closely with the precepts propounded by Trotski for the ideal aircraft to equip both the Military and Civil Air Fleets. The F.13 was to make a great contribution to the first Soviet civil air services introduced by *Dobrolyot*, and its successor, the W 33, was purchased in numbers in 1928[5]. When the *Reichswehr* ministry refused further subsidies to Junkers in 1925, the undertaking was financed by GUAP and a Russian director, Sergei Gorbunov, installed. While this was far from satisfactory as far as Junkers were concerned, they were reluctant to lose contracts for the assembly of K 30 bombers, a trimotor development of the F.13 which had been demonstrated to the

---

[5]Junkers had flown air services for the Russians between Moscow and Nizhni Novgorod (Gorky) in 1922, and *Junkers-Luftverkehrs AG* later co-operated with the Soviet Civil Air company, *Dobrolyot* formed in 1923 in setting up passenger services in southern Russia and the Caucasus. The Junkers Air Transport Enterprise was, in fact, eager to gain concessions here as part of its circular route Berlin-Moscow-Baku-Teheran-Bagdad-Cairo-Rome-Paris-Berlin. The Russians, sensitive about foreign overflights in this area, insisted on the employment of Russian crews for flights over the Caucasus and these services were taken over by *Dobrolyot* soon after. *Deruluft*, a Russo-German company formed in November 1921 to operate air services between the two countries, lasted until 1937 and was briefly revived after the Non-Aggression Pact had been signed in 1939.

Russians that year in its civilian guise as the G 24[6]. Built under the designation JuG-1 (Junkers-Gorbunov), the K 30 was used to equip the first two multi-engined bomber squadrons of the new Heavy Bomber Brigade in 1926-27 as a stop-gap measure pending delivery of the first Soviet twin-engined all-metal TB-1 bombers.

The Russians, meanwhile, did not delay in putting the lessons learned from Junkers to practical use on their own account. A special group to design all-metal aircraft and aero-sleighs had been formed at TsAGI in 1922 under Andrei Tupolev which received the title of Aviation, Hydroaviation and Special Design (AGOS) three years later. After Tupolev's first essay in all-metal design, the ANT-2 of 1924[7], work was at once begun on the ANT-3 (R-3) all-metal two-seat reconnaissance biplane as a replacement for the R-1. The prototype ANT-3 flew in April 1926 followed by thirty production exanples at GAZ No. 5, Moscow, during 1927-28 and a further seventy-nine at Fili over 1928-29. The first ANT-3 machines were triumphantly used for ODVF-sponsored prestige flights; in the late summer of 1926 Mikhail Gromov took the 'Proletariat' (*Proletari*) on a tour of European capitals and the following August Semyon Shestakov flew 'Our Reply' (*Nash otvet*) across Siberia to Tokyo. An enlarged and revised version of the ANT-3, the ANT-10 (R-7), was intended to benefit from the more powerful BMW VI engines later available but development was terminated in 1930 in favour of Polikarpov's competing R-5.

The ANT-3 gave the Soviet aircraft industry its first taste of original success but the greatest *éclat* was reserved for Tupolev's next design, the ANT-4. With features clearly derived from the Junkers design school, the prototype twin-engined cantilever low-wing monoplane first flew in November 1925 and Soviet directorship of the Fili factory was swiftly utilised to move in forty AGOS staff the next year to prepare for series production. After making ineffectual complaints that the Russians had infringed their patents, Junkers finally vacated Fili in March 1927 when the last JuG-1 trimotors had been completed and the factory was then fully integrated into the

---

[6]Between July and October 1926, two G 24 aircraft made a proving flight between Berlin and Pekin to investigate the possibilities of starting scheduled flights to the Far East via Siberia. A number of the K 30 bombers built at Fili were converted for passenger use with *Ukrvozdukhputi*, Ukrainian Airlines, in 1931.

[7]Aircraft produced by AGOS (later KOSOS) were denoted by the initials of Tupolev's name followed by a series number. After Tupolev's arrest, this designator was retrospectively changed to that of TsAGI.

Soviet aircraft industry as GAZ No. 22, the 'Tenth Anniversary of October Factory', although it was later usually referred to as the Gorbunov plant. Imported BMW VI engines were installed in the ANT-4 prototypes and delays in starting licenced series production of the BMW VI as the M-17 held back the completion of the first TB-1 heavy-bomber versions until June 1929. In August that year Shestakov flew the ANT-4 'Land of the Soviets' (*Strana Sovetov*) across Siberia to Khabarovsk where its wheels were exchanged for floats before the flight across the Pacific to San Francisco. From San Francisco, Shestakov flew over the USA to New York where his arrival was timed to coincide with the visit of a Soviet air delegation led by Baranov. The destination was not without significance. The Russians were already looking further afield than Germany in their search for powerful radial engines and new ideas in airframe design.

Excluding the floatplane variant with floats produced on the basis of examples supplied by the British firm of Short Brothers, 216 ANT-4 aircraft were built before manufacture ended in 1932, the machine remaining in Red Air Force service until 1936 and subsequently with the Civil Air Fleet (GVF) as the superannuated G-1 transport. A smaller and lighter version, the ANT-7, was also produced as a three-seat long-range escort fighter or reconnaissance bomber in answer to the demand for a multi-role 'air cruiser' and 'air battle' machine embodying the single type versatility (*odnotipnost'*) philosophy of the early twenties. The prototype flew in 1929 and production at GAZ No. 22 was begun two years later. Forty-five were built at Fili before production was farmed out to smaller factories including GAZ No. 31, Taganrog, where a dutiful quota of floatplane versions was manufactured in accordance with the policy of providing floatplane counterparts of Red Air Force machines for naval air duties. Four hundred ANT-7 aircraft were supplied as the R-6 until 1936 and, when obsolete as a military aircraft, remaining examples, like the ANT-4, were handed down to GVF.

These first successes in the design of bomber and reconnaissance aircraft were not matched by comparable progress in fighter design in spite of the priority given to it. Even while the R-1 was being hastened into production, a crash fighter-design programme was instituted at GAZ No. 1, the ODVF factory, where two competing design teams were set to work. The first of these was directed by Nikolai Polikarpov, a young engineer who had worked under Sikorski at the aircraft division of the Russo-Baltic Carriage Works and had already distinguished himself at the *Dux* factory during the Civil War and in preparing the R-1 for series production. His ambitious single-seat low-wing I-1 monoplane fighter fitted with a Liberty engine flew in 1923, but with all the marks of an over-hasty design. In spite of strenuous efforts to rectify them, the aerodynamic problems of the I-1 led to such difficult handling characteristics that not one of the thirty-three built was cleared for squadron service. The second team under Dmitri Grigorovich was more successful with a conventional biplane similarly powered and also initially designated I-1, whose second prototype made its maiden flight in the spring of 1924 as the I-2. Although its cockpit was cramped and its service performance suffered from inept manufacture and excessive structural weight, the fighter went into production as the I-2*bis* with 164 built at GAZ No. 1 and 47 at GAZ No. 23 between 1926 and 1928 as the first fighter of Soviet design to be manufactured in series.

The crash fighter-design programme had yielded only limited benefits, but on the other hand the results had been gratifyingly immediate and seemed to indicate the advantages to be gained from the creation of other adequately staffed and directed experimental design bureaux. There was, moreover, a pressing need to relieve the burdens imposed on Tupolev's AGOS as the only organised establishment for aircraft design. In 1925 at Baranov's request and with the backing of the Aviation Trust, the Central Design Bureau (TsKB) was formed consisting of two divisions responsible for landplane and floatplane development; the former (OSS) under Polikarpov being accommodated at GAZ No. 25, Moscow, and the latter at GAZ No. 23, Leningrad, under Grigorovich as the Experimental Floatplane Division (OMOS). Grigorovich was in fact primarily a flying boat specialist whose M-5 and M-9 flying boats had been built in quantity for the Imperial Russian Navy and had served with distinction. Diverted from his true vocation by the directive to produce a fighter, he now set to work to provide sorely needed replacements for the few obsolete flying boats still in naval service.

For the next two years Grigorovich and his staff of forty designers and engineers worked on a series of ill-fated new prototypes and projects, always hoping that the next would bring a change to their fortunes. The MR-2 reconnaissance seaplane crashed on its first test flight in 1926, and the MUR-1 and MU-2 flying boat trainers and the ROM-1 and ROM-2 long-range reconnaissance flying boats that followed were no more successful. In common with AGOS and

Polikarpov's OSS, OMOS took on too much design work at the same time; unlike them it was not able to produce the two or three viable types that compensated for the time and effort devoted to the failures, and flying boats had to be bought from abroad until well into the thirties. Sixty Dornier *Wal* flying boats were acquired in 1925, supplemented later by Italian Savoia S-16*bis* and S-55 machines. The Savois S-62*bis* was subsequently bought in limited numbers together with the manufacturing rights, production being undertaken between 1932 and 1933 as the MBR-4 at GAZ No. 31, Taganrog, a centre that was to replace Leningrad as the focus of floatplane and flying boat manufacture. Two Heinkel He 5c floatplanes obtained for the Yeisk Naval Air School were followed by an order for forty He 55 reconnaissance flying boats built specially for the Red Navy in 1930[8].

Foreign designers as well as aircraft were imported to assist in the task of re-equipping the Naval Air Forces. The French aircraft designer Paul Aimé Richard was given the facilities of the deposed Grigorovich together with an augmented design staff which included such ultimately famous names as the future floatplane and flying boat designers Ivan Chetverikov, Vadim Shavrov and Georgi Beriev, the rotating-wing aircraft specialists Nikolai Kamov and Nikolai Skrzhinski, fighter designers Mikhail Gurevich and Sergei Lavochkin, and the pioneer of Soviet space achievements Sergei Korolyov. A three-year scheme of work was drawn up but Richard's main responsibility, the TOM-1 torpedo bomber, was unsuccessful and the design bureau was dissolved. Other foreign designers drawn to work in the USSR at this time experienced diverse fortunes, few of which proved satisfying either for them or their Soviet employers[9].

---

[8]The He 55 (with the Soviet designation Kr.1) was intended for catapult launching from warships of the Black Sea Fleet, the catapult assemblies also being built by Heinkel. A number of Kr.1 flying boats were adapted to carry ski undercarriages and experiments were made in operating them from ice. The Kr.1 remained in service until replaced by Beriev's KOR-1 shipborne reconnaissance flying boat in the late thirties.

[9]After the German designer Rohrbach had declined the terms offered for work in the USSR, ten French designers were invited to Moscow in August 1928 to discuss terms. Only three including Richard decided to stay on. After Richard's bureau was disbanded in 1930, his deputy André Laville formed his own New Design Bureau (BNK) to develop the DI-4 two-seat fighter. Laville later worked briefly for GVF, carrying out the preliminary design studies in what was later to be the PS-89 civil transport, before returning to France. Italy also contributed its share of designers. General Umberto Nobile accepted a commission to design airships for Russia in 1929 after the scandal of the 'Italia' disaster, and Vittorio Izacco came to Russia in 1932 to build his wildly ambitious autogyro with engines mounted on the tips of the rotor blade. The most outstanding Italian designer was Roberto Bartini who went to work in Russia in the mid-twenties and later designed a number of outstanding aircraft in the STAL' series before his arrest on charges of being an agent for Mussolini.

To compensate, Tupolev was obliged to revive a project for a twin-engined long-range reconnaissance flying boat, the ANT-8 (MDR-2), drafted in 1925 and shelved due to the pressure of other commitments. The prototype was completed by January 1931, largely due to the expedient of adopting the wing and tail structures of the ANT-9 trimotor transport, but Tupolev's flying boat was turned down by the Navy on the grounds that its landing and take-off speeds were too high and that its design was already dated. In any case Tupolev was already engrossed in a more grandiose project, a twin-hulled six-engined flying boat that was to be nothing less than a naval counterpart to the Red Army's TB-3 heavy bomber[10].

Polikarpov was at first more successful than Grigorovich in managing to produce designs suitable for series production. After a first set-back when the 2I-N1 two-seat biplane fighter prototype crashed during tests in March 1926, the result of a construction fault, the design was revised as the I-3, Polikarpov's first successful single-seat fighter. Powered by the M-17 inline engine, the I-3 was placed in production at GAZ No. 1 in 1928 and a total of 399 assembled there over the next four years. AGOS had also been directed to submit fighter designs, Tupolev delegating this responsibility to the young Pavel Sukhoi who, under his chief's supervision, produced the I-4 (ANT-5) using one of the newly acquired 420 hp Gnôme-Rhône Jupiter radial engines in the prototype of 1927. An attractive sesquiplane with a high proportion of metal components and drawing on design features proven in the ANT-3, the I-4 fighter remained in front-line Red Air Force service until 1933 by which time 369 examples had been turned out by GAZ No. 22 fitted with the M-22 engine, the licence-built version of the Jupiter[11].

While the I-3 served to establish Polikarpov as a leading fighter-plane designer, his more lasting successes of the twenties lay in the creation of more modest types. The first and foremost of these was the U-2 two-seat basic training biplane (on Polikarpov's death in 1944 the designation was changed to Po-2 in honour of its late

---

[10] This was the ANT-22 or MK-1 'Sea Cruiser' completed in 1934. Although promising results were shown by tests conducted between August 1934 and May 1935, the Navy refused to accept the flying boat and work on it was broken off. Two load-to-height records were set up on the MK-1 towards the end of 1936.

[11] The M-22 was a licence-manufactured Gnôme-Rhône Jupiter 9ASB, itself a licenced version of the Bristol Jupiter VI engine. Imported examples were used in the Soviet Union until 1930 when production of the M-22 began at Zaporozh'e.

designer) produced in answer to a NTK-VVS requirement of 1925 for a U-1 replacement. With its 100 hp five-cylinder M-11 radial engine designed by Arkadi Shvetsov and Nikolai Okromeshko at GAZ No. 24 on the basis of the Lorraine 5P, the U-2 represented a partnership between airframe and engine which lasted well into the nineteen-fifties. Production began in 1930 at GAZ No. 23 and with its simple pine, plywood and fabric construction the U-2 proved itself highly adaptable for manufacture in small and austerely equipped provincial factories. These virtues together with the U-2's ease of handling and immense versatility were exploited to the full a decade later when the humble basic trainer was promoted to the status of a frontline combat aircraft. Not only did the U-2 see wide-scale service as a Red Air Force and *Osoaviakhim* trainer, but in modified land and floatplane variants it served as a passenger, cargo, ambulance and agricultural utility aircraft; and to these must be added its later wartime roles as a liaison, communications and artillery-spotting machine and its service as a 'utility' *shturmovik* and night bomber. Easy to fly and maintain in the field under the most primitive conditions, the U-2 was one of the most important and successful aircraft ever designed and built in the USSR. It was the essence of the cheap, simple and reliable versatility advocated for Red Air Force machines and in numerous ways the absolute vindication of *odnotipnost'*.

Polikarpov's second triumph was the R-5 two-seat reconnaissance-bomber biplane, the replacement for the ageing R-1 and R-3. With a 650 hp M-17 engine, the R-5 was built at GAZ No. 1 from 1929 and remained in production in a series of revised and modernised variants over the next nine years. From 1930 the 730 hp M-17F was installed, and in 1935 the basic R-5 was adapted to take the more powerful M-34N engine and a partially-enclosed cockpit as the R-Zet ground-attack bomber. In frontline service with the Red Air Force between 1931 and 1937, the R-5 biplanes were already obsolescent when they were committed in the Spanish Civil War and they were hopelessly obsolete by mid-1942 when *Luftwaffe* fighters decimated them over the Don in their last desperate hours as day bombers. Thereafter, the R-5 was withdrawn for transport and partisan-support work although a considerable number were used to equip the first night bomber regiments and the R-5 was still hitting back as a night nuisance raider in 1944. Some of the 7,000 built were handed over to GVF in the second half of the thirties for conversion into feeder transports on local passenger routes and the last were still flying several years after the end of World War II.

Polikarpov resumed his post as chief designer at GAZ No. 1 in 1928 under instructions to design a new fighter for the Red Air Force which could be mass produced to end the glaring deficiency in modern fighterplanes — in 1929 82% of all Red Air Force machines were classified as reconnaissance[12] — and take the place of the variegated fighter force assembled over the past six years and now largely obsolete. Adapting the I-3 airframe for the newly acquired Jupiter VI radial engine, Polikarpov supervised the construction of two prototypes of the new I-6 biplane fighter and it was decreed by Stalin that both should take pride of place in the 1930 May Day flypast over Moscow. At this critical moment things went badly for Polikarpov. One of the prototypes was lost when the pilot baled out, apparently prematurely, during tests in the spring of 1930 and Polikarpov was arrested and imprisoned together with a number of his design staff on charges of conspiring to sabotage the aircraft industry[13].

Polikarpov was not the first aircraft designer to suffer in this way. In September 1928 Grigorovich had been dismissed from his post as Head of the Third Experimental Division (OPO-3), the new title for OMOS on its humiliating return from GAZ No. 23 that year, on accusations of deliberately failing to meet the requirements for new naval aircraft. Shortly after his dismissal Grigorovich was interned with several of his closest associates including I.M. Kostkin, formerly head of the Technical Division at GAZ No. 1, and V.L. Korvin who had been responsible for production planning at OMOS and OPO-3. The dismal failures of OMOS and the pre-revolutionary careers of Grigorovich and his colleagues in the Russian aircraft industry appear to have been the primary factors behind this punitive action

---

[12] *Istoriya Velikoi Otechestvennoi Voiny Sovetskovo Soyuza, 1941-45* (IVOVSS), Vol.I

[13] Polikarpov's 'sabotage' included the DI-2, a two-seat fighter evolved from the I-3, which crashed during tests and the P-2 intermediate trainer which had to be taken out of production at GAZ No. 23 when its handling characteristics proved too formidable for trainee pilots. Polikarpov's essay in multi-engined aircraft design at this time, the TB-2, showed little edge in performance over the TB-1 when it was completed in 1930 and development was abandoned.

taken by Stalin through the agency of the OGPU[14].

The imprisonment of aircraft designers did nothing, however, to solve the problems they were alleged to have induced. The purchase of aircraft abroad on the scale required would have been both expensive and undermined Soviet military prestige in the eyes of potential enemies; in any case, the growing productive capacity of the First Five-Year Plan had to be supported and exploited by the provision of indigenous designs for aircraft capable of matching those in service with foreign air forces. A solution was found by setting up a special design bureau for interned designers, administered by the OGPU as part of its technical division. The location chosen was GAZ No. 39, formerly named the *Aviarabotnik* (Aircraft Industry Worker) but now retitled the Menzhinski factory after the head of the OGPU, where the OGPU Internee Design Bureau No. 39 was formed under the directorship of Paufler. It was here that Grigorovich and Polikarpov were brought together in company with other interned aircraft industry specialists, notably Vladimir Denisov, an authority on wooden airframes, the armament engineer Aleksandr Nadashkevich and the unfortunate design team which had been working on the abortive I-39 Fokker fighter development and which found itself imprisoned in its own factory. The internee staff were supported by 'free' draughtsmen, technicians and assembly workers to give the disgraced Central Design Bureau a total of three hundred personnel by late 1930 and some five hundred a year later.

Stalin's orders to Paufler were that a viable prototype based on Tupolev's ANT-12 fighter project, drawn up originally in the AGOS design offices but overshadowed by multi-engine design commitments, should be realised within a month by the internee TsKB 39 design bureau as the I-5 fighter. In all three prototypes were produced, the first of which was ready for flight testing in April 1931 with seven pre-production examples following in the late summer. A tubby biplane of mixed construction, the I-5 soon evinced evidence of its enforced creation and most of 1931 was spent in exhaustive trials to cure the fighter of its worst vices and prepare it

---

[14]The OGPU as an organ to oppose 'counter-revolutionary activities' replaced the *CheKa* in 1922 and was itself retitled the NKVD (People's Commissariat for Internal Affairs) in 1934. Between 1927 and 1931 the OGPU conducted a campaign of arrests against technical specialists and engineers who were held to blame for the 'sabotage' frustrating Soviet industrial development. Among others in 1928, fifty-five non-communist mining engineers were put on trial and found guilty of 'wrecking' at Shakhty in the Donets basin. Five were executed.

for series production. As a precautionary measure the licence was obtained from Heinkel for the production of the He 37 biplane fighter at GAZ No. 1 where 134 were subsequently built between 1932 and 1934.

Both Stalin and Alksnis were frequent visitors to Khodinka airfield adjacent to GAZ No. 39 where the I-5 prototypes were tested and Alksnis, made directly responsible for ensuring the new fighter's success, insisted on making a number of test flights himself. By late 1932 the I-5 had been eased into mass production under Kostkin's supervision at the extensive new fighter plant, GAZ No. 21, Nizhni Novgorod (Gorky), which was later named after the People's Commissar for Heavy Industry, Sergo Ordzhonikidze. Powered by a nine-cylinder 480 hp M-22 radial engine built under licence from Gnôme-Rhône at GAZ No. 29, Zaporozh'e, the production I-5 carried four 7.62mm PV-1 machine guns specially evolved from the infantry Maxim Model 1910 by Nadashkevich. Despite piloting difficulties and hazards in spin recovery, the besetting sin of most Soviet fighters, the I-5 remained on the production lines until the mid-thirties and was still in Red Air Force service until shortly before the German invasion. The Gorky plant turned out 803 examples of the I-5, more than double the production total for any previous Soviet fighter and one which prepared the way for the mass production of the I-15 and I-16 fighters from 1934.

The design team responsible for the I-5 were given their liberty as their 'reward'[15] and the Central Design Bureau (TsKB) placed under the overall direction of Sergei Il'yushin to complement and extend the work done by AGOS, on the whole, as it transpired, in the field of fighter, ground-attack and long-range bombers. The association between the aircraft industry and the OGPU/NKVD was to be revived again in the late thirties when Stalin was once more faced with a crisis in re-equipping his air force. This time the purges were to be on a more sweeping scale and to strike most severely at the man who had done most to modernise aircraft design in the USSR, Andrei Tupolev himself.

---

[15]Yakovlev in *Tsel' Zhizni* adds to his brief description of 'TsKB No.39 OGPU' the comment — 'It should be noted that after the first flights by the I-5 Polikarpov, Grigorovich and those interned with them were set free'.

3 Higher! Faster! Further!

The enigma of Soviet Russia yielded few facts but evoked many guesses, not least as regards the faltering rise of Soviet air power. Western estimates that the USSR had almost a thousand military aircraft by 1925 more than doubled the real size of the Red Air Force[1], but a dramatic increase was to occur in the decade covered by Stalin's first two Five-Year Plans; from less than a thousand aircraft in 1928 the number of Red Air Force machines rose to some 2,700 by January 1933 and to over 5,500 by 1938. When the League of Nations Armaments' Handbook gave Soviet military air strength as 750 aircraft in January 1930, it erred as much on the conservative side as other western estimates made a few years later were to be inflated. Official Soviet figures for 1936 admitted to a total of 4,700 combat aircraft, and on this basis the Germans assessed Soviet frontline air potential as consisting overall of 6,000 aircraft in March 1938.

The composition of the Red Air Force also underwent great changes. The proportion of classified reconnaissance aircraft declined from 82% in 1929 to 26% by 1934 and again to 9.5% by 1938 as the proportions of bomber and fighter aircraft increased. Between 1934 and 1938 bombers accounted for about half the combat total with the percentage of fighters rising steadily from 25% to 39% over the same period.

To meet the needs of this major programme of expansion, Alksnis was promoted from Deputy to Head of GU-VVS in June 1931 allowing Baranov to concentrate fully on his responsibilities for aircraft production as Head of GUAP, aircraft production being subsequently placed under Ordzhonikidze's People's Commissariat for Heavy Industry (NKTP) with Baranov as his special deputy from

---

[1] Jane's *All The World's Aircraft* for 1927 credited the Red Air Force with 987 aircraft and 1,210 flying personnel as of July 1925.

35

Soviet Air Force

January 1932. By 1933 the Soviet Union possessed six major airframe and four major aeroengine plants and the policy of expansion was extended during the Second Five-Year Plan with some emphasis on strategic dispersal as recommended by Tukhachevski. The dense concentration of the industry in the Moscow area was offset by the construction of new factories in eastern and southern Russia, notably the new Gorky fighter plant, GAZ No. 21, the 'Ordzhonikidze' factory, and the Voronezh bomber plant, GAZ No. 18. Of the four large aeroengine plants only one, GAZ No. 24, the 'Frunze' factory, was sited in Moscow although research and design organisations continued to expand in the immediate vicinity of the Soviet capital.

Output increased steadily as the new factories began production and established factories were enlarged and made more efficient. Over 1930-31 the average annual production of military aircraft was 860, over 1932-34 it rose to 2,595 and between 1935 and 1937 it was increased to 3,576 machines a year, although comparable figures for aeroengine production remain unquoted[2]. Over these seven years fighter production increased tenfold and bomber production well over five-fold, and with the clouding of the international situation output was more steeply accelerated in the late thirties. In 1938 the *Luftwaffe* High Command advanced a Soviet productive capacity of 8,000 military aircraft a year, a figure which credited the Russians with a greater output than they had as yet attained. After his visit to the USSR in 1937 the French industrialist and aircraft designer Henri Potez reported that the Soviets had produced 7,000 aircraft and 40,000 aeroengines the previous year. Such statements, prompted no doubt by what Potez had been told on his tour, were particularly welcome to the Russians at this time in impressing Germany with the Soviet Union's military and industrial might.

The Red Air Force enjoyed a uniquely strong representation on the *Revvoensovet* between 1931 and 1933 as Alksnis was given a seat on it as Head of GU-VVS while Baranov retained his place as Head of GUAP. This, together with the continuing intimate link between air force and aircraft industry, provided an excellent basis for the first phase of expansion which was to be interrupted by the sudden death

---

[2]IVOVSS, Vol.1

of Baranov in September 1933[3] and the dissolution of the *Revvoensovet* the year after. The new People's Commissariat for Defence under Voroshilov did not include the Head of GU-VVS among its eleven deputies until January 1937 when the need to include the Red Air Force in the highest council of the Red Army was again recognised. The loss of Baranov was in itself a severe blow to Red Air Force standing and influence. Baranov had worked to lay a modern productive foundation for military aviation in the USSR and its successes as compared to the generally sluggish development of the armaments industry had been singled out for special praise by Voroshilov in December 1927. Baranov also had a discreet but well rooted political backing and had been made a candidate member of the Central Committee at the 16th Party Congress held in the summer of 1930. Alksnis, on the other hand, was comparatively isolated from the mainsprings of political power. His connections were with Tukhachevski and the more progressive command elements in the Red Army, and his fortunes and his fall were closely associated with theirs. In the autumn of 1935 when command ranks were introduced into the Red Army, Alksnis was made an army commander (*komandarm*) second rank[4] — on a par with the commanders of the less strategically important military districts.

Facilities for research and aircraft design were also amplified and reorganised in readiness for the Second Five-Year Plan. New premises for an enlarged TsAGI were built at Stakhanovo (later Zhukovskaya) south of Moscow where two new, full-scale wind tunnels had been completed by 1939. TsAGI was also relieved of its responsibilities for research and development in aeroengines and structural materials with the creation of the Baranov Central Institute for Aeroengine Design (TsIAM) to co-ordinate work formerly carried out at the Scientific Automotive Institute (NAMI)

---

[3]Baranov was killed in an air crash on 5 September 1933 while flying from Moscow to the Crimea as a passenger on the prototype civil conversion of the R-6. Amongst those who also lost their lives were Baranov's wife, Abram Gol'tsman, Head of GU-GVF, his deputy Petrov, V.A. Zarzar, Chief of the Aviation Section of the State Planning Commission and S.P. Gorbunov, the director of GAZ No. 22.

[4]The Commanders of the Moscow, Leningrad, Belorussian and Ukrainian Military Districts were made army commanders, first rank, and the commanders of five other military districts, the Head of the Frunze Military Academy and Alksnis army commanders, second rank. In November Budyonny, Voroshilov, Yegorov, Blukher and Tukhachevski — the last three liquidated in the subsequent purges of the Red Army — were raised to the new rank of Marshal of the Soviet Union.

Soviet Air Force

and at GAZ No. 24 as well as at TsAGI's Aeroengine Division, and the All-Union Institute for Aviation Materials (VIAM). The development of aircraft equipment was undertaken by the new Scientific Institute for Aviation Technology (NIAT, later redesignated GKAT).

At VIAM a considerable amount of work was done on methods of producing moulded plywood and bonded birch airframe sections. The wooden fuselage of the I-16 was made of *shpon* — strips of birchwood impregnated with phenol-formaldehyde, moulded and pressed into shape on a wooden block pattern. When firm and dry, the two moulded fuselage halves so formed were detached and mounted on the airframe structure with metal plates along the dorsal and ventral joins. A similar process was later used in the fuselage of the LaGG fighters. Measures were also studied at VIAM for increasing the longevity and reliability of wooden airframes, and the later inability of the Soviet metallurgical industry to supply suitable alloys in quantity for stressed metal skinning and the problems posed by the loss of much of its resources during the Great Patriotic War were to render VIAM's services in this field specially valuable.

Aircraft engines, however, remained the weakest aspect of the industry and a cause for persistent concern. In 1928 70% of all the aeroengines used in the USSR were imported and attempts to develop new models of engines and increase the power output of the faithful M-5 based on the Liberty engine proved unsuccessful. The M-17 based on the BMW VI was already obsolescent when quantity production was finally achieved in 1929 and had been supplemented by the purchase of 480 hp nine-cylinder Gnôme-Rhône 9ASB radial engines from France and their eventual licence-manufacture as the M-22. Air-cooled radials with their high output and suitability for Russian climatic conditions offered most promise to the new generation of Soviet combat aircraft and the USA was approached as a source of supply as well as France. A Soviet air delegation headed by Baranov and including Andrei Tupolev and Boris Stechkin, then Head of TsAGI's Aeroengine Division, visited the USA to negotiate the purchase of aircraft and engines in 1929. They managed to obtain a number of 600 hp Curtiss Conqueror inline engines, but only in limited quantities, which were used for installation in prototype and experimental aircraft. For the time being only the M-22 was available to designers wishing to incorporate radial engines in their designs.

A second delegation to the USA in 1932 was more successful and

Higher! Faster! Further!

manufacturing rights for the 700 hp Wright Cyclone SGR-1820-F3 nine-cylinder radial were secured together with a number of examples used to power the prototypes of the I-14, I-15 and I-16 fighters. In 1934 preparations were made to produce the Wright-Cyclone engine as the M-25 at GAZ No. 19, Perm (Molotov) under the supervision of Arkadi Shvetsov who later developed the M-25 into the more powerful M-62 series in 1937 and undertook development of the fourteen-cylinder two-row Wright Cyclone R-2600 radial at the same factory as the celebrated M-82 of the war years.

In spite of the acquisition of the Wright Cyclone patent, contacts with the French aeroengine industry were not neglected. In 1933 Vladimir Klimov and Sergei Tumanski were sent by TsIAM in a delegation led by Sergei Il'yushin to discuss deals with the firms of Gnôme-Rhône and Hispano-Suiza. Two engines were chosen for production in the USSR, the 800 hp fourteen-cylinder two-row Gnôme-Rhône Mistral 14 radial and the twelve-cylinder Hispano-Suiza 12Y inline engine developing 860 hp, as the M-85 and M-100 respectively. Tumanski was despatched to GAZ No. 29 to instal the M-85 in production and Klimov, an experienced engineer who had headed Soviet purchasing delegations to BMW and Gnôme-Rhône in the twenties, was sent to GAZ No. 26, Rybinsk (Shcherbakov) where the M-100 was to be manufactured[5]. But while these three engines built under licence were destined to play crucial roles in the future development of Soviet aircraft engine technology, the first years of the thirties were dominated by the M-34, developed from the M-17 by Aleksandr Mikulin at GAZ No. 24 and used to power multi-engined and long-range aircraft as well as later versions of the R-5. Design work was begun in 1929 and after bench tests in 1931 the first flight tests were successfully carried out the next year. The twelve-cylinder M-34 inline engine had the distinction of being the first Soviet aeroengine to be built on a production line with versions

---

[5]GAZ No. 26, the *Amstro* (Aeroengine Construction) factory, was established on the basis of the former Moscow Renault plant reopened in 1921 as GAZ No. 6. When the factory was moved to Rybinsk in the early thirties, its number was changed and it became GAZ No. 26. In the late thirties Rybinsk became the biggest centre for aeroengine production in the USSR with the building of GAZ No. 16, also for the production of Klimov engines derived from the Hispano-Suiza 12Y. Members of the German air delegation visiting Rybinsk in the spring of 1941 reported on the existence of two aeroengine plants there. See Schwabedissen *The Russian Air Force in the Eyes of German Commanders*.

developing from 700 to 1,200 hp appearing between 1932 and 1938 when manufacture ended.

The two military aircraft design establishments serving the Red Air Force during the Second Five-Year Plan period (1933-38) were Tupolev's Experimental Aerodesign Division attached to TsAGI (KOSOS, the new title for AGOS from 1932), and the Central Design Bureau (TsKB) under Il'yushin based on the TsKB-39 OGPU which had produced the I-5 fighter. A planned merger in 1931 between these two organisations was abandoned before it had been fully implemented, but it was decided that they should co-operate and co-ordinate their design activities to achieve the best results without undue duplication of time and resources. In general it was envisaged that KOSOS should be largely concerned with multi-engined, long-range and maritime aircraft while TsKB would concentrate on fighter, ground-support and tactical bomber types. Within each establishment design teams (*brigady*) were formed to work on selected designs, or aspects of the design in the case of multi-engined aircraft, under the general direction of the bureau's head. At KOSOS Tupolev and his main wing designer, Vladimir Petlyakov, headed the multi-engined design team, Arkhangel'ski concentrated on tactical bombers, Pogosski on flying boats until his death in April 1934 during tests of the MDR-4 trimotor flying boat, and Sukhoi was charged with preparing studies for long-range aircraft. At TsKB where personnel were scattered through several Moscow factories, Polikarpov at GAZ No. 1 was primarily responsible for fighter design, with Grigorovich and Kocherigin engaged on a mixture of design work which ranged from fighters through reconnaissance types to special ground-attack aircraft. Chetverikov, later Beriev, was included in the TsKB group as flying boat designer, and the fact that both KOSOS and TsKB included flying boat design *brigady* gives some indication of the important place then given to naval aircraft in Soviet military thinking. In reality the demarcation of design territory between KOSOS and TsKB was never sharply delineated, and, where the urgency of demand dictated, competing design teams would be set to work. The attentions of designers were liable, too, to range beyond the limits of intent originally imposed on their *brigada*; fighter prototypes were produced by Sukhoi and Chernyshev at KOSOS as well as by Polikarpov and Grigorovich at TsKB, Tupolev was closely involved in the design of multi-engined flying boats and Il'yushin's long-range bomber *brigada* at TsKB was set up to succeed

Higher! Faster! Further!

where Sukhoi's at KOSOS had failed.

At heart there was rivalry, at times even jealousy and bitterness in the relationships between these two design establishments, and both Tupolev and Polikarpov as their champions were uncompromising personalities. With the death of Baranov there was no longer an experienced hand at the helm of GUAP to steer a far-sighted course and later heads of GUAP, notably Korolyov and Kaganovich, lacked Baranov's experience and authority. New designs by Aleksandr Yakovlev, an *Osoaviakhim* protegé, were resented and impeded, and backing for the development of Bartini's Stal'-6 high-speed monoplane as a fighter was stoutly resisted by GUAP on the grounds that Bartini was a designer at NII-GVF and therefore his province must be solely that of civil aircraft[6]. Aleksandr Yakovlev had already made a name for himself with a series of successful and original light aircraft built with *Osoaviakhim* funds before joining the design staff at GAZ No. 39 in 1931. There he refused to work in Kocherigin's *brigada* and insisted on the right to continue his own individual design projects. His high-speed AIR-7 attained a top speed of 330 kph in late 1932, but soon afterwards the machine shed an aileron during a speed test and the pilot, Piontkovski, only managed to land the aircraft with difficulty. An enquiry found Yakovlev guilty of faulty design work and he was expelled from the factory and denied alternative facilities by GUAP. Yakovlev's AIR-6 was placed in production in 1934 and 468 examples built, but Yakovlev was only rescued from the wilderness when his successful UT-1 and UT-2 trainers came to Stalin's notice. Thereafter, Yakovlev enjoyed the special confidence and patronage of Stalin.

Tupolev and Polikarpov emerged as autocratic figures in the field of aircraft design, albeit in a paternalistic way. Polikarpov modelled his control of his design staff on Stalin's handling of the Politburo while Tupolev's view, it is recorded[7], was that small design bureaux served only to dissipate the fund of experience and talent and that only the huge KOSOS could cope adequately with the complexity of

---

[6] During tests in 1933 the Stal'-6 with a Curtiss Conqueror engine reached a top speed of 420 kph and Ordzhonikidze overruled GUAP's objections to developing the machine as a fighter. The Stal'-8, its all-metal fighter development, was expected to reach 630 kph and possess a climb-rate of twenty metres a second with a M-100 engine installed, but antagonism between GU-GVF, GUAP and NKTP brought the aircraft's development to a halt in 1934.

[7] Ozerov *Tupolevskaya sharaga*

Soviet Air Force

modern aircraft design. Tupolev was quite correct in that only an organisation like KOSOS could have produced the multi-engined aircraft in which it specialised. At the same time, the hierarchical nature of KOSOS and TsKB frustrated the eager new graduates from the aviation institutes as much as it did the older engineers who found their talents and ideas restricted as mere components in a creative machine. Where Polikarpov and Tupolev were deeply divided was in their basic design philosophies. For Polikarpov, successful design meant creating aircraft equal, or if possible superior, to those in service with the western air forces. Nothing less would do, and he was tormented by that pursuit as much as by the failings of an aircraft industry whose productive skill incessantly lagged behind the demands he made upon it. Tupolev, on the other hand, held that such competition was pointless and harmful. A successful aircraft was one that the industry could produce and which fulfilled a function required of it by the overall military doctrines of the Red Army. Research and development must, of course, be maintained, but divorced from the short-term applications which ensued when it was considered merely an adjunct to series production. These divergent viewpoints are particulary significant when we come to consider why Tupolev was held to blame for the aircraft industry's failings as the Chief Engineer of GUAP and interned, while Polikarpov, despite the lack of practical success he enjoyed later, escaped the direct results of Stalin's displeasure.

Among the newer semi-autonomous research organisations created by TsAGI to extend its aerodynamic development programme was the Special Design Division (OOK) under A.M. Izakson which concentrated on rotating-wing aircraft. In 1933 OOK contained a helicopter *brigada* under Ivan Bratukhin and three autogyro *brigady* led by Vyacheslav Kuznetsov, Nikolai Kamov and Nikolai Skrzhinski. Although an energetic start had already been made[8] and a series of prototypes produced by OOK, only a small batch of Kamov's A-7 autogyros had been built for the Red Army when the organisation was disbanded.

One of the Red Army's most urgent needs was not for autogyros

---

[8]The first Soviet autogyro, the Kaskr, was designed by Kamov and Skrzhinski and built with *Osoaviakhim* funds in 1929. Test flights were eventually made in 1930-31 after a more powerful engine was installed in place of the original one. The first Soviet helicopter, the TsAGI-1EA, was flown in August 1932 by its designer, Aleksei Cheremukhin, but lacked stability and later crashed during tethered tests.

Higher! Faster! Further!

but for effective anti-tank aircraft in the new conditions of armoured warfare prophesied by Tukhachevski, with both the major design bureaux being directed to submit prototypes for evaluation. At TsKB four low-level ground-attack or *shturmovik* prototypes were built on the basis of the R-5 while Tupolev proposed a heavy twin-engined biplane and a modification of the R-6. None of these were accepted by the NTK-VVS and the only original *shturmovik* design, the TSh-3 low-wing monoplane submitted by Kocherigin and Gurevich, was ultimately rejected in 1934 after prolonged tests on the grounds of inadequate speed. In fact its top speed of almost 250 kph at sea-level was only marginally lower than that specified but its generous armour protection for crew and engine gave the TSh-3 an empty weight of 2,665 kgs and brought its flying weight to slightly over 3,500 kgs. Given the armament and bomb-load the TSh-3 was expected to carry, it was considered that the output of its 830 hp M-34F engine would be insufficient to give viable attack speeds with weights of this order. The problem was that the NTK-VVS expected the *shturmovik* to possess the turn of speed of a heavy single-seat fighter while incorporating extensive armour plating and carrying a heavy armament load. The modest output of available engines in the first half of the thirties frustrated these essentially incompatible requirements and *shturmovik* development lapsed until 1938 when Il'yushin produced the TsKB-55. Even then production was delayed and hindered by Stalin's insistence that the design should be revised as a faster, single-seat machine and by quibbles with NTK-VVS so that the Red Air Force was denied early familiarity with what was to be one of its fundamental types of combat aircraft. The policy remained one of adapting existing types; a *shturmovik* version of the R-5, the R-5Sh, was built in several hundreds while a number of Kocherigin's DI-6 two-seat fighter biplanes were converted to serve in the ground-attack role. Two attempts were also made to adapt the I-16 for ground attack, but these did not proceed beyond the prototype stage.

One of the basic factors retarding *shturmovik* development was the lack of any effective anti-tank weapon. Batteries of 7.62mm machine-guns were useless against armour and low-level horizontal bombing at speed was hopelessly inaccurate. A breakthrough appeared to have been made when it was suggested that the new large-calibre recoilless cannon devised by Leonid Kurchevski for the Red Army could be adapted for installation on aircraft. After Stalin and Tukhachevski had witnessed impressive demonstrations of Kurchevski's recoilless cannon the designer received vast funds to develop the weapon for all services and was made head of a Special Weapons' Development Directorate attached directly to Ordzhonikidze's Commissariat for Heavy Industry[9]. The aircraft industry was directed to work closely with Kurchevski in the design of a special aircraft to carry two 76mm APK-4 cannon and Sukhoi was instructed to mount weapons of the same calibre on the I-4 fighter for preliminary tests. The I-4 with its Kurchevski cannon was demonstrated in December 1931 and, despite a number of accidents during earlier test firings, the results were considered encouraging enough for Grigorovich to press on with his special 'Z' fighter. Grigorovich had decided to use the I-5 airframe for this purpose but converted it into a low-wing monoplane on which the explosive reactionary gases expelled from the cannon caused particular problems, necessitating the provision of protective metal sheathing under the wings and the raising of the tailplane so that control would be unaffected by the blast. Aerodynamic problems resulting from this held back the completion of the prototypes' tests; a first prototype in 1931 was followed by a second the next year, and it was only in 1933 that the first three top-secret 'Z' fighters were demonstrated by a NII-VVS *zveno* under Tomas Suzi in front of Stalin, Voroshilov, Tukhachevski, Ordzhonikidze and Tupolev. Production was ordered at once, but the staged demonstrations had masked a series of problems and setbacks which no one, it would appear, had the temerity to mention to Stalin. Not only did the 'Z' fly badly and require expert handling, the Kurchevski cannon had proved highly unreliable — jamming, bursting and with a muzzle velocity far below that needed for accurate air-gunnery. Nonetheless, 21 'Z' machines were built at GAZ No. 1 in 1933 and a further 50 at GAZ No. 135, Khar'kov, over the next two years.

Meanwhile Kurchevski and Grigorovich became increasingly unhappy with their enforced partnership when Stalin insisted that they were to continue work together on a new fighter project, the IP-1 (DG.52), and Grigorovich was not the only designer who was bent unwillingly to work with the new wonder of the Soviet armaments industry. At KOSOS Sukhoi was told to include provision for two APK-4 cannon in his new I-14 fighter — the outcome of which was ultimately to handicap the more promising machine in its contest

---

[9] Kurchevski was also given direct access to Stalin and a Lincoln limousine to convey him between his experimental factory and the Kremlin.

Higher! Faster! Further!

with the I-16 — while Arkhangel'ski and Chernyshev were ordered to work on heavier aircraft capable of carrying a pair of 102mm recoilless cannon. Chernyshev's I-12 was an ambitious twin-boomed fighter powered by two Jupiter VI radials, one in the nose and the other in tandem behind the pilot's cockpit and driving a pusher airscrew. Objections from NII-VVS test pilots to the hazards involved in baling out and falling into the rear propeller dampened enthusiasm from the start and further development work was terminated in 1933. Arkhangel'ski's two-seat DIP (ANT-29) fighter was a more conventional, twin-engined aircraft but priority given to the development of the SB bomber — with which the DIP had certain features in common — delayed work until Kurchevski's ideas had been discredited and his design facilities appropriated in February 1936. A number of other highly adventurous and unconventional fighter designs intended to carry Kurchevski cannon, including a fighter with a retractable cockpit cover by Lyushin and Lavochkin, the BICh-7 flying-wing fighter by Cheranovski and a project by Grushin at the Moscow Aviation Institute, were begun but subsequently abandoned.

Kurchevski himself was arrested in 1936, either for execution or to perish anonymously in one of GULAG's labour camps. There can be little doubt that the Kurchevski fiasco enraged Stalin and made him deeply suspicious of all other Soviet engineers and designers engaged on the more unconventional aspects of military technology. It triggered off a wave of arrests which were soon compounded by the 'failings' of the Soviet aircraft industry to match the new *Luftwaffe* in the skies of Spain. The full effect of Stalin's vengeful purging of the Soviet military research establishment over the next three years has still to be adequately assessed.

Despite the failure to produce satisfactory ground-attack aircraft in the Second Five-Year Plan period, the impetus in fighter design imparted by the I-5 was well maintained. Polikarpov's most notable contribution here lay in the rapid design and testing of the world's first cantilever low-wing fighter monoplane with a fully retractable undercarriage, the I-16, whose first prototype was flown by the *enfant terrible* of Soviet test pilots — Valeri Chkalov[10] — on 31

Valeri Pavlovich Chkalov, born in 1904, became a fighter pilot in the Leningrad Military District in 1924. After several reprimands for dare-devil flying he was banished to a fighter squadron near Bryansk, but discharged from the Red Air Force in 1929 after crashing his fighter in an attempt to fly under telephone wires. With the aid of his friend, Mikhail Gromov, Chkalov was appointed as a test pilot with NII-VVS in 1930 but left in 1933 to become Polikarpov's chief test pilot and remained in this post until death five years later on the I-180. Chkalov became respectable and a national figure after his long-distance flights to the Soviet Far East in 1936 and across the North Pole to the USA in 1937 on the ANT-25 (RD).

45

December 1933 and proudly displayed in the 1934 May Day flypast. At that time the world's fastest as well as the smallest and lightest fighter — the I-16 had a wingspan of nine metres and an overall length of six and the TsKB-12 prototype (M-22 engine) had a flying weight of only 1,345kg — Polikarpov's *yastrebok* or 'little hawk' with its blunt nose and cockpit set well back on the short, stubby fuselage was to serve as the standard Soviet single-seat fighter for the next seven years with the last of the many still operational in early 1944. It was also a triumph for the stocky, taciturn Nikolai Polikarpov and the zenith of his career; for the next four years he was to be the undisputed and uncontested master of Soviet fighterplane design.

Observers at the 1935 May Day flypast were astonished by the formations of new fighters which swept over the domes of St. Basil's Cathedral and sped in hot pursuit of the massed TB-3 heavy bomber squadrons. The appearance of the I-16 in numbers at such an early date emphasised the importance Stalin attached to the immediate full-scale production of the fighter. Chkalov had reached a top speed of 359 kph on the first prototype, the TsKB-12, fitted with a 480 hp M-22, but even better results were expected from the second, the TsKB-12*bis*, with its 630 hp Wright Cyclone SGR 1820-F3 radial which Chkalov flew in February 1934. Polikarpov was not diappointed when Chkalov reported a maximum speed of 455 kph at a height of 4,000 metres. Stalin, too, was elated — making its designer a personal gift of a limousine and decorating him with the Order of Lenin the year following. Pending deliveries of the first Soviet licence-built copies of the Wright Cyclone engine as the M-25, production of the new fighters went ahead at GAZ No. 1 and GAZ No. 21 using either M-22 engines or imported examples of the SGR-1820-F3.

The first I-16 fighters began to reach Red Air Force fighter squadrons in 1935 but its service introduction was not to be without problems. Pilots used to the more docile I-5 and I-7 biplane and the I-4 sesquiplane fighters were disconcerted by the monoplane's faster landing and take-off speeds; pilots misjudged landing speeds and stalled on approach, they under-estimated take-off runs and careered off runways, and when they tried to put the I-16 into the tight turns they had been accustomed to it fell into a vicious spin. They disliked its cramped, enclosed cockpit and the exacting concentration it demanded of its pilot so that aversion grew as the accident rate climbed. An immediate programme to lengthen fighter airfield

Higher! Faster! Further!

runways was put in hand and Polikarpov was directed to prepare a two-seat conversion trainer version, the UTI-4, with an initial production ratio of one UTI-4 for every three I-16 fighters As a concession to pilot protest — evoked by the poor quality of the plexiglass used and the need to see and 'make hand signals in the absence of radios — the cockpit canopy was removed and Red Air Force fighter pilots continued to fly with open cockpits throughout the thirties.

At NII-VVS, the top fighter specialists carried out exhaustive spin-recovery tests on the I-16 and prepared an instruction manual on the correct procedures for handling the new fighters. In late 1935 Chkalov with Pyotr Stefanovski and Stepan Suprun toured the newly converted fighter squadrons instructing, advising, demonstrating and equally as important, giving virtuoso flying displays to inspire confidence and boost the morale of apprehensive pilots.

By 1936 the I-16 with its wooden airframe had vanquished its all-metal rival, Sukhoi's I-14. Like the I-16, the I-14 was also a low-wing monoplane with a retractable undercarriage, but development problems due initially to the requirement to instal Kurchevski cannon and handling difficulties evinced under test were not resolved until Polikarpov's fighter had already established itself in service. Of fifty-five I-14 fighters ordered, only eighteen were completed in 1936-37 and the remainder scrapped. While this decision no doubt represented the best interests of the Red Air Force at the time, its repercussions on later attitudes to fighter airframe design were more questionable. The death of the I-14 and the ascendency of wooden over metal airframes, simple, robust and suited to the capability of the aircraft industry as the former were, involved the penalty of weight and placed the onus for maintaining fighter speeds and climb-rates on the aeroengine industry which, under constant pressure for more and more powerful engines, was still mastering the techniques essential for the mass production of sophisticated modern engines and was to remain heavily reliant on continued access to the latest developments abroad.

The accommodating I-16 lent itself easily to continual modifications with more powerful engines and heavier armament. The I-16 Type 5 with the M-25 and the Type 6 with the more powerful 715 hp M-25A engine were built in quantity between 1935 and 1937 when the Type 10 with the improved M-25B was introduced. The I-16 Type 10 also incorporated heavier armament

Soviet Air Force

with the installation of two synchronised ShKAS machine-guns in the nose to supplement the two wing-mounted ShKAS on earlier models, and with the introduction of the Type 17 the following year, the two synchronised ShKAS were replaced by 20mm ShVAK cannon[11]. The heavier M-62 radial derived from M-25 offering 1,000 hp for take-off and 800 hp at 4,000 metres was fitted from the Type 18 onwards, this version having four ShKAS machine-guns like the Type 10 while the Type 24, the last variant to be built in series for the Red Air Force, had the same armament as the earlier Type 17.

When the last of the 6,554 I-16 fighters left the production lines at GAZ No. 21 in 1940[12], its top speed was 156 kph greater than the TsKB-12 which Chkalov had flown in December 1933 and its flying weight had risen by 567 kg. It was, however, essentially the same fighter whose adaptability had discouraged the trauma of introducing a new machine as its replacement from 1936 onwards when advances in inline-engined fighter design abroad had begun to show the way ahead. In fact Polikarpov had applied himself to the task of providing a faster successor to the I-16 using the Hispano-Suiza 12Y inline engine by 1935. The I-17 was to attain a top speed of 500 kph but the first prototype, the TsKB-15, tested late in 1934 yielded a maximum speed of only 424 kph and disgraced itself at an official demonstration when the undercarriage jammed. After a series of aerobatics to try to free a reluctant undercarriage leg, Chkalov landed on one wheel — impressing the spectators with his flying skill although their reaction to the new fighter was less cordial. A second prototype, the TsKB-19, with a M-100 engine (licence-built Hispano-Suiza 12Y) was tested by Chkalov the next year and vindicated itself by touching the required top speed of 500 kph at a height of 9,700 metres. The machine was sent for exhibition in Paris and Milan in 1937 but official interest had waned. The I-16 had shown itself amenable to improvement and Chkalov was obliged to interrupt flight tests to prepare for his trans-polar flight in the ANT-25. A third prototype, the TsKB-33, was praised by its test pilots for its responsive handling

---

[11] The 7.62mm ShKAS machine-gun was first produced in 1933. Early models had a rate of fire of 1,100 rpm, but this was increased on later models to 1,800 rpm. The 20mm ShVAK cannon was tested in 1937 and first installed on the I-16 the year after. With a rate of fire of 800 rpm, the ShVAK was first used operationally in the air battles against the Japanese over Khalkin Gol.

[12] This figure represents the pre-war total, but the later production of 450 I-16 fighters as an interim measure in late 1941 has been reported.

Higher! Faster! Further!

qualities and its virtues as a steady gun platform, but Polikarpov's decision to incorporate wing-surface evaporation radiators had already damned it in the eyes of the NTK-VVS and the I-17 programme petered out[13]. So the reliable 'little hawk' confirmed Stalin in his policy of maintaining production of a proven and familiar machine as best suited to the productivity of the aircraft industry and the numerical strength and confidence of Red Air Force fighter squadrons, and when a more radically revised version of the I-16 was attempted in 1938 it resulted in the ill-fated I-180. The realisations of this error in 1939 precipitated the 'emergency' fighter design competitions of that year and toppled Polikarpov in favour of the younger fighterplane designers of the Great Patriotic War.

This refusal to contemplate radical changes in fighter policy was most clearly reflected in the career of the I-15, the I-16's biplane contemporary developed from the I-5 and also designed by Polikarpov. First flown by Chkalov three months before the TsKB-12, the I-15 was an insurance against the failure of the more advanced monoplane. Apart from its 'gull' upper wing faired into the fuselage forward of the cockpit, it represented little that was disturbingly new with a fixed undercarriage, more modest speeds and more tractable handling. Production of the I-15 was undertaken from 1934, the first 404 of the 674 examples built[14] being fitted with M-22 engines as supplies of the more powerful M-25 were allocated for the I-16s. The first ShKAS 7.62mm machine-guns also went to arm the I-16s, and the I-15 had two PV-1 machine-guns — a weapon designed originally for the I-5. Production was brought to a stop in 1936 after Red Air Force objections to the 'gull' wing as an obstacle to the pilot's forward vision and Polikarpov redesigned the fighter as a conventional biplane with an increased armament of four PV-1 machine-guns. Yet in spite of the more powerful M-25B engine fitted to the I-15*bis*, its climb-rate and ceiling proved inferior to the I-15 and its career might easily have ended if it had not been for the impression produced on

---

[13] Wing-surface evaporation cooling systems were incorporated into the design of Bartini's Stal'-8 in 1934 and Il'yushin's I-21 (TsKB-32) fighter in 1937. Problems of over-heating and fears of vulnerability to incidental combat damage made the idea generally unacceptable to NTK-VVS. Similar cooling systems were used on the Heinkel He 100 and He 119.

[14] Yakovlev *50 let sovetskovo samoletostroeniya*. Nemecek in *Sovetské Letadla* gives the number of I-15 fighters produced as 733, to include 59 examples fitted with imported Wright Cyclone engines.

49

Soviet Air Force

Soviet fighter pilots in Spain by the agile Italian CR 32 biplane fighter. This persuaded the Red Air Force Command that the future of fighter warfare might well devolve on a planned symbiosis between the slower but more manoeuvrable biplane able to engage in the traditional dog-fight with its tight turns and twists and the faster monoplane relying on speed for dive attacks and able to break off combat at will. Experience in Spain had also indicated — at least during the first nine months of the conflict — that the I-15 was suited to the role of ground attack aircraft, given adequate top cover and opposed from the ground only by sporadic infantry fire. Therefore, although the failings of the I-15*bis* to compete with its modern fighter counterparts on equal terms were very soon to become apparent, 2,408 examples were built for the Red Air Force and Polikarpov and other designers persisted in more advanced biplane figher projects[15].

In 1938 the I-15*bis* was redesigned once more, this time reverting to its 'gull' upper wing but with a retractable undercarriage, a M-62 radial engine and an armament of four 12.7mm Berezin machine-guns and two ShVAK cannon to increase its potency in the ground attack role. Production of the I-153, the *Chaika* (seagull), was begun early in 1939 at GAZ No. 1 and GAZ No. 156, Moscow. Its first commitment in combat came that summer in action against the Japanese Air Force at Khalkin Gol but after a few initial successes, allegedly when Japanese pilots were tricked into mistaking the new fighters for the slower I-15*bis*, the I-153 was more of a liability than an asset. Highly manoeuvrable in the hands of an independent, confident pilot the I-153 was inferior in speed to the Nakajima Ki-27 fighter, so that pilots who lost their nerve and tried to break off combat by diving clear were easily overtaken and despatched. It was soon evident too that it was vulnerable to ground fire, especially if incendiary ammunition was used, since it carried no defensive armour forward or below. As, however, there was no new fighter to replace it, production of the I-153 continued into late 1940 by which time 3,437 examples had been supplied to the Red Air Force. Many were fated to burn on the ground in the first few days of *Barbarossa*

---

[15]Later Russian biplane fighter projects included the OKB-7 and its development the I-207 by Borovkov and Florov in 1937-38, the I-220 (IS-1), able to convert in flight from biplane to shoulder-wing monoplane configuration, by Nikitin and Shevchenko in 1939-40, and Polikarpov's I-190 derived from the I-153 but to be fitted with a M-88 engine. None of these was accepted for series production.

Higher! Faster! Further!

and others, pressed into service as *shturmoviks*, fell victims to the German flak.

The I-15 and I-16 fighters were paralleled by the SB bomber, the outcome of a 1933 requirement for a new, fast tactical bomber to replace the ageing TB-1, R-5 and R-6 machines still in service. Designed by Aleksandr Arkhangel'ski under Tupolev's supervision at KOSOS as the ANT-40, two prototypes of the all-metal mid-wing twin-engined bomber were built in 1934. The first, powered by two Wright Cyclone SGR 1820-F3 radials was flown by Gromov on 7 October followed on 30 December by the second with two Hispano-Suiza 12Ybrs inline engines. The performance of the second prototype, due mainly to the reduced resistance offered by the inline engines and a fuel capacity increased from 940 to 1,670 litres, was markedly superior to that of the first with a top speed of 420 kph at 5,000 metres, improved ceiling and a greatly extended range of 1,250 kms with the same 500 kg bomb-load. Testing did not proceed smoothly and an acrimonious quarrel over the new bomber's failings broke out between Arkhangel'ski and Konstantin Minder, the NII-VVS test pilot. This reached such a pitch that Ordzhonikidze was asked to intervene, and when he and Tupolev arrived at the test airfield they were confronted by the SB prototype plastered in home-made posters proclaiming its defects. Eventually the affair came to Stalin's ears and he rebuked Arkhangel'ski for refusing to listen to Minder's complaints. State tests of the SB were finished in July 1935 and production of the bomber began at GAZ No. 22, Fili, and GAZ No. 18, Voronezh, with the first examples reaching Red Air Force bomber squadrons early in 1936. At peak output thirteen SB bombers were built each day and manufacture was still in progress when the Germans invaded the USSR in June 1941. In common with the I-15 and I-16, the SB was updated throughout the thirties with the installation of the 840 hp M-100A and 960 hp M-103 engines in later versions. With a total of 6,456 produced, the SB came second only to the R-5 as the most widely-built Soviet bomber of the pre-war years. Although the SB with its monocoque fuselage frame and duralumin covering for wings and fuselage represented a significant advance in Soviet aircraft design techniques, its greatest defensive advantage — speed — became invalidated as fighter performance surged forward abroad; as events in Spain were to show, the SB was by no means safe from attack by the new generation of fighters represented by the *Luftwaffe's* Bf 109. The SB needed height to see

Soviet Air Force

and elude intercepting fighters, but at the cost of any accuracy in bombing.

Civil aviation, although in theory a separate entity, was in practice intimately tied to the Red Air Force during the nineteen-thirties. During the formative years of the nineteen-twenties the Deputy Head of GU-VVS had also served as Deputy Head of the Council for Civil Aviation and, in effect, exercised control in consultation with the Council's Chief Inspector. In February 1932 a Chief Directorate of the Civil Air Fleet (GU-GVF) was formed under Abram Gol'tsman and, after his death in 1933, Iosif Unshlikht. The new GU-GVF was modelled closely along the lines of GU-VVS with various specialist departments, including a Deputy Head as Chief of the Political Department, a Chief Inspector and a Civil Air Scientific-Test Institute (NII-GVF) to evaluate new designs. From 1934 civil air regions were defined and administered after the manner of military districts with GVF responsible for crop-spraying and pest control as well as passenger and cargo services. There was also a GVF section administered by the NKVD for VIP transport and the conveyance of special prisoners — the service being greatly extended during the purge of the Far Eastern Army in 1938. Certain aspects of civil aviation remained, however, independent of GU-GVF[16]. New GVF flying schools were opened at Bataisk, Tambov and Balashov and training schools for mechanics at Saratov and Gorky. More advanced technical instruction was given at the new Moscow, Kiev and Khar'kov Aviation Institutes, at the Voronezh Aeronautical Technical College and at the Leningrad Institute for Civil Air Force Engineers.

The new aviation institutes at once became the centres for a surge of independent experimental design work and one of the most urgent concerns was for the development of new civil aircraft. In 1932 GVF was operating twenty-seven different types of aircraft powered by nineteen types of engines. Resolves to produce specifically civil machines were nonetheless constantly impeded by the priorities given to military aircraft production, the sheer lack of any civil aircraft design tradition in the USSR and the tendency of aspiring

---

[16]These included the Air Ambulance Service (*Sanitarnaya aviatsiya*) which came under GVF jurisdiction in 1939, and aircraft used for forestry and fishery patrol work in 1948 and 1949 respectively. In 1960 arctic aircraft of *Aviaarktika* attached to the Chief Directorate for the Northern Sea Routes were incorporated into GVF as the new *Polyarnaya Aviatsiya* (Polar Aviation).

Higher! Faster! Further!

young designers to think in terms of versatile aircraft suitable for either civil or military roles. In the pursuit of prestige and performance economics fell by the wayside, and many designs were patently projected with air force service in mind. At the Kiev Aviation Institute Zelman Itskovich produced his first design, the KAI-1, as a bomber crewtrainer while Iosif Neman at the Khar'kov Aviation Institute designed the first Soviet aircraft with a fully retractable undercarriage in his KhAI-1 which reached a top speed of 300 kph. Only forty-three were built for GVF and Neman's later KhAI-5 and KhAI-6 were more overtly military machines. The KhAI-5 was built for the Red Air Force as the R-10 reconnaissance-bomber from 1937 and, although its bomb-load was small and its design concept dated, 490 were produced. After the disappointment of the Stal'-8 fighter project, Bartini designed the Stal'-7 as a high-speed long-range transport. Flight tests were made in 1935, but the prototype was developed as a bomber under the designation DB-240 and after Bartini's arrest the machine was produced as the Yer-2 long-range night-bomber and credited to his deputy, Vladimir Yermolaev.

Few specifically civil aircraft were built in quantity[17] and the majority of GVF's machines were Red Air Force cast-offs; over two hundred R-5 reconnaissance-bombers were converted into P-5 civil transports at GVF's Bykovo workshops, and these were supplemented by numbers of twin-engined R-6 machines under the civil designation PS-7. Discarded TB-1 and TB-3 bombers were used by GVF as the G-1 and G-2 freighters, and a civil version of the SB was introduced in the latter half of the thirties as the PS-40. This utilisation of ex-Red Air Force bombers as civil transports ensured the exploitation of obsolete military machines and facilitated the priority production of fighters and bombers, but it did not provide a viable civil air transport service as such along economic lines. Incidentally, the policy paid off in the Great Patriotic War when

---

[17]The notable exceptions were Kalinin's K-5 of which 260 were built at GAZ No. 135, Khar'kov, in 1931-34 and Putilov's Stal'-2 and Stal'-3 transports of which 190 were produced by GAZ No. 81, Moscow, in 1932-36. All three of these designs were single-engined monoplanes with limited passenger accommodation. The PS-9, a twin-engined development of Tupolev's ANT-9 trimotor, was built in some seventy examples of which a high proportion were allocated to the Red Air Force as paratroop and VIP transports. Later twin-engined transports — Arkhangel'ski's PS-35 (ANT-35), Kulev's PS-89 (ZIG-1) and Rafaelyants RAF-11 — carried between eight and fourteen passengers but were dropped in preference to licence-production of the Douglas DC-3.

Soviet Air Force

GVF pilots were easily absorbed into the Red Air Force to fly types they had already known in civilian guise. In other words, GVF — in common with *Osoaviakhim* — was yet another aspect of military aviation, while the policy of evolving civilian from military types, as the Tu-104 and Tu-114 were to show, was to persist well into the post-war years.

4 The Fortunes of Soviet Air Strategy

On 31 October 1930 the tram services in Moscow's suburb of Fili were unexpectedly suspended for the day. Passengers who decided to continue their journey on foot past the 'Gorbunov' aircraft works discovered that the overhead power lines had been taken down to allow the largest Soviet aircraft yet built, the ANT-6, to be transported to the Central Aerodrome for flight testing. The all-metal four-engined monoplane with a wingspan of nearly forty metres and bearing the unmistakable hallmark of Junkers engineering was the product of four years' work by Tupolev's AGOS design bureau, and it was to play a major role in Soviet defence planning over the next six.

Mikhail Gromov as Head of the AGOS Flight-Test Team first lifted the ANT-6 prototype with its four imported Curtiss Conqueror engines into the air on 22 December 1930, and towards the end of the following year preparations for the aircraft's series production with M-17 engines were well under way at Moscow's GAZ No. 22 and GAZ No. 39, the 'Gorbunov' and *Aviarabotnik* factories. Soon after the first production model had been delivered for State acceptance trials under NII-VVS test-pilot Andrei Yumashev in January 1932, Stalin ordered the immediate completion of a further eight machines so that a formation of his new bombers could be flown in that year's May Day flypast. Despite the persistent unreliability of the M-17 engines, Yumashev led his formation of nine ANT-6s, each crewed only by a pilot and flight engineer, over Red Square in company with seventy TB-1 twin-engined bombers, fifty-nine R-5 and R-6 reconnaissance bombers and twenty-seven fighters. The era of the mighty Russian bomber had begun.

Large-scale production of the ANT-6, predominantly in its heavy

55

Soviet Air Force

bomber version as the TB-3[1], reached its peak in 1933-34 when up to fifty examples a month left the Moscow assembly lines. After a short break in manufacture between the autumn of 1934 and the spring of 1935 while preparations were made for the production of the new SB-2 tactical bomber, assembly was resumed on a smaller scale until 1937 by which date 818 ANT-6s in various versions and with various modifications had been built[2]. Symbolising the huge and menacing heavy bomber forces of the Red Army, massed formations of TB-3 bombers were regularly flown over Moscow as part of the May Day military parade or in the annual display to commemorate Red Air Force Day on 18 August[3]. The new TB-3 bombers were formed into special brigades consisting of between three and four squadrons, each of twelve aircraft, and from 1934-35 they were available in sufficient numbers to permit the formation of special heavy-bomber air corps. The first three TB-3 brigades to be formed, some one hundred and fifty bombers, were sent immediately eastwards to reinforce Soviet air power in Eastern Siberia after the occupation of Manchuria by Japanese troops. As early as the summer of 1932 Yumashev, Stefanovski and Nyukhtikov from NII-VVS and Gromov from AGOS, all experienced pilots of multi-engined aircraft, were sent to advise Albert Lapin', then Head of the Special Far Eastern Army's Air Force, on the best methods of preparing bases and the necessary servicing facilities for heavy bombers. The significance of this gesture was not lost upon the Japanese who set to work to improve their air defences and build up their air strength on the Asiatic mainland, while Stalin made plans for the creation of the *Aviatsiya osobovo naznacheniya* or Special Purpose Air Arm (AON) whose strategic

---

[1]The only heavy bombers in the TB series which were not ANT designs were the prototypes of Polikarpov's TB-2 twin-engined biplane completed in 1930, and Grigorovich's four-engined TB-5 monoplane tested in the spring of 1932.

[2]The TB-3 series of 1933-34 had M-17F engines, but from late 1933 onwards the more powerful M-34 was fitted. The final production series of 1936-37 had four 900 hp M-34FRN engines and developed a maximum speed of 300 kph at 3,000m. The TB-3 saw active service during the air battles at Khalkin Gol, during the Winter War and in the early stages of the German-Soviet War — notably during the Battle for Smolensk and on the Northern Front. The remaining TB-3s were used by ADD or modified to serve as transports.

[3]The first Air Force Day display was held on 18 August 1933 at the Central (Frunze) Aerodrome and was opened by Alksnis and Yegorov, then Chief of Red Army Staff. Subsequent displays were held at Tushino and became the major occasions for demonstrating Soviet air power and new types of aircraft.

potential would parallel the tactical function of the VVS-RKKA.

Stalin chose as Head of the AON one of the most able Red air commanders of the Civil War, Vasili Vladimirovich Khripin, a man deeply and consistently interested in the strategic use of air power whose rise and fall were closely related to those of Alksnis and Tukhachevski. Khripin had served in the Imperial Air Force and had been one of the few flying officers in it to give his total allegiance to the Bolshevik cause; in 1919 he distinguished himself in command of the Red air *otryady* attached to the 10th Red Army at Csaritsyn, and was Commander of all RKK-VVF units on the Caucasian Front when the war ended. He would have been a good candidate for selection as the new Head of RKK-VVF, but there were rivals with more 'ideologically sound' backgrounds and for a time Khripin disappeared from upper command echelons and turned his attention to questions of theory, publishing a series of articles on the role of air power in future wars in the Red Air Force journal *Vestnik Vozdushnovo Flota*, writing his own introduction to the Russian translation of Douhet's treatise on air warfare, and contending insistently that modern military operations could not be carried out successfully without an independent air arm[4]. Khripin shared the adventurous, progressive view of air power held by Tukhachevski and Alksnis, and when Tukhachevski was appointed Chief of Ordnance and Deputy Chairman of the *Revvoensovet* under Voroshilov in 1931 he began to implement on a wider and more practical scale the ideas contained in his treatise on warfare[5] and assisted in the re-establishment of his former Air Commander on the Caucasian Front. In the late twenties Khripin was already Head of

---

[4] General Giulio Douhet's *Il dominio dell' aria* (Command of the Air) first appeared in 1921 with a second, enlarged edition six years later. The first Russian edition with Khripin's introduction was published in 1935. Russia's other outstanding air theoretician was Aleksandr Lapchinski who, like Khripin, had held a commission in the Imperial Air Force and commanded Red air units during the Civil War. Lapchinski was replaced as Chief of Air Staff in 1925 and became Professor of Air Tactics at the Frunze Military Academy, maintaining in his later works on air power a spirited defence of the strategic bomber. Like Khripin, Lapchinski was liquidated in the pre-war purges.

[5] Entitled *Voina kak problema vooruzhyonnoi bor'by* (War as a Problem of Armed Conflict) and appearing in 1938, Tukhachevski's work advocated, among other measures, the encouragement of close technical liaisons with foreign armed forces, the dispersal of the Soviet armaments industry to reduce its vulnerability to strategic air attack, and the need to develop new techniques in facilitating rapid and well co-ordinated offensive operations.

Soviet Air Force

the Operations Section at GU-VVS, and soon after Alksnis took over from Baranov he replaced Sergei Mezhenikov in the key post of Chief of Air Staff. Under Khripin the bomber component of VVS rapidly increased; addressing the Eighth Congress of Soviets in 1936 he claimed that 60% of the Red Air Force which had quadrupled in size over the previous four years now consisted of bombers[6]. As Head of the AON created in 1936 and made directly subordinate to the Defence Commissariat, Khripin enjoyed near parity with Alksnis although he remained at the lower rank of Corps Commander.

The AON was not planned, however, as an exclusively heavy bomber force. Its function lay equally in the support and supply of the Red Army in the new age of fast, mechanized warfare foreseen by Tukhachevski who through his close association with many officers in the *Reichswehr* was particularly aware of the new doctrines of *blitzkrieg*. As Commander of the Leningrad Military District for three years from 1928, Tukhachevski encouraged the creation of the Red Army's first parachute detachment which took part in demonstrations and exercises over the Voronezh battle range in 1930. In August 1931 nineteen parachutists were dropped near Krasnoe Selo to seize a landing area on which a TB-1 squadron landed troops and guns, and the exercise was repeated that autumn in the Kiev Military District at the invitation of its Red Army Commander, Yakir. The detachment was then expanded to become the first airborne brigade. In May 1933 Alksnis circulated a memorandum to all Military District Air Commanders urging them to collaborate in establishing airborne forces and by 1935 brigades had been formed in the Moscow, Kiev and Belorussian Military Districts. Parachuting was promoted as a mass sport by *Osoaviakhim*, with teams making demonstration drops during Red Air Force Day displays at Tushino and travelling abroad on prestige tours. Two hundred *Osoaviakhim* parachutists made a mass descent over Tushino in 1936 and the crowd of half a million was also treated to the glamorous spectacle of twenty-five girl parachutists using brightly coloured canopies.

The new airborne brigades played a prominent part in the extensive Red Army training exercises held during the summer and early autumn. In 1934 three hundred and twenty VVS machines took

---

[6]Loktionov in his statement on Red Air Force strength in August 1939 claimed that 55% of Soviet combat aircraft based in the West were bombers. The *Luftwaffe* estimate of some months earlier had concluded that bomber, reconnaissance and ground-attack aircraft made up 50% of Soviet air strength.

The Fortunes of Soviet Air Strategy

part in manoeuvres in the Belorussian Military District and mass parachute drops were made by the 'attacking' force, and in 1935 six hundred aircraft were involved in manoeuvres in the Kiev Military District together with an entire airborne brigade. This operation consisted of three phases; in the first six hundred men were dropped to secure a landing area and permit a second wave of aircraft to land infantry support as phase two — the final phase being the delivery of light artillery and supplies by a third wave of transports. The German observers were disconcerted by the speed of Soviet developments in airborne operations, reporting later that year that an entire rifle division had been air-lifted from Moscow to Vladivostok. When British military observers attended Red Army manoeuvres in Belorussia in 1936, parachute troops again cleared a landing area to which ANT-6 transports brought field artillery and light tanks, and similar exercises were held on a more extensive scale the next year in the North Caucasus and Belorussia — the last to which foreign attachés were invited. The latter, in August, included the better part of two airborne brigades and was entitled, 'Operations by Frontal Air Forces and the Supreme Command's Special Purpose Air Arm in the Opening Phase of Battle and under the Conditions of a Developing Front'. In 1938 German Intelligence assessed Soviet airborne strength as consisting of at least four brigades of a thousand men each in the Leningrad, Kiev and Belorussian Military Districts and the Far East, and reported two years later that a thousand Soviet paratroopers were used in the seizure of Bessarabia and Northern Bukovina from Rumania.[7]

This, but probably more the German airborne successes of 1940, appears to have encouraged the Russians to increase the size of their own airborne forces in spite of the calamities experienced when they had been used during the Winter War with Finland. By early 1941 the airborne brigades were being formed into corps by the new Directorate for Airborne Forces (U-VDV). Three airborne corps, the III, IV and V Airborne Corps in the Kiev, Belorussian and Leningrad Military Districts were each intended to have three brigades, but only the original brigade in each corps appears to have been fully equipped by June 1941[8].

---

[7] Schwabedissen

[8] See the excellent but brief monograph *Soviet Airborne Troops* by J.M. Mackintosh in *The Soviet Air & Rocket Forces*.

Soviet Air Force

A series of experiments were made to improve equipment and techniques for the airborne forces, a large part being allocated to the special research and development group under Pavel Grokhovski formed by GUAP in 1932 to collaborate with the Red Army. Grokhovski's devices included a novel 'tipping cradle' to facilitate the dropping of parachutists in clusters from the bomb-bay of the ANT-6, and also special containers for troops or equipment dropped on multiple parachutes. A glider to be towed by a R-5 and carry eighteen troops, the *Yakov Alksnis*, was tested in 1934 and later developed as the G-31 motorized glider with a M-25 engine. None of these projects proved viable, nor did Grokhovski's special underwing containers for the TB-1 enabling twelve parachutists to be carried in conditions of extreme discomfort under each wing. These containers were in effect a series of simple 'pens', open at the front and just large enough for the occupant to lie prone until the time came to wriggle forward against the slipstream and tumble downwards. The weight and the immense drag penalty involved made a serious reduction in the TB-1's already humble speed inevitable and the idea was abandoned. It was, however, revived by GVF for accommodating excess passengers under the wings of P-5 biplanes for short flights, and inspired the two underwing coffin-shaped boxes, each housing one stretcher case, fitted to later versions of the U-2 ambulance biplane. The most perilous of Grokhovski's ideas was for suspending light tanks on special platforms under ANT-6s and dropping them at low speed on to water while the aircraft themselves went on to land close by and act as refuelling bowsers for the forward light tank units they had thus delivered. To ensure success, the free drops had to be made over rivers and lakes at almost stalling speed and no higher than one metre from the surface. The tests were ended after a heroic series of preliminary experiments carried out by highly unwilling NII-VVS test-pilots. The sentiments of the tank crews involved have not been recorded but can be vividly imagined.

The success of the ANT-6 as a heavy bomber and military transport fired Soviet aspirations to build even larger multi-engined aircraft. Even before the first ANT-6 prototype had been completed Petlyakov, Tupolev's wing designer, had made preliminary studies for a six-engined aircraft to carry a 10,000 kg bomb-load, almost five times more than the TB-3. Gromov made the maiden flight of the ANT-16 (TB-4), with two M-34 engines installed in the leading edge of each wing and two more mounted back to back in tandem on girders above the fuselage, on 3 July 1933, but serious vibration in the rear fuselage and tail surfaces had brought flight tests of the giant aircraft with a fifty-five metre wingspan to a halt by September and they were not resumed. The ANT-16 had already been surpassed by the ANT-20, an even larger eight-engined aircraft which was to become more widely known as the *Maksim Gorky*.

The *Maksim Gorky* itself was not a military aircraft — although a bomber variant was proposed — but a proud manifestation of Soviet aeronautical achievement and the flagship of the *Maksim Gorky* Propaganda Squadron[9].

Financed by public subscription to the sum of six million roubles, the construction of the ANT-20 began in July 1933 and was completed the following April. Only two days after Gromov's first flight on 17 June the huge aircraft flanked by two fighters made a surprise appearance over Red Square as part of the flypast celebrating the rescue of the *Chelyuskin* survivors[10]. Six 900 hp M-34RN engines were installed in the wings, spanning sixty-three metres, with the other two engines mounted over the fuselage as on the abandoned ANT-16. The fuselage, thirty-two and a half metres long, contained accommodation for the crew of eight, a saloon for seventy-two passengers, a broadcasting and public address system, a printing press, a cafeteria, sixteen telephones with an exchange and a film projection box in the nose. The *Maksim Gorky* was an immense prestige success and the building of a further seven similar machines, each to be named after a prominent Bolshevik leader, was contemplated until the aircraft's destruction on 18 May 1935 cooled official enthusiasm and terminated support for even more grandiose

---

[9]The Maksim Gorky Squadron was formed in 1933 by GU-GVF with the backing of the Soviet Press to conduct political propaganda campaigns in the more remote areas of the USSR. Some thirty aircraft attached to the squadron were named after Soviet newspapers and periodicals of which the most famous were the five-engined *Pravda* (ANT-14), later the squadron's flagship, and the ANT-9 *Krokodil* with its bizarre crocodile nose. The writer, journalist and editor Mikhail Kol'tsov was made the squadron's honorary commander.

[10]The *Chelyuskin*, a 3,600 ton steamer with a hull reinforced to resist ice pressure, left Leningrad in July 1933 for a voyage via the North-Eastern Sea Route along the Soviet Union's arctic coastline to Vladivostok. In February 1934 the vessel had to be abandoned after having been caught and crushed in the ice and air rescue flights were organised. N.P. Kamanin, V.S. Molokov, M.T. Slepnev, A.V. Lyapidevski, S.A. Levanevski, I.V. Doronin and M.V. Vodopyanov became the first Heroes of the Soviet Union after successful rescue airlifts had been made in March and April of that year.

projects. Responsibility for the tragedy was ascribed to a fighter pilot who recklessly tried to perform a loop around the *Maksim Gorky* during the shooting of a documentary film. Mikheev, piloting the *Maksim Gorky*, had begun to make a cautious turn back towards Tushino after the collision when the debris of the fighter, which had lodged in the *Maksim Gorky*'s wing, broke away and dashed itself against the fin, resulting in a loss of lateral control. Spectators saw the giant aircraft slowly turn over before breaking up in the air with the loss of fifty-six lives[11]. In fact the *Maksim Gorky* was not the first Soviet giant aircraft to come to grief. On 21 November 1933 the K-7, an ambitious flying-wing powered by seven M-17 engines, had already crashed in the Ukraine with the loss of fifteen lives after a structural failure in one of the twin booms supporting the tailplane. The K-7 had been intended by its designer, Konstantin Kalinin[12], as either a passenger or a bomber aircraft, but work on two additional prototypes begun on Baranov's instructions shortly before the crash was suspended in 1935 before either had been finished. A highly adventurous project for a twelve-engined flying-wing tank-transporter with rear-ramp access by Professor S.G. Kozlov at the Zhukovski Air Force Academy was immediately abandoned after the K-7 crash, and Tupolev's biggest design for a seventy-ton twelve-engined bomber and military transport under the designations ANT-26 (TB-6) and ANT-28 was shelved early in 1936 when the decision had been taken to terminate all further work in the field of super-heavy aircraft.

The growth of the Soviet heavy bomber forces raised the question of providing suitable ways of protecting and escorting such large and vulnerable aircraft. One proposal was for the development of special long-range escort fighters based on the 'air cruiser' principle of the ANT-7, but Arkhangel'ski's ANT-21 gunship of 1933 suffered from severe vibration at speed and it was realised, in any case, that a heavy, twin-engined escort fighter would be no match for the speed, climb and agility of the single-seat interceptor. A more radical solution was advanced by a young NII-VVS engineer, Vladimir Vakhmistrov, in

---

[11] A single example of a modified ANT-20 with six engines, all wing-mounted, was later built at GAZ No. 124 under the supervision of Boris Saukke and completed in 1938. After serving on scheduled passenger services between Moscow and the Caucasus it was used as a military transport until it crash-landed in December 1942.

[12] Kalinin, who was known for his high-wing civil aircraft featuring elliptical wing planforms, disappeared during the purges of the late thirties.

The Fortunes of Soviet Air Strategy

the form of 'parasite' fighters which could be carried by the bombers and released when necessary to fight off enemy interceptors on equal terms. An initial series of experiments was authorised by Alksnis in June 1931 and was undertaken by NII-VVS from its Monino airfield with the *Zveno-1* (Combination-1) which consisted of a TB-1 with two I-4 fighters modified as parasol-winged monoplanes and mounted on the upper wing surfaces of the bomber where they were secured by special clamping and release mechanisms. Chkalov and Anisimov made the first airborne take-offs in their I-4 fighters from the TB-1 carrier on 3 December 1931, and Vakhmistrov was allowed to pursue his experiments with a view to equipping each bomber brigade with at least one bomber and parasite fighter combination.

By 1934 the I-4 was already obsolete and the TB-3 had entered service. Accordingly, the *Zveno-2* which flew in August that year consisted of a TB-3 carrier and two I-5 fighters, although Vakhmistrov was eager to exploit the greater size of the TB-3 by increasing the number of fighters carried and to develop specially designed parasite fighters dispensing with the superfluous, conventional undercarriage. Experiments to perfect a satisfactory in-flight attachment system using I-16 fighters were undertaken, but technical difficulties, the growing obsolescence of the TB-3 and declining official interest had already blighted Vakhmistrov's hopes before his arrest and internment[13]. Although Vakhmistrov's plans for equipping Soviet bombers with their own parasite fighters came to nothing, his ideas were adapted to provide VVS with a long-range diver-bomber — two I-16 fighters, each carrying two 250 kg bombs, being released by a TB-3 carrier with full tanks in the vicinity of the target and thus enabled to return to base independently after making their attack. In late 1940 pilots of the 92nd Fighter Regiment were trained in dive-bombing and a special unit of six adapted TB-3 carrier-planes and twelve I-16SPB dive-bombers was formed at Yevpatoria airfield in the Crimea. On the outbreak of war Vakhmistrov was sent to Yevpatoria to advise on preparations necessary for operations against Rumania, the first raid over Constanza being successfully carried out on 1 August. On 10 and 13 August raids were made against the Chernovoda bridge over the Danube, followed by attacks on oil refineries at Ploesti, naval vessels

---

[13] Vakhmistrov later worked on the Tu-2 design in the Tupolev Internee Design Bureau and on the development of drop-tanks.

Soviet Air Force

and installations at Constanza and rail bridges over the Dnieper. About thirty sorties were flown by the unit before it suffered heavy losses in the fierce fighting for the Perekop isthmus and was disbanded, the remaining TB-3s flying east to the Caucasus while the I-16s remained to augment Sevastopol's meagre fighter defences. The unit appears to have acquitted itself well in spite of the obsolescence of its aircraft and the fact that much of its success was due solely to the element of surprise. As the first Soviet 'stand-off weapon', there can be little doubt that Vakhmistrov's brainchild compounded Hitler's fear for his Rumanian oil resources and strengthened his determination to make the seizure of the Crimea a first priority.

Experiments were also carried out in the use of radio-controlled TB-3s loaded with explosives as flying bombs. Radio control of the TB-3 was taken over by an accompanying SB bomber after the crew of the TB-3 had abandoned their aircraft, and the four-engined bomber was then directed on to its target. Trials were made in August 1941 but the idea was not put into practice operationally[14].

Range was clearly essential as well as bomb-load for the new strategic air force; long-distance flights had been among the most outstanding Soviet aeronautical achievements of the twenties and the military applications were taken up by the *Revvoensovet* with Voroshilov heading a special commission to co-ordinate development work over the winter of 1931-32. Pavel Sukhoi at AGOS was directed to begin design studies under Tupolev for a long-range aircraft and two prototypes of the resulting ANT-25 were begun in the summer of 1932. A single-engined, all-metal monoplane with a retractable main undercarriage and high aspect-ratio wings spanning thirty-four metres, the first prototype ANT-25 or RD (Long-Distance Record), flew on 22 June 1933. But in spite of the huge seven metre long fuel tanks, an integral part of the wing structure, its range of 7,200 kms fell far below the 13,000 kms specified by Voroshilov. The second prototype, its corrugated metal covered by lacquered cotton to reduce drag and its M-34R engine fitted with a reduction gear, made its first flight on 10 September 1933 and, after further measures to reduce drag, it was handed over to Mikhail Gromov for a non-stop endurance flight of 12,411 kms over European Russia between 10 and 12 September 1934.

---

[14] Fyodorov *Aviatsiya v bitve pod Moskvoi*

The Fortunes of Soviet Air Strategy

At this point Stalin decided to commit the aircraft to a record-breaking transpolar flight to the USA using a third prototype built as the forerunner of fifty long-range bomber developments under the designation ANT-36 (DB-1). The machine was prepared for an attempt by Sigismund Levanevski from the specially constructed four kilometre long concrete runway at Shcholkovo, but an oil leak was discovered shortly after Levanevski had taken off on 3 August 1935 and he turned back to land near Novgorod. After this loss of face, Stalin ordered that a preliminary long-distance trial flight should be made inside the USSR before further transpolar attempts were made. This flight was made by Valeri Chkalov in July 1936 over the 'Stalin Route' from Moscow via Franz Joseph Land with the intention of landing at Khabarovsk, although in fact navigational problems compelled Chkalov to land near the mouth of the Amur after covering 9,374 kms. Satisfied, Stalin gave his consent to Chkalov's transpolar flight to the USA in June the following year. In July Chkalov was followed across to the USA by Gromov flying a similar machine, but this time fitted with dual controls[15]. The transpolar records gained had been long delayed but they coincided fortuitously with the impact Soviet air power had produced in Spain. The Red Star had been triumphantly displayed to the world.

While the ANT-25s had brought glory to the USSR and fame to their pilots, the aircraft had no future as the long-range bomber it had originally set out to be. Essentially a cross between a powered glider and a flying fuel tank, able to carry a mere 100 kgs of bombs and with little protection from fighters in either defensive armament, ceiling or its maximum speed of 240 kph, production of the DB-1 was terminated after only twenty had been built. None of these saw squadron service and most were used as experimental aircraft, two

---

[15]Chkalov with his second pilot Baidukov and navigator Belyakov took off from Shcholkovo on 18 June and landed at Portland, Oregon, two days later after flying 8,504 kms and remaining airborne for sixty-three hours, sixteen minutes. They returned to a tumultuous welcome on the *S.S. Normandie*, all three having already been decorated as Heroes of the Soviet Union for their flight over the 'Stalin Route' the year before. Between 12 and 14 July Gromov, his second pilot Yumashev and his navigator Danilin covered 10,200 kms before landing at San Jacinto in California. Yumashev and Danilin were made Heroes of the Soviet Union, Gromov having already received this award after his record flight on the ANT-25 in 1934.

being employed as test-beds for diesel engines[16] and another modified by Vladimir Chizhevski's Bureau for Experimental Designs (BOK) as a high-altitude research aircraft under the designation BOK-1. With a two-seat pressure cabin and a M-34RNV engine with two superchargers, the BOK-1 reached a height of 12,000 metres in 1937 and Chizhevski decided to develop the aircraft into the BOK-11, a long-range high-altitude strategic reconnaissance aircraft, and the BOK-7, a record-breaking long-range machine which was being prepared for a round-the-world flight with one refuelling stop in the USA when Chizhevski was removed and interned. Work was later resumed on two unarmed examples of the BOK-11 under the new designation BOK-15 until the outbreak of war in June 1941 brought the dissolution of BOK in its wake[17]. Aware of the impracticability of the ANT-25 as a military aircraft, Sukhoi switched his attention to the twin-engined ANT-37 powered by two Gnôme-Rhône 14K radials and intended to carry a 1,000 kg bomb-load over 5,000 kms at an average speed of 250 kph as the DB-2 long-range bomber. The first prototype crashed during tests after being completed in June 1935, and the second with more powerful M-86 radials yielded an average speed of only 213 kph over its specified range. A third prototype was built solely as a record-breaker in 1938, and named *Rodina* (Motherland), was flown across Siberia by an all-woman crew later that year[18]. In reality, Sukhoi's work on long-range bombers had already been eclipsed by the success of a new young designer, Sergei Il'yushin.

The thirties was the era of great partnerships between designers

---

[16]Examples of the Junkers Jumo 4 and Packard diesel engines were purchased in the early thirties for study and development by Aleksei Charomski, Head of TsIAM's Diesel Engine Division. A R-5 test-bed with a Jumo 4 was flown in 1935 followed by two examples of the ANT-25 the next year, one powered by a Jumo 4 and the other by Charomski's AN-1 development. Plans to install the 750 hp AN-1 diesel in the TB-3 in 1936-37 were not implemented due to the bomber's obsolescence.

[17]Chizhevski had designed the gondolas for the *SSSR-1 and Osoaviakhim-1* stratostats before turning his attention to experimental aircraft design. After his arrest he worked in the Tupolev Internee Design Bureau and was later credited with the design of the Tu-91 prototype exhibited in 1957.

[18]Valentina Grizodubova, Marina Raskova and Polina Osipenko set a women's long-distance record in September 1938 by flying their ANT-37 *Rodina* 5,908 kms to the Soviet Far East, making a forced landing after spending twenty-six hours and twenty-nine minutes in the air. All three were made Heroes of the Soviet Union — the first women to receive this award and the last before the German-Soviet War.

The Fortunes of Soviet Air Strategy

and test-pilots — Polikarpov and Chkalov, Tupolev and Gromov, Yakovlev and Piontkovski — and Il'yushin was fortunate in having the outstanding Vladimir Kokkinaki to fly his new twin-engined TsKB-26 designed at the Central Design Bureau in the new *brigada* created in parallel with, and then superceding, Sukhoi's at AGOS. After a virtuoso display in front of Stalin on May Day 1936, the designer and pilot of the new aircraft were summoned to the Kremlin and closely questioned about the potential range of the TsKB-26 which had first flown that March. Il'yushin promised that with the same engines as Sukhoi's ANT-37, the TsKB-26 would carry the same bomb-load over 4,000 kms at an average speed of 310 kph and under Kokkinaki's expert hands the bomber fulfilled his promise. Revised as the TsKB-30, Il'yushin's new bomber was placed in full-scale production at GAZ No. 39, Moscow, as the DB-3 and 1,528 examples built. A modernised version, the DB-3F, with more powerful M-87A radial engines followed it on the production lines in 1938 after the completion of State tests in June the previous year; re-designated the Il-4 and fitted with 1,100 hp M-88B radials Il'yushin's design remained the standard Soviet medium-long range bomber throughout the war years and was never seriously challenged by a rival[19]. While Il'yushin's DB-3 established itself as long-range twin-engined bomber over the late thirties, no satisfactory replacement for the ageing TB-3 was forthcoming and Russia's heavy bomber force became more antiquated with each year that passed. Two prototypes of a revised and modernised TB-3 with four M-34FRN engines were built under the direction of Viktor Bolkhovitinov at GAZ No. 22 in 1935, on the first of which Nyukhtikov and Baidukov set up a new series of load-to-height records in November 1936. But although Bolkhovitinov's DB-A promised to carry a far greater bomb-load than the TB-3 — 3,000 kgs over a distance of 4,500 kms — the loss of the second prototype during a transpolar flight by Levanevski in August 1937[20] resulted in

---

[19]An enlarged version of the Il-4 with diesel engines was proposed in 1943 as the Il-6, but the prototype remained uncompleted. Yermolaev's Yer-2 long-range bomber was placed in production in October 1940, but only two air regiments had been equipped with the type before war broke out the following June and series production was suspended.

[20]Levanevski took off from Shcholkovo on 12 August 1937 to make the proving flight for scheduled transpolar services to the USA. Radio contact was lost near the Pole and no trace of the aircraft was found despite an extensive air search.

diminished official interest and only twelve of the sixteen examples ordered had been completed when production ended in 1940. Tupolev and Petlyakov had also started work on a TB-3 replacement in 1934 and Gromov made the first flight on their four-engined ANT-42 (TB-7) in December 1936. Defensive gun positions in the nose, on the upper fuselage, in the tail and in the rear of each inner engine nacelle were incorporated in the design, but it was decreed that the new bomber's ceiling must be bettered to ensure maximum protection against fighters and anti-aircraft fire. The problem was solved by installing an ATsN-2 turbo-compressor powered by an M-100 engine — nick-named 'the nightingale' by its test-crew on account of its peculiar whistling sound — in the bomber's fuselage to boost the height capability of the four M-34FRN engines. The revised ANT-42 flew in August 1937 and in late October Alksnis reported with enthusiasm on the new bomber's performance, adding that its speed of 403 kph at 8,000 metres should render it almost impervious to fighter interception. During further tests in the Crimea, the ANT-42 touched a height of 12,000 metres before a taxiing accident interrupted further tests. The new prototype had acquited itself well in its height capability trials, but the diminished bomb-load resulting from the fuselage-mounted turbocompressor and engine and the decrease in range brought about by the increased flying weight threatened to turn the ANT-42 into yet another record-breaker without practical military application. The ATsN-2 had not always functioned reliably, but the resumption of tests to rectify these failings was delayed by the lack of replacement M-34FRN engines, the production of which was being phased out in favour of the newer M-35, and by the internment of Tupolev and Petlyakov as the two most experienced designers of multi-engined aircraft. When M-35A high-altitude engines were installed in the TB-7 in 1938, tests indicated that the bomber would be capable of a range of 4,700 kms — but with only a 2,000 kg bomb-load. The bomber's fate was discussed at a Kremlin conference early in 1939 after the completion of State tests, and production was staunchly advocated by one of the few remaining supporters of the strategic bomber, Aleksandr Filin — then Head of NII-VVS. Stalin apparently consented to production but is reported to have remained sceptical of the bomber's value[21]. In

---

[21] Yakovlev *Tsel' Zhizni*. Yakovlev writes that Stalin gave in with the words — "Well, have it your own way. But you haven't convinced me at all."

The Fortunes of Soviet Air Strategy

any case, Stalin had concluded from the Spanish Civil War that the value of air power lay in ground support rather than in independent long-range strategic bombing. Delays to the completion of the TB-7 assembly plant at Kazan' and the priority allocated to the MiG fighters for M-35A engine supplies held back the start of production until 1940 and only a handful had been delivered by June 1941. Later versions of the TB-7 (Pe-8) were fitted with M-82 radial engines, but only 79 examples were produced in all, representing the USSR's total output of four-engined bombers during the Soviet-German conflict.

Thus, although the Red Air Force remained proportionately strong in four-engined heavy bombers by the end of the thirties, the Soviet Union's strategic bomber potential had fallen drastically due to the sheer obsolescence of its machines and the correspondingly dated training and experience of its air crews. When the AON was abolished in 1940 a number of its four and twin-engined bomber regiments were handed over to the new Frontal Aviation (*Frontovaya aviatsiya*) and the remainder reorganised as the *Dal'nebombardirovochnaya aviatsiya Glavnovo Komandovaniya* (DBA-GK) or Supreme Command's Long-Range Bomber Arm consisting of five corps, each of two divisions, deployed to the rear of the western military districts and two 'independent' divisions retained for special operations. In all the DBA contained some 800 machines in June 1941, a high proportion of which survived the *Luftwaffe's* first attacks against forwards airfields where the more modern tactical elements of the Red Air Force were based. Over the next two months, the DBA represented the largest Soviet bomber resource and it was expended mercilessly in bids to slow the *Wehrmacht* spearheads over river crossings, airfields and rail junctions where the blazing wreckage of countless lumbering bombers added to the soaring tallies of the Bf 109 pilots and the untiring flak crews.

In August the DBA corps were dissolved and the remaining regiments placed at the disposal of the front air commanders. With the launching of 'Operation Typhoon' in September all DBA units on the Western Front were committed to attacks against the encroaching panzers and by 22 October the overall strength of DBA had been reduced to 439 aircraft[22] including a high proportion of

---

[22] Made up of 310 DB-3F, 92 TB-3 and 9 Pe-2 bombers and 28 escort fighters. (Fyodorov)

69

Soviet Air Force

unserviceable machines. By 5 December the DBA had only 273 machines, 154 of which were damaged or otherwise unfit for operations, and ten days later it could muster only 182 DB-3F and 84 TB-3 bombers in all. Those remnants of the DBA which took part in the Soviet counter-offensive over the winter of 1941-42 were reformed into three divisions, two of which were subordinated to the C-in-C Red Air Force with the GKO retaining direct control only over Golovanov's 3rd Special Long-Range Air Division as the nucleus of the *Aviatsiya dal'nevo deistviya* (ADD), the new Long-range Air Arm inaugurated in March 1942. Retaliatory bombing raids on Germany were ordered by Stalin soon after the outbreak war, and by early July a special long-range bomber group formed expressly to attack Berlin was based on the Baltic island of Saaremaa off the Estonian coast. Consisting of two DB-3F squadrons from the Baltic Fleet Air Force's 1st Mine & Torpedo Bomber Division and two similarly equipped squadrons of the 81st Long-Range Bomber Division, the group was placed under the overall command of Lt. General S.F. Zhavoronkov, Head of the Naval Air Force (VVS-VMF), who was instructed to commence operations as soon as possible. On the night of 7 August 1941 fifteen DB-3F (Il-4) bombers under Colonel Yevgeni Preobrazhenski, Commander of the 81st Mine & Torpedo Bomber Regiment[23], took off to make their way independently to the German capital. It was an expensive gesture with the loss of nine aircraft but the sirens had sounded in Berlin and Stalin ordered a second, larger raid to be prepared. This time, on 11 August, Preobrazhenski's DB-3F squadrons were augmented by eleven TB-7 bombers of the 332nd Special Purpose Heavy Bomber Regiment, their M-35A engines having been hastily replaced by M-30B diesels to give the bomber a range of 7,820 kms. Four TB-7 bombers were lost in the raid and most of the remainder suffered more from the untried and temperamental diesels which had a tendency to cut out or catch fire than from the German anti-aircraft defences[24]. Raids over Bucharest, Constanza and Ploesti were made

---

[23] Preobrazhenski was made a Hero of the Soviet Union six days later, and the regiment subsequently awarded 'Guards' status. By late 1944 Preobrazhenski was Commander of the Northern Fleet's Air Forces and in the post-war period served as C-in-C VVS-VMF.
[24] The 332nd Special Purpose Heavy Bomber Regiment was formed on Stalin's orders 'to bomb Berlin at all cost' by Colonel Mikhail Vodop'yanov, a veteran arctic pilot and Commander of the 1st Long-Range Bomber Division. The regiment's eighteen to twenty TB-7 bombers were crewed by NII-VVS personnel who were trained for their sorties – tacitly agreed to be suicidal – while their machines were undergoing engine refits. Vodop'yanov, whose TB-7 force-landed when it ran out of fuel on the return flight, reported directly to Stalin after having made his way back to base with his crew through the enemy lines. Details of this amazing raid are given in Stefanovski's *Trista Neizvestnykh* and Vodop'yanov's *Druz'ya v Nebe*.

The Fortunes of Soviet Air Strategy

by DB-3F (Il-4) bombers of the Black Sea Fleet Air Force until late July 1941 when they were obliged to fly solely in support of the hard-pressed Southern Front, and attacks by Baltic Fleet Air Force units on Memel, Danzig and Kolberg continued until 4 September. Soviet bombing raids over enemy territory by bombers of the VVS-VMF and the DBA under Colonel Gorbatsevich then came to an end and were not resumed until the creation of the new Long-Range Air Arm (ADD).

Subordinated directly to the *Stavka* and commanded by Lt. General Aleksandr Golovanov[25], the ADD had no pretensions to be a strategic bomber force. The vast majority of its aircraft were unsuitable, its crews inadequately trained and lacking modern navigational and bombing aids, and its few contemporary machines too valuable to be risked for dubious returns. Added to these factors, the pressing requirements of the tactical air force and the limited technical and productive ability of the aircraft industry mitigated against the provision of any real strategic bomber in the forseeable future[26]. Some small token raids were made on Danzig, Ploesti and Königsberg between July and September 1942, mostly by single aircraft or small groups of Il-4 (DB-3F) and Pe-8 (TB-7) bombers, although ADD operations were more widespread against German supply depôts and rail junctions to the rear of the frontline. Later, as the supply of Il-4 bombers increased and Lend-Lease North American B-25s became available, ADD's main bomber function lay in the preliminary night bombing of enemy positions as a prelude to major ground offensives or counter-attacks. No less important, especially during the first year of its formation, was the part ADD aircraft played in flying supplies, ammunition and reinforcements to ground units temporarily isolated or under extreme pressure.

The C-in-C ADD, General Golovanov, had served in the NKVD component of GVF in the pre-war years and was transferred to the

---

[25]The Chief of ADD Air Staff, General Shevelev, was later replaced by General Perminov and took over control of the Transiberian Air Ferry Route. Colonel-General Markov, Chief Engineer of ADD, had previously headed the NII-VVS Bomber Test Section.

[26]The design of a high-altitude, long-range bomber under the designation DVB-102 was begun by Vladimir Myasishchev in parallel with Tupolev's '103' (Tu-2) and Petlyakov's VI-100 (later developed as the Pe-2) in the NKVD Internee KB in Moscow. Work continued after evacuation to Omsk but was impeded by the dearth of suitable engines to enable the bomber to carry its 3,000 kg bomb-load at an acceptable height and over a viable range.

Soviet Air Force

DBA as a regimental commander only in February 1941. By August that year he commanded a division with the rank of colonel. As C-in-C ADD he was promoted Colonel-General in 1943 and in 1944 was made an Air Chief Marshal together with the C-in-C VVS, Novikov[27]. By the summer of 1943 the Germans had identified seventeen ADD divisions and one transport division with PS-84s. The ADD regiment appeared normally to consist of three squadrons, each of fifteen aircraft, plus a command echelon. *Luftwaffe* Intelligence assessed ADD strength as consisting of 860 aircraft in February 1944, 1,100 in June, 1,300 in August, 1,400 in September and 1,600 by January 1945. In mid-September 1944 it was estimated that ADD was composed of nine corps, comprising eighteen divisions with forty-eight regiments. By the end of the year it was reported that the number of ADD regiments listed in the Soviet air order of battle had risen to fifty-eight[28]. While these figures may have been on the high side, at least seven ADD corps had been formed by the end of the Second World War. In May 1942 GVF was subordinated to ADD instead of VVS and the Head of GU-GVF made a Deputy under Golovanov[29] to unify the work of the two arms. In many ways ADD and GVF performed similar functions, not only as transports but also in supporting and supplying the growing partisan units in the rear of the German lines. Composed of civilians and troops who had eluded capture during the sweeping German encirclements, the partisan bands became a growing threat to the attenuated German lines of supply and communication and to bases in the sparsely garrisoned occupied zones. Their raids tied down troops in guarding railway lines and bridges or escorting road convoys, and the indiscriminate and ruthless reprisals made by the Germans merely added to the partisan ranks. The GVF regiments attached to the air armies were responsible for partisan support, often assisted by the U-2 biplanes of the night-bomber regiments; ADD aircraft also brought arms, explosives, radios and trained guerilla leaders, slipping over the German lines under cover of a diversionary

---

[27] Zhavoronkov, C-in-C VVS-VMF, Astakhov, Head of GVF, Vorozheikin, Khudyakov, Falaleev and Golovanov's Deputy, Skripko, were all made Air Marshals at this time.

[28] Schwabedissen *The Russian Air Force in the Eyes of German Commanders.*

[29] Astakhov had previously been a Deputy C-in-C VVS under Novikov responsible for GVF collaboration and support.

The Fortunes of Soviet Air Strategy

air raid[30]. Most important of all while the *Luftwaffe* dominated the skies, ADD and GVF partisan liaison flights brought back intelligence from partisans who were trained to watch and record as well as to shoot and handle explosives. Stalin was quick to realise the value of this 'front' behind the enemy lines and allocated the most modern machines, Lend-Lease C-47 and Soviet-built Li-2 (PS-84) transports, for these operations.

The purely tactical role of ADD led to its reformation in December 1944 as the 18th Air Army, operationally subordinate to VVS, while GVF was recreated as a separate command once more. GVF aircraft continued to provide transport, ambulance and liaison services although they were rarely called upon to perform night reconnaissance and bombing sorties as they had been earlier in the war. In the final battles, the massed bombers of ADD were used to saturate enemy positions and worked in close co-operation with Soviet artillery and rocket units in preparing the way for assaults by tanks and infantry; in the Battle for Berlin 800 ADD bombers were concentrated, representing about half of Golovanov's total strength.

At the same time developments in the air war in the West had not escaped Stalin's attention. The great bomber offensives by the USAAF and RAF against the industrial heart of the Third Reich was a different matter from the *Luftwaffe's* raids on virtually unprotected cities or the pin-pricks inflicted by ADD intrusions. During the Fourth Lend-Lease Protocol period between July 1944 and June 1945 the USSR requested 240 B-17 and 300 B-24 four-engined bombers, but the United States was sceptical of Soviet ability to handle complex modern bombers and wary of sharing its ability to strike harder and deeper into Europe.

The dawn of the atomic age brought a more urgent significance to the development of a truly long-range bomber arm and, left to its own devices, Soviet air power would have suffered the full results of its neglect. But it was saved by the acquisition and copying of the mighty American B-29, the most modern and sophisticated strategic bomber in the world; not through Lend-Lease, but through the sheer fortunes of war. For those who recalled the early days at the Junkers factory at Fili, it was not to be without a certain irony.

---

[30]Captured German ammunition was frequently supplied so that weapons seized from the Germans could be used by the partisans.

5 Stalin's Falcons

The expansion of VVS and the re-equipment of its squadrons with the new generation of I-15 and I-16 fighters and SB-2 bombers had barely begun before Europe was shaken by the first tremors of war. As the news of the military uprising in Spain flashed round the world's telegraphs and hit the morning headlines, the Republican Government of Spain and the insurrectionary Nationalist forces under General Francisco Franco y Bahamonde had already begun to seek military aid from abroad, and while José Giral y Pereira, the new Republican Prime Minister, urgently contacted the French Popular Front Government for arms, Franco's agent was already flying to Rome to enlist the support of Mussolini. Three days later the first Nationalist approaches were made to Hitler, and on 26 July 1936 the *Führer* made his fateful decision to send Ju 53/3m transport aircraft to lift Franco's Moroccan reinforcements over the Republican naval blockade and supply advisers and arms under the guise of forming a Spanish training contingent. The handful of trimotor transports took off for Spain and a number of He 51 biplane fighters were despatched in crates to act as escorts on their arrival; a month later they were joined by an equally modest Italian air contribution.

Stalin was cautious in his reactions. He wanted to protect a sympathetic France from isolation and encirclement by the 'Fascist camp' and he was tempted by a dream dormant since 1920, the creation and control of a socialist state in Western Europe. At the same time he realised that the situation was a delicate one and that any hasty move by the Soviet Union alone might precipitate an unwelcome diplomatic reaction. Moreover, he was about to crush the Bolshevik Old Guard and his attention was focussed on the crucial staging of the first round of show trials. On 23 August Stalin accepted the terms of the Non-Intervention Agreement, but the increasingly perilous position of the Spanish Republic and the probability that any military aid would be both inadequate and hampered by the pacifist factions of even sympathetic foreign governments was making it difficult to delay a decision for much longer. Soon the opportunity would be lost, the Spanish Republic extinguished. His decree of 28 August was, therefore, no more than a gesture to paper diplomacy while preparations for a full-scale Soviet intervention were made.

On 10th September the Soviet freighter *Rostok* put into Cartagena with thirty-three mechanics and fitters as the advance guard to assemble and maintain the crated aircraft being loaded on Odessa's waterfront. The first eighteen crated I-15 fighters were delivered to Cartagena on the *Bolshevik* on 13 October and a further seven were transferred from a Soviet vessel to the Republican *Lavamendi* off Spain's Mediterranean coast three days later. As further shipments of Soviet arms and aircraft arrived at Cartagena, Alicante and Bilbao, the stage was being set for utilising the war in Spain as a weapons' testing-ground.[1] For Stalin as for Hitler and Mussolini, the Spanish conflict was to be an ideal opportunity for evaluating air tactics and equipment and for providing still inexperienced and untried command staffs with authentic battle training. The most promising young VVS pilots and commanders, drawn initially from the Belorussian Military District, were selected and sent on six-month tours of active service in Spain as members of the Soviet 'Volunteer' Air Group after vetting by the Red Army Political Directorate and briefing by Alksnis. Later VVS personnel were 'seconded' from the Kiev Military District and the Baltic Fleet Air Force. The total number of VVS personnel who served in Spain still remains problematical, with Soviet figures ranging from one hundred and forty to over five times that number[2]. Overall command of the Soviet

---

[1] In 1936 the USSR sent 55 I-15 and 31 I-16 fighters with 31 SB and 31 R-Zet bombers to Spain. By 22 March 1937 a further 92 I-15, 31 I-16, 30 R-Zet and 31 R-5 aircraft had been delivered, and by July these had been followed by 80 I-16 fighters and 75 R-5 bombers together with 31 SB bombers to form the new *Grupo* 24. (*La guerra de España desde el aire.*)

[2] *Istoriya Velikoi Otechestvennoi Voiny Sovetskovo Soyuza*, Vol 1, p 113 states that a total of 141 VVS flying personnel served in Spain. However, Semyonov in *Parol'-Ispaniya* p. 7 affirms that 772 VVS flying personnel and 130 mechanics and engineers from Soviet aircraft factories were sent to Spain in the course of the Civil War.

Soviet Air Force

Air Group in Spain was in the hands of 'General Douglas'[3], the *nom de guerre* adopted by Brigade Commander Yakov Vladimirovich Smushkevich, a Lithuanian of Jewish parentage who began his career in the Red Army's Political Commissariat and arrived in Spain as Commander of the *Sovnarkom of the Belorussian SSR Light-Bomber Brigade* flying SB-2 bombers. His declared function was to replace A.I. Bergol'ts as adviser to the Head of the Spanish Republican Air Force, General Hidalgo de Cisneros; in reality he was immediately subordinate to General Shtern, Chief Soviet Military Adviser to the Spanish Republican Government, and Commander of Soviet Forces in the peninsula. While Smushkevich supervised the setting up of bomber operations, his deputy, Pyotr Pumpur or 'Colonel Julio' was responsible for the fighter protection of airfields and ports while the Soviet presence in Spain was being consolidated. Soviet fighter bases were established at Los Alcázares and Carmolí with a headquarters at Alicante, and in the north an air headquarters at Santander was set up to support Republican Basque and Asturian forces.

Air schools for Republican pilots were set up at Albacete, Alicante, Murcia, Palmar, Alhama, Los Alcázares, Lorca and Carmolí — the last for advanced I-16 fighter and night flying training — and later attempts were made to produce I-15 and I-16 fighters in Spain. The I-15 was placed in production at Sabadell-Reus, just outside Barcelona, but only fifteen were completed before the end of the war, 205 examples in various stages of completion being acquired by the Nationalists. The assembly of I-16 fighters at Jerez de la Frontera, Guadalajara and Alicante resulted in about 70 machines finished, together with about ten UT1-4 two-seat fighter trainers.

One of Pumpur's first tasks as Fighter Commander was to provide an air defence for Madrid, and as the SB-2 bombers commenced operations in late October a fighter group under Ivan Kopets was sent to the Central Front to fly in defence of the Spanish capital. On 4 November I-15 fighters of Pavel Rychagov's squadron rose to intercept a reconnaissance aircraft of the Italian *Aviacion Legionaria* over Madrid and on 15 November it was joined by Sergei Tarkhov's I-16 squadron. Tarkhov was shot down and killed soon afterwards, but for the twenty-five year old Rychagov, 'Comrade Pablo', these

---

[3] *Noms de guerre* were used by all Soviet commanders in Spain to conceal their true identities and nationality. Ptukhin was known, for example, as 'General José' and Arzhenukhin as 'General Fedorio'. Commissar Agal'tsov went under the name of 'Comrade Martin'.

Stalin's Falcons

first victories in Castillian skies were the start of a meteoric career. Only recently commissioned as a fighter pilot in the Ukraine, he rose in the space of four short years from squadron leader to Head of the Red Air Force before he was swept away in Stalin's purges barely two months before the German invasion of the USSR. Tarkhov, 'Comrade Antonio' was posthumously decorated as a Hero of the Soviet Union on 31 December together with the Swiss-born fighter ace and squadron leader Ernst Shakht and Sergei Chernykh. These were only the first of such high awards to be conferred on 'Stalin's Falcons' in Spain[4]. The Soviet Air Group had the element of surprise, and the identification of its aircraft gave rise to considerable confusion since the Soviet machines were at first taken to be American and their superficial similarity to recent United States' types led to the I-15 being christened the 'Curtiss', the I-16 the 'Boeing' and the SB-2 the 'Martin' as it resembled the Martin 139 twin-engined bomber. These errors persisted long after the presence of the Soviets had been confirmed and the confusion was further increased when the warring sides began to confer their own nicknames[5]. The German response to the build-up of Soviet air power was the formation of the 'Condor Legion' consisting of a fighter and a bomber group, a reconnaissance and seaplane squadron, anti-aircraft and signals companies and an operations staff. As the He 51 biplane fighter and the Ju 52/3m bomber were now out-matched by the new Soviet warplanes, Göring urged the despatch of the latest *Luftwaffe* aircraft to Spain to regain air superiority and carry out combat

---

[4] Thirty-five VVS pilots and aircrew were made Heroes of the Soviet Union for services in Spain as well as two air advisers. These included Smushkevich, Pumpur, Yeremenko, Rychagov and Brigade Commanders Kholzunov and Proskurov in 1937, Serov in 1938, and Gusev, Gritsevets and Senatorov in 1939. Pavel Rychagov who was credited with fifteen victories in Spain and named as a Hero of the Soviet Union when he took part in the 1937 Air Day Flypast and again as the subject of a brief biographical feature in the Red Army daily *Red Star* in 1963, has been omitted from the special appendix listing all Soviet air personnel so decorated in *Aviatsiya i Kosmonavtika SSSR*.

[5] The Republicans called the I-16 the *Mosca* (Fly), the I-15 the *Chato* (Snub-nose) and the SB-2 and R-5 the *Katyusha* and *Natasha*. The R-Zet ground-attack version of the R-5 was nick-named the *Rasante* (Scraper). The Nationalists, less flatteringly, dubbed the I-16 the *Rata* (Rat), a name that stuck with *Luftwaffe* pilots who encountered it again in 1941. A number of captured SB-2 bombers were later put into service with the *Ejército del Aire* as the *Sofia*. Numbers of R-5, R-Zet, I-15, I-16 and SB-2 bombers were acquired by the Nationalists in 1939 and put into service with the *Ejército del Aire*, the last two types flying under Spanish colours until the early fifties and late forties respectively.

testing. From February 1937 the twin-engined He 111 and Do 17 bombers began to replace the Ju 52/3m and in April the first Bf 109B fighters arrived to re-equip the second squadron of the Condor Legion's fighter group. The spring of 1937 also saw an increase in Soviet air strength in Spain and the arrival of further advisers; in February Colonel Fyodor Arzhenukhin arrived in Bilbao as the Senior Air Adviser on the Northern Front and assistant to Sveshnikov, the Soviet air attaché, followed in April by Regimental Commisar Filipp Agal'tsov, a graduate of the Lenin Politico-Military Academy. His role was supposedly that of political surveillance and the improvement of Marxist-Leninist morale in the Soviet Air Group, but with the introduction of the 'dual command' system whereby political commissars enjoyed equal status with military commanders he had considerable command authority and worked as an equal with successive Chief Soviet Air Advisers and Heads of the Soviet Air Group for the next eighteen months.

Republican air superiority, boosted by the still poorly opposed Soviet squadrons, was instrumental in frustrating the Nationalist drive to sever the Madrid-Valencia road and split the Republican fronts at the Battle of Jarama in February 1937, but its freedom was curtailed with the appearance of the new German aircraft. The I-15 was employed more and more for air defence or with the R-Zet for ground-attack operations supervised by the *Shturmovik* specialist, Aleksandr Turzhanski. The faster I-16 was used increasingly for fighter cover but its effectiveness declined as the Bf 109 pilots gained confidence and experience in exploiting the Soviet fighter's weaknesses and its essentially inferior performance. Even the SB-2 bomber crews found that speed no longer guaranteed immunity from fighter attack and were obliged to operate from altitudes which they negated accurate bombing.

To the north the Nationalists put their airfields on Mallorca to good use, strategically placed as they were to mount air raids against Barcelona and Valencia and command Soviet supply routes from the Black Sea. The delivery of material and equipment became difficult and uncertain. New I-16 fighters bound for Cataluña had to be shipped to Bordeaux or Le Havre and transported south by rail, Soviet replacements were flown from France or sometimes travelled by train through Poland, Germany and France in civilian clothes and with false identities. Yevgeni Ptukhin, Commander of the 142 Fighter Brigade in the Belorussian Military District who replaced

Kopets as Commander of the *Escuadra de Caza* or Fighter Group on the Central Front travelled to Spain in this manner in May 1937, but the journey became more difficult as Geman suspicions were aroused.

In June 1937 two SB-2 bomber squadrons commanded by Aleksandr Senatorov and Oleg Sobolevski flew from the Central Front to reinforce Republican air units hard pressed in the north. Escorted by Yeremenko's and Yevseev's fighter squadrons, they were to hit Nationalist supply lines and raid staging bases on Mallorca. Soviet SB-2 squadrons were frequently criticised, however, for operating independently or even contrary to the orders of the Republican Army Staff and when the German warship *Deutschland* was bombed while at anchor off Ibiza on 28 May 1937, German naval vessels retaliated by shelling Almería three days later. This was not the only instance where illicit Soviet bombing raids evoked reprisals against towns and cities in areas held by the Republicans — throughout the autumn of 1937 and the spring of 1938 the SB-2 squadrons continued to raid Nationalist held cities, including Zaragoza, Sevilla, Valladolid and Salamanca, and to carry out intermittent attacks on Mallorca. According to Nationalist sources, the bombers suffered heavy losses at the hands of the Italian CR 32 fighters defending the island[6].

The most notable Republican air successes in the summer and autumn of 1937 were gained on the Central Front and went to the fighter squadrons. When Ptukhin replaced Smushkevich as Chief Air Adviser in July 1937, Ivan Yeremenko was promoted Fighter Commander on the Central Front and handed over command of his fighter squadron to Anatoli Serov, 'Comrade Rodrigo'. Serov had been credited with ten victories during his first month in Yeremenko's squadron and with his fellow ace, Mikhail Yakushin, mounted night-fighter patrols over Madrid with Yakushin making the first kill on the night of 27 July when he shot down an intruding Ju 52/3m. A second was claimed the following night by Serov and both pilots were decorated with the Order of the Red Banner for sustaining the morale of the beleaguered capital. In October the Soviet Air

---

[6]Sanchis in *Alas Rojas Sobre España* claims that thirty-two SB-2 bombers were brought down over Zaragoza and Palma de Mallorca on 12 October and on 7 and 10 December 1937. He puts the total Republican losses of SB-2 bombers at thirteen in August, twelve in October and twenty-three in December 1937 — eleven of the latter falling to CR 32 fighters over Palma de Mallorca on 7 December.

Soviet Air Force

Group had one of its last major successes with a surprise attack against the Nationalist air base at Garrapinillos outside Zaragoza in which the destruction of some forty aircraft on the ground was later claimed. Planned by Ptukhin and Agal'tsov, the raid was successful largely due to the repeated and unrelenting attacks made by Serov's I-16 squadron. Serov later commanded a I-16 fighter brigade before returning to the Soviet Union in early 1938 to be fêted as a national hero, decorated as a Hero of the Soviet Union and made Head of the Air Force Inspectorate[7].

By August 1938 the Soviet Air Group had begun its withdrawal, handing over its remaining aircraft to Spanish Republican pilots. Losses in the Battle of the Ebro over the late summer and autumn were the largest yet suffered and in reality marked the collapse of Republican air opposition[8]. Arzhenukhin, who had replaced Ptukhin as Chief Air Adviser in the winter of 1937-38, handed over to Brigade Commander N. Andreev, the last occupant of the post, and left for the USSR followed in October by Agal'tsov. The departure of the last SB-2 bomber crews in November brought the Spanish adventure to an end.

Throughout 1937 and 1938 'Stalin's Falcons' returned from their tours in Spain to receive honours and promotions, many visiting VVS units picked to provide replacement 'volunteers' and lecturing on the air war in Spain. Clearly, however, it was not politic to speak too candidly. Ptukhin and Kopets were made Air Commander and Deputy Air Commander for the Leningrad Military District and Pumpur served as Head of VVS Operations Staff before taking up command of the air units attached to Marshal Blukher's Special Red Banner Far-Eastern Army. Smushkevich, now Deputy Head of GU-VVS under General Loktionov, was to have led the flypast over Red Square on May Day 1938 in a parade dedicated to the exploits of the Red Army and Air Force in Spain, but suffered back and leg injuries when his R-10 which was to lead the flypast force-landed after engine failure on 30 April during rehearsals. His place was taken by Ptukhin

---

[7]Serov was twenty-nine when he was appointed to this post with the rank of Brigade Commander. With Yakushin and three other fighter pilots fresh from Spain he gave a display of formation aerobatics at the 1938 Air Day Display, but was killed in May the following year together with the celebrated airwoman Polina Osipenko while taking part in night-flying exercises.

[8]*Sanchis* gives Republican air losses during the Battle of the Ebro between July and November 1938 as 217 aircraft confirmed.

Stalin's Falcons

flying his red-winged I-16. Agal'tsov returned from Spain to be made Head of the VVS Political Directorate as Deputy Head of GU-VVS[9].

It seemed evident that Stalin considered his 'Spanish Falcons' the replacements he needed for those who had been swept away in the removal of Alksnis in November 1937, yet many of these senior appointments were subject to recurring waves of purges over the next three troubled years. Some were executed, other interned or demoted into obsurity. Some who survived were released and re-instated during the command crisis of 1941 and succeeded in recovering their careers in further battles with the *Luftwaffe*. In the main these were men who had occupied intermediate or junior command positions in Spain like Aleksandr Senatorov, Deputy Commander of the 16th Air Army in 1945 and Timofei Khryukin, Commander of the 8th and later the 1st Air Army, who were both SB-2 squadron leaders in Spain. General Zlatotsvetov, Deputy Commander of the 17th Air Army, had commanded the SB bomber *Grupo* 12 on the Central Front in Spain, and Boris Sveshnikov, formerly air attache in Madrid, served as Chief of Staff in the 7th Air Army. Generals Gorlachenko and Arkhangel'ski who commanded III *Shturmovik* and IV Bomber Corps had both gained their first combat experience in Spain, and leading fighter pilots Mikhail Yakushin and Leonid Rybkin re-appeared during the Battle of Moscow as Commander of the Eastern Sector of Moscow's PVO Zone and Commander of the 34th Fighter Regiment.

Even as the parades, decorations and slogans were proclaiming the valour of Soviet arms in Spain, the balance-sheet of intervention was being drawn up in the Kremlin. The USSR had supplied 1,409 military aircraft to Republican Spain as part of the arms deal paid for with the surrender of £63 million of the Spanish gold reserve[10].

---

[9] Agal'tsov occupied this post in 1939 but was subsequently removed — possibly with the fall of Smushkevich early in 1940 — and may have been interned. He later re-appeared as Commander of the 9th Guards *Shturmovik* Division in 1944, organised the formation of and subsequently commanded the First Polish Mixed Air Corps, and served in the post-war years as Chief Inspector and Deputy C-in-C VVS before assuming command of the Long-Range Air Force in 1962.

[10] A total composed of 550 I-15 and 475 I-16 fighters, 210 SB-2 and 130 R-5 bomber and reconnaissance aircraft, 40 R-Zet ground-attack bombers and four UTI-4 fighter trainers. Soviet supplies comprised well over half the 2,460 aircraft utilised by the Republic and consisting of machines extant in the Spanish Air Force in July 1936, requisitioned civil aircraft and aircraft supplied from abroad. France, the largest source of supply after the Soviet Union, contributed 260 aircraft. Sanchis: *Alas Rojas Sobre España*.

Valuable battle experience had been gained and part at least of the senior VVS Command blooded. On the debit side, losses had been high and Soviet pilots had found themselves at a decided disadvantage when faced in battle by the superior training and machines of the *Luftwaffe*[11]. Serov as Chief Inspector for VVS coordinated the reports of commanders returning from Spain and their proposals for improving combat efficiency. There was no lack of criticisms. The I-16 was disliked for its difficulty in handling at low speeds and heights and the I-15 fighter's fixed undercarriage was out of date. Both fighters were considered to have inadequate armament, especially for attacks on bombers, and poor gun-sights. Radios and oxygen equipment were also needed. The SB-2 bomber was criticised for its inadequate defensive armament, low bomb-load and its inline engines which, it was proposed, would be better replaced with more powerful radials. The low standards of flying training, air gunnery and combat tactics were also commented upon, with the recommendation that the three-fighter *zveno* should be replaced by a four-fighter *zveno* consisting of two pairs[12]. On the basis of the report compiled for Voroshilov, Loktionov and Smushkevich, a conference chaired by Voroshilov was called to enable the VVS commanders from Spain to discuss these issues with aircraft designers and representatives from GUAP. There was some hostility to criticism, notably from Polikarpov who insisted that existing fighters could be modified and the rate of production would, therefore, be unimpeded by the introduction of new types. The I-153 and later versions of the I-16 resulted from this conference, as did a number of other aircraft intended to incorporate improvements on the basis of Soviet experience in Spain, among them Shevchenko's remarkable IS figher prototype able to convert from biplane to monoplane configuration in flight.

---

[11]*Sanchis* claims that 496 I-15, 415 I-16, 178 SB-2 and 87 R-5 and R-Zet aircraft were destroyed, listing losses for each type yearly as follows:

Year	I-16	I-15	SB-2	R-5 & R-Zet	Total
1936	15	30	25	10	80
1937	92	140	64	36	332
1938	263	266	84	41	654
1939	45	60	5		110
Total	415	496	178	87	1,176

[12]Gusev: *Gnevnoe nebo Ispanii*

Stalin was at first inclined to treat the criticisms of Soviet military aircraft in Spain as 'scandal' or 'sabotage'. When the test-pilots Suprun and Stefanovski openly attacked GUAP's reluctance to undertake the development of an inline-engined fighter along the lines of the Bf 109, he ordered enquiries to be made about their 'reliability' and Ivan Petrov, Head of NII-VVS had to vouch for them personally[13].

Not long afterwards, however, Mikhail Kaganovich, Commissar for Aircraft Production, was rebuked by Stalin for neglecting to pass on a critical report made by Sergei Denisov on his return from Spain. This substantially reiterated the points made to Serov, but attacked more fundamentally the concept of maintaining and developing the manoeuvrable biplane as an out-moded approach to fighter warfare[14].

By 1938 Spain had, in any case, been eclipsed by events in the Far East and the looming collision with Japanese expansionist ambitions on the Asiatic mainland. The problems posed by the defence of the Soviet Far East with its ill-defined and extensive frontiers and poor communications had been a source of concern to the *Revvoensovet* in the nineteen twenties and in August 1929 it decreed the formation of a Special Far Eastern Army (ODVA) under General Blukher. In October ODVA units saw action against Chinese infringements of declared Soviet territory at the junction of the Sungari and Amur Rivers. The Red Air Force presence, a token thirty-two machines — mainly Fokker D.XI fighters and R-1 reconnaissance bombers — was effective enough to encourage the planning of a larger and more self-sufficient air element, Albert Lapin', Blukher's Chief of Staff, being formally appointed ODVA Air Commander in 1931. The Soviet victory in this relatively minor skirmish with China was taken by Japan as a warning to establish her military position in Manchuria to safeguard her mainland interests and in 1931 Japanese forces

---

[13]Suprun was, however, temporarily expelled from the Party on the grounds that he had been born in the USA and had associated with the discredited former Head of the Red Army's Political Directorate, Yan Gamarnik, who had committed suicide in June 1937. Yakovlev; *Tsel' Zhizni*.

[14]Denisov returned from Spain as a Brigade Commander and a Hero of the Soviet Union and submitted his report to GU-VVS and GUAP. When no action resulted, he wrote directly to Stalin on his return from taking part in the Khalkin Gol air battles. Denisov was later made a Hero of the Soviet Union for a second time during the Winter War of 1939-40. In the German-Soviet War he commanded the 283rd Fighter Division of the 16th Air Army as a Lt. General.

undertook a systematic conquest of Manchuria followed by its conversion into the puppet-state of Manchukuo. Two years later the Japanese were already penetrating Inner Mongolia and threatening established Soviet interests in Outer Mongolia from the south as well as the east.

The Soviets watched these events with apprehension, but the ODVA was still not strong enough to commit itself against the Japanese Kwantung Army and both the USSR and Japan began to appreciate the difficulties involved in any major clash of arms. The Japanese realised the impracticability of attempting any permanent seizure of Soviet territory if they were able to advance against the ODVA and drive it back, while the Soviets were confronted by immense logistical problems in supporting a large army engaged in wide-scale operations in the Far East. From 1931 onwards, therefore, the area east of Lake Baikal along the Manchurian frontier was fortified with feverish speed and the Transiberian Railway double-tracked to eliminate dependence on the Chinese Eastern Railway for communications with the Soviet Pacific coast[15]. In 1933 the Soviet Pacific Fleet and Naval Air Force, both for the time insignificant, were established and a series of experiments made in sending vessels from the White Sea to the Pacific coast via the North-East Sea Route and the Bering Straits. As a bulwark against further Japanese schemes to the west of Manchuria, the USSR made a Mutual Assistance Pact with Outer Mongolia and sent military observers there in 1936, the year of the Anti-Comintern Pact between Germany and Japan.

By 1933 Lapin' had an air brigade at Chita and one at Vladivostok with squadrons based at Khabarovsk, Novosibirsk and Spassk. The following year these were reinforced by three brigades of TB-3 heavy bombers, one hundred and fifty machines, capable of bombing the Japanese Home-land. Air raid alerts were practised in Tokyo and Osaka and the Japanese embarked on a rapid consolidation of their air strength in Manchuria, convinced that air power would be a crucial factor in the inevitable conflict.

When the Sino-Japanese War erupted in 1937 a second Soviet 'Volunteer' Air Group was formed and four I-15 and two SB-2 squadrons sent to China as the forerunners of some four hundred

---

[15]The Chinese Eastern Railway connected Chita with Vladivostok via Harbin in Manchuria and was the shortest link between the Trans-Baikal and the Pacific. Its strategic value was lost when Japan seized control of Manchuria.

Stalin's Falcons

aircraft and forty air instructers and advisers supplied. This time a number of NII-VVS test-pilots were among the contingent; Stepan Suprun and Grigori Kravchenko were among the first to be sent to the main Soviet fighter base and headquarters at Nanchan before being posted to fighter squadrons defending Lanchow, Nanking, Hankow and Chunking. Later they were joined by some of 'Stalin's Falcons' from Spain — fighter groups in China were commanded by Pavel Rychagov and Sergei Gritsevets and an SB-2 bomber group by Timofei Khryukin.

In May 1938 while VVS pilots were fighting in the skies of Spain and China, Lev Mekhlis, Gamarnik's successor as Head of the Red Army's Political Directorate, arrived in the Far East to launch the purging of the ODVA Command ordered by Stalin. Marshal Blukher was arrested and relieved of his command together with Pumpur, his Air Commander, and the ODVA split into three commands[16]. In the Ussuri area the First Red Banner Army was placed under General Shtern with Rychagov recalled from China as his Air Commander; the Second Red Banner Army, with Zhigarev as Air Commander, was established with its headquarters at Kuibyshevka, and the LVII Rifle Corps in Outer Mongolia was supported by forces in the adjoining Trans-Baikal Military District.

Shtern and Rychagov were the first to see action against the Japanese when a clash occurred on the poorly defined Manchurian-Korean-Siberian border in July 1938. During the 'Lake Khasan' incident as it was later called, Rychagov's seventy fighters and one hundred and eighty bombers flew unchallenged by any enemy air activity. After the twelve-day battle both sides prepared for the next confrontation with the knowledge that it would not be long delayed and that its outcome would have to be decisive. It came less than a year later after incidents along the Khalkin River on the border of Manchuria and Mongolia. Here the threat of a determined Japanese push into Mongolia out-flanking Soviet defences along the north Manchurian border evoked immediate and unrelenting action by Soviet forces and from 20 May 1939 a series of air battles developed which grew rapidly in scale and ferocity. The Japanese had about 500 aircraft in Manchuria and estimated that they were faced by an

---

[16]Lapin's fate is still in doubt as it is not clear whether he remained Air Commander for the ODVA until replaced by Pumpur or whether he had previously been transferred to the Belorussian Military District. He was, however, undoubtedly a victim of Stalin's purges of the Red Army.

Soviet Air Force

opposing force of some 1,500 Soviet machines[17]. The Soviets claimed that hostilities found them with only two air regiments in Mongolia — about a hundred aircraft — although these were swiftly augmented by units from the Trans-Baikal to bring Soviet air strength up to no less than five or six fighter regiments, at least three SB-2 regiments and a regiment of TB-3 heavy bombers, around 600 aircraft in all. Air operations were first directed by Aleksandr Gusev, but on 29 May with the battle escalating overall air command was taken over by Smushkevich.

As the scale of the air battles grew, Soviet aircraft were committed in regimental strength. On 22 June a hundred I-15*bis* and I-16 fighters engaged in scattered dog-fights with Japanese Nakajima Ki-27 fighters, and from 26 June the SB-2 bombers joined the offensive, carrying out raids with up to sixty aircraft escorted by as many fighters. By the third week of July the SB-2 bombers were being used at brigade strength for major attacks and the first I-153 fighters were arriving for combat evaluation[18].

While the VVS air regiments had substantial losses in these air battles, the Japanese did not go unscathed and ultimately lost a vital number of experienced pilots. The intensity and persistence of Soviet bomber attacks had also begun to tell. Standing fighter patrols had to be mounted to intercept the SB-2 bombers flying at heights over 6,000 metres and night raids by TB-3 four-engined bombers were hardly countered. The major Soviet offensive was opened by the recently promoted General Zhukov on 20 August, the ground assault being supported by two immense waves of aircraft containing 200 bombers and 300 fighters. Japanese resistance weakened, and the last air battles over Khalkin Gol took place on 15 September — the day preceding the official cease-fire. It seems probable that the Red Air Force lost 207 aircraft and the Japanese Air Force 162 between 22 May and 16 September 1939, although the official claims advanced

---

[17]The Germans, who had assessed Soviet air strength in the Far East at 2,000 aircraft in 1938, revised this to 1,000 the following year — roughly in accordance with the contemporary French estimate of 850 machines.

[18]The Soviets claimed initial successes on the I-153 by flying with lowered undercarriages and posing as the slower I-15*bis*. When the Japanese pilots were tempted into pursuit, the Russian pilots retracted their undercarriages and increased speed as they turned to meet them.

Stalin's Falcons

by both sides were wildly inflated[19]. Sixty VVS pilots were made Heroes of the Soviet Union — Smushkevich, Kravchenko and Gritsevets, the latter killed in action, being the first to receive this award for a second time. Smushkevich was further rewarded by promotion to Head of GU-VVS, a post he was fated to hold for less than seven months. Grigori Kravchenko[20], who had flown with Suprun in China, commanded the legendary 22nd Fighter Regiment[21] at Khalkin Gol which claimed thirty-two Japanese aircraft for the loss of one pilot, gained ten Hero of the Soviet Union awards and fired the new RS-82 rockets for the first time in air combat[22].

The ambitions of Japan in Mongolia had been frustrated, but with the signing of the German-Soviet Non-Aggression Pact on 23 August 1939 Stalin's eyes were once more focussed on the west. On 1st September Hitler's troops invaded Western Poland and on 17 September Soviet air and ground forces crossed the eastern boundaries of Poland 'to liberate the Western Ukraine and Western Belorussia from Polish rule'. The Second World War had begun.

---

[19] The Soviets claimed the destruction of 645 Japanese aircraft, 355 between 22 May and 19 August and a further 290 by 16 September. *Aviatsiya i Kosmonavtika SSSR*. The Japanese claimed 1,260 VVS machines. A detailed account of the Khalkin Gol air battles from the Japanese viewpoint is given by Eiichiro Sekigawa under the title *The Undeclared War* in *Air Enthusiast* for May-July 1973.

[20] Kravchenko later flew against Finland in 1939-40 and served as Air Commander under Loktionov in the Baltic Military District. In June 1941 he was commander of the 11th Mixed Air Division in the Western Military District which was largely destroyed in the first *Luftwaffe* attacks. After commanding a 'special air shock group' he was killed while serving on the Volkhov Front in February 1943 as commander of the 215th Fighter Division. His death was mourned as that of a national hero and his remains buried in the Kremlin Wall.

[21] Also identified as participants in the Khalkin Gol air battles are the 19th, 23rd, 56th and 70th Fighter Regiments, the 32nd, 38th and 150th SB-2 Bomber Regiments and the 21st Long-Range Bomber Regiment flying TB-3s.

[22] Intended for use as an air-to-air weapon, developed in response to requests for a more effective weapon against bombers made by pilots returning from the Spanish Civil War, the RS-82 was first tested by Grigori Bakhchivandzhi against a sleeve target towed by a R-5 earlier in 1939. Five I-16 Type 10 fighters were then adapted to carry four RS-82 rockets under each wing and these were flown by pilots of the 22nd Air Regiment at Khalkin Gol. Subsequently, I-153 fighters were also armed with this weapon. The RS-82 and the larger RS-132 saw wide service in the German-Soviet War, but primarily against ground targets.

6 The Falcons Culled

Over the four years preceding the German invasion of the USSR in June 1941, the effectiveness of the Red Air Force declined as its numerical strength increased. This was due not merely to the loss of much of the technical parity with other European air forces it had striven to achieve in the first half of the thirties, but also to the setbacks of Spain and the Winter War with Finland with their impact on Soviet military confidence and planning and the resulting failure to implement the lessons derived from them quickly enough. In common with the Red Army, these problems were to be compounded by the destruction of its High Command.

Less than a year after the outbreak of the Spanish Civil War Stalin made his first moves against the Red Army, the opening of a devastating purge of its High Command designed to eliminate all potential military as well as political opposition to his dictatorship. The first flash of lightning in the storm came in May 1937 when Marshal Tukhachevski was removed from his post as Head of Red Army Ordnance and demoted to command of the Volga Military District. It is unlikely that he ever reached his headquarters at Samara (Kuibyshev) before his arrest by the NKVD. Alksnis, a deputy commissar for defence under Voroshilov since that January, was reported as having served on the special military tribunal of the supreme court convened to investigate charges of espionage, sabotage and subversive alliance with the Trotskiite-Zinovievite Opposition. On 11 June 1937 Tukhachevski was executed together with Eideman, Chairman of *Osoaviakhim*, Kork, Head of the Frunze Military Academy, the military attache Putna, Uborevich and Yakir, Commanders of the Belorussian and Kiev Military Districts and Primakov, Deputy Commander of the Leningrad Military District.

The fall of Tukhachevski was followed by a ruthless purge of his colleagues, associates and protegés, and Alksnis had been too closely

The Falcons Culled

linked with the executed marshal to escape a similar fate for long. On the evening of 23 November 1937 the 'Commander of the Winged Army' was snatched away to the Lubyanka while on his way to a diplomatic reception in Moscow; he lived for less than a year afterwards[1]. With him went most of the senior Red Air Force Command, including Vasili Khripin, Chief of Air Staff and Head of the Special Purpose Air Arm, Troyanker, Head of the Air Force Political Directorate, Todorski, Head of the Zhukovski Air Force Academy[2] and the military district air commanders Uvarov, Ingaunis, Chernobrovkin, Kushakov and Lopatin. Only the year before these men had received decorations from the hands of Stalin himself[3].

In December Alksnis was replaced as Head of GU-VVS by General Aleksandr Loktionov, a forty-four year old former rifle brigade commander with little more than four years experience in the Red Air Force. After serving as Air Commander in the Belorussian and Khar'kov Military Districts for brief periods in the mid-thirties, Loktionov was brought from the obscurity of the Central Asian Military District as proof of Stalin's determination to promote a new High Command which would be directly reliant on his patronage. Loktionov lacked any operational experience and in September 1939 Smushkevich, Loktionov's deputy since his return from Spain, took over as Head of GU-VVS in readiness for the invasion of eastern Poland. Unlike Alksnis, Loktionov did not immediately fall victim to the NKVD; he retained his inherited office of deputy defence commissar and was made a Colonel-General in 1940, serving as commander of the newly formed Baltic Military District until his removal that December[4]. But Smushkevich failed to repeat his

---

[1] The circumstances of Alksnis's arrest were apparently similar to the fictional account of the diplomat Volodin's in Solzhenitsyn's *The First Circle*. See the account given by Kristina Mednis-Alksnis in *Komandarm Krylatykh*. The date of Alksnis's death given in the third (latest) edition of the *Bol'shaya Sovetskaya Entsiklopediya* is 29 July 1938.

[2] Todorski survived the purges and was alive in 1958 as a Lt. General (retired).

[3] In May 1936 the Order of the Red Star was conferred on Alksnis, Khripin, Todorski, Ingaunis and Zhigarev, and the Order of Lenin on Astakhov, Beryozkin, Borman, Chernobrovkin, Golovnya, Lavrov, Lapin', Lopatin, Pomerantsev, Rudenko, Sinyakov, Suprun and Turzhanski. *Aviatsiya i Kosmonavtika SSSR*.

[4] The *Bol'shaya Sovetskaya Entsiklopediya* gives the date of Loktionov's death as 28 October 1941. It is likely that this was the result of Stalin's decision as to which officers were to be given the opportunity of reinstating themselves in battle and which were to be dispensed with.

Soviet Air Force

Manchurian successes over Finland, and the true condition of the Red Air Force was revealed in the grim Winter War which broke out in November 1939 and dragged on through three and a half months of bitter cold.

The USSR had concentrated some 900 aircraft along the frontier dividing Finland from the Leningrad Military District, but although contested by less than a hundred Finnish machines the Red Air Force suffered heavy losses — particularly of its obsolescent SB, DB-3 and TB-3 bombers. Large-scale bombing raids on Finnish towns, ports and railways failed to disrupt essential troop movements or demoralise the Finnish population and exceptionally severe weather conditions badly affected the Red Air Force's ability to provide consistent and co-ordinated ground support. Soviet air strength had to be increased to 1,500 and latterly to an estimated 2,000 machines before an armistice was forced on the Finns in March 1940. The liberal dispensing of decorations, including sixty-eight awards of Hero of the Soviet Union to the Red Air Force, and laudatory features in the Soviet press could not disguise the fact that Soviet military weaknesses had been displayed for all to see, not excluding the allegedly friendly Third Reich. Available estimates place Soviet air losses in the Winter War at between 700 and 950 aircraft for some sixty or seventy by the Finns[5].

Smushkevich, who had directed air operations from his headquarters at Petrozavodsk, was removed from command in April 1940 to be replaced in his turn by his former comrade-in-arms from Spain, Pavel Rychagov[6]. The debâcle of the Winter War did not put an end to Stalin's 'command changes'. A new wave of purges launched in the spring of 1941 toppled Rychagov in favour of General Pavel Zhigarev, Rychagov's Deputy Head of GU-VVS from the previous December. Zhigarev, forty at the time of his appointment, had begun his army career in the Red Cavalry and was transferred to the Red Air Force in the mid-twenties, graduating in 1932 from the Command Faculty of the Zhukovski Air Force Academy and rising

---

[5]See Richard Condon *The Winter War* and *The Finnish Air Force, 1918-68*.

[6]Despite Vodop'yanov's assertion that Smushkevich died from natural causes during the early part of the Winter War in *Druz'ya v nebe*, Yakovlev in *Tsel' Zhizni* mentions both Smushkevich and Rychagov as victims of the purges who suffered, 'as it later transpired, utterly innocently'. Conquest in *The Great Terror* gives the date of Smushkevich's execution as 28 October 1941; significantly, this coincides with the date of Loktionov's death given in the *Bol'shaya Sovetskaya Entsiklopediya*.

rapidly to become Head of Air Force Operational Readiness Staff before being sent east to take over command of the air forces attached to the 2nd Independent Red Banner Army. Decorated with the Order of the Red Star in May 1936 he survived the waves of purges and in May 1940 was promoted to the rank of Lt. General — on a par with Rychagov — together with K.P. Kravchenko, the hero of Khalkin Gol and S.F. Zhavoronkov, Head of Naval Air Forces. These promotions coincided with Voroshilov's replacement by Timoshenko as Commissar for Defence when a number of interned officers were released and reinstated; several, like Pumpur who was made Air Commander for the Moscow Military District, disappeared once more with the fall of Rychagov.

On the political front, the Winter War brought about an end to the 'dual command' system introduced in May 1937 whereby commissars held equal status with their military counterparts. The commissar's authority not only extended to questions of morale and political indoctrination but also, in alliance with the unit's NKVD attachment, to counter-espionage, security and the selection of personnel for promotion. Under 'collegiate control' the commanders of military districts were obliged to refer their decisions to a council in which the political commissars had the power to change or veto purely military proposals. As a result command effectiveness was gravely impaired since the political commisar had more real power than the military commander and his adverse report could result in a humiliating reprimand, demotion, or worse. Timoshenko reintroduced the 'single-command' system to strengthen Red Army command confidence, and by a decree of August 1940 the political commissar was replaced by the new office of political deputy. The system of 'dual command' returned after June 1941 when the 'dedication' of the Red Army under the shock of its first defeats was suspected by Stalin, but in October 1942 with the Stalingrad crisis looming the commissars were again made deputies for political affairs with Red Army ranks.

Under Loktionov and Smushkevich the first steps had been taken to reorganise the Red Air Force for its planned expansion and bring it more closely into line with the structure of the Red Army. Under the restructuring of the Red Air Force planned in 1938 and introduced from the following April, the air brigade was abolished and replaced by the new air regiment (*aviatsionny polk*). Each bomber regiment

Soviet Air Force

(*bombardirovochny aviatsionny polk*[7]) was to have five squadrons of twelve aircraft while the fighter (*istrebitel'ny*) and ground-attack (*shturmovoi*) regiment was to contain four squadrons of fifteen aircraft. In all cases the squadron was to be composed of the traditional three-aircraft *zven'ya* and the recommendations made by Gusev and other Soviet fighter commanders in the Spanish Civil War that the four-fighter *zveno* with two pairs (*pary*) should be introduced apparently went unheeded.

Although the strength of the new air regiment was to be standardised at sixty aircraft, excluding reserve machines, this target was not invariably met. *Luftwaffe* Intelligence concluded that the strength of the average fighter or ground-attack regiment was likely to be forty-eight aircraft and the average for bomber and reconnaissance regiments thirty-six, with squadrons of twelve and nine machines respectively. Between four and six air regiments formed the new air division (*aviatsionnoya diviziya*), and while purely fighter or bomber divisions went to form the military district air forces, a composite or mixed (*smeshannaya*) air division consisting of fighter and bomber regiments was to be directly attached to each ground army as part of the new Army Air Forces (*armeiskaya aviatsiya*). As before, certain army corps retained their own squadrons attached for reconnaissance or communications duties.

The special purpose aviation armies (*aviatsionnye armii osobovo naznacheniya*) subordinated directly to the Commissariat for Defence were disbanded in 1940 with the demise of the Special Purpose Air Arm (AON), although the Supreme Command retained control of a number of tactical air corps as well as of the *Dal'nebombardirovochnaya aviatsiya GKO* (DBA-GKO) or Long-Range Bomber Arm. Military district air staffs, in particular those in the western frontier districts whose air resources were greatly augmented in early 1941, were faced with the task of co-ordinating various air elements, including army air divisions, GKO air corps and the now tactically deployed long-range bomber corps over which they had no direct command authority, with their own military district (later frontal) air commands. The strains imposed on

---

[7]Bomber regiments were sub-categorised as either a fast bomber (*skorostnoi bombardirovochny*), dive bomber (*pikiruyushchi bombardirovochny*), light bomber (*lyogkobombardirovochny*), close-support bomber (*blizhnebombardirovochny*), long-range bomber (*dal'nebombardirovichny*) or heavy bomber (*tyazhyolobombardirovochny*) polk

The Falcons Culled

operational cohesion, liaison, supplies and services by this fragmentation of control were to become clear over the first weeks of the Great Patriotic War and contribute in no small measure to the ineffectiveness of the Red Air Force.

Naval Aviation had been operationally detached from GU-VVS in 1935, although the latter remained responsible for technical, support and supply matters. In 1939 a new Naval Air Force Directorate was created under General Semyon Zhavoronkov, one time Commissar of the Black Sea Fleet Air Force and later a fleet naval air commander. Zhavoronkov's task was to prepare for the projected growth in function as well as in the size of the Naval Air Forces which were in future to be capable not only of supporting the Red Navy but also the Red Army along the Soviet Union's maritime flanks. The most notable change, therefore, was the relegation of the flying boat and the floatplane and the rise of the landplane, particularly in the expansion of fighter strength and the formation of new mine and torpedo bomber regiments equipped with the DB-3F (Il-4). In the main the landplanes that the Naval Air Forces (VVS-VMF) received were discarded Red Air Force machines consisting of DB-3, SB, TB-1 and TB-3 bombers and I-15*bis*, I-153 and I-16 fighters, so that although the size of VVS-VMF increased by 39% in 1940 alone, the proportion of new types it possessed remained minimal. Apart from its DB-3F (Il-4) torpedo bombers and a few Pe-2 bombers for reconnaissance, VVS-VMF had only seventy-two Yak-1, MiG-1 and MiG-3 fighters in June 1941, less than 10% of its fighter strength. When war with Germany broke out, the three western fleet air forces had 1,445 aircraft of which over half were fighters and just under a quarter torpedo bombers[8].

The overall poor standard of flying skill shown by the Red Air Force in Spain in anything but text-book conditions coupled with inadequate standards of physical fitness, indifferent air gunnery and

---

[8] The breakdown of the three western fleet air forces in June 1941 was as follows (*See Aviatsiya i Kosmonavtika SSSR*).

Fleet	Fighters	Bombers &Torp. Bombers	Recce & Misc	Total	% of Total
Northern	49	11	54	114	7.8
Baltic	368	188	151	707	48.9
Black Sea	346	138	140	624	43.2
Totals	763	337	345	1,445	

lack of any determined personal initiative in combat had already been commented on by senior Red Air Force officers returning from Spain. *Osoaviakhim* no less than the Red Air Force shouldered the responsibility for these criticisms which were confirmed by the Winter War. With a paper membership of thirteen millions in 1935-36, *Osoaviakhim* was still producing too few adequately prepared recruits. The number of aeroclubs leaped from thirty-three in 1935 to one hundred and fifty the following year when it was claimed that 8,000 pilots had gained certificates of competence on powered aircraft and 20,000 on gliders[9]. Standards were, however, generally low. This was due in part to the lack of trained instructors and the fear of criticism in not producing an impressive number of 'passes', and in part to the primitive conditions under which *Osoaviakhim* had often to function and its sheer lack of equipment. The number of training aircraft at its disposal was inadequate since the Red Air Force had prior claims on deliveries of the U-2 trainer, and although *Osoaviakhim* had attempted to make itself at least partly self-sufficient in this respect by setting up its own factory, this turned out specialised sporting and competition aircraft rather than the sorely needed basic trainers. A halt to *Osoaviakhim's* expansion programme was ordered by Stalin in his secret decree of August 1935, and by the following April a general revision and reduction of its collosal membership had been made before the purging of its Central Committee. An editorial attack on Eideman in *Samolyot* was timed to coincide with the announcement of his execution[10] and the Central Kosarev Aeroclub (later renamed the Chkalov Aeroclub) became *Pravda's* target of attack. Many of its staff including its head, Brigade Commander Maks Deich, were arrested on ludicrous charges of being responsible for sabotaging the long-distance light aircraft trials and causing the deaths of display parachutists making delayed drops[11]. In 1938 the Tushino Glider Factory was taken over by GUAP and *Osoaviakhim*'s Scientific-Research and Technical

---

[9]*Khimiya i Oborona* No.8 1936

[10]Eideman was accused of having, 'allowed the distraction of success and self-congratulatory babble to weaken Bolshevik vigilance and permit enemies of the people to insinuate themselves into the society's ranks'. The editorial concluded with a call for 'an immediate and radical reconstruction of *Osoaviakhim's* work from top to bottom on the basis of the directives given at the Central Committee's Plenary Session in February and Comrade Stalin's address'. *Samolyot* No. 6, 1937.

[11]Yakovlev *Tsel' Zhizni*

Society (*Avianito*) formed to promote the design of high-performance light aircraft was dissolved. Yet despite these chastisements the work of *Osoaviakhim* continued. In 1940 it presided over one hundred and eighty-two aeroclubs, four flying schools for instructor training, thirty-six gliding schools and twelve technical clubs and claimed to have trained 24,000 pilots, 22,000 parachutists and 3,107 mechanics — only 4,156 glider pilots were issued with certificates, demonstrating the swing to instruction on powered aircraft[12].

A three-year *Osoaviakhim* course certificate enabled the holder to enter the Red Air Force as a volunteer where a basic three-month course of infantry and aeronautical instruction was followed by twelve to fifteen months tuition on U-2 and UT-2 trainers. At this juncture the most promising were selected for a further six to nine months' training if picked for fighter schools and a year's training if recommended for bombers. By 1938 there were eighteen schools established for Red Air Force flying and technical trainees. There was considerable emphasis on formation flying for both fighter and bomber pilots, with the former carrying out most of their air gunnery exercises against fixed ground targets. Night and bad-weather flying training was largely neglected. Formation flying involved observing and reacting to signals given by the *zveno* or squadron leader — by hand, flares or wing movements — with no encouragement to develop personal judgement or initiative. One result of this was that *Luftwaffe* fighter pilots soon noted that Soviet air formations became confused and usually turned back once the formation leader had been shot down, and bomber regiments lost a disproportionate number of their best crews early in the war.

The chastening experience of the Winter War was followed by feverish endeavours to improve the operational efficiency of the Red Air Force and the standard of aircrew training. From December 1940 it was decided to select Red Air Force entrants from the annual military draft instead of relying on voluntary enlistment from *Osoaviakhim*. On the completion of training, conscripts were chosen to serve as pilots, air-gunners, bombardiers or mechanics; pilots passed out with the rank of sergeant and the practice of awarding a commission to qualified flying personnel was not reintroduced until

---

[12] See *Sovetskie voenno-vozdushnye sily v Velikoi Otechestvennoi Voine* (SVVSVOV) and *Aviatsiya i Kosmonavtika SSSR*.

the war years. All conscripted men up to and including *zveno* commanders, usually with the rank of Senior Lieutenant, serving their obligatory four years were required to reside permanently in barracks. These measures to impress the new conscript airmen that they could no longer expect preferential treatment in the Red Army succeeded in causing widespread resentment without improving morale or enthusiasm. In February 1941 the courses offered by flying schools were standardised in duration — the basic military air school (*aviashkola pervonachal'novo obucheniya*) with a four-month course, the air force pilots' school (*voennaya shkola pilotov*) with a nine-month course and the air force college for flying command staff (*voenno-aviatsionnoe uchilishche komandirov-lyotchikov*) with a course lasting two years. In time of war it was envisaged that these courses would be reduced to periods of three months, six months and one year respectively. To provide for advanced command and technical education, the Command Faculty of the Zhukovski Academy was moved to Monino as the basis for the new Air Force Academy for Command and Navigational Staff (now the Gagarin Red Banner Air Force Academy), and a year later the Leningrad Air Force Engineers' Academy (now the Mozhaiski Air Force Academy) opened its doors for the first time.

To accelerate conversion training, three special reserve air regiments were created in 1940 but a resolution of the Party Central Committee the following February calling for the formation of as many new air regiments equipped with the latest combat aircraft as possible was impeded by the slow introduction of series production. With only 322 LaGG-3 fighters and 460 Pe-2 bombers supplied in the first half of 1941, the planned pilot conversion programmes for these types were only 32% and 72% complete by 1st May. Most successful was the MiG fighter programme which was claimed to be 80% complete, although many pilots remained very apprehensive and avoided flying the MiG-3 whenever possible. By June 1941, therefore, the Red Air Force contained only nineteen air regiments re-equipped with the latest types of aircraft. Air-to-air and ground-to-air radio communications for operational control were in the main lacking or of poor quality — the RSI-3 fighter radios were so unreliable and had such a limited range that little use was made of the few available. The ground communications system relied heavily on telephone and telegraph facilities to which unit commanders rarely had exclusive access. Attempts were made after the Winter War to

The Falcons Culled

improve the shortcomings of the rear services, but little of the ambitious programme had actually been put into practice by June 1941. Military districts were to be divided into a number of air basing regions (*Raiony aviatsionnovo bazirovaniya*) containing one air base for each division and servicing and maintenance battalions for each air regiment. The divisional air base was to consist of a fleet of seventy vehicles to make it fully mobile and able to transport spares, workshop equipment, meteorological and signals apparatus, fuel and rations. The sheer lack of motorised transport frustrated much of the planned re-organisation while the shortage of repair workshops, spares, and adequately trained mechanics and fitters meant that a high proportion of the air division's machines remained unserviceable and had often to be returned to factories for repair. There were also too few properly equipped airfields with hangars and surfaced runways. *Luftwaffe* Intelligence decided that only about a tenth of all Soviet airfields in the west could be considered suitable for bombers. The Russians themselves tended to maintain a fatalistic attitude towards airfield conditions and a decision to discontinue the policy of fitting ski-undercarriages to combat aircraft with a corresponding reduction in performance was vehemently opposed by Zhigarev on the grounds that it would be impossible to keep runways clear of snow in winter.

While the standard of training and equipment in the Red Air Force remained inferior to its western counterparts, it continued to grow in size. In a statement made by Loktionov on 17th August 1939 it was claimed that the Red Air Force had between five and five and a half thousand aircraft in Western Russia, more than the British, French or German estimates drawn up earlier that year[13]. Loktionov also claimed a dramatic increase in aircraft production to give an annual output of between 10,500 and 11,500 machines, excluding civil and training types. Loktionov's pronouncements appear to have been somewhat exaggerated, although the acceleration in production was

---

[13] Discounting naval aircraft, French Intelligence estimated that VVS possessed some 5,200 machines as of 1st January 1939: 3,750 in European Russia, 600 in Central Russia and Siberia and 850 in the Far East. British Intelligence, refusing to commit itself to an estimate for the Far East, advanced the remarkably fastidious figure of 3,361 aircraft for the rest of the USSR on 1st August (*Erikson*). The Luftwaffe Operations Staff estimated Soviet air strength at 5,000 in May 1939 with 1,000 machines in the Far East. The assessed composition was 1,400 fighters, 1,300 bombers and recce, 350 ground-attack, 250 observation and communications aircraft and 700 naval air force machines. (*Schwabedissen* and *Baumbach*).

in itself remarkable. In September 1939 *Sovnarkom*'s defence committee approved a priority measure to build nine new aircraft plants and reconstruct nine existing ones to give an output of over 17,000 aircraft a year by the end of 1941. By late 1940, when a further seven factories had been turned over to the aircraft industry, it was claimed that the industry's productive capacity was almost three-quarters as great again as it had been in 1937. From March 1941 the aircraft industry as a whole was put on a twenty-four hour working day with the aim of producing 1,500 machines a month by July.

The quantity of machines produced, however, was not effectively matched by the introduction of better and newer types in the required numbers. Fyodorov[14] gives the output of military aircraft as 17,745 machines produced between 1 January 1939 and 22 June 1940, of which only 3,719 were new types. Given that 2,653 Yak-1, LaGG and MiG fighters, Pe-2 bombers and Il-2 (or BSh) *shturmoviks* were produced in the first six months of 1941, Fyodorov's figure implies the staggeringly low number of 1,166 new types — accounting presumably for Yak-4, Ar-2, Su-2 and DB-3F (Il-4) production — in 1939-40.

What is certain is that the Germans underestimated Soviet attainments in boosting output and gave a disproportionate significance to the dislocation resulting from the purges. The *Luftwaffe* High Command assessed the Soviet aircraft industry as consisting of fifty airframe, fifteen aeroengine and about a hundred and forty component and equipment workshops with a total workforce of 250,000 in the spring of 1941. Output over 1939-40 was calculated to be about 5,500 aircraft and 14,500 engines annually and to represent less than half the target quotas set[15]. Estimates like these encouraged a dangerously dismissive attitude towards Soviet production potential, regenerative ability and industrial resilience.

As early as March 1939 Voroshilov had informed the 18th Party Congress that the production of light bombers, ground-attack and reconnaissance types had been halved. Clearly, this decision had not been taken because the doctrines of the Red Air Force declared such aircraft to be unnecessary but because the types extant were

---

[14]*Aviatsiya v bitve pod Moskvoi*. The statistical evidence available indicates that the Soviet aircraft industry supplied no more than 7,500 combat machines annually in 1939 and 1940. Shtemenko in *Sovetski general'ny shtab na voine* gives the total aircraft production figures for 1939 and 1940 as 10,382 and 10,563 machines respectively.

[15]Schwabedissen

The Falcons Culled

obviously superannuated. Technical development had been seriously hit by the purges and innovatory or dissenting voices suppressed or ignored. Many prototypes were discarded when they failed to meet the specifications set for them and when they were placed in production they frequently proved incapable of satisfying the demands they had been designed to fulfil. Yakovlev's graceful Ya-22 intended as a high-speed reconnaissance or escort fighter was placed in production in April 1939, but at Smushkevich's insistence as the BB-22 (Yak-4) close-support bomber — in which role its service performance with an unavoidably exterior bomb-load turned out to be so disappointing that a decision to phase out production had already been taken before Germany invaded. Sukhoi's BB-1 (Su-2), placed in production late in 1940 to supplement the obsolescent R-10 reconnaissance and ground-attack bomber, showed its high vulnerability to flak and fighter attack in the first months of the war and was to be dropped from production in 1942 after five hundred had been built.

The most telling blow against the Soviet aircraft industry was the arrest of Tupolev himself as Head of KOSOS and Chief Engineer to GUAP, accused, among other things, with the ludicrous charge of having sold the plans of the Bf 109 and Bf 110 fighters to Germany. He was soon joined by most of his senior design staff including Vladimir Petlyakov and Vladimir Myasishchev. Georgi Ozerov, a member of KOSOS and later of Tupolev's internee design bureau, has estimated that four hundred and fifty aircraft designers, engineers and specialists were interned between 1934 and 1941, of which some three hundred were later set to work in NKVD supervised design bureaux, about a hundred died in GULAG labour camps and no less than fifty were executed[16]. Among the prominent specialists arrested and utilised in the NKVD internee design bureaux were the aeroengine expert Boris Stechkin, the helicopter pioneer Aleksei Cheremukhin, and the designers Iosif Neman, Aleksandr Putilov and Roberto Bartini. The Head of TsAGI, Nikolai Kharlamov, who had visited the USA with Tupolev to secure the licence-production rights for the Douglas DC-3 was also removed, to be replaced briefly by Mikhail Shul'zhenko. After suffering innumerable humiliations at conferences presided over by Stalin, who contended that TsAGI consisted of dispensable theorists, Shul'zhenko was replaced in the spring of 1940 by Ivan Petrov,

---

[16] Ozerov *Tupolevskaya sharaga*

formerly a deputy chief of NII-VVS, and allowed to take up a lectureship at the Moscow Aviation Institute. The Head of NII-VVS, Nikolai Barzhanov, also fell in 1938 to be replaced by the head of its Scientific-Research Division, Aleksandr Filin — a veteran of the ANT-25 long-distance flights who later paid the penalty for championing the Pe-8 four-engined bomber.

Some major aircraft factories lost almost all their key personnel. GAZ No. 1 lost its director, Ivan Kostkin, its chief engineer, his deputy, the heads of two design *brigady* and the heads of four shops, and GAZ No. 156, GUAP's main prototype factory, lost the heads of four design *brigady*. Experimental and research establishments were either closed or decapitated by the removal of directing specialists. The Reaction-Motor Scientific-Research Institute (RNII) where Soviet rocket engine development had been concentrated since 1934 and encouraged by Tukhachevski lost both its head, Ivan Kleimenov, and its chief engineer, Georgi Langemak — the men responsible for the widely used RS-82 and RS-132 air-launched rockets. The deputy scientific head of RNII, Sergei Korolyov — later to be glorified as the pioneer of Soviet space achievements — was also imprisoned, although at the time of his arrest RNII was preparing to test the RP 318 rocket-powered glider and the result of Korolyov's removal was that the first Soviet rocket-powered aircraft flight was delayed by two years. Helicopter and autogyro development was also interrupted when the Special Design Bureau (OOK) was deprived of its director, A.M. Izakson and his deputy Cheremukhin. In January 1941 OOK's remaining staff were divided between the Moscow Aviation Institute where Bratukhin pursued work on helicopter development and a small autogyro team under Nikolai Kamov which was eventually disbanded in 1943. The Bureau for Experimental Designs (BOK) specialising in research into high-altitude flight was closed for a time after the arrest of its chief designer, Chizhevski, and many other smaller design bureaux, including the Experimental Aerodesign Division at NII-GVF and the Special Design Bureau at the Leningrad Institute for Civil Air Fleet Engineers (LII-GVF) were shut down altogether.

The failures of prototypes to meet specified performance figures and accidents during flight tests were classified as sabotage and severe punishments meted out. When Valeri Chkalov was killed on the prototype I-180 fighter on 15 December 1938, the death of the national hero evoked immediate retribution — including the arrest of

The Falcons Culled

Belyaikin, head of the People's Commissariat for the Defence Industry, Polikarpov's deputy, Dmitri Tomashevich who had prepared the design for the new fighter and was later made head of an internee design bureau during the war years, and the director of GAZ No. 156 where the prototype had been built — although the responsibility for the crash was unmistakably the pilot's[17]. Three further prototypes of the I-180 were tested, but after one example had been seriously damaged and two lost in test flights, further development ended and the I-16 remained in production as the standard VVS fighter. According to Aleksandr Rotenburg, then a member of the Polikarpov KB, the abandonment of the I-180 denied the Red Air Force the 3,000 I-180 fighters he estimates would have been in service by June 1941[18]. It was probably as a result of the I-180 engine failures that Sergei Tumanski, designer of the M-87 radial, was removed from his post as Chief Designer at TsIAM supervising the production and development of the M-87 and M-88 radial engines — at that time the most powerful available — at GAZ No. 29. Further work on radial engines was entrusted to Shvetsov. Another of Polikarpov's deputies, Nikolai Zhemchuzhin, was imprisoned when a pre-production example of his VIT-2 anti-tank aircraft broke up during diving tests and he was only released after incontrovertible evidence of imprudent behaviour by the test-pilot was brought to light. Polikarpov himself, while he lost much of Stalin's confidence, remained inviolate. Early in 1939 a special conference was called at the Kremlin and attended by Stalin, Molotov, Voroshilov, Loktionov, Mikhail Kaganovich from GUAP,

---

[17] Vodop'yanov's account of the accident states that Chkalov was told on the morning of the fatal flight that the fighter's M-87 engine had not been protected against frost the previous night although it seemed to be running satisfactorily. Chkalov decided to take off but remain in the immediate vicinity of the airfield in case he needed to make a forced landing. The frost was still keen when Chkalov took off and the engine cut as he brought the I-180 round to land after one circuit of the airfield. Unable to restart the engine, Chkalov attempted a wheels-up landing on littered open ground short of the runway, but in trying to avoid a telegraph pole he brushed the ground with a wing-tip and the aircraft cart-wheeled. Chkalov was thrown out of the cockpit and struck his head on the cable-drum, dying soon after of his injuries on the staircase leading to the operating theatre. His body lay in state visited by military and political dignitaries until its burial in the Kremlin Wall. His native town of Orenburg was renamed Chkalov in his honour. (*Druz'ya v Nebe*).

[18] A. Magid: *Bol'shaya Zhizn'*, Moscow, 1969. In fact the I-180 would appear to have promised only a marginal improvement in performance over the I-16 type 24, and with an armament of two ShKAS and BS machine-guns would have lacked the latter's more potent cannon armament.

101

Soviet Air Force

Shul'zhenko from TsAGI and Filin from NII-VVS. As a result of the resolutions taken, a number of aircraft designers, most of them still relatively unknown, were asked to submit proposals for new designs. There was a particular need for a new fighter and the successful LaGG-1 and Yak-1 medium-level fighters powered by the M-105 engine and the high-altitude MiG-1 fighter with the M-35 were built as prototypes at top speed over the remainder of the year. The Yak-1 was ready for flight tests in January 1940, followed by the LaGG-1 in March and the MiG-1 the month after, the last two being subsequently revised as the LaGG-3 and MiG-3 after some hundred production examples of each had been built. Smushkevich had decided that factory and State tests by NII-VVS should be conducted simultaneously to reduce delays in starting production, and the degree of urgency can be judged by the fact that tooling for series production had begun before the MiG-1 had made its first flight on 5 April 1940, with state tests completed by August and the first twenty MiG-1 fighters built before the close of the year. The improved MiG-3 began to reach Red Air Force fighter regiments in March 1941, less than a month after its introduction onto the assembly lines at GAZ No. 1. The MiG was required with particular urgency to equip the fighter regiments of the new *Protivovozdushnaya Oborona* (PVO) or Air Defence Force created early in 1941 and by the end of June 1941 1,309 MiG fighters had been produced as against 399 Yak-1 and 322 LaGG fighters.

The new PVO zones were established on the bases of the existing military districts but had their own commanders, usually drawn from the artillery, with overall control of anti-aircraft guns, searchlight batteries and barrage balloon defences and supported by the Air Observation, Warning and Communications Service (VNOS). Subordinate to the PVO zone commander were an AA artillery commander and the commanders of attached fighter units who remained subordinate administratively to the military district air commander; fighter corps were in the process of formation for PVO in early 1941. PVO zone commanders were deputies to frontal and military district commanders until 1942 when they were made directly responsible to a PVO Command attached to the Red Army. With the heightened importance of strategic air defence in the postwar years, PVO attained the status of an independent command in its own right.

Il'yushin's Il-2 (BSh) single-seat *shturmovik* had also passed its

The Falcons Culled

flight tests in January 1940 after being revised on Stalin's orders from its original two-seat form, but little further headway was made due to objections about its inadequate armour protection raised by NTK-VVS and preparations for production of the aircraft at GAZ No. 18, Voronezh, were only begun after Il'yushin had appealed directly to Stalin in November. When Stalin criticised Il'yushin for sluggish production the following February, he refused to listen to explanations although the fault was not Il'yushin's but due to the failings of the Leningrad plant responsible for supplying the armour plate. Impressed by the *Luftwaffe's* use of dive-bombers, Stalin ordered similar machines to be provided for the Red Air Force. Arkhangel'ski's SB-RK (Ar-2) — an attempt to revise the SB for a dive-bombing role — was not successful and only two hundred were built in 1940-41. Petlyakov was obliged to revise his VI-100 high-altitude fighter and transform it into the PB-100 (Pe-2) dive-bomber, for which he was 'rewarded' with his freedom. Tupolev, at work on what was to be the Tu-2, was instructed by Beria to produce a four-engined long-range dive-bomber to match the German Heinkel He 177, a proposal he firmly resisted[19].

In January 1940 Stalin finally dismissed Mikhail Kaganovich from his post as Head of GUAP, freed from subordination to the NKTP and made an independent People's Commissariat the previous year, and replaced him with Aleksei Shakhurin, Secretary of the Gorky Regional Party Committee and a man with some experience of the aircraft industry[20]. Yakovlev who had enjoyed Stalin's particular favour and confidence after the design of his successful UT-1 and UT-2 trainers [21] was made Shakhurin's deputy for Research and Development. Yakovlev had already been included in the Soviet air delegation sent to Germany in October 1939 led by Ivan Tevosyan and containing Aleksandr Gusev, Ivan Petrov, Nikolai Polikarpov,

---

[19] Ozerov

[20] According to Khrushchev, Mikhail Kaganovich was later accused of plotting with the Germans and committed suicide (*Khrushchev Remembers*). Kaganovich, who had survived purely through the protection of his brother, Lazar, had been replaced as Head of GUAP for a brief period in 1939 by Sergei Il'yushin. Il'yushin was allowed to resign after prudently pleading pressure of design work to Stalin. See Astashenkov *Konstruktor legendarnykh Ilov*.

[21] The UT-2 two-seat primary trainer was placed in production in 1936 and 7,243 built. It was followed in 1937 by the similar UT-1 single-seat advanced and aerobatic trainer of which 1,241 were built. Both machines were extensively used by the Red Air Force and by *Osoaviakhim*.

Soviet Air Force

Vasili Kuznetsov and Pyotr Dement'ev — the last two subsequently made Shakhurin's deputies for aeroengine development and airframe production problems. The host to the Soviet delegation was Ernst Udet who showed the latest *Luftwaffe* machines to the Russians, facilitated their visits to German aircraft factories and presented Tevosyan with the gift of a Fi 156 *Storch*. The Russians made a return visit in March 1940 to confirm the agreement drawn up that February under which Germany was to sell some thirty-five aircraft to the USSR and to negotiate the production of certain German types in the Soviet Union with the Germans receiving one third of the machines produced in lieu of royalties.

In the event, the Soviet delegation purchased all six existing prototypes of the Heinkel He 100, five examples of the Bf 109E-3, five of the Bf 110C, two Dornier Do 215B-3 bombers and two examples of the Ju 88 together with a small number of other machines, including a Bü 131 trainer[22]. These machines were reluctantly delivered in June 1940, evaluated by NII-VVS and made available for examination by Soviet aircraft designers.

A reciprocal visit by members of the *Luftwaffe*'s Technical Office was arranged by the German Air Attache, Lieutenant-Colonel Aschenbrenner, in April 1941. In Moscow the Germans visited TsAGI, GAZ No. 1 where MiG-3 fighters were being built, the Pe-2 production lines at GAZ No. 22 and the Mikulin engine factory, GAZ No. 24. The delegation later went to the aeroengine factories at Rybinsk (Shcherbakov) and Molotov (Perm) where it was noted that three shifts were working round the clock and that women seemed to comprise half the workforce. These reports and the observations of Werner Baumbach who had visited Aschenbrenner the September before and travelled over the Trans-Siberian Railway en route to Tokyo, were sent to Milch and Göring but largely ignored[23].

But even while the fraternal exchange of delegations was under way the *Luftwaffe* was drawing up its plans for Operation Barbarossa, the codename for Hitler's surprise attack on the Soviet Union. In October 1940 Lt. Colonel Rowehl was instructed to carry out the photographic mapping of western Russia and the frontier military

---

[22] Substantiating evidence cannot be found to confirm Ozerov's claim that examples of the Ju 87, He 111, and Fw 189 were also obtained (*Tupolevskaya sharaga*). According to Yakovlev, the Russians decided against buying an example of the Ju 87 as it was 'obsolete and slow' (*Tsel' Zhizni*).

[23] Schwabedissen

districts using one squadron based on Seerappen to cover Belorussia, a second at Insterburg to cover the Baltic States and a third operating from Bucharest to survey the Black Sea coast. Rowehl's aircraft were supplemented by special high-altitude versions of the Ju 88 flying from Cracow and Bucharest to photograph the area between Minsk and Kiev — the heart of the Russian frontline defences. One of these machines made a forced landing in the Minsk area after engine trouble on 20 June and its crew was subsequently released by the advancing *Wehrmacht*. In fact from October 1939 until the morning of Operation Barbarossa, the Soviets claimed that some five hundred overflights of Soviet territory were made by *Luftwaffe* machines, one hundred and fifty of these in the six months immediately before the German invasion. That these incursions went unmolested was later blamed on Beria who had apparently prohibited any aggressive reply to German overflights in March 1940[24]. Stalin, however, was clearly responsible for these instructions with his fear of providing Hitler with a 'provocation'. Fighter regiment commanders in the Odessa Military District were reprimanded for allowing their MiG-3 fighters to make 'unauthorised' interceptions of the intruding *Luftwaffe* reconnaissance flights.

As the deadline for Barbarossa drew near, the *Luftwaffe* prepared its last estimates of the air opposition it expected to meet. Between 5,700 and 9,300 combat aircraft were thought to be available to the Red Air Force in the west, and it was assumed that about half these aircraft would be modern types, with about two or three hundred MiG fighters in service and representing the greatest threat to *Luftwaffe* air superiority. An estimate of between 13 to 14,000 aircraft based in western Russia advanced by Signals Intelligence was deemed to be exaggerated, but in any case sheer weight of numbers meant nothing to the conquerors of Poland, France, Belgium, Holland, Denmark and Norway. On 21 June 1941 the *Luftwaffe* was ready for its most testing commitment so far in the Second World War — the destruction of Stalin's mighty Red Air Force.

---

[24] IVOVSS, Vol II

Army Composite Air Division — 1940

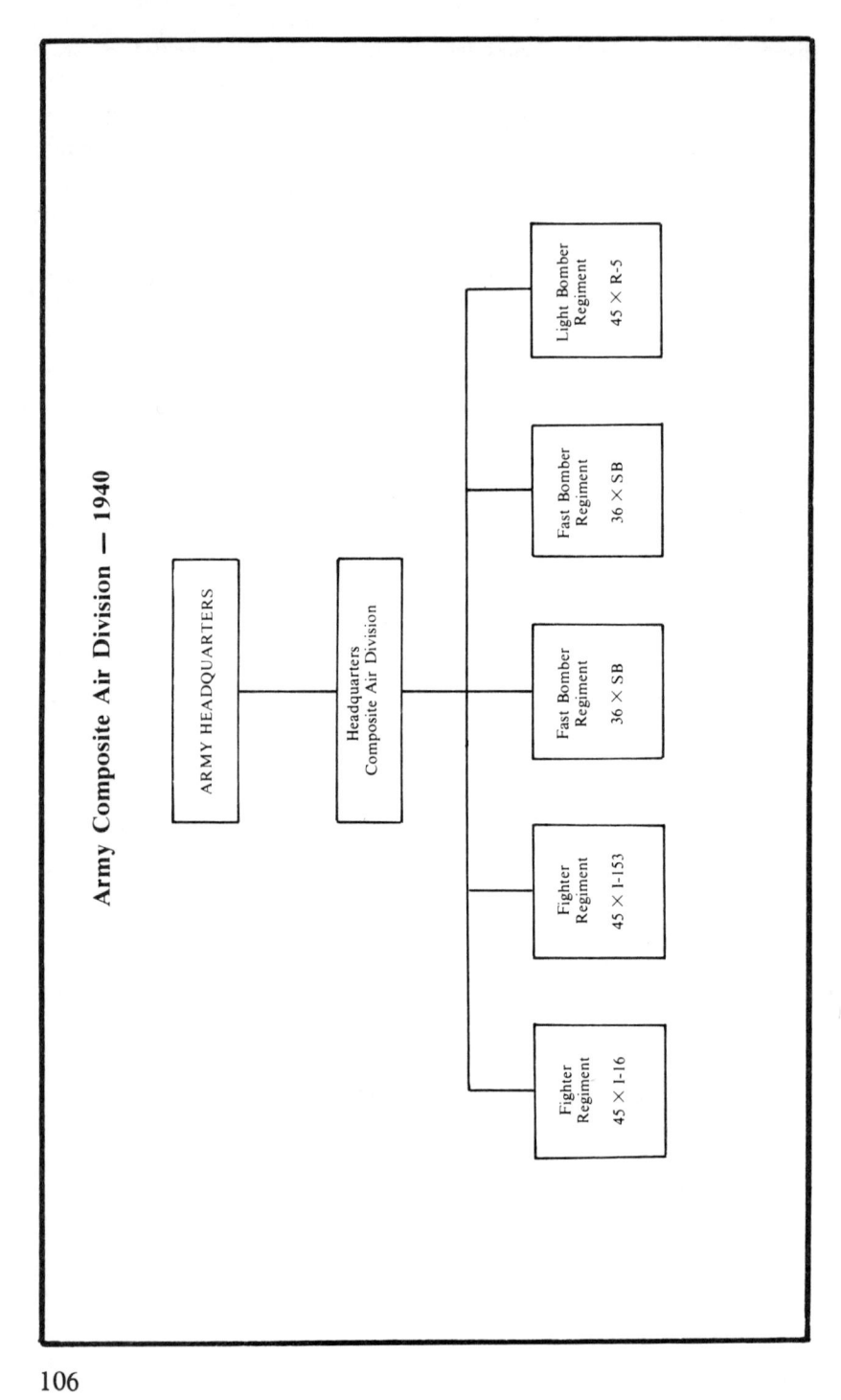

```
ARMY HEADQUARTERS
        |
Headquarters
Composite Air Division
        |
   ┌────────┬────────┬────────┬────────┐
Fighter   Fighter   Fast      Fast      Light
Regiment  Regiment  Bomber    Bomber    Bomber
                    Regiment  Regiment  Regiment
45 × I-16 45 × I-153 36 × SB  36 × SB   45 × R-5
```

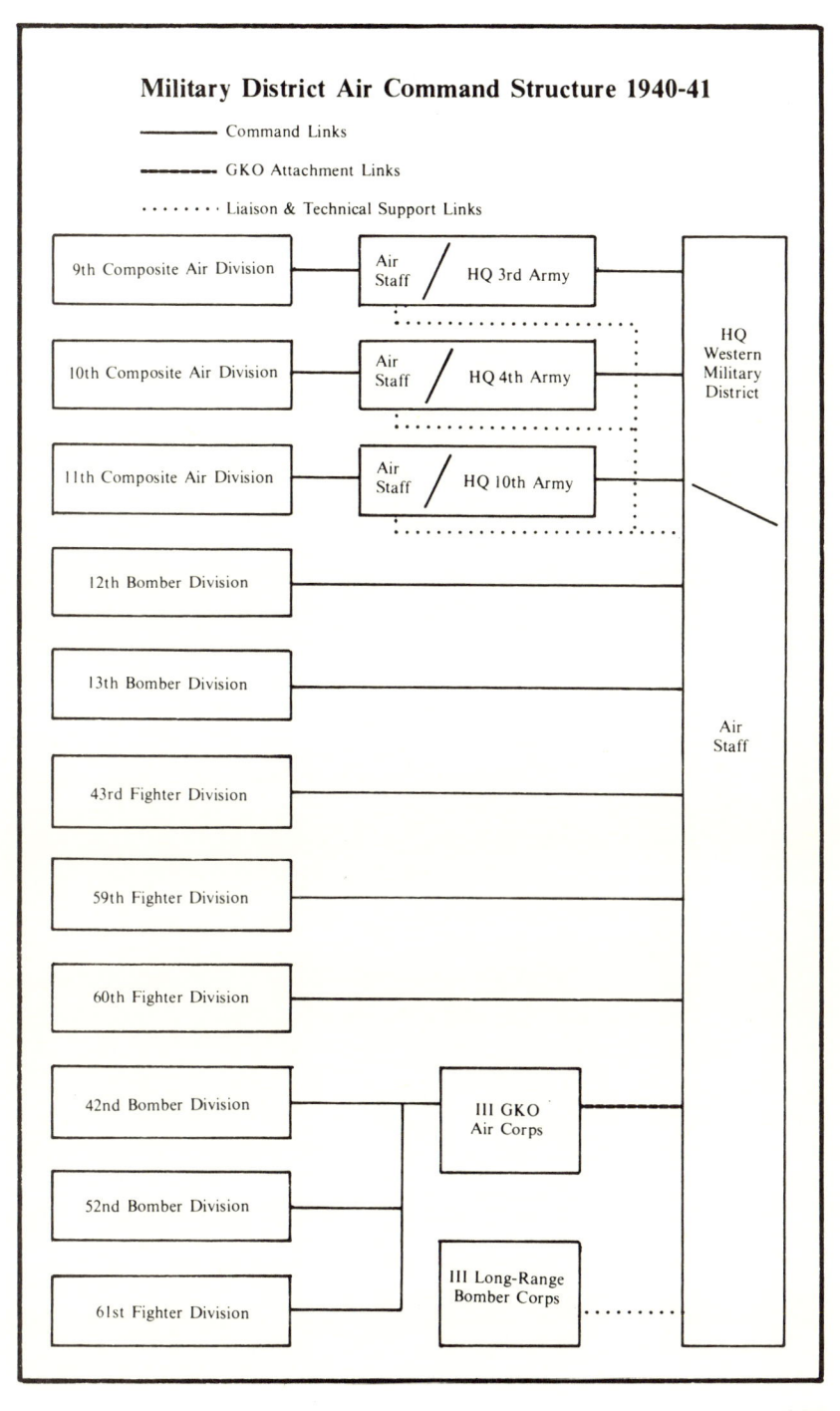

Military District Air Command Structure 1940-41

——— Command Links
⎯⎯⎯ GKO Attachment Links
········ Liaison & Technical Support Links

- 9th Composite Air Division — Air Staff / HQ 3rd Army
- 10th Composite Air Division — Air Staff / HQ 4th Army
- 11th Composite Air Division — Air Staff / HQ 10th Army
- 12th Bomber Division
- 13th Bomber Division
- 43rd Fighter Division
- 59th Fighter Division
- 60th Fighter Division
- 42nd Bomber Division — III GKO Air Corps
- 52nd Bomber Division
- 61st Fighter Division — III Long-Range Bomber Corps

HQ Western Military District

Air Staff

7 Barbarossa

At 3.15 am on Sunday, 22 June 1941, picked crews of *Kampfgeschwadern* 2,3 and 53 released their first SD 2 fragmentation bombs over Soviet territory, announcing the launching of Hitler's *blitzkrieg* invasion of the Soviet Union. In accordance with Hitler's Directive No. 21, 'Case Barbarossa', that the first task of the *Luftwaffe* in the new campaign should be the destruction of the Red Air Force, their bombs fell among neatly parked Soviet machines on airfields in the northern salient of the Western Military District, recently part of eastern Poland. This handful of He 111, Ju 88 and Do 17Z bombers formed the spearhead of a day's unrelenting attacks against sixty-six airfields in the western military districts of the USSR where 70% of their air resources, predominantly fighters[1], were massed in close proximity to the border. These dense concentrations gave the *Luftwaffe* its chance to launch the most devastating pre-emptive attack ever visited by one air force upon another, and to annihilate the bulk of an adversary it knew to be its superior in numbers if not in the quality of its aircraft or the training and experience of its aircrews.

Its task was made easier by the failure of last-minute orders for dispersal and concealment, sent out from Moscow less than two hours before the first *Luftwaffe* bombers struck, to reach air commanders in the frontier districts — although even these orders concluded with the words, 'no other measures are to be taken without specific instructions'[2]. Even if these orders had been received, it is

---

[1]The composition of Soviet air strength in the Baltic, Western, Kiev and Odessa Military Districts is reported to have been 59% fighters, 31% bombers, 4.5% ground-attack and 5.5% reconnaissance aircraft (SVVSVOV). By comparison, Fyodorov gives the general composition of the Red Air Force at this time as 45% bombers, 42% fighters and 13% reconnaissance and reserve aircraft.

[2]*IVOVSS*, Vol II

May Day 1918. Lenin and Trotski watch a Nieuport fighter flying over the military parade on Moscow's Red Square.

Top Left: Nikolai Zhukovski, founder of the Central Aero & Hydrodynamics and Air Force Scientific-Test Institutes and the Air Force Engineering Academy.

Top Right: 'Sergo' Ordzhonikidze, People's Commissar for Heavy Industry 1930-37 and responsible to Stalin for aircraft production.

Bottom Left: Pyotr Baranov, Head of the Red Air Force Chief Directorate 1924-31.

Bottom Right: Yakov Alksnis, Baranov's successor as Head of the Red Air Force Chief Directorate until purged by Stalin in 1937.

Top Left: Robert Eideman, Chairman of *Osoaviakhim*'s Central Committee 1932-37.

Top Right: Iosif Unshlikht, Secretary of the Central Executive Committee when he was purged in 1938, was closely involved in the development of *Osoaviakhim* and the Civil Air Fleet.

Bottom: With Marshal Voroshilov, People's Commissar for Defence, and Head of the Red Air Force Chief Directorate Alksnis (seated) stand (left to right), Todorski - Head of the Zhukovski Air Force Academy, Ingaunis - Military District Air Commander, Khripin - Head of the Special Purpose Air Arm, Lavrov - Chief of Red Air Force Staff, Lapin - Commander of the Far Eastern Air Forces, and Bergstrem - Assistant to Red Navy Chief Admiral Orlov for Naval Air Forces. A photograph of 1937 taken before the sweeping purges of that year.

Top Left: Yakov Smushkevich, first Head of the Soviet Air Group in the Spanish Civil War and Head of the Red Air Force Chief Directorate in 1939-40, was purged after Soviet air failures in the Winter War with Finland.

Top Right: Sergei Tarkhov, one of Stalin's 'Spanish Falcons', was shot down near Madrid in November 1936 and posthumously decorated as a Hero of the Soviet Union.

Bottom Left: Valeri Chkalov, the leading Soviet fighter test-pilot and celebrated long-distance record flier. A photograph of 1938, the year Chkalov met his death testing the ill-fated I-180 fighter.

Bottom Right: Marina Raskova, famous airwoman and organiser of the three women's air regiments, died in an air crash in January 1943.

Top Left: Grigori Kravchenko, twice decorated as a Hero of the Soviet Union in 1939 after serving in China and commanding the outstanding 22nd Fighter Regiment in battles against the Japanese over Mongolia. After commanding air divisions and a special GKO 'Air Strike Group', Kravchenko was killed in action in February 1943.

Top Right: Grigori Bakhchivandzhi lost his life testing the first Soviet rocket-powered fighter in 1943, and was posthumously made a Hero of the Soviet Union thirty years later.

Bottom: Decorated as Heroes of the Soviet Union after bringing down Luftwaffe bombers in first *'taran'* (ramming) attacks in June 1941, fighter pilots Zhukov, Zdorovtsev and Kharitonov.

Top Left: Twice Hero of the Soviet Union Stepan Suprun, a leading test-pilot and commander of the 'special' 401st Fighter Regiment composed of NII-VVS test-pilots, was credited with four victories before his Yak-1 fell to Luftwaffe fighters in July 1941.

Top Right: Ivan Kozhedub, officially the highest-scoring Soviet fighter pilot of the Great Patriotic War with 62 victories.

Bottom: Aleksandr Pokryshkin, officially the second highest-scoring Soviet fighter pilot with 59 victories. In the background, his Lend-Lease P-39 Airacobra fighter.

Top Left: Andrei Tupolev, patriarch of Soviet multi-engined aircraft design, on the eve of his eightieth birthday in 1968.

Top Right: Nikolai Polikarpov who monopolised Soviet fighter design in the 1930s with his almost legendary I-16.

Bottom Left: Sergei Il'yushin. A photograph of 1936 when Il'yushin was developing his DB-3 long-range bomber for the Red Air Force.

Bottom Right: Vladimir Petlyakov, designer of the Pe-2, the standard tactical day bomber of the Red Air Force during the Great Patriotic War years.

Top Left: Aleksandr Yakovlev, the youngest of Soviet military aircraft designers of immediate pre-war years and creator of the Yak fighters. He was Deputy People's Commissar for Aircraft Production 1940-46.

Top Right: Artyom Mikoyan in 1962. Together with Mikhail Gurevich he initiated the now world-famous MiG series of fighters in 1940.

Bottom Left: Semyon Lavochkin. He achieved immense success with his wartime radial-engined fighters but retreated into obscurity in the post-war jet era. A photograph of 1958.

Bottom Right: Pavel Sukhoi, designer of the Su fighters and fighter-bombers whose early career was plagued by setbacks.

Top Left: Vladimir Klimov, designer of the VK-series of inline engines which powered the Yak fighters and Pe-2 bombers of the war years. Later he was the brains behind the Soviet development of the Rolls-Royce Nene centrifugal turbojet.

Top Right: Arkadi Shvetsov. His ASh-82 radial engine married to Lavochkin's revised LaGG-3 airframe resulted in the highly successful La-5 and La-7 fighters.

Bottom Left: Aleksandr Mikulin, whose inline engines carried the *shturmoviks* into battle, later developed the first powerful Soviet axial-flow turbojet engines.

Bottom Right: Arkhip Lyul'ka. Pioneer developer of the first Soviet turbojet engines whose later products power Sukhoi's Su-7, Su-11 and Su-15 fighters.

Top Left: Air Marshal Sergei Rudenko. Photographed in 1965 when he was First Deputy C-in-C Soviet Air Forces.

Top Right: Air Marshal Vladimir Sudets in 1965 as C-in-C Soviet Air Defence Command. The year following he was replaced by Marshal of the Soviet Union Pavel Batitski.

Bottom Left: Air Chief Marshal Aleksandr Novikov, C-in-C Red Air Force 1942-46, was interned by Stalin and rehabilitated in 1953. During the 1960s, when this photograph was taken, he was Head of the Advanced Civil Air School near Leningrad.

Bottom Right: Air Chief Marshal Aleksandr Golovanov was C-in-C Long-Range Air Arm 1942-47. A protégé of Stalin, he was 'retired' in September 1953.

Top Left: Air Chief Marshal Konstantin Vershinin in 1965 as C-in-C Soviet Air Forces, his second term in is command.

Top Right: Air Chief Marshal Pavel Zhigarev, serving in 1965 as Head of the Air Defence Staff Academy.

Bottom Left: Air Marshal Filipp Agal'tsov. C-in-C Long-Range Air Force in 1965.

Bottom Right: Air Chief Marshal Pavel Kutakhov, C-in-C Soviet Air Forces since March 1969.

The Soviet aircraft carrier *Kiev* in the Mediterranean in July 1976. This photograph by an RAF Nimrod reconnaissance aircraft from Malta shows two of the latest Soviet V/STOL fighters and four Kamov Ka-25 ASW helicopters on the after deck.

doubtful if they could have been acted upon as Soviet dispersal capability was still handicapped by the limited number of airfields operational in the newly acquired territories of the Baltic States, Poland and Bessarabia. A decision to build one hundred and ninety new airfields in the western military districts taken in February 1941 was followed by an even more ambitious edict in March — and this extensive programme was embarked upon while existing airfields were being enlarged and new runways laid. Few had been completed by June, and the blame for this was later to be laid at the door of the NKVD which was responsible for organising forced labour in the building of runways and protected dispersal points[3]. The Air Observation, Alert and Communications Service (VNOS) also became a scapegoat for the débâcle although it lacked an adequate signals system and telephone lines were still being laid.

Astonishingly, the whole question of camouflage and concealment from the frequent *Luftwaffe* reconnaissance flights had not been raised until early June, allegedly as a result of an anonymous letter from an airman addressed to the Party Central Committee protesting that, 'our camps adjoining the frontier are set out as if for inspection with white tents in rows, clearly visible from the air'[4]. At the same time it was discovered that SB bombers were being sent out from their factories with a reflective silver finish often retained in squadron service, and that the lacquered finish applied to the fabric covering on most Russian fighters made them easily distinguishable from above. On Stalin's orders work was put in hand to devise camouflage schemes for Red Air Force machines, drawing on methods used abroad, but in any case camouflage would have made little difference on the morning of 22 June when Russian aircraft were lined up in rows, wing tip to wing tip, on cluttered and exposed airfields.

According to German sources, the *Luftwaffe* had slightly under 2,000 aircraft available for 'Barbarossa' — in *Luftflotte* 1 under Keller supporting Army Group North, *Luftflotte* 2 under Kesselring (the largest concentration) supporting Army Group Centre, and

---

[3]'In the spring of 1941 organs of the NKVD entrusted with construction work failed to take into account the [international] situation and work was begun on the majority of frontier airfields simultaneously. As a result, a significant proportion were in fact unusable under operational conditions and fighters were concentrated on a small number, restricting their ability to deploy and impeding concealment and dispersal.' (*IVOVSS*, Vol I)

[4]Yakovlev *Tsel' Zhizni*

Soviet Air Force

Luftflotte 4 under Löhr supporting Army Group South — of which 1,300 were serviceable on 22 June. The Soviets have claimed that over 3,500 aircraft were available for Hitler's invasion of the USSR[5]. Soviet air strength has never been officially admitted, but 1,540 new types of aircraft in production since 1940, representing approximately 20% of Soviet air power in the west, were in service when the Germans invaded[6]; it is reasonable, therefore, to assume that there were at least 7,700 aircraft in western Russia, although this may not include the 1,445 aircraft of the three western naval air forces. It has been estimated than an additional 3,500 to 4,000 aircraft were in service in the interior or in the Far East at this time representing a considerable reserve, albeit almost entirely of obsolescent types.

The *Luftwaffe* achieved a degree of success on 22 June which surpassed its wildest hopes; by noon 1,200 Red Air Force aircraft had been accounted for, three-quarters of them while sitting on their airfields, and by nightfall the toll had reached a figure of 1,811 — of which 1,489 had been destroyed on the ground — for the loss of thirty-five *Luftwaffe* aircraft. Erhard Milch, Göring's deputy, recorded a tally of 3,820 Russian machines destroyed by the end of the campaign's fifth day and on 29 June the German High Command proclaimed the destruction of 4,017 Soviet for the loss of only *150*

---

[5] A comparison is given below of the strengths of the *Luftflotten* engaged against the USSR on 22 June 1941 according to German and offical Soviet sources:

Luftflotte	German sources (a)	Soviet sources (IVOVSS)
1	430	1,070
2	910	1,680
4	600	800 (b)
Total	1,940	3,550

(a) Plocher *The German Air Force versus Russia, 1941* and Bekker *The Luftwaffe Diaries*. Bekker gives details of the aircraft serviceable as consisting of 510 bombers (Ju 88, He 111 and Do 17Z), 290 dive-bombers (Ju 87), 440 single-seat fighters (Bf 109E and Bf 109F), 40 twin-engined fighters (Bf 110) and about 120 reconnaissance aircraft (Ju 88, Do 17P and Do 215).

(b) The Soviets contend that an additional 500 Rumanian aircraft were also available to support the *Luftwaffe* in this sector.
In claiming an overall German and satellite air strength of 4,950 aircraft arrayed against the Soviet Union for 'Barbarossa', the Soviets also include *Luftflotte* 5 in Finland and Norway with 400 machines backed by 500 Finnish aircraft. *Luftflotte* 5 was not, however, engaged on 22 June and is credited by Plocher with only 60 aircraft at this time.

[6] See *Pyatdesyat let vooruzhyonnykh sil SSSR* and Kravchenko *Ekonomika SSSR v gody Velikoi Otechestvennoi Voiny*.

Barbarossa

Luftwaffe aircraft to date[7]. It was unthinkable to admit the magnitude of such losses to the Soviet public which, indoctrinated in the invincibility of its armed forces, was astounded when Radio Moscow later announced that 374 aircraft had been lost by the Red Air Force in the first three days of the war. On 5 October a more accurate and stunning admission was made by the candidate Politburo member A.S. Shcherbakov that 5,316 Soviet machines had been lost[8].

Marshal Timoshenko's directive to the Red Army despatched four hours after 'Barbarossa' had begun that it was, 'to engage the enemy's forces and destroy them in those zones where they had crossed the Soviet frontier.....but not advance beyond the frontier without special orders', reflects the bewilderment of the Soviet High Command in trying to grasp the situation at all and Stalin's stubborn refusal to concede that anything more than 'provocations' was taking place. As for the Red Air Force, Timoshenko's instructions were, 'to determine the areas of enemy groupings, to destroy enemy aircraft on their airfields and bomb the main concentrations of enemy ground forces'. Königsberg and Memel were to be raided, but incursions limited to a depth of between a hundred and a hundred and fifty kilometres west of the frontier; flights over Finland and Rumania were prohibited without explicit instructions from Moscow. By the time they reached the western military districts, Timoshenko's directives had taken on an air of grim absurdity. The Red Air Force was no longer in a position to carry out defensive, far less offensive, operations and German bombers were raiding Kiev, Riga, Kaunas, Vilnius, Grodno, Zhitomir and Sevastopol.

In the Western Military District containing eleven air divisions, twenty-six airfields were attacked and 387 fighters and 351 bombers

---

[7]See Plocher *The German Air Force versus Russia, 1941* and David Irving *The Rise & Fall of the Luftwaffe*. According to Milch's records, 1,800 Soviet machines were claimed on 22 June, 800 on the 23rd, 557 on the 24th, 351 on the 25th and 300 on the 26th.

[8]Yakovlev *Tsel' Zhizni* and Erickson *The Soviet High Command*. Shpanov's 'fictional documentary' novel about the Red Air Force in which an attacking force of German bombers was utterly routed was published under the title 'The First Blow' (*Pervy udar*) in 1939. It was read widely and popularly believed to demonstrate the complete superiority of Soviet air power.

Barbarossa

of their 1,560 aircraft[9] — of which 1,086 were serviceable on the morning of 22 June — destroyed. The three divisions to suffer most were the 9th, 10th and 11th Composite Air Divisions supporting the 3rd, 4th and 10th Armies in the frontier zone; the 9th Air Division losing 347 of its 409 aircraft, the 10th Air Division 180 out of 231 and the 11th Air Division 127 out of 199 machines. By the time the last German bomber had departed westwards, the official strength of the three divisions had been reduced from 839 to 185 aircraft. Inevitably, most of the newer types were in the divisions which had suffered the greatest losses — and a number of aircraft were even destroyed by shell fire when *Wehrmacht* field artillery bombarded Russian airfields within sight of the border. Least affected on 22 June was the III Long-Range Air Corps whose 265 machines were based well to the east of the military district. By the end of the month, air losses on the Western Front* amounted to 1,163 aircraft[10].

Twenty-three airfields were surprised at dawn in the Kiev Military District and 277 aircraft destroyed. Between 22 June and 26 July Lörzer's II Fliegerkorps supporting Army Group Centre claimed the destruction of 915 Soviet aircraft in this sector and by the end of August, according to a *Luftwaffe* High Command summary dated 9 September, the score had risen to 2,660, almost half of which had been destroyed on the ground. To the north in the Baltic Military District the picture was no brighter. A number of air regiments had been carrying out night training flights and had barely landed with empty tanks before the first bombers with their ominous black crosses thundered overhead. Offensive operations got under way by the late morning, but so swiftly had von Leeb's panzers bitten into Lithuania that the remnants of the advanced Red Air Force divisions

---

[9]Fyodorov gives the numbers of types in service with these air divisions as follows:

Bomber, Ground-Attack & Recce		Fighter	
SB	377	I-16	424
Su-2	75	I-153	262
Pe-2	42	I-15	73
Yak-4	24	MiG-3	233
Ar-2	22	Yak-1	20
Il-2	8		
Total	548		1,012

[10]Fyodorov

*Shortly after the outbreak of war the Leningrad, Baltic, Western, Kiev and Odessa Military Districts were designated the Northern, North-Western, Western, South-Western and Southern Fronts.

Soviet Air Force

had to be hastily pulled back and regrouped in the areas of Riga and Daugavpils (Dvinsk) in Latvia. Flying in support of Army Group North, Förster's I *Fliegerkorps* claimed to have disposed of 2,514 Soviet aircraft by 23 August, 1,594 of these during strikes on airfields[11].

The *Luftwaffe* had least success against the Red Air Force in the Odessa Military District where some air regiments had been prudently redeployed and fighter patrols mounted. Well over a hundred of the district's 827 combat aircraft were MiG-3 fighters, most of which escaped the first fury of the German raids and were able to oppose the bombers of von Greim's V *Fliegerkorps*. The destruction of forty *Luftwaffe* aircraft for the loss of twenty-three Soviet fighters was subsequently claimed for the first day of the war[12]. It was here that Senior Lieutenant Pokryshkin, then a *zveno* leader in the 55th Fighter Regiment and later acclaimed as the second highest-scoring Soviet fighter ace, prepared to mark up his first victory. Ironically, it was a Red Air Force Su-2 that he dived upon in his MiG-3, part of a formation on its way to bomb German troops crossing the Pruth and a type he had never seen before. He had assumed automatically that its unfamiliar shape denoted a German aircraft and was horrified to make out red stars on its fuselage as he closed in to attack. He was not the only Soviet fighter pilot to make this kind of mistake; later one of his comrades complained bitterly that the Su-2 bombers based at Kotovsk could be seen any day by peasant women on their way to market but were kept 'secret' from fighter pilots in the same air division[13].

The 20th, 21st and 45th Composite Air Divisions and a reconnaissance regiment were sent to the Southern Front on 1 July but losses mounted as the Germans pressed forward. Over the first four days of fighting V *Fliegerkorps* claimed 910 victories, primarily during strikes against airfields, although by 10 July the Red Air Force

---

[11]Plocher *The German Air Force versus Russia, 1941*.

[12]*Chetvyortaya vozdushnaya armiya*. Captain Afanasi Karmanov of the 4th Fighter Regiment was credited with having destroyed two Ju 88 bombers and three Bf 109 fighters in his MiG-3 before being shot down and killed late in the morning of 23 June. Karmanov was posthumously decorated as a Hero of the Soviet Union in March 1942.

[13]Pokryskhin *Nebo voiny*. A recognition handbook of Red Air Force machines published by the People's Commissariat for Defence went to press on 21 June 1941. Captured copies were much appreciated by the *Luftwaffe*.

113

Barbarossa

still fielded 734 aircraft on the Southern Front and claimed 238 victories over the *Luftwaffe*.

Shock and confusion combined with disrupted communications and the paralysing reluctance of local commanders to take any kind of independent action aided the *Luftwaffe* greatly. There was no tradition of personal initiative at junior command levels to cope with this kind of crisis, and the most obvious and elementary measures were often neglected by officers who did not know how or did not dare to act independently. As late as 9 July, when the *Luftwaffe* had already provided ample proof of its ferocity and effectiveness, divisional and regimental air commanders had to be instructed from Moscow to base no more than nine to a dozen aircraft on any one airfield, to disperse and conceal aircraft immediately after they landed, to provide trenches for shelter during air raids and to prohibit personnel and vehicles from crossing the open airfield or congregating on it. One legacy of the past four years was that officers were more afraid of the NKVD than of the Germans.

Certainly at the higher command echelons there was justification for these fears and the NKVD was soon on hand to punish senior officers for their 'mistakes'. In the Odessa Military District the Air Commander had been removed from his post shortly before 22 June, the hastily assembled headquarters staff being informed simultaneously of General Michugin's posting and the German attack. His replacement, Major-General Shelukhin, only arrived in Vinnitsa to which the Air HQ Southern Front had been evacuated on 25 or 26 June, and then in total ignorance of the military situation[14]. In the Western Military District the Air Commander, Major-General Kopets, is said to have committed suicide on 23 June[15] but it is more likely that he fell victim to a NKVD firing party as did General Pavlov, Commander of the Western Military District, his Chief of Staff, General Klimovskikh, and Kopets' former comrade-in-arms from Spain and Finland, Air Commander for the Kiev Military District Major-General Ptukhin[16]. In the Baltic Military District, Air Commander General Ionov also disappeared, most probably to share the fate of his comrades to the south.

---

[14]*Chetvyortaya vozdushnaya armiya*

[15]See Conquest *The Great Terror* and Erickson *The Soviet High Command*

[16]Revealed in a brief but candid biography of Ptukhin in the periodical *Aviatsiya i Kosmonavtika*, September 1963.

Barbarossa

Russian bomber attacks begun on the afternoon of the 22nd in response to Timoshenko's directive and aimed largely at German columns and river crossings were followed up by more massive efforts on the 23rd. The regiments of SB bombers, mostly without fighter escort, were massacred by flak and the Bf 109 fighters as they flew in steady, level formations as if they were on routine training flights over the bombing range. Even the exultant Germans were shaken to witness wave after wave of Russian bombers fly in to be destroyed piecemeal. Nonetheless, during the first week to ten days of hostilities Red Air Force bombers continued to fly at regimental strength in formations of up to sixty aircraft and hardly ever with proper fighter cover. Bombing, carried out at first from regulation heights of between 2,000 and 3,000 metres was found to be ineffectual and attacks were pressed home at heights between 600 and 1,000 metres with even greater losses from the merciless and ubiquitous flak. The destruction of so many Red Air Force machines on the ground during the first days of the war had meant a loss of largely obsolescent aircraft rather than aircrews, a fact which might have tempered the *Luftwaffe's* jubilation. In the main, however, they were fighter and ground-attack pilots who escaped unscathed and the subsequent rash expenditure of bombers in these initial and futile mass raids was to mean a severe reduction in the number of experienced bomber crews later on. Replacements came forward from GVF and *Osoaviakhim*, but all too often they were committed to battle without the training or operational initiation necessary for survival.

After early July bomber units were ordered to operate at no more than squadron or *zveno* strength — an injunction hardly necessary after the attrition of the past week — escorted by fighters whenever possible and with some attempt to neutralise the German anti-aircraft defences beforehand; in practice these conditions could rarely be implemented. Unescorted bombers were in theory to operate solely by night as lone intruders and at high altitude. Since, however, by January 1941 only 60% of tactical bomber crews had received any kind of bad weather flying training and only 30% tuition in night-flying[17], bombing by night was normally undertaken by DBA aircraft pending the formation of special night bomber units. Daylight operations by the DBA were at first prohibited by the GKO

---

[17]*Aviatsiya i Kosmonavtika SSSR*

after a grevious sacrifice of vulnerable and obsolete TB-3 and DB-3 bombers, but the order was countermanded as the disasters of the late summer gathered momentum and the need to hold back the *Wehrmacht* became increasingly urgent — over the first three months of the war the DBA carried out 70% of its sorties by day. In fact nightbombing had little more than the satisfaction of hitting back at the Germans due to the small scale on which raids could be mounted, the inability of bombers to maintain formation in darkness and the sheer paucity of navigational expertise.

The danger to Leningrad posed by the still inert *Luftflotte* 5 was countered by raids against nineteen German airfields in Finland and northern Norway from 25 June, and against ports, bridges and railways in a bid to stall the anticipated Finnish offensive. The co-ordination of these operations was undertaken by General Aleksandr Novikov, Air Commander on the Northern Front, drawing on elements of the Baltic and Northern Fleet Naval Air Forces. The worsening situation on the North-Western Front, however, had necessitated the withdrawal of three air divisions from Novikov's strength before the Finnish drives towards Petrozavodsk and Olenets had begun. With the arrival of aid from Great Britain, the port of Murmansk and the Murmansk railway took on an added strategic significance and the danger to both was acute. The responsibility for their defence was undertaken by the Northern Fleet Air Force, the smallest of all three western fleet air forces in June 1941 with only a hundred and fourteen machines. In July it was reinforced by a squadron of SB bombers transferred from the Baltic, but its real need — for modern fighters — was met by two RAF squadrons, Nos. 81 and 134 of 151 Fighter Wing, equipped with Hurricanes and sent to cover the arrival of the first British convoy. As well as instructing Soviet pilots on the Hurricane, the two RAF squadrons escorted SB and Pe-2 bombers in attacks on Finnish ground forces before handing over their fighters to the 72nd (later 2nd Guards) Fighter Regiment later commanded by Lt. Colonel Safonov, one of the first Soviet fighter aces of the war who was twice decorated as a Hero of the Soviet Union before being shot down over the Barents Sea in May 1942. When the RAF pilots returned to Britain in October, their Hurricanes were already being flown operationally by the Red Air Force as the forerunners of 210 Hurricane IIA and 1,542 Hurricane IIB fighters delivered to the USSR.

To the south, Soviet fighter pilots flying for the most part out-

Barbarossa

classed I-16s were endeavouring vainly to cover the retreating remnants of the Soviet armies. The ramming of *Luftwaffe* machines dated from the first few hours of 'Barbarossa', although its first instances were as often acts of desperation or accidents of the dogfight as the considered sacrifice of one obsolete Russian fighter for a modern *Luftwaffe* bomber and its crew. At 4.30 am on 22 June Lieutenant Kokorev of the 124th Fighter Regiment, part of the 9th Composite Air Division, took off in a group of twenty-eight fighters from his airfield in the Western Military District. After exhausting his ammunition to no effect, he rammed a Bf 110 and managed to make a forced landing after the enemy machine had fallen out of control. An hour later, over the Kiev Military District, Junior Lieutenant Butelin rammed the tail of a Ju 88 at low level and Senior Lieutenance Ivanov, a *zveno* leader in the 46th Fighter Regiment, after making five sorties and being engaged in combat four times, drove the propeller of his I-16 into the tail of a He 111 bomber and was posthumously made a Hero of the Soviet Union after paying for the attempt with his life. Such first examples of air ramming showed that *Luftwaffe* bombers could at least be brought down in this way by I-16 fighters, and that if he possessed sufficient height the fighter pilot stood a reasonable chance of jumping clear or force landing his crippled machine.

As the air situation deteriorated the practice of ramming (known as *taran* by Soviet pilots) became increasingly laudable. On 27 June Junior Lieutenant Zdorovtsev of the 158th Fighter Regiment on the North-Western Front rammed the Ju 88 he was attacking and parachuted to safety from his spinning I-16; two fellow pilots, Zhukov and Kharitonov, followed his example and each claimed a German bomber for their I-16. As members of the *Komsomol* they set an example to be followed; all three were decorated as Heroes of the Soviet Union and had their deeds widely publicised. Lieutenant Boris Kobzan, a Hero of the Soviet Union in 1943, became the highest scorer with four successful ramming attacks — the first in October 1941 while flying with the 184th Fighter Regiment and the second three months later when he brought down a Ju 88 over the approaches to Moscow. Aleksandr Khlobystov came second with three victories gained in air rams, and seventeen other Soviet fighter pilots were credited with having destroyed two *Luftwaffe* machines each in this way. In all, some two hundred ramming attacks on *Luftwaffe* aircraft were made with an additional seventy recorded instances of aircraft being deliberately crashed into the targets they were attacking — the example here being set by Captain Gastello of the 207th Long-Range Bomber Regiment who dived his Il-4 onto a German motorised column on 26 June 1941 after his bomber had been set ablaze by flak. Ramming was frowned upon when precious modern fighters were being flown and was expressly forbidden over enemy-held territory; in the *Luftwaffe* the rumour circulated that Soviet fighters were fitted with special armoured propellers.

While the I-16 and I-153 had only their manoeuvrability to fall back on in combat, even the newer and faster Red Air Force fighters failed to match the Bf 109, due often to the need for modifications, better piloting and more intelligent and determined commitment. The fighter regiments in the frontier military districts had 886 MiG and only 94 Yak-1 and LaGG-3 machines at the outbreak of war, but not only was the high-altitude MiG-3 quite unsuited for the low and medium level roles it was called upon to perform, it proved to be inadequately armoured and armed; with its armament of two 7.62mm ShKAS and one 12.7mm Berezin machine-gun it was easily out-gunned by the cannon-armed Bf 109. The design problems inherent in using the heavy M-35 engine in as light an airframe as possible gave rise to handling difficulties and a distinct aversion to the new fighter on the part of apprehensive pilots who tried to avoid flying the newly delivered MiG-3s whenever they could. So serious was this dislike that special NII-VVS fighter teams were touring fighter regiments to promote and advise on conversion training when war broke out. Two of the six test-pilots' regiments formed shortly afterwards were equipped with MiG-3s[18]. After the Battle for Moscow, the MiG-3's finest hour, it was relegated to service with interior PVO and tactical reconnaissance squadrons where its good turn of speed at high altitudes made it particularly valuable.

The LaGG-3 suffered hardly less than the MiG-3 in its share of faults and frustrations although it was built in greater quantities than any other Soviet fighter over the second half of 1941. The original prototype had been revised to include wing fuel tanks which added to the already considerable flying weight of the wooden airframe, and since the 23mm cannon mounted between the cylinder banks of the

---

[18]These were the 401st and 402nd Fighter Regiments commanded initially by Stepan Suprun and Pyotr Stefanovski. One other regiment was equipped with Il-2s, two with Pe-2s and the sixth, the 332nd Heavy Bomber Regiment, with Pe-8s. See Stefanovski *Trista neizvestnykh*.

M-105 engine and firing through the propeller hub made it one of the most useful ground-attack aircraft late in 1941, its armament was frequently supplemented to make it more effective in this role. This, no less than the need to camouflage the fighter by masking the highly-polished finish on which it relied for its edge of speed, sadly depleted its original virtues. It showed a vicious tendency to flip over into a spin if put into a tight turn and its ill-humour grew with its weight. Pilots were disconcerted to find their fighters resting on their bellies after the undercarriage had given way and the required reinforcements only added yet again to the weight. The LaGG-3, once christened the 'grand piano' in honour of its gleaming finish now earned the grimmer nick-name of the 'varnished guaranteed coffin' — a new interpretation of the designation LaGG as *lakirovanny garantirovanny grob.*

The LaGG-3's one outstanding quality was its ability to absorb battle damage, but its robustness could not compensate for mounting losses, not just in combat when flown by raw and nervous pilots, but in a multitude of airfield accidents — especially on take-off when the LaGG-3 practiced some of its nastier vices. By early 1942 it had been decided to phase the LaGG-3 out of production — although in fact this was not accomplished until 1943 with the later production series converted to carry a 37mm hub-cannon — and to boost the output of the one proven fighter the Red Air Force possed, the Yak-1. Light, adequately armed and easier to fly, the Yak-1 soon established itself as the most promising aircraft to have emerged from the 1939 fighter design competition. Over 58% of all Soviet single-seat fighters produced during the Great Patriotic War were products of the Yakovlev design bureau and the offspring of the Yak-1.

Lieutenant-General Zhigarev, titled as Commander of Red Army Air Forces (*Komanduyushchi VVS-RKKA*) from 29 June instead of Head of Chief Directorate, a redesignation which reflected no shift towards any greater air force autonomy, was assisted by two deputies, Generals Petrov and Stepanov, in his planning of air support for the Soviet ground armies. Neither deputy had any operational experience as Petrov had been quickly promoted from second-in-command of NII-VVS and then Head of TsAGI in 1940 while Corps Commissar Stepanov was technically in charge of the Air Force Political Directorate. On 10 July when Stalin created an additional command echelon interposed between the *Stavka* and the fronts with Voroshilov, Timoshenko and Budyonny given overall control in the

Soviet Air Force

North, Centre and South, air force operational expertise was improved with the appointment of Novikov, Naumenko and Falaleev as their respective Air Commanders. All three were to prove their worth over the war years that followed.

With Novikov's appointment as overall Air Commander in the North, the first serious attempts were begun to provide for the air defence of Leningrad. As Chief of Staff under Ptukhin, Novikov had been one of the more astute young air commanders during the Winter War against Finland and he had been made Ptukhin's successor when the latter was transferred from the Leningrad Military District. Since Novikov remained happily unimplicated in the disasters of 22 June and had recommended himself by organising offensive operations over Finland, he already enjoyed the favour of the *Stavka* that was to make him Zhigarev's first deputy in February and his successor as Commander of Red Army Air Forces in April 1942. Now Novikov found himself required to scrape together the remnants of air units formerly in the Baltic Military District, the resources of his own front, naval air forces of the Baltic and Northern Fleets, the fighters of Leningrad's VII PVO Fighter Corps and elements of the I Long-Range Bomber Corps to counter German thrusts threatening Novgorod and ultimately Leningrad itself. He was faced with the task of providing some cover for the attempted Soviet regrouping on the eastern bank of the Luga while trying to halt the German armour and hit communications and concentrations in the enemy rear. It was a losing battle and Novikov had to play for time, ruthlessly sending in his older types of aircraft with heavy losses and giving what cover he could with the few new fighters he had. The eventual and decisive battle for Leningrad loomed nearer day by day and he could look forward to very little in the way of reinforcements. He was allocated four extra air regiments in August by the *Stavka* and nine more in September, but there were never enough of the right kind of aircraft operating effectively in the right place at the right time.

The immediate threat to Novgorod on the northern shore of Lake Ilmen and the line of the Luga river was complicated by Finnish advances, menacing Leningrad with a drive between Lake Ladoga and Lake Onega and ultimate encirclement. Despite this prospect, Novikov had to commit most of his resources to the sector north-west of Lake Ilmen in support of the Soviet 11th Army's counter-offensive in the Soltsy area. Between 14 and 18 July Novikov's dwindling resources, including three frontal composite air divisions, the Northern Fleet's 2nd Composite Air Division flying SBs and bombers of the I Long-Range Bomber Corps, were thrown against the tanks of the 7th Panzer Division. After a dearly bought respite, the Soviets were faced with a renewed blow against Novgorod on 10 August and an attempted counter-blow south of Lake Ilmen failed. On 16 August Novgorod fell and five days later the Germans had reached Krasnogvardeisk, forty kilometres from the outskirts of Leningrad. On 23 August Novikov's responsibilities were lightened with the creation of a separate Karelian Front with its own air command under General Khryukin and he was able to give his full attention to the impending struggle for Leningrad; on 31 August when Soviet troops east of the Luga were trapped in the German pincers, little remained to bar the way to Russia's northern capital on the banks of the Neva.

With 600 Army Air Force and 200 Baltic Fleet aircraft supported by Colonel Danilin's VII PVO Fighter Corps, Novikov prepared for concentrated air attacks on Leningrad before the storming of the city. Schlisselburg on the southern tip of Lake Ladoga fell on 8 September, isolating the city, but Leningrad had been reprieved by Hitler's decision to break the Soviets in the Centre. *Luftwaffe* units were withdrawn, although raids on the city continued with the destruction of the penned Baltic Fleet given high priority. Confined in the Kronshtadt roadstead, the warships were still a threat to German seaborne supplies to Baltic and Finnish ports as well as in giving the support of their heavy guns to ward off any further German incursions towards Leningrad from the direction of Oranienbaum and the southern shore of the Gulf of Finland. The larger vessels were subjected to repeated attacks between 22 and 24 September and the battleship *Marat* was sunk by Ju 87 dive-bombers based at Tyrkovo on the 23rd, but as far as Leningrad itself was concerned it had become a war of siege. *Luftwaffe* raids were aimed primarily at breaking morale rather than reducing the city by systematic bombing. Cold and starvation became the most telling weapons in the months ahead with GVF transports running the German blockade to evacuate sick and wounded and technical specialists, and to fly in desperately needed supplies. Six thousand tons of food, medical supplies and ammunition were flown into Leningrad between 10 October and 25 December by a special GVF unit of thirty Li-2 (PS-84) transports which also flew out over 50,000

Soviet Air Force

casualties, technicians and army staff personnel.[19].

In the South where Falaleev supervised air operations on the South-Western and Southern Fronts assisted by their respective air commanders, Generals Astakhov and Shelukhin, five air divisions supported by IV and V Long-Range Bomber Corps were thrown into the defence of Kiev. Most of these aircraft, together with the South-Western Front's Air HQ, were lost during the intensive bombardment of the encircled Soviet forces by II and V *Fliegerkorps* which the Red Air Force proved unable to impede. The *Stavka*'s reaction was to summon Shelukhin to Moscow and relieve him of his command. He was replaced, officially from 24 September, by Colonel Vershinin, an infantry veteran of the Russian Civil War. Astakhov was also replaced, but to be made Deputy Head of GU-GVF under the former long-distance arctic flier, Vasili Molokov, whom he replaced in May 1942, with Falaleev himself taking over air operations on the South-Western Front in his place. Naval air force machines of the Black Sea Fleet joined in the persistent but unavailing attacks against enemy bridgeheads on the Desna and Dnieper where the Germans were taken aback by the stubborn fury of the Soviet air strikes. As the retreat continued, Odessa was evacuated by sea under constant raids by bombers of Pflugbeil's IV *Fliegerkorps* with forty Red Air Force fighters and three naval fighter squadrons scraped together to provide air cover. But Soviet air resistance was totally unable to prevent the German breakthrough into the Crimea and seizure of Kerch, leaving the mighty naval fortress of Sevastopol to its protracted martyrdom.

When the battle for Smolensk opened in the second week of July, the overall strength of the Red Air Force had been reduced to 2,516 aircraft of which 638 were unserviceable. Its losses had been enormous, but it had not been destroyed. The *Luftwaffe* boasted the destruction of over 7,500 Soviet aircraft in the first month of the campaign alone, and when Hitler gave a total of 17,322 Soviet machines destroyed, captured or damaged in his address to the Reichstag on 11 December 1941, even these incredible figures seemed feasible to his audience in their triumphant euphoria[20]. It was true that the *Luftwaffe* had annihilated thousands of Red Air Force

---

[19]*Grazhdanskaya aviatsiya SSSR*.

[20]See Erickson *The Soviet High Command* and Schwabedissen *The Russian Air Force in The Eyes of German Commanders*.

machines, and it was on the Eastern Front that the *Luftwaffe* fighter aces would claim staggering scores; the most famous, Major Erich Hartmann, achieved 352 victories on the Eastern Front between November 1942 and May 1945 and seven other fighter pilots claimed over two hundred. On the other hand, many of the Soviet aircraft lost in 1941 and 1942 were obsolete or obsolescent and the *Luftwaffe* did not destroy the factories to provide modern replacements or the crews to fly them. In the process it had exhausted itself and it had certainly not gone unscathed. The number of serviceable *Luftwaffe* aircraft in the East had fallen to about a thousand even by the end of June, and its declared losses of 774 machines with 510 others damaged by 19 July had risen to 1,023 lost and 657 damaged by 2 August[21]. From 25 June the *Luftwaffe* had been directed to turn its attention to army support on the assumption that the Red Air Force had ceased to exist as any kind of effective opposition. For the moment this was indeed true, but the continual demands made upon *Luftwaffe* crews with fighter pilots flying five to nine sorties a day, Ju 87 pilots seven or eight and bomber crews up to six, combined with the growing stubbornness of Soviet ground fire, told heavily even before the crucial battle for Moscow had got under way.

General Naumenko, Air Commander on the Western Front[22], had 389 aircraft on 20 July[23] supported by 120 bombers of III Long-Range Bomber Corps and an extra 150 aircraft of the Reserve Front, commanded by General Pogrebov until 1 August and then by General Nikolaenko, devoted to the immediate task of holding Smolensk. Red Air Force units operated in close proximity to the frontline, but the harsh lessons of 22 June had already had some effect with small groups of three to six aircraft deployed over a number of tactical airstrips. Even these tactics, their value admittedly decreased by the lack of communications and co-ordination, did not prevent alarmingly high losses with operational capability eroding day by day. The crisis made necessary the creation of two supporting fronts — the Central with seventy-five aircraft on 24 July and the Bryansk

---

[21] See Carell *Hitler's War on Russia*, Vol I, and Bekker *The Luftwaffe Diaries*.

[22] As a colonel, Naumenko had replaced General Tayurski on the Western Front on 2 July. Between 16 August and 25 December as overall air commander in the Centre, Naumenko relinquished his frontal command to General Michugin.

[23] Consisting of 48 fighters and 118 bombers of the frontal air command and 55 fighters and 168 bombers and ground-attack aircraft attached to the ground armies. Fyodorov.

Soviet Air Force

with a hundred and thirty-eight on 16 August under air commanders Vorozheikin and Polynin, and on 29 August air elements from all these fronts —466 machines — were co-ordinated by General Petrov as Zhigarev's deputy in support of Yeremenko's attempted counter-offensive to block Guderian's panzer divisions.

Failure brought sharp criticism from Stalin. The expenditure of aircraft had not given anything like the results hoped for, due often to inexperienced pilots and navigators, the lack of measures to counter German flak and the poor escort provisions for the handful of day bombers still available. This was to be the largest Red Air Force offensive operation before the counter-offensive of December. Now all resources went to the defence of the Soviet capital. 'Barbarossa' had reached the gates of Moscow.

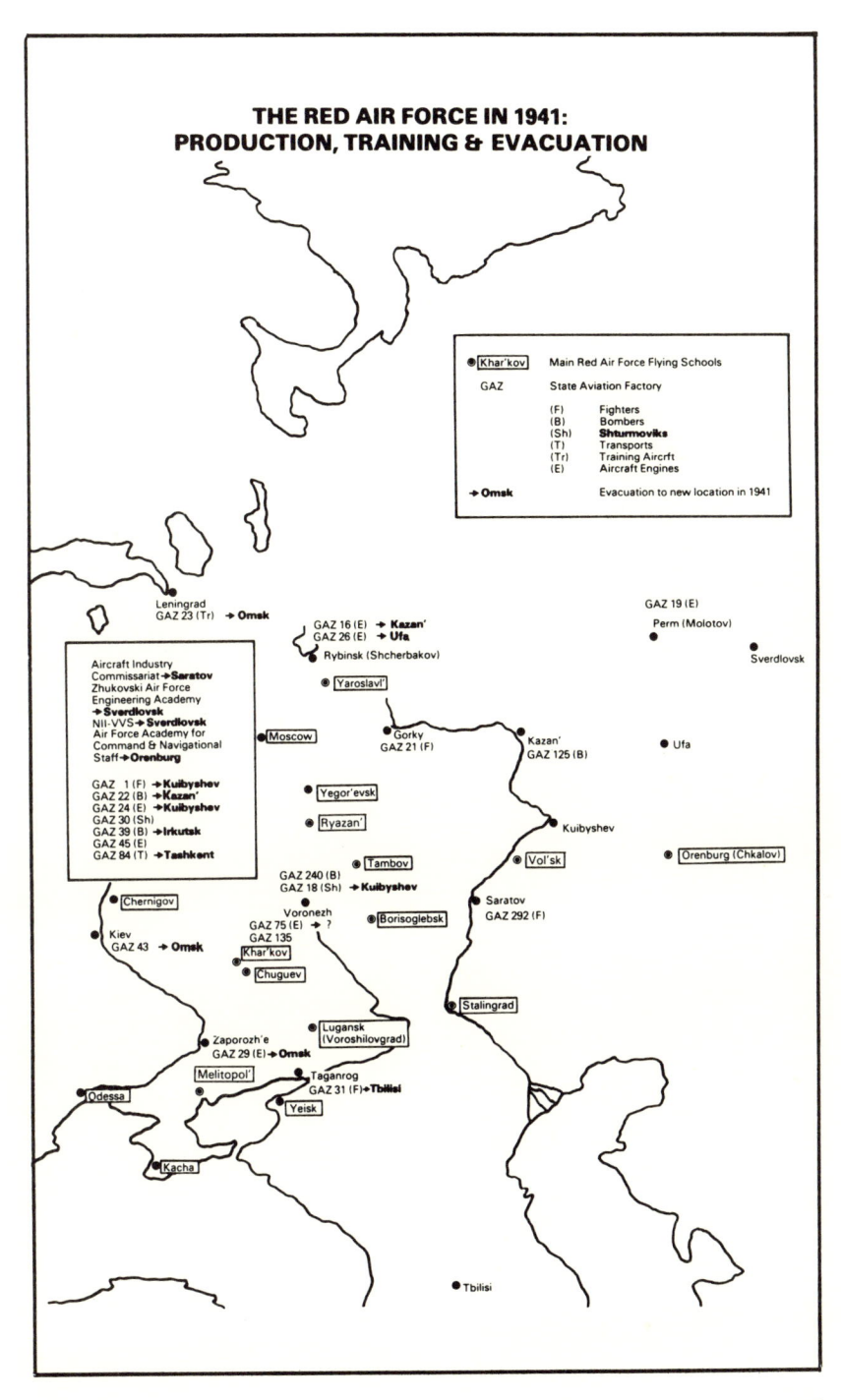

THE RED AIR FORCE IN 1941: PRODUCTION, TRAINING & EVACUATION

● Khar'kov — Main Red Air Force Flying Schools

GAZ — State Aviation Factory

(F) Fighters
(B) Bombers
(Sh) **Shturmoviks**
(T) Transports
(Tr) Training Aircrft
(E) Aircraft Engines

→ **Omsk** — Evacuation to new location in 1941

Leningrad
GAZ 23 (Tr) → **Omsk**

GAZ 16 (E) → **Kazan'**
GAZ 26 (E) → **Ufa**

Rybinsk (Shcherbakov)

Yaroslavl'

GAZ 19 (E)
Perm (Molotov)

Sverdlovsk

Aircraft Industry
Commissariat → **Saratov**
Zhukovski Air Force
Engineering Academy
→ **Sverdlovsk**
NII-VVS → **Sverdlovsk**
Air Force Academy for
Command & Navigational
Staff → **Orenburg**

GAZ 1 (F) → **Kuibyshev**
GAZ 22 (B) → **Kazan'**
GAZ 24 (E) → **Kuibyshev**
GAZ 30 (Sh)
GAZ 39 (B) → **Irkutsk**
GAZ 45 (E)
GAZ 84 (T) → **Tashkent**

Moscow

Gorky
GAZ 21 (F)

Kazan'
GAZ 125 (B)

Ufa

Yegor'evsk

Ryazan'

Kuibyshev

Orenburg (Chkalov)

GAZ 240 (B)
GAZ 18 (Sh) → **Kuibyshev**
Voronezh
GAZ 75 (E) → ?
GAZ 135

Tambov

Vol'sk

Borisoglebsk

Saratov
GAZ 292 (F)

Chernigov

Kiev
GAZ 43 → **Omsk**

Khar'kov

Chuguev

Stalingrad

Zaporozh'e
GAZ 29 (E) → **Omsk**

Melitopol'

Lugansk
(Voroshilovgrad)

Taganrog
GAZ 31 (F) → **Tbilisi**

Yeisk

Odessa

Kacha

● Tbilisi

The Shturmovik Regiment: Late 1941

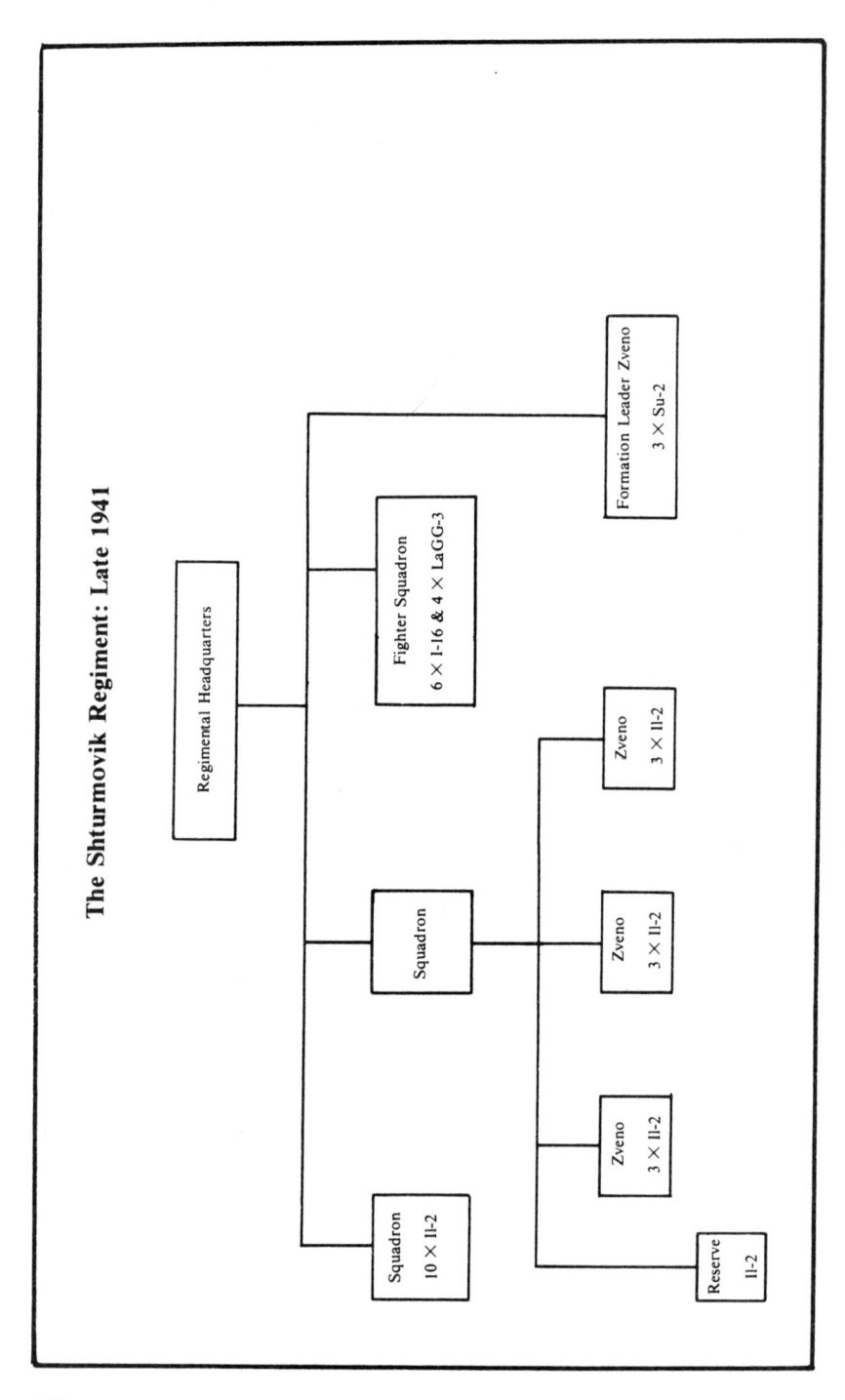

```
Regimental Headquarters
├── Fighter Squadron
│   6 × I-16 & 4 × LaGG-3
│   └── Formation Leader Zveno
│       3 × Su-2
├── Squadron
│   ├── Zveno — 3 × Il-2
│   ├── Zveno — 3 × Il-2
│   └── Zveno — 3 × Il-2
│       └── Reserve Il-2
└── Squadron
    10 × Il-2
```

8 The Battle for Moscow

The rout of the Soviet armies in western Russia and their immense losses of men and equipment over the first weeks of 'Barbarossa' persuaded Hitler that the complete collapse of the Soviet armed forces could not be delayed for long. With the fall of Smolensk to Army Group Centre on 16 July, Moscow seemed to be exposed to an easy German conquest — and it appeared certain that Stalin would commit the bulk of his remaining resources to its defence, placing them ideally for yet another planned encirclement which would clear away finally and utterly all further organised resistance in the centre. But Hitler had decided, in the face of protests from Army Group Centre, to postpone the blow and consolidate the flanks of the German advance before possessing the 'geographical concept' of Moscow itself. As Guderian's panzers were sent rumbling south to complete the subjugation of the Ukraine, *Luftflotte* 2 — under the terms of Hitler's Directive No. 33 issued from *Führer* Headquarters on 19 July — was ordered to commence massive air attacks on the Soviet capital. These raids — 'reprisals for Russian attacks on Bucharest and Helsinki' — intended to disrupt administration and supply as well as undermine civilian morale in the city were to be the prelude to Army Group Centre's forthcoming assault.

On the night of 21-22 July four waves of *Luftwaffe* bombers drawn from KGs 3, 53, 54 and 55 bombed Moscow for the first time, dropping one hundred and four tons of high-explosive and forty-six thousand incendiary bombs over a period of five and a half hours[1]. The results from the *Luftwaffe*'s view were disappointing. No concentrated area of devastation was inflicted, the Kremlin emerged unscathed and the Ju 88 and He 111 raiders were greeted by a spirited

---
[1] Bekker in *The Luftwaffe Diaries* gives the number of bombers involved in this raid as 127 while official Soviet sources assert that between 220 and 250 bombers attacked Moscow.

wall of anti-aircraft fire which claimed ten of them while twelve others fell to the guns of Soviet night-fighters working in conjunction with searchlight batteries. Clearly this was not going to be a Warsaw or a Rotterdam. Further mass raids were mounted on the nights of 22-23 and 24-25 July, but thereafter the bombers of *Luftflotte* 2 were apparently too heavily committed to army support over an extensive front to carry out raids on a similar scale during the late summer and autumn[2].

In fact the Russians had been expecting a blitz on Moscow and while the hard-pressed fronts were starved for air cover Major-General Gromadin, the Commander of the Moscow PVO Zone, had at his disposal I PVO Anti-Aircraft Artillery Corps with 796 76mm and 85mm guns capable of putting up an avenue of fire against approaching *Luftwaffe* bombers and Colonel Klimov's newly-formed VI PVO Fighter Corps with nearly 600 fighters[3]. The Russians had learned the lessons of the London blitz and had already turned the Moscow Metro stations into air-raid shelters and organised civilian anti-incendiary pickets. Decoy fires were ignited when German formations approached the outskirts of Moscow and a group of special 'decoy pathfinders' flying Pe-2 and SB bombers attempted to lead the enemy aircraft astray; these machines also picked out the *Luftwaffe* bombers with specially mounted searchlights so that they could be engaged by Russian night-fighters. Among the one hundred and fifty to two hundred fighters sent up nightly to oppose the German raids were fighters of the 2nd Independent Night Fighter Squadron led by Hero of the Soviet Union Andrei Yumashev and composed of leading test-pilots; as the *Luftwaffe* bombers returned to their bases, Soviet bombers tagged on behind in the hope of bombing their airfields as they landed.

On the ground civilian labour was used wholesale in camouflaging and in the erection of entire 'mock' factories built out of fabric and plywood to mislead the *Luftwaffe*, and German pilots on daylight

---

[2] As might be expected, Soviet and German accounts — the latter notably by Bekker and Carell — are at variance as regards the scale of these and subsequent raids on Moscow. Bekker, for example, gives the number of bombers involved on 22-23 and 24-25 July as 115 and 100 while the Soviets cite corresponding figures of 150 and 180. In general both Bekker and Carell maintain that later *Luftwaffe* attacks on Moscow were made by far fewer bombers than do the Soviets.

[3] VI PVO Fighter Corps was officially formed on 20 June 1941 from the 24th Fighter Division (formerly the 57th Fighter Brigade) responsible for Moscow's air defence augmented by the 78th Fighter Division.

The Battle for Moscow

reconnaissance sorties over Moscow were astonished at the elaborate measures taken to disguise the centre of the city. The walls of the Kremlin had been painted over to resemble house-fronts, the golden domes of its cathedrals boarded over and Lenin's mausoleum on Red Square cocooned in sandbags. Several major thoroughfares had their surfaces painted to resemble roof-tops and bomb-damaged buildings had been 'restored' with canvas screens on which doors and windows had been crudely daubed[4]. All this painstaking artifice was no protection at all against night raids, although a rigorous blackout was maintained, while by day *Luftwaffe* pilots were able to orientate themselves with ease using the distinctive bends of the Moscow River and the concentric layout of the city's central area. These attempts at urban camouflage gave the *Luftwaffe* sorely needed amusement, but for the bomber crews flying by day in support of the *Wehrmacht* the night flights of around a thousand kilometres from their bases at Minsk, Bobruisk, Orsha, Mogilev and Vitebsk were anything but a joke. The raids were a telling ordeal for already over-worked aircrews, and the results hardly justified when Moscow seemed fated to fall to ground assault in the near future. Nor did the raids seriously harass the evacuation of vital production facilities eastwards. If the Soviet armies before Moscow should evade containment now and fall back towards the Urals, fresh supplies of equipment would go on bolstering their resistance to an already fatigued and extended German advance.

The ferocity and determination of the Russian air defences came as an unwelcome surprise to the *Luftwaffe*. The Red Air Force still existed and it was evident that Stalin had retained most of its latest fighters to guard his capital. Well over half of Colonel Klimov's fighters were modern types[5] and at peak strength VI PVO Fighter Corps had thirty-four regiments with twenty-nine more on call from the adjacent fronts. Between July 1941 and January 1942 up to 2,000 fighters were involved in the defence of Moscow so that each of the four sectors of the Moscow PVO Zone had the equivalent of a fighter corps in the number of machines available and VI PVO Fighter Corps resembled more an air army in size. The Western Sector under

---

[4] Uebe *Russian Reactions to German Air Power*

[5] On 9 July VI PVO Fighter Corps contained 585 fighters, comprising 170 MiG-3, 75 LaGG-3 and 95 Yak-1 fighters backed up by 200 I-16 and 45 I-153. Later additions included Hurricanes and P-40s. By the end of December only one in five of its fighters was an obsolete type. See *Voiska protivozdushnoi oborony*.

Soviet Air Force

Colonel Stefanovski had eleven main fighter regiments of which only two were equipped with out-dated I-153 and I-16 fighters. Of the remaining nine, four had Yak-1s, two MiG-3s, two Hurricanes and one LaGG-3s with a twelfth regiment in reserve flying Lend-Lease P-40s[6]. The Southern Sector under Colonel Trifonov was almost as strong, although correspondingly smaller resources were allocated to the Northern and Eastern Sectors under Colonels Mitenkov and Yakushin.

Fighting spirit and patriotic zeal were as crucial for the defence of Moscow as modern fighters. Pilots paraded past their regimental colours before kneeling in the snow beside their machines to repeat the oath, 'I swear to you my country and to you my native Moscow that I will fight relentlessly and destroy the Fascists'. When Junior Lieutenant Talalikhin rammed a crippled He 111 west of Moscow on the night of 7-8 August and parachuted from his I-16, he was decorated as a Hero of the Soviet Union the very next day although air ramming had ceased to be an audacious novelty and similar awards had already been liberally dispensed in its recognition. Talalikhin's terse account of his victory, widely publicised before he was killed that October, was plainly intended to remind other Red Air Force fighter pilots of what was expected from them...

> 'I managed to hit the bomber's port engine and it turned away, losing height. It was at that moment that my ammunition ran out and it struck me that, although I could still overtake it, it would get away. There was only one thing for it — to ram. If I'm killed, I thought, that's only one, but there are four fascists in that bomber. I crept up under its belly to get at its tail with my propeller, but when I was about ten metres away a burst of fire hit my 'plane and shot my right hand through. Straight away I opened the throttle and drove right into it....'

As the frontline fell back towards Moscow, VI PVO Fighter Corps regiments flew from bases in and on the outskirts of the capital, from Vnukovo, Fili, Tushino, Khimki and the Central Aerodrome. They were able, therefore, to fly from long-established and comparatively well-equipped airfields in support of Soviet ground forces as well as intercepting raiders. The premises of the evacuated aircraft factories provided facilities for repair and maintainance which the *Luftwaffe*,

---

[6]This was the 126th Fighter Regiment at Shcholkovo, the first Soviet fighter regiment to be equipped with this American fighter. Fyodorov.

The Battle for Moscow

flying from the ruts and quagmires of rural airstrips, might well have envied.

Elsewhere the picture was less encouraging. The losses in the Ukraine had been enormous with 100,000 Soviet troops caught in the Pervomaisk encirclement of 8 August and a further 500,000 were claimed by the Germans when the Kiev trap was sprung a week later. Unaware of Hitler's Directive No. 34 of 30 July which had called for a halt in the centre and might have given the *Stavka* time to consider its position more cooly, Stalin ordered Timoshenko to retake Smolensk. Timoshenko's failure and the loss of 300,000 more men seriously weakened Soviet infantry strength and only served to hearten the *Wehrmacht* in its push forward. The shortage of day bombers and ground-attack aircraft was now a grave drawback in harassing German concentrations. On 25 September Colonel-General Konev, Commander-in-Chief on the Western Front, sent an urgent request to the *Stavka* for a regiment of Pe-2 bombers and a regiment of Il-2 *shturmoviks* since of his sixty-three bombers still flying, forty-three were TB-3 and SB machines only suitable for night operations[7]. Night-bombing remained the main offensive weapon of the Red Air Force and from 1 October special night-bomber regiments equipped with obsolete machines were formed in accordance with GKO instructions. Of the first night-bomber regiments planned and prepared for operations in October and November, seventy-one were equipped with the fragile U-2 biplanes, thirty-two with R-5 and R-Zet light-bomber biplanes and five with SB bombers. Eventually the U-2 (Po-2) was to become the standard workhorse of the night-bomber regiments, with pilots making their way individually to the designated target area at heights of between 400 and 800 metres with engines throttled right back to shower grenades or small bombs on any light or sign of activity beneath. The U-2 was first used in this role while undertaking night reconnaissance sorties in September 1941, and during the Battle for Moscow, when small fragmentation bombs were often in short supply, bags filled with combustible material were often ignited and dropped over the side instead. Such raids were of little more than nuisance value, but they served a useful purpose in the war of nerves.

When the drive on Moscow — 'Operation Typhoon' — was launched by the German Army Group Centre on 30 September,

---

[7] *Fyodorov*

Soviet Air Force

Colonel-General Zhigarev had 373 aircraft available on the Western, Bryansk and Reserve Fronts[8] backed up by five long-range bomber divisions, units from the Moscow Military District under the command of Colonel Sbytov, regiments detached from VI PVO Fighter Corps and special GKO Reserve Air Groups. In all half a dozen GKO Reserve Air Groups consisting of four to six air regiments were formed over the autumn of 1941. Like the DBA-GKO these air groups were directly subordinated to the *Stavka* and allocated by it, with frontal air commanders exercising tactical control on a temporary basis only. Intended to form the shock spearheads of the counter-offensive, they were grudgingly committed by Stalin during the desperate defensive battles of October and November in the knowledge that his reserve air power was being depleted and that the supply of new aircraft from the evacuated factories was unlikely to improve before the following March. The first blow of 'Typhoon' fell against the Bryansk Front where General Polynin's aircraft were reinforced by the five regiments of General Demidov's 6th Reserve Air Group. This threat from the southern claw of the German pincers seemed at first the most dangerous. All available GVF and DBA units were utilised to fly in thirteen tons of ammunition and 5,500 additional troops — including Major-General Lelyushenko's I Guards Rifle Corps which was supported by Demidov's air regiments in the fierce but futile battles which ensued.

Oryol fell to the Germans on 3 October and with the fall of Bryansk soon afterwards Tula and ultimately Moscow were exposed to Guderian's panzers. The full gravity of the situation was not, however, brought home until 5 October when a pilot of the 120th Fighter Regiment on a reconnaissance sortie discovered an eighteen-kilometre long German armoured column moving towards Yukhnov between Vyaz'ma and Kaluga. This indication of a German breakthrough splitting the Western and Bryansk Fronts was at first not believed, even after two further confirmatory reconnaissance

---

[8]Fyodorov details the distribution of this air strength as follows:

front	fighter regts.	bomber regts.	shturmovik regts.	total serviceable aircraft
Western	8	4	2	206
Bryansk	3	5	2	102
Reserve	7	3	1	65

sorties had been made. Sbytov who had forwarded the report was interrogated by the NKVD as a 'panic-monger' on Beria's instructions and pressure brought upon him to withdraw his report[9]. Vindicated by events almost immediately, Sbytov was elevated to the command of the air elements in the Moscow Military District and the Moscow Defence Zone on 12 October. Yukhnov fell on the night of 6 October and air attacks against German troops occupying the town commenced the following morning — but only by pairs of U-2 and I-15*bis* biplanes whose pilots were as much protected as hampered by the swirling mist.

Air units later committed included the 120th Fighter Regiment flying I-153 fighters, a regiment of SB bombers, another of Pe-2s and a *shturmovik* regiment equipped with Il-2s reinforced by a light-bomber regiment whose R-5s were flown by instructors and trainees from the Yaroslavl' School of Bombing and Air-Gunnery and a squadron from the Yegor'evsk Flying School. Subsequently these regiments were joined by a further Pe-2 and two additional Il-2 regiments as the GKO Reserve Air Group under Sbytov to support the Soviet 5th Army on the Mozhaisk Defence Line where the remaining twenty-eight aircraft of the Reserve Front were transferred to the army air commands of the Soviet 43rd and 49th Armies.

To the north, the Western Front was supplied with SB and TB-3 regiments from the Central Asian Military District — almost the last that the interior districts could scrape together — but the loss of Kalinin on 14 October necessitated the formation of yet another front with its air units under Major-General Trifonov and a further division of evaporating tactical resources. Although all-out day and night bombing of *Luftwaffe* airfields at Oryol, Vitbsk, Smolensk, Severskaya and Dugino was ordered by the *Stavka* in the second week of October, the Red Air Force continued to suffer heavy losses and frequently proved unable to carry out its primary task of giving token air support to the Red Army. Totally inadequate radio communications between ground and air units meant that much liaison had to be done by U-2 biplanes and air commanders often had little idea of the latest disposition of their own and enemy units.

---

[9] See Erickson *The Road to Stalingrad*. One reason for this reaction to Sbytov's report may have been that air operations in this sector were under the overall control of Commissar Stepanov and that only via him could 'acceptable' notification of such a crisis be made.

Soviet Air Force

Zhigarev's instruction that air commanders should control operations from the ground rather than flying with their regiments was generally frustrated by the lack of radios, and the demoralising confusion was not helped by the Red Army's trigger-happy tendency to fire at anything flying overhead.

The heavy autumn rains which turned roads and runways into seas of mud, the legendary *rasputitsa*, was clearly to the Soviet advantage in impeding the *Wehrmacht* in what it hoped was the final push and wheels and tracks were only able to turn freely once more when the frosts of early November had hardened the churned and cratered earth. Moscow was still taking the threat of a massive *Luftwaffe* air attack seriously and on 6 November Stalin delivered his address commemorating the twenty-fourth anniversary of the Bolshevik revolution from the depths of the Mayakovski Square Metro station. The next day, the tanks and troops parading in front of Lenin's mausoleum were sent straight to the front while five hundred PVO fighters stood by at No. 1 alert. The Red Air Force continued to suffer punishing losses in November, not least in halting the German breakthrough south-west of Tula in the middle of the month. Discovered again by pilots of the 120th Fighter Regiment and hit by the Il-2s of Vitruk's 65th *Shturmovik* Regiment, the thrust was countered by General Kravchenko's reserve air group and every serviceable machine pushed into battle.

The *Luftwaffe* too was faltering as incessant ground support sorties took their toll of machines lost and damaged[10]; even damaged aircraft were as good as lost since the shortage of spares meant a prolonged period before they could be made airworthy once more. Veteran pilots failed to return and their replacements were not yet the equals of the experienced and confident élite which had hounded Stalin's Red Air Force that summer. The *Luftwaffe's* strength in the East was being run down rather than augmented. Even as the fateful Battle for Moscow was nearing its climax the headquarters of *Luftflotte 2 and II Fliegerkorps* were withdrawn from the support of Army Group Centre on Hitler's orders for transfer to the Mediterranean theatre.

When the Soviet counter-offensive was launched on 5-6 December, some 750 machines were available on the Kalinin,

---

[10]The Soviets claimed the destruction of 1,020 Luftwaffe machines between 30 September and 14 November (IVVSVOV, Vol 2)

The Battle for Moscow

Western and Bryansk Fronts and numerical superiority to the confronting *Geschwader* was the more telling due to the relatively high proportion of modern types involved[11] although day bombers were still in very short supply and SB bombers were manned by two crews, one for day and one for night operations. Poor weather conditions negated much of the air support hoped for during the first few days of the counter-offensive, and as the Germans fell back its effectiveness remained far below what had been anticipated. This was due in part to the lack of *shturmoviks* for effective ground-attack and the resulting over-use of fighters in this role. Fighters flying from established airfields near and in Moscow when the counter-offensive opened were soon forced by growing distances from the front line to rebase on the field strips recently vacated by the *Luftwaffe* and contend with the same unfavourable conditions. It was a factor which was to convince Stalin that range must be of paramount importance in the design of future fighters and cause friction more than once with his fighter designers[12]. A second factor was that, as in November, the lack of spares, trained technical staff and repair and maintenance facilities in the field soon depleted the quantity of serviceable machines. Before long more than half the Soviet combat aircraft were standing on their airfields, damaged in combat or in airfield accidents, without the parts, fitters or mechanics to get them flying again.

The supply of new aircraft had also slumped as the impact of the industrial upheavals was felt. Even when new machines did arrive at the frontline air regiments they were so plagued by defects resulting from hasty and inadequately inspected production that many were unfit to be flown in combat. The necessary adjustments and corrections imposed yet another burden on the over-taxed ground crews which were called upon to do work that should have been done

---

[11]As of 1 December the three fronts had 762 aircraft of which only 22% were classed as 'old types'. By contrast, the Red Air Force as a whole on this date had 2,495 combat aircraft (excluding 295 R-5 and 710 U-2 machines) of which 43% were 'old types'. *50 let Vooruzhonnykh Sil SSSR.*

[12]Lavochkin's fighters were particularly criticised by Stalin on this count. During a Kremlin conference in March 1943 Stalin compared the range of Soviet fighters unfavourably with that of the Spitfire. When Yakovlev tried to correct him by telling him that it was the unarmed Spitfire reconnaissance version on which he was basing his figures, Stalin exploded... 'What rubbish are you telling me? Do you take me for an infant? I'm talking about the fighter not the reconnaissance version. The Spitfire has a bigger range than our fighters and we must do something about it.' Yakovlev *Tsel' Zhizni.*

Soviet Air Force

at the factory. The situation was no better in the early spring of 1942 and most regiments were fortunate if they could operate at standard squadron strength. On the Kalinin Front the 6th Guards *Shturmovik* Regiment consisted of three Il-2s in April 1942 and the 4th Shock Army's four fighter regiments could muster no more than a dozen LaGG-3s between them. The only consolation was that the *Luftwaffe* was little better off and even by the end of December many bomber *Staffeln* were flying at a third or even a fifth of their strength[13].

Brought officially into the framework of the Red Air Force on 23 June 1941, GVF under Major-General Molokov and subsequently Major-General Astakhov[14] had been called upon to fulfil a wide variety of support tasks including the transportation of munitions and troops, the supply of encircled armies, the evacuation of wounded and of senior commanders, reconnaissance sorties and even bombing raids. Early in October 1941 the Moscow Special Purpose Air Group transported elements of the Soviet V Airborne Corps to reinforce the Bryansk Front, its elderly G-2 (converted TB-3) transports carrying up to twice their regulation payload on flights from Vnukovo. Other sorties entailed dropping fuel supplies to detached tank units and long-distance courier flights to the Caucasus, Siberia and northern Russia.

As the Soviet counter-offensive developed momentum, all available GVF transports were concentrated in the Moscow area to carry the paratroopers of Major-General Glazunov's Airborne Forces[15] with the objective of sandwiching the retreating *Wehrmacht* in the Olenino-Rzhev-Sychevka area between the 10,000 troops of IV Soviet Airborne Corps under Major-General Levashov and the advancing forces of the Kalinin and Western Fronts. This operation was to be as ill-omened as it was ambitious. The sheer delay in assembling the corps and the transport aircraft alerted the Germans so that the G-2 transports of Colonel Georgiev's 23rd Transport Division were harassed by the *Luftwaffe* in the air and on their base airfields. Few of the paratroops had combat experience and the drops

---

[13]Plocher *The German Air Force versus Russia, 1942.*

[14]Replaced as Head of GU-GVF in January 1942, Molokov retained his rank but was 'demoted' to the command of the 213th Night-Bomber Division. In 1945 Molokov was made Deputy Chief of the Air Meteology Service and from 1947 until his retirement in 1955 was Head of the Senior GVF Certifying Commission.

[15]As Commander of the Airborne Forces (*Vozdushnodesantnye voiska*) or VDV, General Glazunov was directly subordinated to the GKO.

were far from accurate; only half the 2,500 paratroops managed to reach their assembly points and then without most of their supplies and heavy equipment before the operation was called off with the slowing of the Soviet advance. A new air drop west of Yukhnov by troops of V Soviet Airborne Corps was intended to reinforce the Soviet 29th Army and to coincide with the dropping of the rest of IV Airborne Corps south-west of Vyaz'ma. Over 7,000 men were dropped in this operation between 17 February and 24 February when it was terminated after the G-2 carrying General Levashov and the IV Airborne Corps command staff had been shot down by *Luftwaffe* fighters. The *Wehrmacht*, suffering greater losses from the extreme cold than Soviet action, slipped away from the encirclements.

The Soviet airborne operations were not quite total failures, but they did not bring about the grand encirclements planned for them. They were always handicapped by the lack of enough transports which prolonged the process of dropping troops and made it more vulnerable to enemy interdiction, poor navigation and dropping accuracy and the sheer adversity of weather conditions. The inability of the Red Air Force to maintain an adequate supporting presence over forward areas, its paucity of escorting cover and the lack of diversionary raids contributed in no small measure to the disappointing showing by Glazunov's Airborne Forces. Indicative of Stalin's disillusionment was the later conversion of eight airborne corps into guards rifle divisions in the summer of 1942, most of which were to fight a very different battle from the one they had been trained for among the rubble and craters of Stalingrad.

To the north-west, however, the Soviet counter-offensive did succeed in temporarily containing two pockets of German troops, both of which were relieved after the Soviet encirclements had been breached from the west in May. At Kholm 3,500 German troops were cut off from their lines on 21 January 1941 and they were only reunited with them on 5 May. These troops were supplied by the *Luftwaffe* using DFS 230 and Go 242 cargo-gliders when it became evident that the proximity of Russian field batteries and anti-aircraft guns made landings within the restricted area of the pocket by transport aircraft impossible. Even then it proved necessary at last to resort to containers dropped by parachute when losses of aircraft to Soviet ground fire during glider-launch approaches became unacceptable. The situation at Demyansk was far more serious.

Soviet Air Force

There four Soviet armies had breached the lines of the German 16th Army between Demyansk and Staraya Rusa, trapping six divisions totalling around 100,000 men. *Luftwaffe* transport units were concentrated on Pskov, Korov'e Selo, Ostrov and Riga to fly in a scheduled 300 tons of supplies per day brought from Germany across Eastern Prussia on a variety of antiquated and converted transports[16]. The first flight by Ju 52/3m transports into Demyansk, a former advanced tactical airfield with few facilities, was made on 20 February 1942, but flights at low-level by single aircraft or small formations as planned soon had to be curtailed. Single transports were pounced upon by groups of patrolling Soviet fighters and at low-level the formations had to pass through a fifty-five kilometre long corridor of anti-aircraft fire to gain the pocket. Formations of twenty to thirty transports had to be organised, flying at heights around 2,000 metres and whenever possible with fighter escort.

The Soviets were unsure how to deal with their enormous catch which had taken them almost as much by surprise as it had the Germans. It was at first proposed that airborne troops should be dropped into the pocket as a diversion while the defensive wall was stormed from outside. Three fighter regiments flying Yak-1, MiG-3 and Hurricane fighters were seconded from VI PVO Fighter Corps to oppose *Luftwaffe* intervention and neutralise anti-aircraft fire from the pocket, but the idea was abandoned. Bad weather, the shortage of transports and the failures of January and February argued against the further use of the airborne corps and held the Soviets back. Their hopes of landing their catch ended when Demyansk was relieved in mid-May. From the German standpoint the Demyansk operation had been successful — but at a cost. An average of 273 tons of supplies per day had been flown into the pocket but 262 Ju 52/3m transports had been lost[17]. Experienced aircrews had been expended and the pilot training programme seriously affected since instructors were drafted to serve on the extensive supply route. The losses of Ju 52/3m transports amounted to over half the total production of the

---

[16]These included Ju 86, Junkers W 34 and Focke-Wulf FW 58 Weihe machines. See Morzik *German Air Force Airlift Operations*.

[17]Smith & Kay *German Aircraft of the Second World War*. Figures for the tonnage supplied and the number of personnel flown in and out of the Demyansk pocket vary. Morzik in *German Air Force Airlift Operations* records an average daily supply of 302 tons, fully meeting the scheduled quota, for the loss of 265 Ju 52/3m transports and 383 aircrew.

The Battle for Moscow

aircraft for 1941[18] and the demand for escorts had taxed the energies of the already heavily committed Bf 109 fighter units. The need to fly in large formations for mutual protection and economise on fighter escorts had caused additional difficulties in handling, accommodating and unloading such a large number of tranports simultaneously with the limited facilities at Demyansk and provided a tempting target for *shturmovik* intruders. Cold had added to the *Luftwaffe's* hardships. Engine life between overhauls was sadly reduced, adding to the maintenance load of minor repairs during taxiing accidents on ice-covered runways and from incidental combat damage. Hydraulic systems and tyres deteriorated and there was little in the way of protective insulation, special lubricants or de-icing equipment.

The *Luftwaffe* transports had suffered their heaviest attrition in Soviet anti-aircraft fire during their flights into the pocket, while making landing approaches and, to a lesser degree, from low-level air attacks while unloading. Fighter interception was limited usually to attacks on isolated transports with bigger formations largely unmolested. To the surprise and relief of the *Luftwaffe*, the Red Air Force made no effort to attack the supply bases outside the pocket where determined air strikes would have had the most damaging effect. The Russians and the Germans were to make their own conclusions from the Demyansk episode and draw upon them when the German 6th Army found itself trapped at Stalingrad. Victory at Demyansk was to cost the *Wehrmacht* and the *Luftwaffe* dearly less than a year later.

---

[18] A total of 502 Ju 52/3m transports were produced in 1941 and an equivalent number in 1942. In 1943, the year which saw the greatest annual output of this already outdated trnasport, 887 examples were built. Baumbach *Broken Swastika: The Defeat of the Luftwaffe.*

9 The New Command

With the exhaustion of the Soviet counter-offensive and the consolidation of the German defensive line in early 1942, both sides took advantage of the brief respite to take stock of the situation and prepare for the next phase of the campaign. As far as the Red Air Force was concerned, Stalin was far from satisfied with its performance during the Moscow counter-offensive and a series of command changes were made over the winter and spring. On the Kalinin Front General Trifonov was replaced on 4 January by General Rudenko, promoted rapidly from command of a fighter regiment over the previous six months and a divisional commander during the Battle for Moscow, and on 17 February General Naumenko on the Western Front handed over to General Khudyakov who had been singled out for special praise by Zhukov. Naumenko remained in the Western Front Air Command for a short period, now as deputy to his former Chief of Staff, before being sent to the North Caucasus. Then in April came the most fundamental change of all. General Zhigarev was dismissed as C-in-C Red Air Force and relegated to a Far Eastern air command. He was replaced by his deputy of three months' standing, General Aleksandr Novikov, formerly Air Commander on the Leningrad Front, who was to head the Red Air Force for the next four years.

Zhigarev's deputies were also moved from the front rank of Red Air Force command — Petrov to liaise between the air force and the aircraft industry and Stepanov to southern Russia where he later organised the formation of the 16th Air Army until replaced by Rudenko in late September 1942. Novikov created a new command staff and his prestige rose with its success; promoted first to Colonel-General, Novikov was made Air Marshal in 1943 and Chief Air Marshal the following year. His immediate deputies included General Grigori Vorozheikin who had served as Zhigarev's Chief of

The New Command

Staff between August 1941 and March 1942 when he was sent to command a special air strike force. Appointed Novikov's First Deputy in May, he served in that capacity for the remainder of the war. General Falaleev who succeeded Vorozheikin as Chief of Air Staff until June 1943 when he was replaced by Khudyakov also served as Operational Deputy under Novikov. These three men were Novikov's closest lieutenants and played with him a major part as GKO representatives in the planning and co-ordination of major Red Air Force operations. Other deputies to Novikov in the new Red Air Force command included the Head of Rear Services, General Zharov, the Head of the Engineering-Technical Service, General Repin, the Inspector-General of the Air Force, General Turkel', the Head of the Political Directorate, General Shimanov, the Head of the Air Formations Directorate, General Nikitin, the Head of the Air Operations Section, Geneal Zhuravlev and from 1943 the Head of the Navigation Section, General Sterligov, a veteran of the thirties who had served under Alksnis. It was these deputies who planned and nurtured the resurgent Red Air Force and saw it through to eventual victory.

Changes were also made in the organisation and structure of the Red Air Force based on the experience of the first six months of the war. In place of the frontal air command (*VVS fronta*) the new air army (*vozdushnaya armiya*) was established on its basis. Like the frontal air command it replaced, each air army supported an army group engaged on a designated front but it was designed to be more flexible to enable rapid augmentation or reduction in strength to be made in response to a strategic situation so that air power could be quickly consolidated for defensive or offensive operations in whatever sector they might occur. The lessons of 1941 had demonstrated that working relationships and adequate command communications had barely existed between ground army air commanders and frontal air headquarters and that Soviet air operations had been hampered or confused as a result. Henceforth the practice of providing ground armies with their own attached air divisions as the *armeiskaya aviatsiya* was abolished and all authority and control was concentrated in the hands of the air army commander who was directly responsible to the front's army group commander and worked under him as his deputy.

In the summer of 1942 the average air army numbered two or three hundred machines at most with the air division as its largest

Soviet Air Force

component. The 4th Air Army had 208 aircraft when it was formed in May from the Southern Front Air Command, almost a third of these U-2 night-bombers, and the 8th Air Army which inherited the South-Western Front Air Command, contained about three hundred aircraft by mid-July, a month after its inception. By the end of 1942 thirteen tactical air armies had been formed in the west and four more were subsequently created from the air forces remaining in the interior and progressively developed in the Far East. The Germans assumed that the new air army structure portended a progressive independence from Red Army control, but in fact the decision to extend the scope of the GKO Reserve — which came under direct *Stavka* control — from the handful of reserve air groups which took part in the Battle for Moscow emphasised that the authority of the C-in-C Red Air Force was to be confined to a supervisory and tactical command role.

In September 1942 General Nikitin, Head of the Air Formations Directorate, was instructed by Stalin to form three air corps, one each of fighters, bombers and *shturmoviks*, and by the middle of November — at the cost of starving the harassed and still feeble air armies of new crews and aircraft — four air corps were available and a further six were under formation, representing a third of all Soviet tactical air strength. By 1 January 1945 the GKO Air Reserve constituted 43% of tactical air power[1]. General Beletski, who commanded the air defence of the Crimea and later the *Stavka's* 1st Aviation Army (or Special Air Group No. 1) thrown against the German bridgeheads on the Don, was chosen to command I Fighter Corps, I Bomber Corps was placed under the command of General Sudets, formerly commander of the DBA's IV Long-Range Bomber Corps, and General Ryazanov was given command of I *Shturmovik* Corps. By late November General Blagoveshchenski's II Fighter Corps had joined the GKO Air Reserve and all four air corps were sent to reinforce General Gromov's 3rd Air Army on the Kalinin Front.

All air corps remained in the GKO Air Reserve and were allocated in accordance with the *Stavka's* strategical planning and, although tactical control was exercised by the commander of the air army to which they were attached, it was emphasised that they were to be used for major air operations only and withdrawn for regrouping and

---

[1] SVVSVOV

The New Command

re-equipment once these were completed. Of the thirty tactical air corps created by the end of 1944, fourteen can be identified as fighter, nine as *shturmovik* and six as bomber corps. A number were originally formed as composite air corps. General Shevchenko's I Composite Air Corps operational in the summer of 1943 had one *shturmovik* and one fighter division, two independent *shturmovik* and two night-bomber regiments and various other minor elements. All the composite air corps were, however, later converted into fully fighter or *shturmovik* air corps and renumbered; General Danilin's IX Composite Air Corps, the last to be formed, consisting half of fighter and half of *shturmovik* regiments became the XIV Fighter Corps while attached to the 15th Air Army in 1944. There were in addition seven long-range bomber corps subordinated to GU-ADD, later the 18th Air Army.

The air corps possessed no autononous support or service facilities other than those at divisional level, these being supplied by the host air army while under its operational command. Most air corps were very mobile. Beletski's I Fighter Corps (from 1943 I Guards Fighter Corps) was attached to the 3rd Air Army in October 1942 and transferred to the 6th Air Army in February 1943. It later flew for successive periods with the 15th, 3rd and 1st Air Armies before joining Rudenko's 16th Air Army for the Battle of Berlin. Corps commanders were given tactical command or liaison tasks in ground control centres during air operations and it was unusual for them to fly with their regiments, the notable exceptions being Major-General Ivan Polbin who was killed in action over Breslau in February 1945 while leading the Pe-2s of his II Guards Bomber Corps and Lieutenant-General Yevgeni Savitski who led the fighters of his III Fighter Corps into battle over the Kuban. With better radio communications, the rule was for divisional commanders and above to exercise command from the safety of the ground rather than attempt to direct and lead their formations in the air.

Supplemented with new aircraft and fresh aircrews and with the contingency transfer of air corps and smaller formations — including independent air divisions and regiments — from the GKO Air Reserve, the air armies grew in size. By the summer of 1943 the air armies in the Centre had from three to five corps each and contained about a thousand aircraft. The 4th Air Army expanded from 459 to 1,665 machines between August and December 1944 in preparation for the offensive on the Second Belorussian Front[2], and during the

---
[2]*Chetvyortaya vozdushnaya armiya*

Soviet Air Force

drive into Poland the 2nd and 16th Air Armies on the First Belorussian and First Ukrainian Fronts fielded a total of 4,770 aircraft between them[3]. The 16th Air Army formed to defend Stalingrad in August 1942 began its existence with no more than three hundred aircraft but had been expanded to contain 2,183 machines by the opening of the Battle of Berlin and was thus numerically superior to what remained of the *Luftwaffe*.

Air divisions — fighter, *shturmovik*, bomber or composite — were normally attached directly to an air army headquarters or indirectly via the headquarters of their air corps if they formed part of the GKO Air Reserve. Divisions like the 257th Independent Composite Red Banner Air Division on the Karelian Front allocated directly to the 7th Air Army by the GKO Air Reserve without the intermediate corps echelon were more rarely encountered. An air army might possess one or two fighter, one or two *shturmovik* and up to three night-bomber divisions, but the air corps usually had two, occasionally three, divisions with the average air division consisting of two or three regiments. The larger air divisions, usually *shturmovik* or night-bomber divisions, could contain up to six air regiments and the larger *shturmovik* divisions often included a regiment of fighters for escort and reconnaissance. Few day bomber divisions were attached directly to air army headquarters and the tendency was to concentrate the modern machines available in the bomber corps and convert the air army's existing bomber division for night-bombing.

The revision of the air regiment had been begun in August 1941 when close-support bomber regiments were reformed to consist of two bomber squadrons and a squadron of fighters, all of ten aircraft, with two bombers acting as formation leaders. *Shturmovik* regiments included two squadrons of *shturmoviks* and one of fighters with three Su-2s to act as formation leaders and fly reconnaissance sorties — giving a regimental total of thirty-three machines. Shortly afterwards, however, all regiments equipped with new types were standardised to consist of two squadrons of nine aircraft with two Su-2 or Pe-2 bombers serving as formation leaders[4]. The heavy losses of 1941 and early 1942 meant that in practice most air regiments had less than a squadron and at best contained no more than a score of serviceable machines, but with the growth of aircraft production and

---

[3] *Aviatsiya i Kosmonavtika SSSR*

[4] Fyodorov

the assistance of Lend-Lease, regimental strength was increased from the winter of 1942-43 to an average complement of three squadrons, although no attempt was made to restore the air regiment to its former size. This was felt, correctly, to have proved too cumbersome and the new air regiment was modelled on the lines of the *Luftwaffe Gruppe*. In the new fighter regiment with, on average, thirty machines, the *zveno* of three was replaced by a four-fighter zveno made up, like the *Schwarm*, of two pairs or *pary*. The new *para* with its Number One (*vedushchi*) and his Number Two (*vedomy*) to cover him was introduced into fighter regiments on conversion to new types in the summer of 1942 and that autumn was introduced as standard practice in all fighter, and subsequently *shturmovik*, regiments. Each fighter squadron contained two of the new *zven'ya* plus an additional *para* consisting of the squadron leader and his Number Two. Fighter regiments usually comprised three such squadrons, sometimes four in the case of guards fighter regiments, with two Pe-2s attached as formation leaders. *Luftwaffe* intelligence assessed the total personnel of the new Red Air Force fighter regiment as around two hundred, of which thirty-four were pilots, a hundred and thirty fitters and mechanics and the remainder engaged on miscellaneous duties[5].

The day bomber regiment retained the three-aircraft *zveno* with three *zven'ya* forming a squadron — commonly called 'a nine' (*devyatka*) — to give an overall strength of twenty-seven bombers with three to five other machines in reserve. Regiments equipped with the Pe-2 contained about a hundred aircrew but ADD regiments flying the larger Il-4 and Lend-Lease North American B-25 bombers had up to two hundred aircrew and three hundred ground staff. *Shturmovik* regiments, in common with fighter regiments, had about two hundred pesonnel of which, on average, thirty-three were pilots with an equal or slightly smaller number of rear-gunners depending on the proportion of two-seat Il-2s it contained.

The air army, in addition to its complement of air divisions, normally had at least one reconnaissance and one artillery-spotting regiment, a communications and liaison regiment, a GVF transport regiment and squadrons responsible for command liaison, pilot recovery and ambulance duties. Certain liaison, VIP transport and special operations GVF regiments worked directly under the *Stavka*,

---

[5] *The Russian Air Force in the Eyes of German Commanders*

the special operations regiments carrying out important partisan liaison sorties, the landing and recovery of agents and deep—penetration night reconnaissance flights[6].

In 1942 the air army was commanded by a Major-General, later promoted to Lieutenant-General and eventually, in the more important air armies, to Colonel-General by the close of the war. His senior staff consisted of a Deputy Commander, a Chief of Staff, a Deputy for Political Affairs (Corps Commissar until October 1942), a Deputy for Rear Services and a Chief Engineer of the Engineering-Technical Service (ITS). From 1943 it became the practice to post the deputy air army commander with a small staff in a forward control centre or auxiliary control point (VKP) linked to the frontal command centre to ensure the fullest tactical awareness of the air situation and the closest support for ground forces during major air battles. Corps and divisional air commanders were also posted in this manner to the headquarters of key ground armies in advisory, liaison or tactical control capacities. Under the Air Army Commander and his Chief of Staff in the main control centre came the Operations Section responsible for planning, co-ordination and, from 1943, the preparation of monthly reports based on the air army's combat records which were collated by the Section for the Utilisation of Combat Experience under Lieutenant-General N.A. Zhuravlev's Operations Directorate at Red Air Force Command Headquarters in Moscow. The heads of sections covering Intelligence and Reconnaissance, Navigation, Communications, Meteological Data, Cypher and Air Gunnery were also located under the Chief of Staff in the main air army control point. From 1943 a special Advance Staff Echelon was formed to facilitate the setting up of new advanced headquarters for the air army as the tide flowed westwards.

From December 1943 the air army's Chief Navigator was also made a Deputy Commander. His tasks also embraced the checking and improvement of bomb-aiming and the Ground Assistance to Air Navigation Service (ZOS) which used homing beacons, flares, lights in arrowhead patterns, searchlights and bonfires to guide aircraft onto targets at night and indicate the fluctuating frontline. During the advances of 1944 and 1945, ZOS also indicated key navigational points by painting figures on the ground or using white fabric to

---

[6]In 1942 the GVF air groups were retitled 'independent' GVF regiments if attached to air armies, or air transport divisions when subordinated to frontal commands or higher echelons.

The New Command

guide Soviet aircraft over unfamiliar territory. Needless to say, the *Luftwaffe* also took frequent advantage of the services offered by ZOS. The Political Deputy presided over education, indoctrination and the maintenance of a healthy fighting and political morale. His assistants supervised Party and *Komsomol* activities and produced the air army's daily newspaper[7]. The Deputy for Rear Services with his own Chief of Staff was based in a rear control centre where he was responsible for the work of the Air Basing Regions (RAB). Each RAB served an air corps or the equivalent number of air divisions with maintenance facilities and contained from six to eight airfield servicing battalions (BAO), with one BAO for each one or two air regiments. He also supervised the sections for airfield construction, medical and transport services, fuel and lubricants, supply and the provision of armaments and ammunition. Working closely with him was the air army's Chief Engineer under whom came the mobile air repair workshops which undertook the recovery of damaged aircraft and carried out repair work. The Chief Engineer's job was to keep as many of the air army's machines operational as possible, and to report on the effectiveness or defects of the new aircraft supplied by the aircraft industry.

The new 'shock élite' of the Red Air Force were the guards air regiments, the first six of which were created to coincide with the opening of the Moscow counter-offensive on 6 December 1941. Air divisions and corps were also later given guards' titles although it was not conferred upon any of the air armies[8]. The conferment of this title for distinction in battle was followed by an elaborate ceremony. The proclamation from the People's Commissariat for Defence was read aloud to the assembled unit with officers and men kneeling while their commander received and kissed the new colours. They then repeated after him the oath — 'In the terrible years of the Great Patriotic War, I swear to you my country and to you my party to fight to the last drop of blood and my last breath — and to conquer. Such is the guards' creed. Forward to victory! Glory to the Party of Lenin!'.

---

[7] In addition to the Red Air Force periodicals *Vestnik Vozdushnovo Flota* (Air Fleet News) and *Stalinski Sokol* (Stalin's Falcon), each air army and naval air force had its own daily. The 4th Air Army's was entitled *Kryl'ya Sovetov* (Wings of the Soviets).

[8] Regiments and divisions were renumbered on being given guards status, the 29th Fighter Regiment becoming the 1st Guards Fighter Regiment and the 210th Fighter Division the 3rd Guards Fighter Division. Air corps retained their original numbers with three fighter, three *shturmovik* and four bomber corps receiving the guards title.

Soviet Air Force

Guards units, usually equipped with the latest aircraft and often larger in size than the conventional air regiment, were expected to serve as the shock spearheads of the Red Air Force and to set an example to others in overcoming the once dreaded *Luftwaffe*. There was certainly a need for inspiration in the Red Air Force as a whole. Throughout 1942 propaganda, exhortations and threats were liberally and doggedly applied in efforts to educate commanders and discipline aircrews. Fighter pilots had to be taught to be more aggressive, more determined, more capable of exploiting the potential of their new fighters and vanquishing their instinctive fear of the *Luftwaffe*. Against bombers they were instructed to hold their fire at extreme ranges and, as the premature expenditure of ammunition was only too common, to use short, well-placed bursts instead of prolonged, generally directed streams of fire while keeping safely clear of the rear-gunner. In combat with fighters they had to learn to fight on the dive and climb and develop skill in deflection shooting instead of relying perpetually on the stern chase. They had to be taught to use sun and cloud cover. Attack and cover groups were to be clearly allocated and adhered to as escorting fighters had become notorious for deserting their charges at the first signs of trouble. Now disciplinary measures were to be enforced against fighter pilots who broke off engagements or turned back without command instructions, and a sortie was only to be counted as such when the escorted bombers or *shturmoviks* got through to the target.

Soviet fighter aces toured the fronts giving lectures and practical 'master classes' and the most experienced regiments — primarily guards or those in the new fighter corps — were chosen to be re-equipped with the latest fighters, to be responsible for their optimum exploitation and establishing confidence in their ability to match the *Luftwaffe*'s machines. A great deal of work was undoubtedly needed if Soviet fighter pilots were to shed their fears not only of the *Luftwaffe* but of their own machines, since the traumas of the MiG-3 and the LaGG-3 were still fresh in their minds. In 1942 and 1943 air commanders, endeavouring to provide the maximum fighter presence, often sent out too high a proportion of inexperienced new pilots on the same sortie with disastrous results. Now the number was to be reduced and regimental commanders and squadron leaders were expected to fly with their units and keep a close eye on the well-being, performance and aptitude of their new pilots. Under attack, Soviet fighter formations tended to scatter and provide easy prey for

The New Command

the more confident and better organised Luftwaffe pilots; now they were educated to keep together and fight as a *zveno*. In spite of all these measures, many weaknesses were never completely eradicated and the Soviet fighter regiments became dominant largely through the demise of the *Luftwaffe* in the face of overwhelming odds. The *Luftwaffe* continued to cherish a poor opinion of the average Soviet fighter pilot, contending that — 'the characteristic features of the average Soviet fighter pilot were a tendency towards caution and reluctance instead of toughness and stamina, brute strength instead of genuine combat efficiency, abysmal hatred instead of fairness and chivalry...'[9].

The *shturmoviks*, on the other hand, won German respect for the sheer stubborness of their pilots who pressed home attacks through lethal walls of flak, and the courage of their rear-gunners who kept on firing from a burning aircraft or with a dead pilot behind them. In 1941 the squadrons of R-10 and Su-2 bombers and I-153 and I-16 fighters employed for ground-attack had suffered severe losses from anti-aircraft fire, and although the armoured single-seat Il-2 (BSh) had proved almost impervious to light ground fire it had been readily vulnerable to fighter attack from astern. In 1942 the Il-2 *shturmoviks* appeared in greater numbers and towards its close the modified two-seat version had appeared. These were best dealt with by fighter attack from behind and above where the crew were unprotected, or, if the rear-gunner could be silenced, the fighter could close in to place an accurate burst in the wing tanks or disable the tail control surfaces. In 1943 when the Il-2m3, fitted with a more powerful engine and heavier armament, came into its own at last, the *Luftwaffe* no longer had sufficient fighters left to deal with them adequately. From late 1943 it became common for *shturmoviks* to operate at regimental or even divisional strength in groups of six to a dozen aircraft, while pairs or *zven'ya* undertook 'free hunt' sorties, attacking targets of opportunity at tree-top level and using the contours of the landscape for surprise and escape.

In comparison Soviet bomber effectiveness remained at a comparatively low level. Less than 10% of all Red Air Force bombers were new types in July 1942 and day bombing capability was minimal. The bulk of the remaining bomber force, mainly SB and R-5 bombers, were used primarily at night and were committed to

---

[9] Schwabedissen *The Russian Air Force in the Eyes of German Commanders.*

Soviet Air Force

daylight operations only *in extremis* — notably in the desperate raids over the Don bridgeheads. Most daylight sorties were indifferently escorted and beset by poor navigation, inaccurate bomb-aiming, inadequate pre-sortie briefings and a shrinking refusal to run the gauntlet of German flak. Bombers were often sent out in total ignorance of the situation on the ground and attacked any likely target of opportunity at the decision of the squadron or *zveno* commander. From March 1942 front commanders were directed to set specific targets and request results that could be reasonably expected and assessed, bomber crews were to be briefed as fully as possible and provided with maps and photographs and reports were to be brought back for analysis. But poor prior target reconnaissance and the dearth of meteological support remained as handicaps. Efforts were increased from May 1942 onwards to provide each air army with a tactical reconnaissance regiment, including at least one squadron of Pe-2s and a squadron of MiG-3s. Later in the war the reconnaissance regiments were often enlarged to include five or six squadrons, each equipped with a different kind of aircraft ranging from fighters to Pe-2s, Il-4s, Li-2s, Tu-2s and Lend-Lease Bostons. In 1942 most reconnaissance aircraft still lacked radio transceivers and had to return to base for verbal reports before any action could be taken. Meanwhile the Germans, aware of the implications after spotting a lone Soviet machine, had either dispersed or prepared flak defences in anticipation of a raid. Captured German aircraft were carefully preserved and used for reconnaissance sorties as well as other special missions[10]. Frontline reconnaissance at night was carried out by R-5 and U-2 biplanes from the night bomber regiments but the results it afforded were perforce limited. The Red Air Force had, however, made great strides in improving their provision for extensive air reconnaissance by the summer of 1943 and it was to prove an important factor in the Battle of Kursk.

The best day bomber available to the Red Air Force, the Pe-2, continued to be built in relatively small numbers in 1942 due to the *Stavka's* decision to expand *shturmovik* production and the shortage

---

[10] The test-pilot Fedor Opadchi organised a special reconnaissance group in late 1941 or early 1942 containing twelve German aircraft — three examples each of the Ju 88, Do 215, Bf 110 and Bf 109 — some of which were very probably among those supplied by Germany in 1940. Stefanovski *Trista neizvestnykh*. At least one captured Bf 109 was used for tactical reconnaissance during the Battle of Stalingrad and others were retained for combat instruction and evaluation.

The New Command

of Klimov inline engines required for fighters. Nor had the Red Air Force yet learned to use the Pe-2 to best effect. By 1943 both the Red Air Force and the *Luftwaffe* realised that they had over-specialised in the development of their close-support aircraft — the *Luftwaffe* by relying too heavily on the Ju 87 dive-bomber at the expense of an anti-tank aircraft while the Soviets, who had successfully nurtured the *shturmovik*, needed a precision bomber for attacks on bridgeheads, gun emplacements and small laterally-protected targets against which a high degree of bombing accuracy was essential. Although the Pe-2 had been intended from the outset for use as a dive-bomber, the *Luftwaffe*'s complete air superiority had dictated its employment as a fast horizontal bomber in which role, while it gained some immunity from fighters, its inherent value was lost. The real potential of the Pe-2 was pioneered and demonstrated by Colonel Polbin's 150th Bomber Regiment whose attacks on the Don bridges had been the most formidable aspect of Soviet air opposition. Polbin's method was to keep the target and its flak defences under constant and concentrated attack by flying in a squadron carousel or *vertushka* whereby one bomber followed another onto the target before climbing to rejoin the circle for a repeat attack. In this way, argued Polbin, ground-fire could be intimidated and suppressed and the most intensive attack sustained over the shortest period, but it all depended on sureness and determination and on the domination of surrounding air space.

The new air armies were to prove themselves staunch supporters of the Red Army in the field. Their newer and better aircraft were backed by better reconnaissance and tactical control, the latter aided substantially from 1943 by improved radars[11] and radio communications. Training received the urgent attention it required with entrants spending nine to twelve months in primary flying training before going on for courses lasting about a year in specialised flying schools for fighter, bomber and *shturmovik* aircrews[12]. After graduating, they were posted to replacement air regiments in the

---

[11] The Soviets had developed the rudimentary RUS-1 and more sophisticated RUS-2 air defence radars shortly before the German invasion, but they were available only in limited numbers. The evacuation eastwards made the resumed production of radar equipment impossible before the late summer of 1943.

[12] *Luftwaffe* Intelligence estimated that there were sixty fighter, thirty *shturmovik* and thirty bomber schools for the Red Air Force and eight ADD air schools. *The Russian Air Force in the Eyes of German Commanders.*

interior before being sent to the front. Once attached to an air army, the newcomer spent from one to four months in a special training regiment under the supervision of the Deputy Air Army Commander before being committed to operations[13]. By the end of the war it became more usual to do away with training regiments attached to the air army and to import regiments *en bloc* from the interior.

Air weapons were also improved. The 7.62mm ShkAS machine-gun was replaced by the more effective 12.7mm Berezin which could be installed in swivel, turret, wing or synchronised mounts, and the 20mm ShVAK cannon by the 23mm VYa and later NS-23 and NS-37 23mm and 37mm cannon which were more able to deal with armour[14]. The RS-82 and RS-132 air-launched rockets were supplemented by the PTAB anti-tank bomb and wider use was later made of incendiary bombs by Red Air Force bombers. New bombsights, the OPB-1D for horizontal and the PBP-4 for dive bombing, were introduced in 1944 and improved the accuracy of Soviet bombing.

On the debit side, the overall quality of Soviet aircraft, equipment and flying acumen remained inferior to those of the *Luftwaffe*. Air supremacy was not won without courage, persistence and sacrifice but it was more the result of weight of numbers and the flagging *Luftwaffe*'s inability to remain an effective fighting arm on the Eastern Front.

---

[13]The *Luftwaffe* reported that these training regiments usually consisted of five squadrons, two fighter, one bomber and one *shturmovik* with a fifth for potential *zveno* leaders. *ibid*

[14]The VYa had a higher muzzle velocity than the ShVAK — 900 metres per second as opposed to 800 — but its rate of fire at 600 r.p.m. was 200 r.p.m. slower than the weapon it replaced.

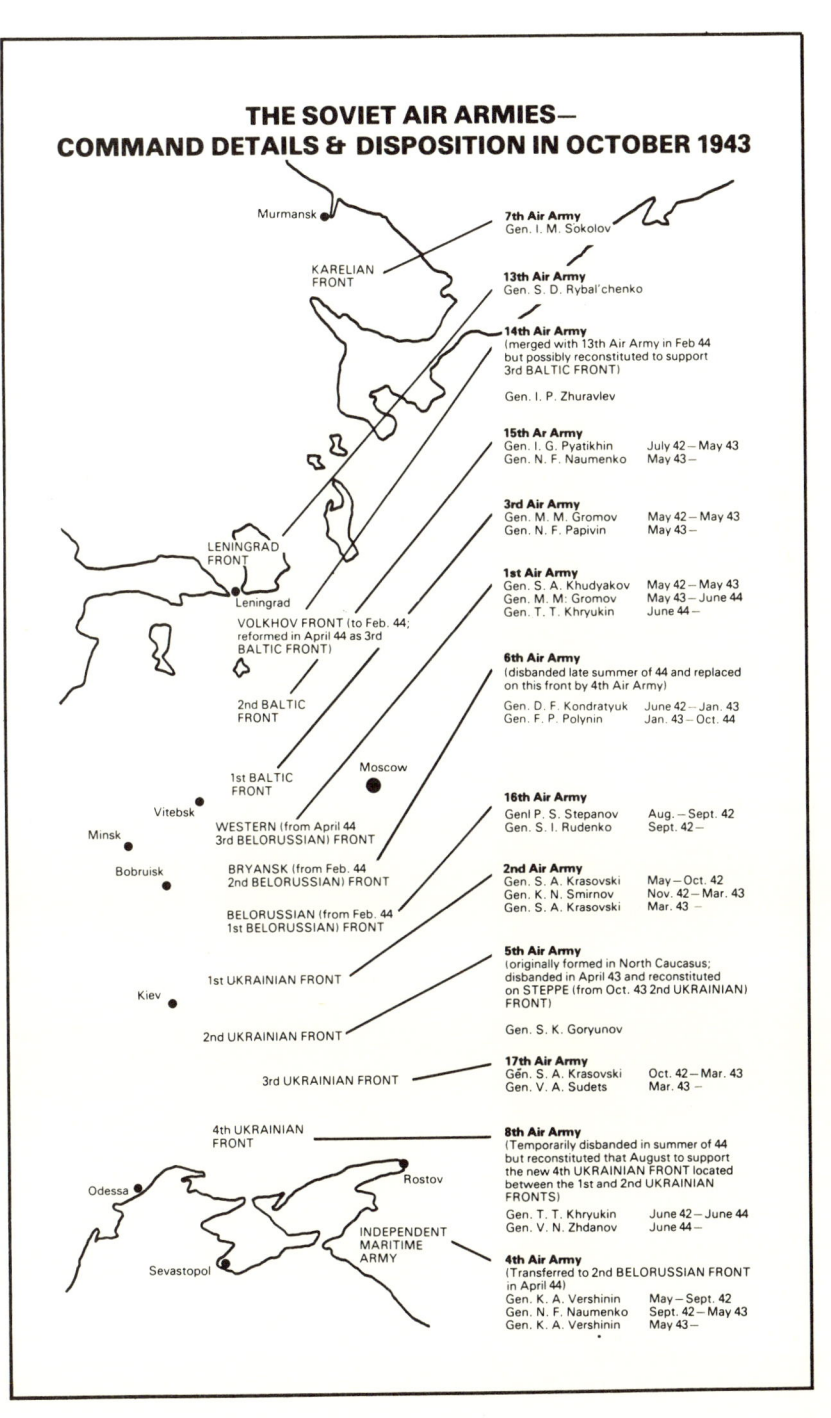

THE SOVIET AIR ARMIES—
COMMAND DETAILS & DISPOSITION IN OCTOBER 1943

Murmansk

KARELIAN FRONT

7th Air Army
Gen. I. M. Sokolov

13th Air Army
Gen. S. D. Rybal'chenko

14th Air Army
(merged with 13th Air Army in Feb 44 but possibly reconstituted to support 3rd BALTIC FRONT)

Gen. I. P. Zhuravlev

15th Ar Army
Gen. I. G. Pyatikhin — July 42 – May 43
Gen. N. F. Naumenko — May 43 –

3rd Air Army
Gen. M. M. Gromov — May 42 – May 43
Gen. N. F. Papivin — May 43 –

LENINGRAD FRONT
Leningrad

1st Air Army
Gen. S. A. Khudyakov — May 42 – May 43
Gen. M. M: Gromov — May 43 – June 44
Gen. T. T. Khryukin — June 44 –

VOLKHOV FRONT (to Feb. 44; reformed in April 44 as 3rd BALTIC FRONT)

6th Air Army
(disbanded late summer of 44 and replaced on this front by 4th Air Army)
Gen. D. F. Kondratyuk — June 42 – Jan. 43
Gen. F. P. Polynin — Jan. 43 – Oct. 44

2nd BALTIC FRONT

1st BALTIC FRONT
Moscow

Vitebsk
Minsk
Bobruisk

WESTERN (from April 44 3rd BELORUSSIAN) FRONT

16th Air Army
Genl P. S. Stepanov — Aug. – Sept. 42
Gen. S. I. Rudenko — Sept. 42 –

BRYANSK (from Feb. 44 2nd BELORUSSIAN) FRONT

2nd Air Army
Gen. S. A. Krasovski — May – Oct. 42
Gen. K. N. Smirnov — Nov. 42 – Mar. 43
Gen. S. A. Krasovski — Mar. 43 –

BELORUSSIAN (from Feb. 44 1st BELORUSSIAN) FRONT

Kiev

1st UKRAINIAN FRONT

5th Air Army
(originally formed in North Caucasus; disbanded in April 43 and reconstituted on STEPPE (from Oct. 43 2nd UKRAINIAN) FRONT)
Gen. S. K. Goryunov

2nd UKRAINIAN FRONT

3rd UKRAINIAN FRONT

17th Air Army
Gen. S. A. Krasovski — Oct. 42 – Mar. 43
Gen. V. A. Sudets — Mar. 43 –

4th UKRAINIAN FRONT

Odessa
Rostov

8th Air Army
(Temporarily disbanded in summer of 44 but reconstituted that August to support the new 4th UKRAINIAN FRONT located between the 1st and 2nd UKRAINIAN FRONTS)
Gen. T. T. Khryukin — June 42 – June 44
Gen. V. N. Zhdanov — June 44 –

Sevastopol

INDEPENDENT MARITIME ARMY

4th Air Army
(Transferred to 2nd BELORUSSIAN FRONT in April 44)
Gen. K. A. Vershinin — May – Sept. 42
Gen. N. F. Naumenko — Sept. 42 – May 43
Gen. K. A. Vershinin — May 43 –

153

The Soviet Air Command Structure c. 1943

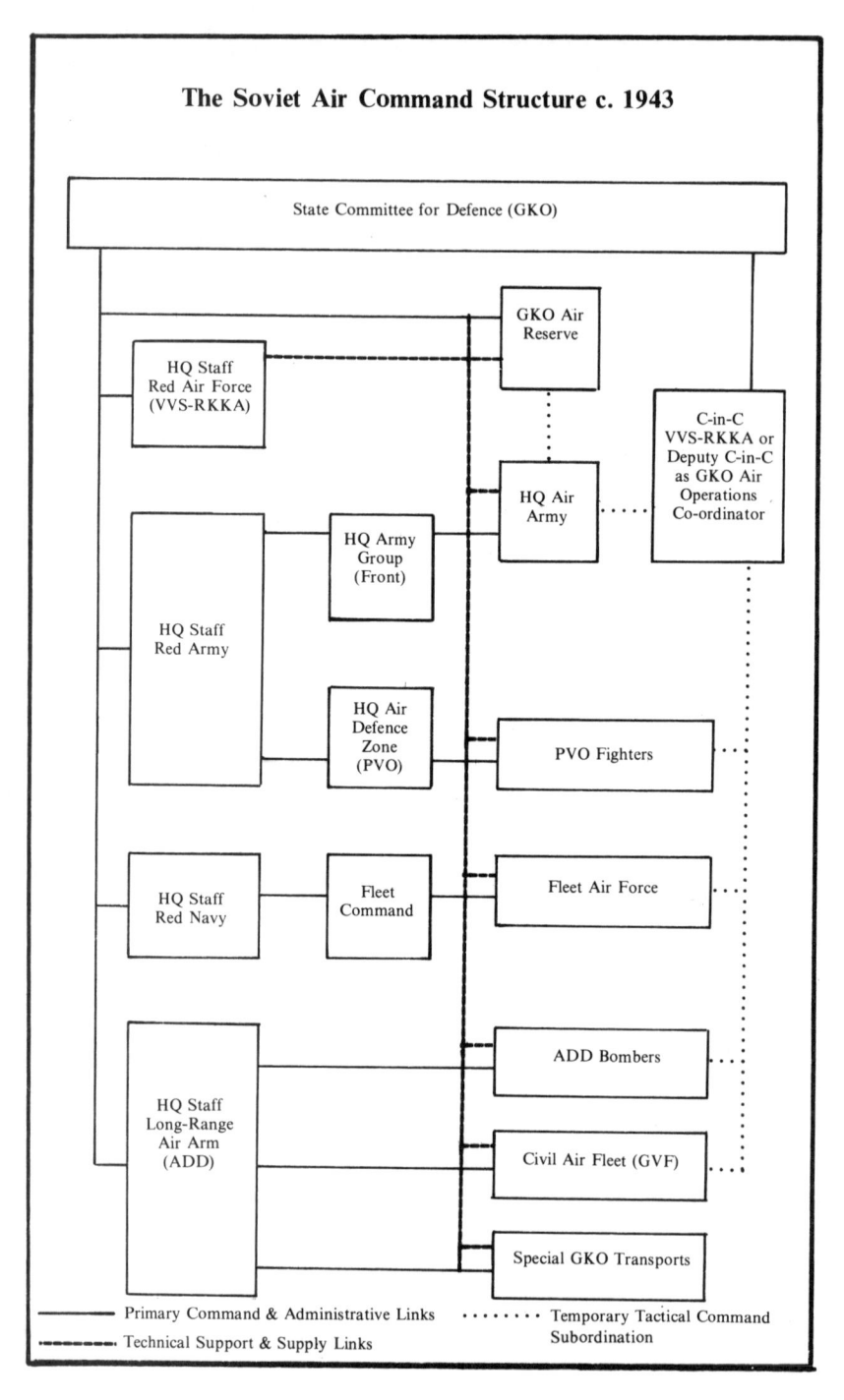

```
                    State Committee for Defence (GKO)
                                  │
        ┌─────────────────────────┼──────────────────────┐
        │                         │                      │
        │                    GKO Air                     │
        │                    Reserve                     │
   HQ Staff                       │                  C-in-C
   Red Air Force ─────────────────┤                  VVS-RKKA or
   (VVS-RKKA)                     │                  Deputy C-in-C
        │                    HQ Air                  as GKO Air
        │                    Army                    Operations
        │                                            Co-ordinator
        │              HQ Army
        │              Group
        │              (Front)
   HQ Staff
   Red Army
        │              HQ Air
        │              Defence
        │              Zone              PVO Fighters
        │              (PVO)
        │
        │              Fleet
   HQ Staff            Command           Fleet Air Force
   Red Navy
        │
        │                                ADD Bombers
   HQ Staff
   Long-Range
   Air Arm                               Civil Air Fleet (GVF)
   (ADD)
        │
        │                                Special GKO Transports
```

─────── Primary Command & Administrative Links   ········ Temporary Tactical Command
─ ─ ─ ─ Technical Support & Supply Links   Subordination

10 Directive No. 41

Spring was late in 1942 and when it came at last in May it did not smile on the fortunes of the Red Army, German resistance at Demyansk went unbroken and in an attempt to retake Khar'kov 240,000 Soviet troops were lost to the German pincers. This was not only a blow to Soviet manpower reserves; the victory at Khar'kov secured for Hitler the Donets Basin as a staging area for his planned summer offensive in the South, his Directive No. 41 of 5 April having called for a concentration of all available forces there with the ultimate objective of destroying the remaining Soviet armies west of the Don and seizing the rich prize of the Caucasian oilfields. The first phase of this campaign was to be the complete occupation of the Crimea and the reduction of its stronghold at Sevastopol. Sevastopol, with its reputation as the world's most impregnable naval base, had already been detailed for special attention in Hitler's Directive No. 39 the previous December, and its capture would not only secure the entire peninsula as an area behind the German front but also guarantee the whole southern flank against any Soviet naval or air interdiction as well as releasing the German 11th Army for operations elsewhere.

The *Luftwaffe*, aided by a formidable array of siege artillery and mortars, was given a leading role in the storming of the steel and concrete bastions guarding the Sevastopol roadstead. Richthofen's VIII *Fliegerkorps* was moved south from Air Command East[1] in the Centre to replace the hitherto ineffectual Special Air Staff Crimea formed under *Luftflotte* 4, and presided over the final route of Soviet

---

[1] After the transfer of *Luftflotte* 2 headquarters and II *Fliegerkorps* to Italy in November 1941, Army Group Centre was left with the support of *VIII Fliegerkorps*. In April 1942 an Air Command East was set up in the Centre, briefly under VIII *Fliegerkorps* headquarters, and then, after the latter's transfer south, under the Luftwaffe High Command.

Soviet Air Force

incursions on the Kerch Peninsula before giving its undivided attention to the smashing of Sevastopol itself. Only meagre Soviet air resources consisting of some seventy aircraft of the Black Sea Fleet Air Force under Major General Yermachenkov[2] and General Beletski's Special Crimean VVS Command were left to impede the work of the powerful VIII *Fliegerkorps* whose operations were directed by Richthofen from his headquarters in the ancient khans' palace at Bakhchisarai. The remaining Soviet airfield at Khersones was under unflagging German observation and the dust clouds raised by Russian aircraft taking off were the cue for German artillery to open fire on predetermined co-ordinates while patrolling Bf 109 fighters were directed by radio to pick off survivors. The Soviet airfields at Rostov and at Krasnodar, Anapa, Gelendzhik, Tuapse and Poti along the eastern Black Sea coast were in a better position to lend air support, but the *Luftwaffe* was able to keep them under constant surveillance and intercept raiders over the sea before they had even reached the Crimea.

On 2 June VIII *Fliegerkorps* began a massive softening-up operation against Sevastopol and its garrison with 723 machines airborne and virtually no Soviet air opposition. Over the next four days an average of 580 *Luftwaffe* machines a day took part in the devastating air raids, pounding the Sevastopol forts with 2,264 tons of high-explosive and 23,800 incendiary bombs. Once fuelled, the Ju 88 and Ju 87 bombers could fly three or four strikes from their bases at Saki and Nikolaev without their crews even leaving their machines[3]. On 7 June the ground assault, *Unternehmen Störfang* (Operational Sturgeon Catch), was launched with continued and full *Luftwaffe* participation. During the latter stages of the siege with complete German control of all land and sea approaches, attempts were made to supply the Sevastopol garrison by air using Black Sea Fleet Air Force transports based in the North Caucasus augmented by twenty Li-2 transports from Mosolov's Moscow-based Special Purpose Transport Command. Without escorts, running the gauntlet of patrolling night fighters and flak, 288 night supply flights were flown between 21 June and 1 July when Soviet resistance finally

---

[2] Yermachenkov, formerly Commander of the Baltic Fleet Air Force, replaced Major General Ostryakov in April after the latter was killed in a Luftwaffe raid over Sevastopol.

[3] Plocher *The German Air Force versus Russia*, 1942.

Directive No. 41

collapsed[4]. One hundred and forty-one Soviet aircraft were claimed by the Germans during the siege of Sevastopol for the loss of thirty-one *Luftwaffe* machines[5].

Timoshenko's ill-fated spring offensive to retake Khar'kov in May had been supported by the air forces of the South-Western and Southern Fronts, but neither Astakhov or Vershinin had been able to provide adequate backing or protect the encircled Soviet troops from a ruthless bombardment by Pflugbeil's IV *Fliegerkorps*. When the 8th Air Army was formed in June, Astakhov was retired from his air command and sent back to Moscow. His successor, Lt. General Khryukin, previously Air Commander on the remote Karelian Front, was thirty-two — a veteran of Spain and China and already a Hero of the Soviet Union. For Vershinin, ten years his senior, who retained command on the Southern Front when the 4th Air Army was formed in May[6] the recent past was less illustrious. A youthful soldier in the Russian Civil War, Vershinin had been transplanted from the infantry and after graduating from the Zhukovski Air Force Academy in 1932 held various Red Air Force command positions until the waves of Stalin's purges had cast him aside. Reinstated in the dark autumn of 1941, Vershinin was to establish a reputation as a resilient and untiring air commander over the long, dispiriting and dusty summer of 1942.

The 4th and 8th Air Armies were composed of three *shturmovik*, three bomber and five fighter divisions together with eight other air regiments — rather less than 600 combat aircraft in all — to counter the combined strength of IV and VIII *Fliegerkorps*. The Stalingrad Front under Timoshenko was declared on 12 July and two days later the order came for the 8th Air Army to withdraw to the east bank of the Don in preparation for the German attempt to establish bridgeheads. Under incessant *Luftwaffe* attack, the withdrawal soon became a débacle. Bowsers, trucks and equipment were destroyed by enemy action or simply abandoned. Unserviceable aircraft, stores of petrol, oil and tyres had to be burned before they could fall into enemy hands. When the Germans captured the Don bridge at Kalach, the disorganised 8th Air Army was further required to throw

---

[4]Grazhdanskaya Aviatsiya v SSSR, 1917-67.
[5]Plocher *The German Air Force versus Russia*, 1942.
[6]The 4th Air Army was officially formed on 22 May 1942 with 208 aircraft and 437 aircrew, the preliminary organisational work being carried out by General Naumenko. By July its strength had been raised to 400 aircraft.

Soviet Air Force

in all its resources and once more formations of up to 160 bombers, mostly SBs and R-5s, were sent in full daylight to be massacred by the flak and the fighters of JG 3 'Udet'. They were joined by the GKO's 'Special Group No. 1' consisting of two picked fighter regiments and Polbin's 150th Bomber Regiment with Pe-2 dive-bombers, but to no avail. For the first time in this air battle a special forward air command post was set up, linked by radio with the main air army headquarters and manned by a special team under the Deputy Air Army Commander. It was a system that was to be developed and successfully applied at Stalingrad in the months ahead.

To the south Rostov fell after desperate resistance to von Kleist's panzers supported by IV *Fliegerkorps* and again the battle focussed on the Don crossings. The 4th and 5th Air Armies, the latter assembled from remaining air elements in the North Caucasus Military District and containing about two hundred aircraft, fell back into the bleak Sal'sk Steppe and could do little to stop the triumphant German drive towards the oilfields in August. The confusion fully equalled the panic of the previous summer. Reconnaissance sorties were flown whenever possible to try to discover the speed and direction of the German thrusts, but pilots frequently lost their way or were unable to fix the locations of the German units they had seen. One squadron leader in the 88th Fighter Regiment landed his I-16 beside a Russian column on the march to ask his whereabouts but fortunately he did not switch off his engine. Shouts from the column that they were prisoners-of-war sent him running back to his machine under a fusilade of bullets from the German guards[7].

On 5 August the Stalingrad Front, now over 700 kilometres long, was split into the South-Eastern Front to the south of the city supported by the 8th Air Army with 300 aircraft, and a new Stalingrad Front to the north-west to which the 16th Air Army was attached. As the Germans pressed forwards towards the Volga, the fronts were again retitled. On 29 September the South-Eastern became the Stalingrad Front, while the ex-Stalingrad became the Don Front where General Stepanov was replaced by General Rudenko as the 16th Air Army Commander. In October a new South-Western Front was formed linking the Don to the Voronezh Front and with yet another new air army, the 17th under General Krasovski. Although VIII *Fliegerkorps* supporting the German 6th

---

[7] Chetvyortaya Vozdushnaya Armiya.

Directive No. 41

Army was faced, on paper, with three Soviet air armies, all three were enfeebled, poorly equipped and still preoccupied in constructing the airfields and support facilities they needed. When Richthofen's Ju 88 and He 111 bombers burned the city of Stalingrad they met little of the fierce fighter opposition encountered over Moscow and the few operational Soviet airfields were easily kept under observation and attack.

Often obliged to release elements in support of IV *Fliegerkorps* to the south or assist German units on the Voronezh Front, VIII *Fliegerkorps* was otherwise fully committed to the struggle for the ruins of Stalingrad, pounding the Soviet positions on the west bank of the Volga and harassing the life-line ferries which supplied them. This total tactical absorption mitigated, as it had done during the Battle of Moscow, against operations of a more strategic nature. Strikes against Soviet supply routes to Stalingrad from the east and against Astrakhan, Kamyshin and Saratov — vital staging points for supplying the Stalingrad and Don Fronts — were only half-hearted due to the growing shortage of bombs and ammunition. Yet again, as before Moscow, the fall of the desired objective to German ground forces semed so close and so inevitable.

The Soviets, for their part, offered little serious fighter interdiction, refusing to fritter away their precious aircraft in small-scale air battles against superior odds. Instead reserves were built up with feverish speed, the 8th Air Army alone receiving 984 new aircraft between September and November. Everything possible was done to ensure full air support for the Soviet counter-offensive once German energies had begun to flag; new bases were constructed, decoy airfields prepared[8], air regiments reinforced and machines overhauled and replaced. In readiness for the counter-offensive, Colonel General Novikov accompanied by the C-in-C ADD, General Golovanov, was sent to Stalingrad to supervise and co-ordinate the work of the air armies. From now on Novikov's main function was that of GKO air representative working closely with Zhukov. Drawing on the lessons learned in the battles for the Don, Novikov instructed Rudenko to set up a forward command headquarters under General Zhdanov, the Air Commander on the

---

[8]Nineteen decoy fields and twenty-five operational ones were built by the 8th Air Army alone. The Soviets used decoy airfields extensively throughout the war, often reverting or proceeding to use them operationally once their decoy function had been discovered.

159

Soviet Air Force

Leningrad Front transferred to serve as Rudenko's deputy, who worked with a team of reserve air regiment commanders in organising the most immediate and effective air support required by the frontline.

When the trap was sprung and the Soviet counter-offensive opened on the South-Western and Don Fronts on 19 November and on the Stalingrad Front itself a day later, the 8th, 16th and 17th Air Armies with elements of the 2nd Air Army on the adjoining Voronezh Front, ADD support and two mixed air corps and seven air divisions from the GKO Reserve had 1,414 aircraft at their disposal, of which 575 were *shturmoviks* and 426 U-2, R-5 and SB-2 night-bombers. During the Battle of Stalingrad 47% of all bomber sorties were made at night by ADD and VVS units, mostly by U-2 biplanes in the LNB light night-bomber form[9] with their crew of two. The LNBs, frail, slow and unarmed but for their small loads of bombs or grenades, were the true heroes of Soviet air endeavour during the summer of 1942 and in the first phase of the Stalingrad Battle, and they continued to be used extensively throughout the war. From two to six sorties were flown each night, the LNBs taking off and making their way towards the target area at timed intervals and carrying out bombing runs from different directions, usually at heights under a thousand metres, in the hope of confusing enemy flak. The increasing amount of Soviet nocturnal air activity, most threateningly in partisan support and supply flights, impelled the Germans to form special 'flak circuses' with between one and two dozen 37 mm antiaircraft guns supported by a searchlight platoon. The 'flak circus' remained hidden by day and moved into a predicated area for Soviet air attack shortly after dusk to lie in wait for the *Nähmashinen* or 'sewing-machines', the *Wehrmacht*'s nick-name for the U-2 which was characterised by the distinctive popping of its five-cylinder radial engine. When the degree of Soviet night-bomber activity became even more uncomfortable, rail-transported radars and fighter control teams were brought in to direct *Luftwaffe* night-fighters onto the intruders. This, however, did not deter the Russians and radars turned out to be of little use in picking up the U-2 with its largely plywood and fabric construction. The normal direction of German-

---

[9]The LNB was similar to the U-2VS light day-bomber but lacked the latter's ShKAS machine-gun mounted in the rear cockpit. Another development, the LSh light *shturmovik*, was armed with four RS 82 rockets in place of the four 50 kg bombs carried by the U-2VS and the LNB.

Directive No. 41

Soviet plagiarism was reversed for once when the *Luftwaffe* formed its own *Nachtschlachtgruppen* in October 1942. Equipped with obsolete Fw 58, Ar 66, He 45, He 46 and Go 145 machines as well as the Fi 156 *Storch* normally used for liaison and artillery-spotting, these 'flying museums' recruited from flying schools were to be used even more extensively in 1943 during anti-partisan operations.

Air activity at the start of the Stalingrad counter-offensive was badly impeded by low cloud and fog with only occasional reconnaissance sorties and raids by small groups of *shturmoviks*, mainly against enemy airfields, being undertaken. In any case, Novikov was holding back his resources until the Soviet pincers had snapped to at Kalach on 23 November trapping the German forces between the Volga and the Don. Thereafter all air power was used fully against the encircled German 6th Army, a special effort being demanded from the 8th Air Army on 20 December against Manstein's relief spearhead while the rest of the 8th and the 16th Air Armies directed their assaults against the pocket itself. The *Luftwaffe* had started to make supply flights into the Stalingrad pocket on 25 November using Ju 52/3m transports from Tatsinskaya airfield, some 240 km to the west, but on 30 November VIII *Fliegerkorps* was instructed to order KG 27 and KG 55 at Morozovsk to undertake additional supply flights using their He 111 bombers as transports in an effort to deliver a daily 300 tons of food, ammunition and medical supplies promised to the Sixth Army[10]. In spite of objections raised by Richthofen[11] as to the feasibility of this undertaking with the quantity of material specified, the numbers of transport aircraft available and the uncertain duration of the airlift, he was overruled. Göring's fateful decision to mount such an ambitious airlift was influenced not only by Demyansk earlier in the year, but also by the fact that VIII *Fliegerkorps* had already used nine Ju 52/3m *Gruppen* and a He 111 *Gruppe* to fly supplies to advance elements of the 4th Panzer and 6th Armies as well as forward *Luftwaffe* units during the

---

[10]The requirements of the encircled forces at Stalingrad were fixed first at 750 tons, then at 500 tons a day. At a conference between Göring and Jeschonnek held on 23 November a goal of 350 tons a day was proposed. Morzik *German Air Force Airlift Operations*, p 185.

[11]Richthofen had assumed command of *Luftflotte* 4 to 19 July 1942 and handed over command of VIII *Fliegerkorps* to General Fiebig.

Soviet Air Force

battles for the Don[12]. The Soviets were fully aware that a successful resolution of their encirclement would depend on denying supplies to the trapped 6th Army once the odds against a breakthrough from the west or a breakout from within the pocket had been sufficiently reduced. On 4 December Novikov telegraphed his air commanders that, 'although we hold complete air superiority over the area of encirclement, German transports are still getting through and landing inside the pocket.....The destruction of the enemy transports is our prime concern'.[13] Day and night attacks on the airfields inside the pocket and the interception of transports along the approach corridors were this time reinforced by ADD raids against the main German supply bases at Voroshilovgrad (Lugansk), Novocherkassk and Rostov. The Soviet had learned the lessons of Demyansk. The well-armed and faster He 111 formations were rarely molested in any determined fashion, but the slower Ju 52/3m and Ju 86 transports suffered increasing losses. By 9 December, thirty-two Ju 52/3m transports had been lost and a further eleven rendered unoperational due to combat damage while the He 111 *Gruppen* had lost fifteen of their aircraft[14]. Soviet fighters, for so long hounded by the *Luftwaffe*, now enjoyed their first taste of revenge. On 28 November three Yak-1 fighters of the 287th Fighter Division intercepted and shot down four Ju 52/3m transports, and on 11 December sixteen Ju 52/3m transports escorted by four Bf 109 fighters were attacked by eight La-5 and nine Yak-1 fighters of the 235th Fighter Division[15] and nine of the transports brought down. The Soviet fighter-pilots had a field-day. They could spot the German transports as they approached and, after a leisurely take-off and with full tanks, attack at will. Even Il-2 *shturmoviks* were used to destroy the lumbering Ju 52/3m trimotors.

On the ground the Red Army's task was to deny the *Luftwaffe* its staging bases nearest to the pocket. On 23 December the Soviet advance on Morozovsk necessitated a partial evacuation to Novocherkassk with some of the He 111 bombers remaining to stem

---

[12]These entailed the delivery of 33,397 tons of *Wehrmacht* and 9,233 tons of *Luftwaffe* supplies, the transportation of 27,044 troops to the front and the evacuation of 51,018 wounded. Plocher *The German Air Force versus Russia, 1942.*

[13]From *Vozdushnaya blokada* in *Aviatsiya i Kosmonavtika*, January 1973.

[14]Plocher *The German Air Force versus Russia, 1942.*

[15]The 235th Fighter Division, re-equipped with the first La-5 fighters, was detached from Beletski's I Fighter Corps on the Kalinin Front.

Directive No. 41

the Russian tanks. The following day shells fell on Tatsinskaya where, after an agonising delay while instructions were sought, a hasty evacuation took place. A hundred and eight Ju 52/3m and sixteen Ju 86 transports were saved, miraculously, out of a total of one hundred and eighty transports, the staff of VIII *Fliegerkorps* being the last to leave under enemy fire[16]. After evacuation to Rostov and Sal'sk, the Ju 52/3m transports were regrouped on the latter airfield, some 330 kms south-west of Stalingrad. Tatsinskaya was retaken from the Russians on 28 December, but its security as a transport base remained in danger and Sal'sk used therafter as the main Ju 52/3m base. On 2 January 1943 Morozovsk was abandoned, the He 111 bombers of KG 55 flying out in thick fog to Novercherkassk which was abandoned a week later for Taganrog, the headquarters of *Luftflotte* 4.

The He 111s flying 360 km from Novocherkassk, and ultimately 450 km from Taganrog, made one flight into the pocket a day. Although well defended from fighters in their formations, their simultaneous arrival at the relatively cramped airfields in the pocket created problems in rapid unloading and made them vulnerable to *shturmovik* attacks. The Ju 52/3m transports, able to operate by night only, came under constant attack at Sal'sk by the ubiquitous night-bombers of the 4th Air Army. By day the *shturmoviks* were becoming bolder, drawn by the over-crowded airfields the *Luftwaffe* was obliged to use. Fighter escorts could no longer be provided with the loss of airfields within their range of the pocket, and the first nine Bf 109 and five Bf 110 fighters with long-range tanks only arrived at Stalingrad on 27 January, too late to be of any use. When Air Marshal Milch arrived at Richthofen's headquarters on 16 January, he found the situation worse than he had imagined. Very few of the transport aircraft remained operational, Sal'sk had been abandoned for Zverevo, which had no facilities for either aircraft or personnel, and Pitomnik airfield — the main supply airfield inside the pocket — had fallen to the Soviets. The increase in supply rate hoped for when larger transport aircraft had been allocated to the airlift had not materialised[17]. Under Milch's energetic measures, supplies into the

---

[16]The Soviets had hoped to catch all the Junkers transports on the ground and use ramming by tanks to immobilise them.

[17]These included eighteen four-engined Fw 200 patrol bombers brought from France and flying from Stalino, He 177 bombers undergoing winter trials at Zaporozh'e and a special transport unit consisting of seven Ju 90s, two Ju 290s, a Ju 252 and a Fw 200B.

163

pocket resumed, this time to Gumrak airfield. When Gumrak airfield fell to the Soviets on 21 January air drops were maintained until 3 February, by which time all resistance in the pocket had been extinguished and Field Marshal Paulus and his staff had surrendered.

The losses in *Luftwaffe* transports had been serious, and six hundred aircraft had been taken from flying schools to serve at Stalingrad, many of them — as were the VIP transports also appropriated — quite unsuitable for the winter operations they encountered. In all, between 24 November and 31 January, the *Luftwaffe* had lost 488 aircraft[18] and around a thousand aircrew. An average daily supply of 116 tons had been flown in over the seventy-two days and nights of the airlift — a total of 8,350 tons.

This blow to the *Luftwaffe*, equivalent to losing an entire *Fliegerkorps*, did not signify the end of German air supremacy as the Soviets were to discover in the spring of 1943 when their main efforts were directed at trying to dislodge the enemy from the North Caucasus. There General Vershinin, who had been appointed Air Commander for the Caucasian Front in September 1942 after temporarily handing over his 4th Air Army to the command of his deputy, General Naumenko[19], had some six hundred aircraft at his disposal including those of the 4th and Goryunov's 5th Air Army, elements of the Black Sea Fleet Air Force and ADD units under Golovanov's deputy, General Skripko. The disaster at Stalingrad made a German withdrawal back behind the Kuban prudent, but when the Soviets attempted to establish a beachhead just south of the Kuban near Novorossiisk the *Luftwaffe* responded with heavy air attacks launched by I *Fliegerkorps*. When the Russians sought to defend the beachhead, large-scale air battles broke out on 17 April. Determined to gain air superiority, the GKO reinforced Vershinin with Ushakov's II Bomber Corps, Savitski's III Fighter Corps and

---

[18]This figure included 266 Ju 52/3m, 165 He 111, 42 Ju 86, nine Fw 200, five He 177 and one Ju 290 aircraft of which there were 166 complete losses, 214 machines damaged beyond repair and 108 missing — a high proportion of these due to airfield accidents, weather conditions and mechanical failure. The Soviets later renovated 80 Ju 52/3m transports abandoned in the pocket and used them for GVF duties in Siberia. See *Grazhdanskaya Aviatsiya v SSSR*, p 142.

[19]Naumenko was officially made Commander of the 4th Air Army in February 1943. When Vershinin returned to take command in May, Naumenko was sent to the Bryansk Front to take over the 15th Air Army in preparation for the expected German offensive against the Kursk salient.

Directive No. 41

Yeremenko's II Mixed Air Corps together with other reserve elements on 20 April, bringing Soviet air strength up to nine hundred aircraft, including 370 fighters, 170 *shturmoviks*, 165 day and 195 night bombers. As many new types as possible were committed to the Kuban air battles, and the Germans noted a high proportion of Lend-Lease aircraft, including British Spitfires and American P-39 Aeracobras in action. Novikov, despatched by the *Stavka* to supervise air operations, attained periods of air superiority but was unable to retain it. The great weakness was in the performance of the Soviet fighters, often as a result of scrappy ground control and guidance. To remedy this Vershinin sent General Borman, Commander of the 216th Fighter Division, to co-ordinate and direct fighter operations from a forward fighter command post as his Special Deputy. Before his recall from the Kuban and appointment as Commander of the First PVO Fighter Army defending Moscow, Borman made a number of proposals regarding fighter control methods; these included his belief that centralised fighter control from an advanced command post to direct resources along the main line of thrust was advantageous, that an adequate system of radio relays was essential to ensure fighter control over a wide battle area, and that air command posts needed to be adequately defended and dug-in. Many of Borman's ideas were later applied at the Battle of Kursk.

Air operations on both sides were hampered by the spring rains which turned airstrips and roads into quagmires and by the utter lack of well equipped airfields from which to operate. The humble night-bomber was widely used in the battles over the Kuban and Kerch Straits, one of the regiments, the 588th (later 46th Guards) Women's Night-Bomber Regiment, being crewed entirely by young women. This air regiment, one of three women's air regiments[20], was

---

[20] The three women's air regiments were formed in late 1941 by Marina Raskova drawing on *Osoaviakhim* instructresses, women GVF pilots and navigators and a number of women already serving in the air force. These were the 588th (46th Guards) Night Bomber Regiment, the 586th Fighter Regiment which flew Yak fighters and formed part of Saratov's PVO defences during the Battle of Stalingrad, and the 587th (125th Guards) Bomber Regiment, first trained on Su-2s but ultimately operational on Pe-2s with mixed crews and male command staff. Other women flew in predominantly male air regiments, like Lidiya Litvyak, the Soviet girl fighter ace who was credited with twelve victories before being shot down and killed in 1943 at the age of twenty-two, served as ferry pilots or flew transports for GVF. Thirty women were made Heroes of the Soviet Union during the war; in addition to the twenty-three awards made to the 46th Guards Night Bomber Regiment and five to the 125th Bomber Regiment, two women *shturmovik* pilots were so decorated.

assembled and trained at Engels and, since most of the pilots had flown the U-2 as flying instructors with *Osoaviakhim,* it was ready for operations late in May 1942 when it was sent to join the 4th Air Army's 218th Night Bomber Divison. Raids over the German lines were begun in June and continued until the end of the war when some 24,000 sorties had been flown. For the young pilots and navigators the raids were a perpetual ordeal. Exposed in their open cockpits to the mercies of wind and rain as their LNBs crawled through the sky at 100 kph, they were an easy prey if caught by prowling night-fighters. Darkness was their only protection and once picked out by the vigilant searchlights or caught against a light sky by a fighter their only recourse was to sideslip out of the beam or sham dead in the hope of pulling out of their spin near the ground. One of the regiment's specialities was the bombing of the 'flak circuses' themselves, with one LNB drawing the flak while its companion slipped in undetected to bomb the guns and searchlights. Losses were not infrequent and in spite of the girls' attempts to copy the grim stoicism of their male counterparts, deeply felt. The bond between a pilot and a navigator who risked their lives together nightly and who were intimately interdependent for surivival was especially strong[21].

In the renewed Soviet offensive on 26 May, 188 bombers and *shturmoviks* and 150 fighters were thrown against the Kuban, and after 380 night-bombers had carried out raids on 28-29 May the Soviet ground attacks were supported by 465 aircraft. The battles continued until August when the setback at Kursk and the worsening German position in the Ukraine made an evacuation of the Kuban area inevitable. In October 1943, as the Kuban was being evacuated, plans were already being made by the Germans to evacuate the Crimea. It was not, however, until April 1944 when the Crimea had been in German hands for nearly two years that it was re-occupied by Soviet forces with the 4th Air Army flying in support of the Independent Coastal Army's attack across the Kerch Straits while the 8th Air Army on the Fourth Ukrainian Front struck southwards along the Perekop Peninsula.

But these were by now side issues. As the spring of 1943 moved into summer attention was again focussed on the Centre where Hitler was preparing to light the 'beacon' which would illuminate the way to ultimate victory in the East.

---

[21] *V Nebe Frontovom* is the most comprehensive account of the three women's air regiments yet to appear.

11 The Falcons Swarm

The spring of 1943 brought a dramatic increase in the size of the Red Air Force, from 3,200 machines in November 1942 to 8,300 by July 1943 — over twice the size of the *Luftwaffe* on the Eastern Front. This was due not only to the output of the now re-established aircraft industry but also to the military air supplied by the Western Allies. Under the terms of the four Protocol Agreements almost 20,000 aircraft were supplied to the USSR by the USA and Great Britain between 1941 and 1945, the USA supplying 14,833 aircraft, including 2,999 on Britain's account, while Britain sent 4,570 aircraft of her own manufacture and reshipped over 200 American machines[1].

Even before the full measure of Soviet air losses became known, pledges of aid were made by Prime Minister Winston Churchill who promised the Russians 400 fighters, half Hurricanes and half P-40s supplied or to be supplied to Britain, while President Roosevelt promised forty P-40 fighters and five B-25 twin-engined bombers as the precursors of more substantial deliveries of the P-39. More P-39 fighters were supplied than any other lend-lease type — in all 4,750 machines representing almost half the total production went to the USSR. Nicknamed *britchik* or 'little shaver', the P-39 proved ideal as a fighter-*shturmovik*, and its 37mm cannon firing through the propeller hub was emulated by similar installations on the LaGG-3 and eventually on the Yak-9T. The P-39 was flown by Aleksandr Pokryshkin, credited as the second highest-scoring Soviet fighter ace with fifty-nine victories, but recovery from flat spins remained one of the fighter's most serious failings. In 1943 the NII-VVS test-pilot Andrei Kochetkov was sent to the USA to carry out flight tests in

---

[1] For a more detailed appraisal of aircraft supplied to the USSR under Lend-Lease see *Foreign Aircraft in Russian Service* by J. P. Alexander and D.J. Voaden in *Air Pictorial*, January 1960.

consultation with Bell engineers at Buffalo, remaining there on detachment for over a year[2].

The P-39's development, the P-63 Kingcobra, was also supplied in quantity to the USSR in 1944 and 1945 — a total of 2,421 examples representing over two-thirds of the number produced. As Soviet fighter production was by this time fully capable of meeting the needs of the Red Air Force, many P-63s were used to re-equip the Far Eastern Air Force and saw action against the Japanese in 1945. The P-40 proved far less acceptable to the Soviets although 2,097 examples were supplied, 1,800 of these by the end of March 1944. Considered very much a 'cast-off' from the Allied Air Forces, most of the P-40s were sent to serve with interior PVO districts or put to work as fighter trainers. About two hundred P-47 Thunderbolt fighters were sent to the USSR in 1944-45, and other types supplied by the USA during the course of the war included 2,908 A-20 Havoc light and 825 B-25 Mitchell medium bombers, 707 C-47 transports, 185 PBY-6A amphibians and PBN-1 flying boats and some eighty AT-6 trainers[3]. From 1943 onwards, the Soviets were more enthusiastic about receiving bombers and transports than fighters — the B-25 deliveries going almost exclusively to ADD regiments and the C-47s acting as an invaluable addition to the USSR's inadequate production of transport aircraft.

The British contribution consisted largely of 2,950 Hurricane fighters, almost a quarter of the total built in Britain and Canada, but a specific request for Spitfires in October 1942 was met by the delivery of 143 Spitfire VB fighters by March the following year, most of which saw action in the air battles over the Kuban. They were followed by 1,188 Spitfire IX fighters between the summer of 1944 and the spring of 1945 when production was maintained exclusively for the USSR. A request for Mosquito bombers made by the Soviets in 1943 was not met, however, and none were sent to the USSR.

Supply routes for the delivery of aircraft under Lend-Lease were by water on the North Russian convoys to Akhangel'sk or Murmansk, to the Persian Gulf for collection by Soviet ferry pilots at Abadan or Basrah, by air over the South Atlantic Ferry Route or over the

---

[2] See Kovalev's article *Pryzhok nad Niagrom* in *Aviatsiya i Kosmonavtika*, September 1970.

[3] An earlier version of the PBY-6A 'Catalina', the PBY-4, had been placed in licence-production in the USSR in 1939 as the GST. The C-47 (DC-3) was licence-built as the PS-84 (Li-2).

Alaskan-Siberian Ferry Route established in 1943. In 1942 the North Russian convoy route was the most immediate mode of delivery but was highly vulnerable to enemy interdiction; convoy PQ 16 which sailed in May 1942 lost 77 of its cargo of 201 aircraft and convoy PQ 17 suffered even greater losses, delivering only 87 of the 297 aircraft it carried. Most of the American bombers were flown over the South Atlantic from Florida to Abadan on the Persian Gulf, but from the summer of 1943[4] the most heavily used route was via Alaska with Soviet pilots collecting the aircraft at Fairbanks.

The Soviets have tended to disparage the contribution made by Lend-Lease to the resurgence of their air power and, in the case of fighters where the latter half of the war saw the plentiful supply of Soviet machines of equal or superior quality, assistance from the West was clearly not essential. As regards day bombers and transports, of which the Soviets remained permanently in need, such an attitude is less defensible. In spirit, it is a poor return for the heroic and tragic sacrifices of the northern convoys to the USSR in its hour of need.

The Soviet counter-offensives over the winter of 1942-43 had not only led to the German defeat at Stalingrad and an eventual evacuation of the Kuban, putting an end to Hitler's dream of possessing the Caucasian oil-fields, they had also driven a blunted wedge between Kluge's Army Group Centre and Manstein's Army Group South forming a salient with the city of Kursk at its centre. This was to be the decisive battleground on the Eastern Front in 1943 and witness Hitler's last desperate gamble to annihilate the unkillable Red Army. The Battle of Kursk was to become legendary as the most crucial and concentrated confrontation of German and Soviet armour, and yet it was also a decisive air battle involving almost five thousand combat aircraft whose outcome was to be as portentous as that of the struggle between the Tigers and the T-34s below.

Once again the *Luftwaffe* was to spearhead the irresistible thrust of the panzers, to sweep the Red Air Force from the sky and lay waste the advancing waves of Soviet infantry and tanks. It braced itself to meet Hitler's demands with depleted resources. There were fewer

---

[4]The Trans-Siberian Ferry Route was set up in 1943 under the command of Lt. General I.S. Semyonov, formerly deputy head of GVF. In 1944 he was replaced by the Chief of ADD Staff, Lt. General Shevelev. By 31 March 1944 3,442 aircraft had been delivered via the Alaskan-Siberian Ferry Route compared with 2,882 and 1,142 by water to the Persian Gulf and North Russia and 810 over the South Atlantic Ferry Route. By the end of the war over half the aircraft supplied to the USSR by the USA under Lend-Lease had been delivered over the Alaskan-Siberian Ferry Route.

Soviet Air Force

combat aircraft available on the Eastern Front than the summer before and many of the veterans of Barbarossa had already found unmarked graves in the snow, mud and dust of the Russian plain. The Red Air Force it confronted was not the air force of June 1941. Bitter experience, the costly lessons of defeat, had been absorbed and morale had been raised by the victories over the Volga and Kuban. New aircraft were flowing from the factories and arriving from the Western Allies to replace the vulnerable and ineffectual fighters and bombers with which the Red Air Force had been obliged to meet the *Luftwaffe* during the harassed withdrawals and retreats of 1942. Both Hitler and Stalin resolved to exploit the Kursk salient to strike a mortal blow in the Centre; Hitler by another surgical pincer operation to sever the salient and isolate the two fronts it contained — Rokossovski's Central Front in the north and Vatutin's Voronezh Front to the south, and Stalin by waiting for the German thrusts, absorbing them and replying with an even more ambitious encircling movement from the Western and Bryansk Fronts to the north of the salient and the South-Western Front immediately below it, supported by a counter-stroke from within the salient itself backed up by forces held expressly in reserve.

Hitler had planned his blow against the Kursk salient, code-named *Zitadelle* — for May, but it was postponed until June to allow Model's 9th Army which was to attack from the north and Hoth's 4th Panzer Army with Army Detachment Kempf which were to strike from the south to build up their tank forces. In June *Zitadelle* was again postponed with the news of the defeats in North Africa and Hitler's apprehensions as to subsequent Allied moves in the Mediterranean, and it was not until 2 July that the *Führer* informed his generals of his decision to begin *Zitadelle* in three days time. Their reactions were not enthusiastic. Several maintained, with justification, that *Zitadelle* had been delayed too long already and that the Soviets had been given the time necessary to prepare defences in depth and concentrate reserves. What they did not know, and what would have made them even less enthusiastic, was that Stalin had been closely informed of the progress of *Zitadelle* via the 'Lucy' spy-ring[5] and was confidently expecting the Germans to open their offensive against the Kursk

---

[5]'Lucy' was the code-name of Rudolph Rössler, an anti-Nazi German living in Switzerland and a Soviet agent. Rössler's spy ring consisted of officers highly placed in the OKW who supplied him with the latest top secret information for transmission directly to Moscow.

salient between 3 and 6 July. This invaluable intelligence enabled Stalin to plan well ahead, to rest, prepare and rehearse his troops, to overhaul and replace equipment and to reinforce the armies holding the salient as well as those designated to take the counter-offensive when the moment came. Meanwhile, as the preparations for *Zitadelle* went ahead, Hitler's generals in the East were becoming more and more uneasily aware of the degree to which the Soviet armaments industry had recuperated and expanded as new tanks and aircraft appeared in growing numbers. By May 1943, the Red Air Force was three times as large as it had been a year before and the percentage of obsolescent types in frontline service had fallen drastically.

Generaloberst von Greim, in command of *Luftwaffe* Command East (retitled *Luftflotte* 6 at the end of May 1943), advocated a more energetic and co-ordinated policy for the bombing of Soviet industrial targets but Jeschonnek could offer little assistance or support. From January 1943, on his own initiative, von Greim took temporary control of the bomber units attached to the neighbouring *Luftflotten* to augment his own in spasmodic raids over key industrial centres within range of the purely tactical bombers at his disposal. Targets associated with the aircraft industry which came under attack included the fighter plants at Gorky and Saratov, the synthetic rubber plant at Yaroslavl, and Rybinsk as a presumed key centre for aeroengine production, although in fact both major plants there had been evacuated. The *Stavka* took the threat seriously enough to create two PVO fronts, the Western with its headquarters in Moscow and the Eastern with its headquarters in Kuibyshev, and to divert a greater proportion of modern fighters into their PVO fighter divisions.[6] Stalin also directed that elements of the 1st, 2nd and 15th Air Armies should make specific strikes against twenty-eight *Luftwaffe* bomber bases in the Oryol-Bryansk and Khar'kov-Belgorod areas in collaboration with ADD night bombers between 8 and 10 June. As the summer progressed and *Zitadelle* became more imminent, von Greim was obliged to switch his bombers against airfields and railway junctions in the enemy rear to impede the

---

[6]Major-General Klimov's newly created Central PVO Fighter Aviation Staff was responsible for over 1,000 fighters on the Western PVO Front commanded by Colonel-General Gromadin, and for somewhat less than 500 on the Eastern PVO Front under Lieutenant-General Zashikhin. The strength of the Eastern PVO Front was soon reduced, however, and many of its resources diverted to reinforce frontal PVO forces during the Soviet advances from the autumn of 1943. The Soviet PVO fronts were twice reformed in 1944. See *Voiska protivovozdushnoi oborony.*

obvious build-up within the salient itself. On 2 and 3 June heavy concentrations of *Luftwaffe* bombers hit the vital rail junction at Kursk, inflicting considerable damage despite interception by fighters of the 101st PVO Fighter Division (shortly afterwards reformed as IX PVO Fighter Corps) responsible for the defence of the rear supply area. On 13 June the marshalling yards at Yelets were raided, and on 4 July, the eve of *Zitadelle*, supply depots and rail installations at Yelets and Valyuki feeding the salient were attacked.

The *Stavka* too was alive to the need to hinder German preparations and night raids by ADD units equipped with recently delivered Il-4 and Lend-Lease B-25 twin-engined bombers were directed against the most important rail centres serving the German fronts. On 3 May over a hundred ADD bombers attacked the rail junction at Minsk; the next night it was the turn of Orsha and then Gomel and Bryansk. On 21 July, in the aftermath of *Zitadelle*, ADD was able to send a hundred and fifty bombers against the railway installations at Bryansk to frustrate an orderly German withdrawal. Partisan units, larger and better-equipped, concentrated their attentions on railway lines and bridges making every journey by train across the German rear an ordeal, while the overcrowded sidings and junctions set up targets for ADD night raids. The partisan operations hampered German communications and required the allocation of men to deal with them, reducing German frontline strength although the operations were only marginally successful. Once delivered to the front to await the signal for *Zitadelle*, the German troops suffered the nightly attentions of seemingly innumerable U-2 night bombers which were rarely idle after dusk had fallen.

Luftwaffe bases were also kept under constant surveillance. Between 6 and 8 May a concerted series of strikes on seventeen airfields were made by 112 day bombers, 156 *shturmoviks* and 166 fighters. Six Soviet air armies contributed to this operation extending over five army fronts, in which a leading part was played by the 16th and 2nd Air Armies on the Central and Voronezh Fronts. Intermittent intruder raids against forward *Luftwaffe* airfields were kept up by these two air armies throughout the next two months. Both were commanded by men whose experience had been acquired in the Battle of Stalingrad; General Rudenko retaining command of the 16th Air Army and General Krasovski replacing General Smirnov in the command of the 2nd Air Army after handing over the 17th Air Army on the South-Western Front to General Sudets. To their immediate rear lay Konev's Reserve (later retitled Steppe) Front where five ground armies were supported by General Goryunov's 5th Air Army, reconstituted after its move from the North Caucasus where most of its air regiments had been transferred to Vershinin's 4th Air Army or the Black Sea Fleet Air Force. Rudenko and Krasovski were also reinforced by air corps from the GKO Air Reserve, the 16th Air Army receiving Yumashev's VI Fighter Corps, Karavitski's III Bomber Corps and Antoshkin's VI Composite Air Corps, while the 2nd Air Army was bolstered by Podgorny's IV Fighter Corps, Polbin's I Bomber Corps and Ryazanov's I *Shturmovik* Corps. Together with the flanking 17th Air Army and supporting ADD corps, some 2,500 to 3,000 Soviet aircraft were ready for the German offensive.

In one respect at least the Soviets were unprepared. The most threatening thrust was expected from the north, but *Luftflotte* 6 with bases in the Oryol-Bryansk region had only 730 aircraft of the 1st *Fliegerdivision* whereas *Luftflotte* 4 supporting Manstein in the south had 1,100 aircraft of VIII *Fliegerkorps* and the 1st Hungarian Air Division, although it had lost the experienced leadership of von Richthofen sent, despite Manstein's protests, to take command of *Luftflotte* 2 in Italy and replaced by General Dessloch. The Red Air Force held a clear numerical superiority, possessing twice as many fighters as the *Luftwaffe* — largely due to Zhukov's insistence that fighter strength should be substantially increased to meet the German offensive — and with many times the German number of ground attack aircraft. Only in its day bombers was the Red Air Force inferior with only about half the number available to the *Luftwaffe*. Soviet air operations against the *Wehrmacht* were, therefore, to rely heavily on the persistence of the newer, better-armed and better-engined *'Ilyushas'* (Il-2s) for success.

As at Stalingrad, overall co-ordination of air operations was the responsibility of Air Marshal Novikov, subordinate to Zhukov as Stalin's deputy, assisted by his First Deputy, General Vorozheikin, and his newly appointed Chief of Air Staff, General Khudyakov[7]. A network of secondary command and control centres was set up inside the salient and deputy air army commanders were posted to the headquarters of those ground armies primarily involved in meeting

---

[7] Khudyakov handed over command of the 1st Air Army, formerly the Western Front Air Command, to General Gromov in May 1943 and was made Colonel-General on taking up his new appointment as Chief of Air Staff.

the first onslaught of the German offensive — Rudenko's deputy, Major-General Kosykh, was stationed with the headquarters of Pukhov's 13th Army confronting Model with first priority in summoning air support and allocating strikes in the interests of Pukhov's army. Large numbers of auxiliary and emergency airstrips were prepared and existing airfields enlarged, one third of these as decoy or dummy fields to deceive the *Luftwaffe*. On the whole Soviet tactical fields were further back than those prepared by the *Luftwaffe* and while German *Staffeln* flew into airfields 18-20 kms behind the frontline on 4 July with some advanced fighter strips only five kilometres from the front, Soviet fighters were based 35-40 kms behind the front, *shturmoviks* 60-70 kms and bombers 120-130 kms to the rear of the frontline. While this was in accordance with the planned Soviet defence posture, it also showed a clear respect for the *Luftwaffe's* talent in hitting forward airfields unexpectedly and hard and it was preferred to maintain patrols of between eighteen to thirty fighters over the front rather than run the risk of losing fighters waiting on standby on frontal airstrips.

Final preparations included the designation and timing of *rendezvous* for fighter escorts, arrangements for co-operative support between neighbouring air armies, the allocation of call-signs and the readying of repair and recovery services. In general, the subdued level of *Luftwaffe* activity immediately prior to the breaking of *Zitadelle* enabled a good deal of preparatory work to be done, although, as events proved, not enough to prevent breakdowns in effective air control under pressure. In the waiting air regiments the political officers tuned the fighting spirit of their aircrews. When one pilot received a letter from relatives in recently reoccupied territory recounting the atrocities committed by the SS, the *politruk* read it aloud to the assembled unit and exhorted everyone to avenge themselves in the coming battle. Many aircraft carried slogans painted on the side of the fuselage in which the words 'vengeance' and 'dammed fascists' figured more frequently than expressions of patriotic zeal.

On 5 July 1943 the day dawned bright and warm, a typical languid summer's day in central Russia but one that was soon to be marred by the bursting of innumerable shells and smudged by the oily smoke from burning tanks and aircraft. On the dusty runways of Belgorod, Khar'kov, Poltava and Dniepropetrovsk the Ju 88 and He 111 bombers of VIII *Fliegerkorps* were lining up for take-off as the first waves of the *Zitadelle* air offensive when the wireless monitoring service reported a considerable increase in Soviet radio air traffic and soon afterwards the *Freya* radar at Khar'kov detected the approach of large air formations from the east. These formations contained 132 *shturmoviks* and 285 fighters of the 2nd and 17th Air Armies detailed to destroy the German bombers on the ground when their fighter escorts were not yet airborne. But the masterstroke was not to succeed. The Soviet regiments were intercepted by the Bf 109G fighters of JG 3 'Udet' and JG 52 scrambled from Khar'kov East and Mikoyanovka which claimed 120 victories in this opening air battle[8]. Even Soviet military historians have been obliged to indicate the magnitude of this initial setback. In the northern sector, the Germans reported that Soviet fighter reaction to 1st *Fliegerdivision* operations began only in the late afternoon and the Fw 190 fighters of JG 51 and JG 54 had claimed 110 Soviet aircraft by nightfall[9]. The commital of fighters to the abortive pre-emptive strike in the early morning left the Red Air Force unable to contest *Luftwaffe* supremacy on the south flank of the salient, and in the north Soviet replies to the *Luftwaffe* attacks were tardy and ineffectual. The two fighter corps designated to give frontline cover, Yumashev's VI Fighter Corps over the Central Front and Klimov's V Fighter Corps on the Voronezh Front proved quite unable to cope. Without adequate air cover, the Soviet ground forces lost confidence and the *Wehrmacht* began to make the rapid headway hoped for. Novikov had to give his first attention to the failings of his fighters and as a result of his investigations Yumashev and Klimov were both replaced — VI Fighter Corps being taken over by Major-General Yerlykin and V Fighter Corps by Major-General Galunov.

Nor were the Soviet attacks on German armour initially successful. Despite the new PTAB anti-tank bombs, their RS-82 rockets and more formidable 37mm cannon, the Il-2 *shturmoviks* failed to get through and stop the panzers rolling forward. Flying in small groups of one or two *zven'ya*, the Il-2s and Pe-2s often lacked fighter escort or were abandoned at the first sign of trouble. On Khudyakov's orders the *shturmoviks* began to fly in much larger formations of regimental size to make escort easier and to enable the Il-2s to break

---

[8] VIII *Fliegerkorps* claimed 432 victories on 5 July and 637 by the evening of the next day. Carrell *Hitler's War on Russia*, vol II.

[9] Plocher *The German Air Force versus Russia, 1943*

through and suppress ground fire by sheer weight of numbers and persistence of attack. Flying in *peleng* formation — staggered line abreast — the Il-2s no longer made hasty passes at low level under favourable condtions but carried out calculated dive approaches from under 1,000 metres at angles of thirty to forty degrees, releasing their bombs and rockets when 200 to 300 metres from their target and making repeat passes with cannon and machine-guns. By 8 July Khudyakov was able to report on the improvement in *shturmovik* potency as the German advance slowed and the *Luftwaffe's* power to control air space over the battle areas declined. Already the *Luftwaffe* was running out of replacements to maintain its *Staffeln* at full strength, and as its vigour flagged the Red Air Force began to range more freely and deeply behind the German lines to hit concentrations and supply centres.

By 12 July Zhukov decided to begin the first phase of the counter-offensive with the Western and Bryansk Fronts supported by Gromov's 1st and Naumenko's 15th Air Armies. Between them the two air armies had two fighter, two *shturmovik* and one bomber corps, and they were joined by Rudenko's 16th Air Army on 15 July as the Central Front went over to the offensive. As if to demonstrate the inexhaustable Soviet air reserves, Naumenko was reinforced by Blagoveshchenski's II Fighter Corps and Danilov's XI Composite Air Corps from the GKO Air Reserve on 1 August. On the southern flank of the Kursk salient the start of the Soviet counter-offensive was delayed. Begun by the South-Western, Southern and North Caucasus Fronts with the 17th, 8th and 4th Air Armies on 16 July, it was joined by the Voronezh and Steppe Fronts until 3 August for the assault on Belgorod. On 5 August both Oryol and Belgorod fell to the Red Army and the salutes of guns, now to sound with increasing regularity as more and more cities were retaken, roared out in Moscow. But Model, yielding the Oryol salient, retreated to the prepared Hagen Line. Army Group Centre withdrew successfully but with much of its force spent and at the cost of irreplaceable men and equipment.

To the south the next Soviet objective was Khar'kov and while Khryukin's 8th Air Army struck at German armour brought up to reinforce the German positions, the 2nd and 17th Air Armies assisted by the 5th Air Army on the Steppe Front kept up a continual sequence of attacks. *Luftwaffe* opposition was not absent, and Zhukov had to request the replacement of ninety fighters, forty Pe-2 bombers and sixty Il-2 *shturmoviks* for the 2nd and 5th Air Armies in preparation for the assault on Khar'kov which fell to him on 23 August. Victory had eluded Hitler. Operation *Zitadelle* had failed. The German armies had escaped destruction in the trap Stalin had set for them, but only by surrendering their positions of advantage and by well-organised withdrawals. From now on the *Wehrmacht* had to fight delaying, defensive battles in the East and its major triumphs were in securing retreats and evacuations with the minimum loss. The *Luftwaffe*, too, was no longer capable of holding air superiority for any length of time over a wide battle area. It was to remain victorious in many localised encounters with the Red Air Force over the course of the next two years, but it could no longer hope to destroy its opponent or prevent his continual penetration over German occupied territory.

Kursk had shown how desperate the *Luftwaffe's* need was for an effective anti-tank aircraft since, although the Hs 129 with its armour-piercing 30mm cannon had proved its worth, it was built in woefully small numbers when compared with the ubiquitous *shturmoviks*[10].From now on the obsolete Ju 87 had to be adapted for the anti-tank role and while still lethal in the hands of a virtuoso like Ulrich Rudel it was in every respect a makeshift. Expensive tactical bombers like the Ju 88 and He 111 had to be used at heights where they were most vulnerable and by June 1944 even the He 177, envisaged as a long-range strategic bomber, was being expended in low-level attacks on the swarming T-34s. The Bf 109G and Fw 190 fighters could more than hold their own still, but they were to find themselves increasingly outnumbered by fighters which began to rival them in performance. It was more often the failings of Soviet pilots rather than the inferiority of the new La-5FN and Yak-9 fighters which had made the Soviet fighter presence at Kursk so inauspicious. In the hands of the rising Soviet fighter aces, the new Russian machines were opponents to be respected.

Too late the *Luftwaffe* realised the wisdom of those who had urged a policy of strategic bombing against the Soviet armaments industry and in August 1943, as Operation *Zitadelle* was written off, it was decided at last to form the strategic bomber corps that von Greim had urged. The formation of this unit was entrusted to the headquarters

---

[10]Only 411 Hs 129 ground-attack aircraft were produced in 1943. Baumbach *Broken Swastika*

Soviet Air Force

of IV *Fliegerkorps* under the title *Wiederauffrischungsstab Ost* or Rehabilitation Staff East under *Generalleutnant* Meister and when, in November, the *Luftwaffe* issued its short study — 'The Battle against the Russian Armament Industry' — Meister had the main elements of KG 3, KG 4, KG 55 and KG 100 flying Ju 88 and He 111 bombers with the promise that one day the new corps would be equipped with the He 177, a promise few took seriously. Operations scheduled to begin in February 1944 never took place. Every bomber was by then needed to stem the tide of Soviet armour as it rolled inexorably westwards.

For the Russians the next objective was the occupation of the eastern Ukraine and the establishments of bridgeheads on the western bank on the Dnieper. The offensive was opened in late August by the Central, Voronezh and Steppe Fronts whose 16th, 2nd and 5th Air Armies fielded a total of 1,450 aircraft and, as in 1941, the Dnieper became the scene of fierce and stubborn air battles. Heavy formations of bombers and *shturmoviks* were hurled against the German river crossings and several paratroop operations were mounted over the western bank of the Dnieper but these did not prevent the German withdrawal from being accomplished by 30 September. To the south, the Donbass was the objective of the South-Western and Southern Fronts supported by the 17th and 8th Air Armies with 1,400 machines. The 8th Air Army faced its old adversary, VIII *Fliegerkorps*, now reduced to using obsolete Hs 123 ground-attack biplanes to support the *Wehrmacht*. In January that year Richthofen had requested that the Hs 123, long outdated but invaluable for close support, should be put back into production, but to no avail; even worse, in 1944 production of the Hs 129, the Luftwaffe's only aircraft specifically designed for low-level close-support, was halved.

Kiev fell to the Soviet armies on 6 November, and four days later the Russians had shattered the German defences over a 160 kilometre front between Dniepropetrovsk and Kremenchug. Weather conditions made air operations an ordeal for both the Red Air Force and the *Luftwaffe*. Airfields became seas of mud with *Luftwaffe* pilots riding out to their machines on horseback and only aircraft with wide-track tyres like the Ju 87 were able to take off from many airstrips. The Soviet offensive directed against the western Ukraine which opened in December 1943 was composed of four army groups backed by 2,360 combat aircraft. The First and Second Ukrainian

The Falcons Swarm

Fronts* supported by Krasovski's 2nd and Goryunov's 5th Air Armies with 768 aircraft between them were committed to the destruction of seven divisions of the German 8th Army temporarily encircled at Cherkassy on the Dnieper, and VIII *Fliegerkorps* was again called upon to mount a supply airlift and fly into the pocket's airfield at Korsun'-Shevchenkovski in the teeth of unrelenting ground fire, frequent *shturmovik* strikes against the landing area and constant fighter incursions. As at Stalingrad, the Soviets devoted the bulk of their air power to the task of smashing the German transports. On one flight alone twelve Ju 523/m transports were shot down, and the eventual cost of the airlift operation between 31 January and 16 February 1944 was 32 Ju 52 3/m transports lost and a further 113 damaged[11].

The Third and Fourth Ukrainian Fronts were supported by the 17th Air Army under Sudets and the 8th Air Army under Khryukin, the latter taking part with Vershinin's 4th Air Army based in the North Caucasus in the reconquest of the Crimea in April 1944. The Perekop isthmus had, in fact, been sealed off by the Soviet advance in late October 1943 and airlifts by Ju 52 3/m and later He 111 aircraft of *Luftflotte* 4 were used to supply the trapped German 17th Army. Surprisingly, these were carried out with very few losses from enemy action[12]. Intensive night-bombing attacks over Kerch were a prelude to the 4th Air Army's mass strikes in support of the Special Maritime Army's invasion with a special forward command post established from which the Deputy Air Army Commander, General Slyusarev, controlled and directed fighter cover over the beach-head. At the end of April 1944, its task completed, the headquarters of the 4th Air Army were transferred to the Second Belorussian Front and Vershinin's air regiments, now absorbed into the 8th Air Army, remained to take part in the storming and capture of Sevastopol in early May.

In the north 1944 opened with the offensive to break the German blockade of Leningrad, besieged since September 1941, backed by General Rybal'chenko's 13th Air Army on the Leningrad Front, General Zhuravlev's 14th Air Army on the Volkhov Front, General

---

*Formerly the Voronezh and Steppe Fronts and retitled in October 1943.
[11]Morzik *German Air Force Airlift Operations*
[12]Five Ju 52 3/m transports were lost between 5 November 1943 and 2 February 1944 and six He 111 aircraft between 12 April and 11 May when the Crimea was abandoned by the Germans. *German Air Force Airlift Operations*.

Soviet Air Force

Antoshkin's II PVO Guards Fighter Corps, aircraft of General Samokhin's Baltic Fleet Air Force, three ADD corps and elements of the 15th Air Army on the neighbouring Second Baltic Front — some 1,200 aircraft in all. Once the Germans had been driven back and the blockade broken, the 14th Air Army was dissolved and merged with the 13th Air Army which, with Antoshkin's fighter corps and General Sokolov's diminutive 7th Air Army on the Karelian Front, pursued the Soviet offensive against Finland in June 1944. Red Air Force operations in the north, however, received comparatively low priority and the Red Air Force there was, in the dismissive verdict of one *Luftwaffe* officer, 'not to be taken seriously as an aerial opponent'[13].

Although the size of the Red Air Force remained fairly static over the last half of 1943 at about 8,500 aircraft, from January 1944 it again expanded rapidly so that by June that year the Soviets were able to field just under 13,500 machines and by January 1945 the total had risen to over 15,500[14]. In April 1945 with the war at its close, the *Luftwaffe* High Command assessed the Soviet air strength deployed against it at about 17,000 machines — of which 8,000 were fighters, 4,000 *shturmoviks* and 5,000 bombers (including night-bombers and the 18th Air Army, formerly the ADD) — but gave the overall total of combat aircraft available to the Soviet Union as 39,700 machines, representing a very substantial reserve[15]. Thus, in spite of the high attrition rate attributed by the Germans — 2,700 machines per month in the last phase of the war of which 1,500 were combat losses[16] — the Soviets were able to mount numerically superior air forces for their offensives on an increasing scale. While the air armies were able to commit *shturmoviks* or bombers at divisional or even corps strength with adequate fighter escort, the *Luftwaffe* found daylight

---

[13] Plocher *The German Air Force versus Russia, 1943*

[14] IVOVSS. Yakovlev in *Tsel' Zhizni* gives the somewhat higher figures of 8,800 aircraft in January and 14,800 in June 1944 rising to 15,800 in January 1945. German estimates of February — March 1944 credited the USSR with a total of 11,800 combat aircraft composed of 4,500 fighters, 2,700 *shturmoviks* and 4,600 bombers — including U-2 night-bombers and ADD machines.

[15] *The Russian Air Force in the Eyes of German Commanders*

[16] The Germans estimated Soviet *shturmovik* and bomber losses as 6,900 and 5,100 in 1943 and 7,300 and 5,200 in 1944. *ibid*. The Soviets claimed an increasing loss ratio due to enemy action from one aircraft in 32 sorties in 1941 to one in every 165 sorties in 1945 (SVVSVOV).

bombing on the whole impossible from the summer of 1944 and the ability of its reconnaissance aircraft to range over Soviet territory greatly reduced.

The major air operation of the summer of 1944 was in Belorussia where the Third, Second and First Belorussian Fronts were supported by the 1st Air Army under Khryukin[17], the 4th under Vershinin and the 16th under Rudenko. These three air armies with elements of Papivin's 3rd Air Army on the First Ukrainian Front to the north and Polynin's 6th Air Army to the south contained 6,000 aircraft — the largest tactical concentration of Soviet air power so far. Half of these aircraft belonged to the eleven air corps allocated from the GKO Air Reserve; Khryukin's 1st Air Army which played a major role in the offensive had been augmented by three fighter, one *shturmovik* and one bomber corps to bring its combat strength up to 1,881 machines[18]. One third of this gigantic force consisted of *shturmoviks* with 1,100 day and night bombers and 1,900 fighters. To the south Krasovski's 2nd Air Army on the First Ukrainian Front was enlarged to contain nine air corps, three fighter, three *shturmovik*, two bomber and one composite, totalling over 3,000 aircraft to prepare for the break-through into Poland. For this major push forward which began in July, the 2nd Air Army's staff was amplified with officers from the disbanded 8th Air Army and its resources split into two main components — a northern under General Slyusarev in the Rava-Russkaya sector with four air corps containing 1,200 aircraft, and a larger southern component with five air corps and 1,400 aircraft under General Krasovski in the Lvov sector. To the south again, the Second and Third Ukrainian Fronts with the 5th and 17th Air Armies — 1,760 aircraft — supported by elements of the Black Sea Fleet Air Force drove forwards into Rumania and a re-established Fourth Ukrainian Front was provided with the reconstituted 8th Air Army under General Zhdanov.

As they advanced westwards, the Soviet air armies now contained non-Russian air formations of increasing size. The French fighter

---

[17] General Khryukin, transferred from the command of the 8th Air Army after the capture of Sevastopol and the Soviet occupation of the Crimea, replaced General Gromov as Commander of the 1st Air Army from June 1944. General Gromov then headed the newly formed Frontal Aviation Operations Directorate until appointed Deputy C-in-C of the new Long-Range Air Force (DA) in 1946.

[18] Detailed as 840 fighters, 528 *shturmoviks*, 459 bombers and 54 reconnaissance aircraft. Kostenko *Korpus Krylyatoi gvardii*

squadron was first, and expanded into the *Normandie-Nieman* Fighter Regiment in August 1943 flew its Yak fighters in support of the 1st Air Army as part of the 303rd Fighter Division. Czech elements were subordinated to Krasovski's 2nd Air Army on the First Ukrainian Front. The 1st Independent Czech Fighter Regiment, equipped with twenty-two La-5 fighters in June 1944, flew from Tri Duby airfield in support of the Slovak uprising three months later and in December it formed the basis of the 1st Czech Composite Air Division consisting of two fighter regiments, each equipped with thirty-six La-5s, and a *shturmovik* division with thirty-four Il-2s as the nucleus of the post-war Czechoslovakian Air Force. A Polish fighter squadron formed in 1943 was later expanded into the 1st Warsaw Fighter Regiment, and by April 1944 it had been joined by the 2nd Crakow Night-Bomber Regiment as the basis for the 1st Polish Composite Air Division established that August. Shortly afterwards the Polish air presence was again developed into the 1st Polish Composite Air Corps consisting of one bomber, one *shturmovik* and one fighter division and headed by General Filipp Agal'tsov, a 'rehabilitated' veteran of the Spanish Civil War and previously commander of the 9th Guards *Shturmovik* Division. When the 6th Air Army on the Second Belorussian Front was dissolved in October 1944, its command staff took over the organisation of the new Polish Air Force with General Polynin serving as C-in-C Polish Air Force until April 1947.

Over 2,400 aircraft were concentrated for the storm of Königsberg in April 1945. Co-ordinated by Novikov and Falaleev, Khryukin's 1st and Papivin's 3rd Air Armies were reinforced by loaned elements from the 4th and 15th Air Armies, bombers of Golovanov's 18th Air Army and units of the Baltic Fleet Air Force, while the drive through Poland and into the Third Reich was backed by the 4,770 machines of the 2nd and 16th Air Armies. For the last battle, the Battle of Berlin, the Red Air Force assembled a force of 7,500 combat aircraft, 6,700 of the 4th, 16th and 2nd Air Armies together with at least half of Golovanov's 18th Air Army — 800 bombers. Rudenko's 16th Air Army was by far the largest; its two bomber, two *shturmovik* and four fighter corps plus four bomber, two *shturmovik* and five fighter divisions were deployed over one hundred and sixty-five airfields. Overall control of the operation was taken by Chief Air Marshal Novikov with, significantly, Rudenko serving as his tactical deputy. An eastern and a northern air control point were set up to handle the mass of aircraft involved, the first under General Senatorov, Deputy Commander of the 16th Air Army, and the second under General Tokarev, Commander of VI *Shturmovik* Corps. When the red flag was at last hoisted above the *Reichstag* on 30 April, the Soviets claimed the destruction of 1,232 *Luftwaffe* machines for the loss of 527 of their own [19] during the last fortnight of hostilities.

When Hitler had been dealt with, Stalin turned his attentions eastwards where he had unfinished business with the Japanese. On 8 August 1945, two days after Hiroshima had been obliterated by the first A-bomb, the Red Army launched its offensive against Japanese forces in Manchuria and Korea with air support provided by three air armies and the machines of Colonel-General Lemeshko's Pacific Fleet Air Force. On the First Far Eastern Front Colonel-General Sokolov, recently in command of the 7th Air Army on the Karelian Front, headed the 9th Air Army with 1,162 aircraft and on the Second Colonel-General Zhigarev, ex-C-in-C of the Red Air Force, commanded the 1,095 aircraft of the 10th Air Army. They were supported by Marshal Khudyakov on the Trans-Baikal Front, whose 12th Air Army with 1,307 machines was numerically superior, and the 1,431 naval aircraft of Lemeshko[20]. Careful preparations had been made for the air offensive including the construction of ninety-six new airfields, fifty-six of which were within twenty kilometres of the Soviet border. The Far Eastern air units had also been re-equipped with the latest Yak-9 and La-7 fighters and Tu-2 bombers as well as Lend-Lease aircraft, and a number of air regiments were

---

[19] SVVSVOV. The Soviets claimed that the Luftwaffe lost a total of 77,000 aircraft on the Eastern Front, 57,000 of these to Soviet action.

[20] The composition of these air armies and the Pacific Fleet Air Force in August 1945 is detailed below

	9th AA	10th AA	12th AA	Pacific FAF
Comp. Air Corps		1		
Bomber Divs.	3	1	6	2(i)
Shturmovik Divs	2	1	2	1
Fighter Divs	3		3	1
Comp. Air Divs		2		
Transport Divs			2	
Smaller elements	11	3	27	8

(i) Including one mine and torpedo bomber division

See *Sovětské letectvo v bojích na Dálném Východe* by Josef Novotný in *Letectví + Kosmonautika*, No. 15, 1975.

Soviet Air Force

transferred from the west — bringing with them their recent experience of combat against the *Luftwaffe*. Extensive bombing operations against Japanese airfields and over Chanchun and Harbin had been carried out before Japan's capitulation on 23 August.

The atomic bombs which brought Japan to her knees were also omens for the Red Air Force. In future warfare the value of sheer weight of numbers had been eclipsed.

Structure of a Soviet Air Army c. 1943

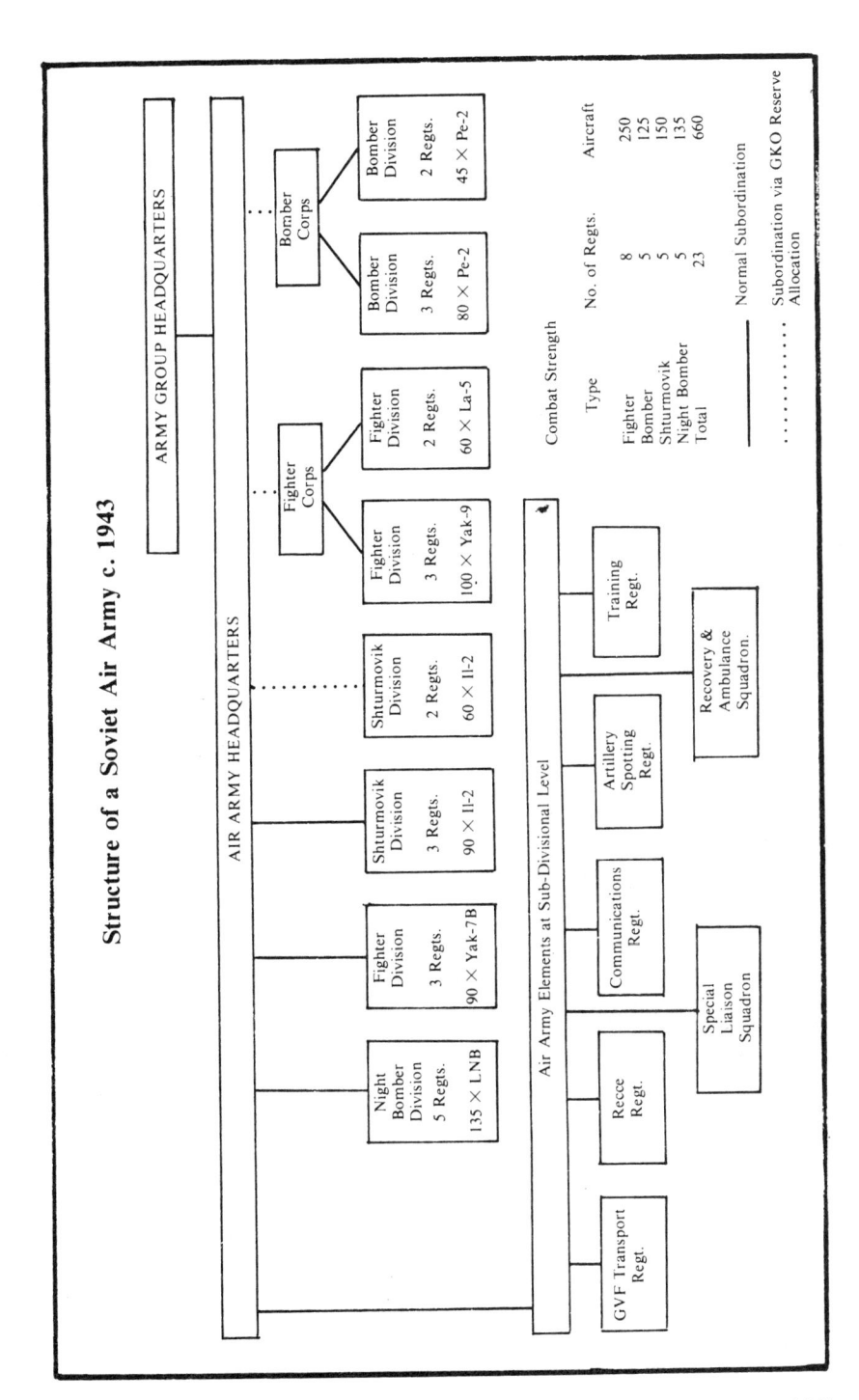

ARMY GROUP HEADQUARTERS

AIR ARMY HEADQUARTERS

- Night Bomber Division — 5 Regts. — 135 × LNB
- Fighter Division — 3 Regts. — 90 × Yak-7B
- Shturmovik Division — 3 Regts. — 90 × Il-2
- Shturmovik Division — 2 Regts. — 60 × Il-2
- Fighter Corps
  - Fighter Division — 3 Regts. — 100 × Yak-9
  - Fighter Division — 2 Regts. — 60 × La-5
- Bomber Corps
  - Bomber Division — 3 Regts. — 80 × Pe-2
  - Bomber Division — 2 Regts. — 45 × Pe-2

Air Army Elements at Sub-Divisional Level

- GVF Transport Regt.
- Recce Regt.
- Communications Regt.
- Artillery Spotting Regt.
- Training Regt.
- Special Liaison Squadron
- Recovery & Ambulance Squadron.

Combat Strength

Type	No. of Regts.	Aircraft
Fighter	8	250
Bomber	5	125
Shturmovik	5	150
Night Bomber	5	135
Total	23	660

——— Normal Subordination

········· Subordination via GKO Reserve Allocation

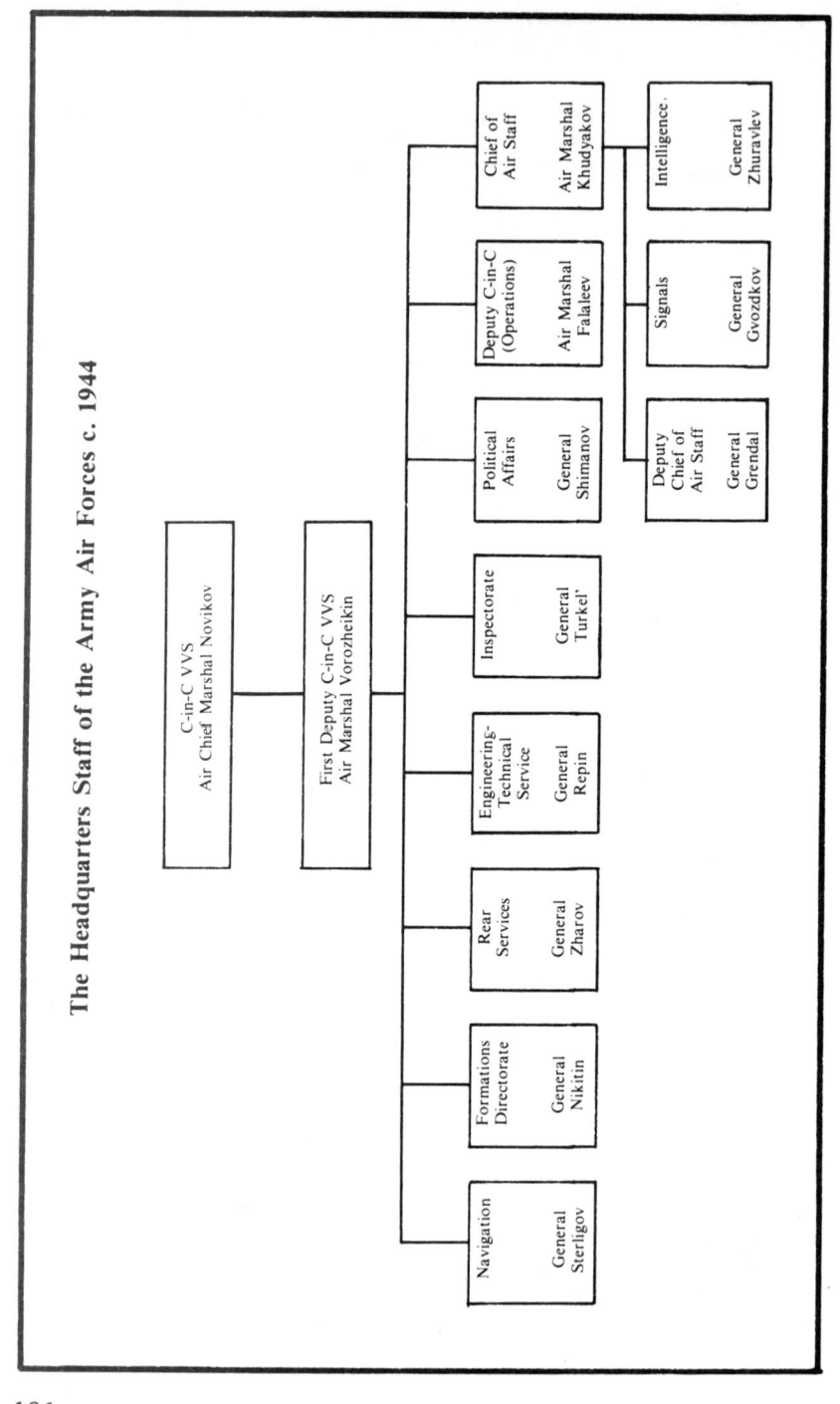

The Headquarters Staff of the Army Air Forces c. 1944

```
                        C-in-C VVS
                   Air Chief Marshal Novikov
                            |
                   First Deputy C-in-C VVS
                   Air Marshal Vorozheikin
                            |
   ┌──────────┬──────────┬──────────┬──────────┬──────────┬──────────┬──────────┐
Navigation  Formations   Rear     Engineering- Inspectorate Political  Deputy     Chief of
            Directorate  Services  Technical                Affairs    C-in-C     Air Staff
                                   Service                             (Operations)
General     General      General   General     General      General    Air Marshal Air Marshal
Sterligov   Nikitin      Zharov    Repin       Turkel'      Shimanov   Falaleev    Khudyakov
                                                                            │           │
                                                                    ┌───────┴───┬───────┤
                                                                  Deputy     Signals  Intelligence
                                                                  Chief of
                                                                  Air Staff
                                                                  General    General   General
                                                                  Grendal    Gvozdkov  Zhuravlev
```

12 Factories at War

The devastating effects of the German invasion and the speed of the *Wehrmacht*'s advance into Soviet territory posed an immediate threat to the Soviet Union's industrial capability and the means whereby equipment could be produced to replace the immense amount already lost and carry out the necessary expansion of the armed forces. The withdrawal of industrial plant vital to the war effort was, therefore, an absolute priority and on 24 June a Special Evacuation Council headed by Shvernik with Kosygin and Pervukhin as his deputies was formed and shortly afterwards made directly responsible to the GKO, Stalin's State Defence Committee. Its first task lay in attempting to salvage everything of industrial or technical value from the path of the advancing Germans, but its endeavours were frequently restricted and hindered by disrupted and congested railways in the frontal areas and the almost unopposed presence of the *Luftwaffe*. In spite of this, Soviet railways carried one and a half million wagonloads of plant, equipment and personnel eastwards between July and November 1941, and a total of 1,523 factories, installations and research establishments of all kinds had been cleared from areas subsequently occupied by the enemy or likely to be abandoned to him.

Responsibility for the evacuation of the aircraft industry was borne by Shakhurin as Commissar for Aircraft Production assisted by his specialised deputies[1]. The Germans later suspected that the evacuation of key war plants from danger zones in the west had been begun prior to operation Barbarossa, a suspicion supported to some

---

[1]These included Shakhurin's immediate deputy P.V. Dement'ev, P.A. Voronin and A.I. Kuznetsov, responsible respectively for fighter and bomber production, A.A. Zavitaev in charge of aeroengine production, A.S. Yakovlev and V.P. Kuznetsov, the chiefs of prototype aircraft and experimental aeroengine development, and M.V. Khrunichev in charge of factory buildings and raw material supplies.

degree by Ozerov's observation that GAZ No. 23 and GAZ No. 43 had both been re-established in Omsk by the late summer of 1941 after evacuation from Leningrad and Kiev[2].

The German drive towards Moscow dictated a more comprehensive and energetic dispersal policy as the summer passed, but Shakhurin's problems were not easily solved. Factories had to be removed from zones foreseeably in danger and resited, as far as possible, in areas which would permit new machines to be delivered to the fronts as speedily as possible; buildings had to be erected, converted or completed, the supply of engines and parts to assembly plants had to be planned with an eye to existing rail links and crucial questions of production priorities resolved. Full evacuation schedules were ready by August and put into effect over the next two months. In all, 85% of Soviet airframe and aeroengine production facilities were evacuated from western Russia, some factories being uprooted a second time in the summer of 1942 when the Voroshilovgrad (Lugansk), Voronezh and Stalingrad areas were threatened.

Shakhurin was aided in this huge undertaking by two important factors. The first was the *Luftwaffe*'s almost total absorption in army support. It received no directive to switch over to a campaign of strategic bombing and the raids ordered against Moscow were ineffectual in hampering industrial evacuation from the area. Between January and May 1942 Moscow, Gorky, Voronezh and Shcherbakov (Rybinsk) — all centres associated with the aircraft industry — suffered small and spasmodic air attacks which did little more than divert some Soviet resources into a strengthening of the local PVO zones. The second factor lay in the work already done in the building of new aircraft factories in the interior and the construction of plants east of the Urals intended to supply the Far Eastern Air Force, although several of these were still far from finished in the summer of 1941.

Even so, the evacuation was an exhausting and demanding operation which taxed everyone from factory directors and chief engineers down to the humblest assembly worker. The long trains of forty or fifty boxcars and platform wagons arrived after journeys lasting up to a fortnight to unload machines and workers beside roofless workshops or bare foundations. These trains had often to be unloaded in three or four hours to clear the line for the one behind so

---

[2]Uebe *Russian Reactions to German Airpower* and Ozerov *Tupolevskaya Sharaga*.

Factories at War

that machine-tools dumped beside the track had to be unfrozen and cleared of snow when they were eventually hoisted into place by hand or using agricultural tractors. The evacuation of aircraft plants from the Moscow area had been completed by the end of October but in the remoter areas of western Russia the task was more complicated. At least two factories, GAZ No. 29 at Zaporozh'e and GAZ No. 31, Taganrog, moved out the last of their heavy machine-tools under shell-fire and barges transporting GAZ No. 26 from Shcherbakov (Rybinsk) to Ufa became ice-locked in the Kama, Belaya and Ufa rivers[3].

Special barrack blocks had to be built to house the sudden influx of workers from the west, and in the meantime local billets, schools, hospitals and theatres were all pressed into service to accommodate the thousands of new arrivals in sparsely populated eastern Russia and Siberia. When Yakovlev arrived in Novosibirsk with his fighter plant from Moscow in October 1941, he found no accommodation left anywhere and he was obliged to requisition a cinema, moving his weary workers in as soon as the performance ended so that they could spend the night in the seats just vacated by the audience[4]. Once production was under way, the workers often ate and slept by their machines and it was not uncommon for the first aircraft to leave the assembly line from shops still open to the sky and the falling snow, with workers taking turns during their twelve-hour shift to warm themselves at fires in pits dug into the earth floors. Their food often consisted of soup made from beetroot leaves or freshwater fish from local rivers and nutritional deficiencies had to be met by special rations and medical check-ups in 1942 to prevent a serious drop in manpower from illness. In the stark, hastily erected factories work went on night and day with power provided by generators on railway wagons and beneath slogans urging greater and more determined productivity — For The Front! — For The Motherland! — For Stalin!

The flow of components during the winter of 1941-42 was highly erratic and often frustrated the best efforts of the assembly plants. At GAZ No. 153, Novosibirsk, where Yakovlev was to share the assembly lines with the LaGG-3 fighters already in production, he found the factory choked with uncompleted aircraft waiting for

---
[3]See A.I. Shakhurin *Aviatsionnaya promyshlennost' nakanune i v gody Velikoi Otechestvennoi Voiny* in *Sovetski Tyl*.

[4]Yakovlev *Tsel' Zhizni*

189

undercarriages or propellers. These were not only parked in 'the marsh' — as the storage area for unfinished aircraft was nicknamed — but also scattered over the adjacent airfield. Covered with snow, some were not revealed until the spring thaw came[5].

Shakhurin was taken to task by Stalin for the declining number of aircraft delivered to the Red Air Force as the Battle for Moscow drew near; from over 1,100 machines in August 1941 monthly production rose to over 2,300 in September before falling to 800 in October and less than 450 in November when most aircraft plants were still in transit. An investigatory committee headed by General Petrov was instructed to report on the reasons for congestion in the assembly plants early in 1942 and henceforth factory production totals had to be based on the number of machines 'ready for combat' rather than on the number 'assembled'. The directors of factories whose production was considered inadequate received sharply worded telegrams from Stalin. Shenkman and Tret'yakov, the directors of GAZ No. 18 and GAZ No. 1, were both fiercely reproved in this manner on 23 December 1941 —

> You have let down our country and our Red Army. You are still not facilitating the production of Il-2s. The Il-2 is as vital to our Red Army as air or bread. Shenkman is producing one Il-2 per day and Tret'yakov one or two MiG-3 fighters. This is an insult to our country and our Red Army. We do not need MiG-3 fighters but Il-2 *shturmoviks* instead. If GAZ No. 18 thinks it can fob us off with one Il-2 a day it is cruelly mistaken and will suffer the consequences. Do not make the government lose its patience. I demand the production of more Il-2s. This is my last warning. Stalin[6].

When Shvernik's Special Evacuation Council was dissolved in January 1942, its work was taken over by a Resettlement Council under Anastas Mikoyan formed the previous month to supervise the re-establishment of evacuated industries. Mikoyan's council did not complete its brief until the latter half of 1942, but the aircraft industry enjoyed a high priority and was largely re-established by the end of March. From January monthly production rose from 1,000 machines

---

[5] *Yakovlev Tsel' Zhizni*

[6] *Yakovlev Tsel' Zhizni*

to 1,300 — 1,400 by April with a slight dropback in February[7]. From April 1942 production accelerated steeply with 8,141 combat aircraft delivered in the first half of the year and 13,436 in the second — giving a total of 21,577 out of an overall aircraft production figure of 25,240 machines. By comparison, 15,735 aircraft had been produced in 1941, some 12,000 of which were combat types. In 1943 combat aircraft constituted 30,000 of the 34,884 aircraft built by the Soviet aircraft industry.

In production priorities the most significant shift was from bombers to *shturmoviks*. In 1941 output of the Il-2 (initially known as BSh) *shturmovik* and its unsuccessful rival, the Su-2, comprised just under 10% of all aircraft produced, but the following year *shturmoviks* accounted for a third of the annual aircraft production with the same proportion retained in 1943 when over 11,200 Il-2s rolled off Soviet production lines. Even by the end of the war, one in every four combat aircraft produced was an Il'yushin *shturmovik*. The Il-2 had been first placed in production at GAZ No. 18, Voronezh, in December 1940, but when the plant was evacuated to Kuibyshev on the eastern bank of the Volga in September 1941, the opportunity was taken to co-locate it with the Frunze Aeroengine Works, GAZ No. 24, from Moscow producing Mikulin inline engines. When assembly of the AM-35 engine for the MiG-3 fighter was phased out, the factory concentrated its resources on supplying the AM-38 for installation in the Il-2, producing four times as many engines in 1942 as it had the previous year and becoming one of the seven NKAP plants to be awarded the Order of the Red Banner in 1945. Kuibyshev became the key centre for *shturmovik* production and one of Shakhurin's deputies was given special responsibility for establishing aircraft production there. No buildings were available to house GAZ No. 18 or GAZ No. 24 when they arrived Kuibyshev, and the latter plant was not able to recommence production until late December 1941[8]. A second important Il-2 plant, GAZ No. 30, Moscow —

---

[7]Soviet sources are at variance as regards monthly aircraft production totals for the first four months of 1942. See below for comparative figures derived from Fyodorov and Yakovlev:

	Fyodorov	Yakovlev
January	976	1,039
February	822	915
March	1,352	1,647
April	1,423	not given

[8]Shakhurin

Soviet Air Force

singled out with the huge Klimov engine plant at Ufa, the Moscow M-11 engine factory, GAZ No. 45, and the immense GAZ No. 153 building Yak fighters at Novosibirsk to receive the Order of Lenin in 1945 — also contributed to the 36,163 Il-2 *shturmoviks* sent to the front. At its peak, production reached a thousand machines per month.

With the growth of *shturmovik* production, the output of twin-engined bombers was sharply curtailed. In 1940 twin-engined bombers constituted 34% of Soviet military aircraft production, but this fell to 24% in 1941 and again to 14% in 1942 when 3,500 bombers were built compared with 8,200 *shturmoviks*. At its peak in 1944, annual bomber production barely reached 4,200 machines. The Pe-2, of which 11,427 examples were built, remained the standard Red Air Force bomber throughout the war and was never challenged quantitatively. Only two were produced at GAZ No. 22 in 1940, but these were followed by 438 in the first half of 1941 and 1,409 in the second — representing half that year's output of multi-engined bombers. Production was expanded when GAZ No. 22 was moved to Kazan' in company with GAZ No. 16 from Shcherbakov (Rybinsk) producing the Pe-2's M-105 engines. The shortage of tactical bombers remained, however, present through the war and was felt keenly at the Battle of Kursk in the summer of 1943 when the supply of Lend-Lease B-25 and A-20 bombers — most of the former being allocated to ADD regiments — proved invaluable. In general Soviet bomber production suffered in having to compete for engines; most of the Klimov inline engines were needed for Yak and LaGG-3 fighters — although the phasing out of the LaGG-3 in 1943 eased the situation — and even Tupolev's more sophisticated Tu-2 had to compete with the Lavochkin radial-engined fighters for supplies of the ASh-82 later in the war. The only Soviet bomber which was not handicapped in this way was the Il-4 equipped with Tumanski M-88 radials and built as the standard ADD bomber at GAZ No. 39, re-sited in Irkutsk.

Fighter production, which fell to 40% of the annual output of aircraft in 1942-43, reverted in 1944 to the 45% it had occupied in 1940-41. From just over 7,000 fighters built in 1941, production rose to 9,900 in 1942 — exceeding German estimates by some six hundred machines[9]. In 1943 14,600 fighters were produced and in the following year Soviet fighter production reached its peak with 18,000

---

[9] Schwabedissen *The Russian Air Force in the Eyes of German Commanders.*

machines supplied to the Red Air Force. The Chkalov Factory at Novosibirsk, GAZ No. 153, which was turning out three Yak-1 fighters a day in February 1942, was producing twenty machines daily by the end of the year and at the close of the war it had increased its output to fifty Yak-9 fighters each day. Between January and March 1945 alone this plant assembled 1,500 Yak fighters, one tenth of its total wartime contribution. A second large Yak fighter plant was GAZ No. 292, Saratov, which was awarded the Order of Lenin in July 1942 for early production successes and where the Yak-7B was soon afterwards replaced on the production lines by the Yak-9. Although less than thirty Yak-9 fighters had been delivered by the end of 1943, production thereafter amounted to over 16,700 examples — a quarter of all fighter production during the war years. With the resumption of aircraft production in the Moscow area from 1942, assembly of the new Yak-3 fighter was subsequently centred there and 4,848 examples built.

Of the Lavochkin fighters, the most numerous were the La-5 and its development the La-5FN of which 10,599 examples were built, mainly at the Ordzhonikidze Fighter Plant, GAZ No. 21, Gorky. Fighter factories GAZ No. 31, Tbilisi, and GAZ No. 126, Komsomol'sk-na-Amure may also have been concerned with La-5 production[10] while reconstituted plants at Yaroslavl' and Moscow were associated with the assembly of 5,753 La-7 fighters from 1944 onwards.

The proportion of transport aircraft built, notably the Li-2 (PS-84) at GAZ No. 84, evacuated from Moscow to Tashkent, remained modest and supplies of the Douglas C-47 under Lend-Lease were a welcome addition to the numerous obsolete bombers converted to serve as transports. Although the output of transports rose from 450 in 1942 to 1,260 in 1943 and to just over 1,500 in 1944, the majority were small utility machines, the Shche-2, Yak-6 or transport versions of the U-2. Il'yushin's Il-12 replacement for the Li-2 begun in 1943 was not to fly until 1946. Training aircraft, ranging from the U-2 and UT-2 to conversion-training adaptions of standard fighters and bombers, had an annual output of between 3,000 and 4,000 machines until 1944 when the figure rose to 5,500. This increase in the production of transports and trainers reflected the ability of the Soviet aircraft industry to supply all the combat aircraft the Red Air

---

[10]GAZ No. 126 was awarded the Order of Lenin in July 1942 and GAZ No. 31 the Order of the Red Star in July 1945. *SSSRvVOV: kratkaya khronika.*

Force could take by the autumn of 1944[11]. In 1945 a yearly total of over 8,000 training aircraft had been attained with older models being handed down to *Osoaviakhim*.

Stalin's insistence on increased output in 1942 meant that some obsolete types and even more recent ones which had proved their inadequacies in combat, in particular the Su-2 and the LaGG-3, had to stay in production until such time as the provision of more satisfactory machines could be extended. It had been decided to phase out the LaGG-3 in the spring of 1942, but 2,736 examples were in fact built that year — more than in 1941 when 2,463 were supplied to the Red Air Force — and a further 1,329 were produced in 1943. In 1942 Su-2 production was terminated and a drastic cut made in MiG-3 production, with only forty-eight machines assembled at GAZ No. 1 after over 3,000 examples had been produced in 1941[12]. Production of the MiG-3 for delivery to PVO fighter regiments was increased in 1943 but had been terminated by the end of that year. Stalin's obsession with quantity often made it difficult to get his consent for the introduction of sorely needed modifications on the basis of combat experience, and he was at once suspicious of anything that might impede the flow of aircraft to the fronts. Shakhurin and his deputies were involved in protracted wrangles with Stalin who, in effect, dictated production policy and whose approval was needed for every innovation. The most serious instance was Stalin's refusal to allow the Il-2 production lines to be slowed to enable the *shturmovik*'s modification to carry a rear-gunner, although combat experience had conclusively shown that the Il-2's Achilles heel lay in its vulnerability to fighter attack from astern[13]. Stalin's stubbornness in this case may, however, have been due to the fact that it was he who had insisted on Il'yushin redesigning the original two-seat prototype as a single-seat *shturmovik* for production in 1940. Two prototypes of a revised two-seat Il-2 were flight-tested in March 1942, but the date when production of this model was authorised remains uncertain[14].

---

[11] Shakhurin.

[12] Immediately before its evacuation from Moscow in late September 1941, GAZ No. 1 had been turning out twenty MiG-3 fighters each day. Shakhurin.

[13] Yakovlev *Tsel' Zhizni*.

[14] While most Soviet sources give October 1942 for the first deliveries of the production two-seat Il-2, Kravchenko states that series manufacture did not commence until early 1943. See *Ekonomika SSSR v gody Velikoi Otechestvennoi Voiny*.

During the Battle of Stalingrad a number of Il-2 *shturmoviks* were converted into two-seat models by engineers of the 16th Air Army with fitters and mechanics flying as rear-gunners — a practice later extended to *shturmovik* regiments in other air armies.[15] Other modifications carried out by the over-taxed mobile aircraft repair workshops included the lowering of the rear fuselage on Yak-1 fighters to improve all-round vision and improving the Pe-2's defensive armament.

In the factories there was a shortage of machine-tools, of the duralumin and metal alloys vital to a modern aircraft industry and of skilled labour. By the spring of 1942 conscription into the Red Army had created a dearth of 219,000 workers in the aircraft industry, 137,000 of these trained machinists. Only the great fund of female labour, noted by the German delegation in April 1941, enabled the factories to shoulder the tasks imposed upon them. The shortage of standardised machine-tools meant that many timber airframe sections were finished by hand as the factories supplying them were only able to work to the most liberal tolerances. By the summer of 1942 the grim possibility of further German advances beyond the Volga meant that precedence had to be given to machines which could be built by a Siberian timber-based economy employing a labour force composed almost exclusively of women and girls drafted for industrial work. Emergency 'utility' designs exemplified by Yakovlev's Yak-6, intended to serve as either a transport or a night-bomber, and Tomashevich's 'Pegasus' *shturmovik*, both powered by twin M-11 radials, were prepared. With its ungainly wooden structure, fixed undercarriage and top speed of barely 170 kph, Tomashevich's 'Pegasus' might easily have become as familiar to the *Wehrmacht* as the *'Ilyusha'* if it had taken Stalingrad. Whenever possible metal components were replaced by wooden ones; in late 1941 the airframe of the Il-4 bomber was modified to incorporate wooden front and rear fuselage sections, and in the following year wooden outer wing sections were substituted for the original metal ones.

The widescale use of timber and steel tube in the construction of airframes and of *shpon* — bonded birch strips — to cover them resulted in high structural weights so that fighters, whose airframes

---

[15] General Polynin attributes the first field conversion of the Il-2 to carry a rear-gunner to a *shturmovik* division in the 6th Air Army, an example of this modified Il-2 being inspected in Moscow by Air Force and aircraft industry VIPs on 7-8 September 1942. *Boevye marshruty*

were too heavy for the output of the M-105PF inline engine, suffered particularly in performance. A reduction in flying weight or a substantial increase in engine power was needed for the Yak or LaGG fighters to engage the Bf 109F on equal terms, but pending the supply of metal alloys in limited quantities, flying weights could only be cut by reducing fuel tankage or armament, thus placing the Soviet fighters at an even greater disadvantage. Soviet fighters with wooden airframes also suffered as a result of the poor quality of the paints and lacquers used. These not only caught fire readily[16] but often failed to protect the wooden covering beneath from corrosion. Many Soviet fighters waiting on standby in preparation for the Battle of Kursk in 1943 were found to be unairworthy due to the deterioration of their airframes after long exposure in the open air. When Zhukov complained directly to Stalin, there was all hell to pay in the Commissariat of Aircraft Production and special repair *brigady* were sent out from all the major fighter factories to effect immediate repairs on the spot[17]. Metal wing spars were introduced on the Yak-9 and La-7 fighters in 1943, but the first fighter with an all-metal airframe, the Yak-9U, was only placed in production in 1944 and the first Lavochkin fighter with an all-metal airframe, the La-9, was not supplied to Soviet Air Force fighter regiments until late 1946.

Under the conditions prevailing, particularly during the first phase of the war when the design bureaux were evacuated — the Yakovlev, Polikarpov and Sukhoi KBs to Novosibirsk, the Petlyakov KB to Kazan'[18], the Il'yushin KB to Kuibyshev and the 'internee' KBs of Tupolev and Myasishchev to Omsk — the number and variety of prototype aircraft designed and built were remarkable. Yet very few were accepted for series production. Design ingenuity was thwarted by setbacks in perfecting more powerful engines, by the uncertainty of future supplies of alloys, the limited fund of skilled workers and the reluctance of an embattled aircraft industry committed to maintain

---

[16]Dispiriting rumours about the Yak fighters' readiness to catch fire were prevalent in the early stages of the Battle of Stalingrad. Yakovlev *Tsel' Zhizni*.

[17]Shakhurin. Dement'ev took the worst blast of Stalin's fury on this occasion. Yakovlev records that Stalin shouted at the aircraft industry representitives — Do you know you have put our fighter force out of action? Do you know what a favour you have done Hitler? You are — Hitlerites! *Tsel' Zhizni*.

[18]Petlyakov was killed in January 1942 when the Pe-2 on which he was flying from GAZ No. 22 to Moscow crashed soon after take-off. Stalin ordered a full enquiry into the circumstances of the accident and development work was given over to a series of interned designers with 'liberation' as the reward for success. The subsequent major development of the Pe-2 was carried out by Vladimir Myasishchev.

optimum output to embark on the problems of producing more complex airframes. There were fears that despite the qualities the prototypes displayed under test — qualities often superior to those of their counterparts in production — their introduction would lead to delays in supplies and present new problems in frontline repair and maintenance. Several at least with better range and heavier armament would have been invaluable in 1943 when Stalin was preoccupied with the need for battlefield cover in depth and the fire power to destroy the new Tiger tanks, but Tupolev's excellent Tu-2 was referred for simplification of design and Sukhoi's long-range, hard-hitting Su-8 *shturmovik* was turned down in favour of revamping the Il-2. The unrelenting policy of standardisation and production continuity, while it resulted in proven and robust machines in ample numbers, deprived the Red Air Force of the flexibility more adventurous and aggressive air operations would require. Last, but by no means least, the designers were thwarted by Stalin's own conservatism with its ingrained preference for simplicity and quantity over the uncertain benefits of technological refinement.

It was felt by some designers that Yakovlev as Shakhurin's deputy responsible for prototype development used his position and his access to Stalin's ear to promote his own interests and obstruct theirs. It seems likely that as far as Polikarpov was concerned old scores were settled[19] and when Polikarpov died in 1944 his design bureau was closed down and flight-tests in progress on the TIS escort fighter, the VP high-altitude interceptor and the NB night-bomber were abruptly terminated. Gudkov, Lavochkin's former colleague, wrote directly to Stalin to recommend his projected experimental Gu-1 fighter, adding that he could not rely on Yakovlev's unbiased report. Stalin directed that work on the Gu-1 should go ahead, promising Shakhurin and Yakovlev that he would 'take the sin on his own soul' if the venture failed, but Gudkov's design bureau was promptly disbanded when the Gu-1 broke up in the air during flight tests in July 1943 causing the death of the veteran test-pilot, Nikashin, who had seen the Lavochkin fighters through their teething troubles. Polikarpov was also driven to plead his causes to Stalin, but with varying degrees of success; Stalin had not completely forgotten the

---

[19]These possibly dated from 1933 when Yakovlev was expelled from TsKB after the Ya-7 incident. In *Tsel' Zhizni* Yakovlev dwells rather pointedly on the inauspicious close of Polikarpov's career. It may also be significant that Oleg Antonov, who worked as Yakovlev's first deputy designer from 1943, is nowhere mentioned in this context in Yakovlev's voluminous memoirs.

luckless I-180.

Yakovlev's designs as the basis of Soviet fighter power were evolved in close connection with the aircraft industry's developing potential. With the easing in the supply of metal alloys both the Yak-7B and the Yak-1 were modified to include metal wing spars as the Yak-7DI and the Yak-1M. On the Yak-7DI, produced from late 1942 as the Yak-9, advantage was taken of the increased wing accommodation and the lowered structural weight to raise wing fuel tankage from 415 to 450 litres, giving an increase in range at the expense of any real gain in performance. The Yak-1M was seen as a lighter, high-performance fighter and, modified as the Yak-3, was placed in production late in 1943. These two associated lines of evolution gave the Red Air Force a 'battlefield' fighter in the Yak-9 which was produced in a number of variants[21] and an 'air superiority' fighter in the Yak-3.

Lavochkin experienced greater initial problems in evolving his radial-engined fighters. While his adaption of the LaGG-3 airframe to take Shvetsov's ASh-82, which was also experimentally installed in the MiG-3, Yak-7 and Il-2, proved ultimately successful as the La-5, the harassed Lavochkin spent the summer of 1942 in eliminating one problem after another in the prototypes and pre-production examples. Engine over-heating, lapses from the anticipated performance under test and vibration due to unbalanced propellers were followed by two incidents in which wings broke away in flight. After rumours of sabotage had cast their shadow over the enterprise, which had been beset by official hostility from the start, it transpired that, due to worn drill bits, the holes in the steel wing attachments were slightly too small for their bolts and the assembly workers were helping them home with a few hefty hammer blows, invisibly weakening the structure and rendering it prone to failure under stress[22]. A crash programme to cure the La-5 of its worst ailments enabled the first production examples to undergo combat testing in the skies above Stalingrad and 1,129 had been built by the end of 1942. The La-5's performance was enhanced in 1943 when the more powerful ASh-82FN became available and work was already under

---

[20] Yakovlev *Tsel' Zhizni*.
[21] The two major versions were the Yak-9D escort fighter and the Yak-9T armed with a 37mm or 45mm hub cannon. The Yak-9B fighter-bomber with a small internal bomb-bay, the Yak-9DD long-range fighter and the Yak-9L 'light' fighter were versions produced in smaller quantities.
[22] Arlazorov *Front idyot cherez KB*.

way on a revised airframe which resulted in the La-7 of the year after. A number of fighter prototypes specially intended for PVO regiments were developed by the Mikoyan design bureau, including the I-220 and I-230 series fitted with the AM-39 inline engine also installed in Polikarpov's VP(K) high-altitude intercepter. When the feared German high-altitude bomber offensive failed to materialise in 1943, however, official interest in anything but frontline fighters declined and none was built in quantity.

In *shturmovik* design, Il'yushin's rival was the unlucky Sukhoi whose Su-4 and Su-6, plagued by development setbacks in Shvetsov's M-90 and M-71 experimental radial engines chosen to power them, failed to oust the established Il-2. The most powerful Soviet piston engine then available, Mikulin's 2,000 hp AM-42, powered three competitors to replace the Il-2 in 1944, Sukhoi's improved Su-6 and Il'yushin's Il-8 and Il-10. The Il-10, the more manoeuvrable and less heavily armoured of the two Il'yushin prototypes was selected for series production and some three thousand built by the end of the war. Red Air Force *shturmovik* regiments got their first Il-10s in October 1944 and it was available in numbers for the Battle of Berlin.

The only new bomber to be produced was Tupolev's Tu-2 whose first prototypes had flown in January 1941. A pre-production series of sixty-three was built in 1942 for combat evaluation, but production was then suspended until 1944 when a simplified version had been prepared. Placed in production first at GAZ No. 166, Omsk, and later at GAZ No. 22, Kazan', where it replaced the Pe-2, the Tu-2 was not built in quantity and only 800-1,000 had been supplied by the end of the war. Il'yushin's projected scaled-up development of his Il-4, the Il-6, Myasishchev's high-altitude long-range DVB-102 and Polikarpov's NB(T) prototypes served only to give the Soviet aircraft industry some preliminary experience in contemporary bomber design which was to be of value in copying the US B-29.

On the basis of figures available[23] the USSR produced between 175,000 and 185,000 aero engines during the Great Patriotic War, standardising on four basic types. Mikulin's inline AM-38 and its development, the AM-42, went exclusively to *shturmoviks* while Klimov's VK-105, developed as the VK-107, powered fighters and

---

[23]These are 38,000 engines in 1942, 49,000 in 1943 and 52,000 in 1944. See Kravchenko and IVOVSSSR Vol II.

Pe-2 bombers with production heavily concentrated on Ufa where 97,000 Klimov engines were built[24]. Shvetsov's ASh-82 radial installed primarily in Lavochkin's fighters and the Tu-2 bomber was produced by the Baranov Factory, GAZ No. 29, Omsk, and by GAZ No. 19 at Perm (Molotov) — one of the few major factories not subjected to evacuation. As the only successful high-powered radial engine, production of the ASh-82 failed to meet production requirements in 1942 when the La-5 fighter was being placed in series production and production of the Tu-2 contemplated. In February 1943 Shakhurin was sharply criticised by Stalin on this score, although direct responsibility lay with Zavitaev, Shakhurin's deputy for aeroengine production. The fourth basic type was the venerable five-cylinder M-11 radial — turned out by a host of smaller factories.

Aeroengine development was not, however, an unqualified success and the disappointments and frustrations of the pre-war years persisted. Klimov's twelve-cylinder VK-107 offering four hundred horsepower more than the VK-105 underwent intensive development but hopes that it might regenerate the LaGG-3 were dashed after constant over-heating during tests in 1942. It was only in 1944, the year after the LaGG-3's demise, that Klimov's new engine was ready for installation in the Yak-9U and later series Yak-3. Mikulin's AM-39, developed from the AM-35, promised an output of 1,700 hp and was used from 1943 onwards to power a number of prototypes including the Polikarpov and MiG high-altitude fighters, but production was only undertaken on a limited scale in the post-war years for the Tu-1 night-fighter and Tu-10 tactical bomber, both derived from the Tu-2. The success of the ASh-82 and ASh-82FN fourteen-cylinder radials, the latter with direct fuel injection, was not echoed in Shvetsov's endeavours to provide more powerful replacements. The eighteen-cylinder ASh-71, intended to give an output of about 2,000 hp, was tested on a number of prototypes but never reached production status and although the Ash-83 of comparable power was fitted to experimental versions of the La-7 in 1945, it was apparently not considered suitable for installation in the all-metal La-9 and La-11 fighters of 1946-47.

---

[24]*SSSRvVOV: kratkaya khronika*. On this basis, GAZ No. 26 would have been responsible for about half the USSR's total wartime production of aeroengines. The factory extended over six kilometres and had forty-two kilometres of site railway track. *Shakhurin*.

Factories at War

To fill these gaps, Mikulin, Klimov and Shvetsov were instructed to prepare boosted versions of their engines despite their misgivings about reduced engine life, and research in the field of auxiliary reaction engines — ram-jet and liquid-fuel rocket units — was consistently encouraged. Merkulov's DM-2 and larger DM-4 under-wing ram-jet engines had, in fact, already been successfully tested on I-15*bis* and I-153 test-beds in 1940 and seventy-four test-flights made without incident. In 1941 similar units were tested on the I-207 biplane fighter prototype and on the Yak-1, and in 1942 they were experimentally installed on the LaGG-3 and on the Yak-7. It was soon evident that the penalties of weight, drag and high fuel consumption could not compensate fully for the short-lived boost in speed as far as frontline fighter operations were concerned, although a number of ram-jet equipped Yak-7 fighters were reported to have seen PVO service against high-altitude *Luftwaffe* reconnaissance aircraft in 1944[25]. A later solution devised by Khalshchevnikov was to make the ram-jet an integral part of the airframe by installing it in the rear fuselage and utilising power from the nose-mounted piston engine to drive a compressor. The Su-5 (I-107) and MiG I-250 mixed power-plant fighters with VK-107 engines were designed along these lines and tested in 1945, but although a small number of I-250 fighters were built for 'jet familiarisation' training further development was clearly obviated by the superiority of the gas-turbine.

Liquid-fuel rocket engines were developed concurrently by a team under Valentin Glushko with Sergei Korolyov as his deputy responsible for the installation and flight-testing of the RD-1 unit burning kerosene and nitric acid. After starting problems had been alleviated with the development of the RD-1KhZ using chemical ignition, the unit was installed in the rear fuselage of a Pe-2 and tests concluded by October 1943. It was decided to continue work on the RD-1KhZ to facilitate pursuit, evasion and climb, take-off from short runways or with excessive loads when long-distance flights were being made. When the appearance of *Luftwaffe* reconnaissance aircraft over Moscow in late 1943 reawakened fears of a renewed German bombing offensive, the Lavochkin, Yakovlev and Sukhoi KBs were instructed to prepare rocket-assisted versions of their fighters capable of meeting intruders at altitudes in the order of

---

[25]See *Letouny s pomocnými motory* by Václav Němeček in *Vojenská Technika*, September 1967.

Soviet Air Force

13,000-14,000 metres. The first adaption to be prepared in response to this directive, the La-7R, was ready for testing in 1944 but turned out to be a highly unpleasant and unreliable machine as nitric acid fumes penetrated into the cockpit and leakages from the piping corroded the wooden airframe. A version with a metal rear fuselage and the designation La-120R was tested in 1945 together with rocket-boosted versions of Sukhoi's Su-7 fighter prototype and the Yak-3R, which exploded in mid-air, before further work on auxiliary reaction motors was discounted. Other, unrealised projects by Korolyov included the installation of RD-1KhZ units behind the engines of Pe-3 and Pe-21 fighters to convert them into high-altitude interceptors and an earlier proposal to fit three such units to the La-5 to enable the fighter to reach a speed of 950 kph and an altitude of 17,000 metres[26].

Three designs for target-defence fighters powered purely by rocket motors were also prepared, the first of which, the BI, was flight-tested under power in May 1942 after the airframe had been built in Moscow and the whole enterprise evacuated to Kol'tsovo near Sverdlovsk. Powered by a 1,100 kg thrust Dushkin D-1A engine, flight-tests were carried out reasonably successfully on a series of prototypes until March 1943 when the original BI crashed, killing its test-pilot Grigori Bakhchivandzhi who had made the first test flight less than a year before[27]. Opinions were, in fact, sharply divided as to the merits of the tiny wooden fighter with its fearsome engine; Bakhchivandzhi recorded in his flight-log that 'flight in a reaction-motor aircraft is very pleasant as the pilot has no airscrew in front of him and fumes do not intrude into the cockpit. Engine noise diminishes with the increase in speed and the engine functioned as required on take-off and in flight. The sudden cutting-out of the engine did not affect control, that is — the aircraft showed no tendency to deviate from course, and the pilot felt deceleration as on any conventional aircraft. The ease with which the machine responded to its controls was better than on modern fighters.' Another NII-VVS test-pilot who flew the BI, Kudrin, described the BI less flatteringly as 'the devil's broomstick'. Further flight tests on the BI prototypes were made but, as the reason for Bakhchivandzhi's

---

[26] See Astashenkov's article *Pervye reaktivnye ustanovki na samolyotakh* in *Aviatsiya i Kosmonavtika*, January 1971.

[27] Bakhchivandzhi was posthumously decorated as a Hero of the Soviet Union in April 1973. Obviously his courage was considered by Stalin inferior to the daring of his young *Komsomol* pilots who rammed their I-16 fighters into German bombers.

Factories at War

abrupt loss of control remained unsolved and the RNII engine development team failed to refine the D-1A significantly or develop a multi-chamber unit giving controlled cruising, official interest in rocket fighters declined. An initial production batch of thirty BI airframes being built at Nizhni Tagil was scrapped, and the two other projects terminated.

These were the Polikarpov 'Malyutka', a more sophisticated design than the BI but still in the drawing-board stage and Tikhonravov's all-wooden I-302 which had begun gliding tests in 1943 pending the supply of the 1,500 kg thrust NII-3 rocket engine. Two under-wing jettisonable Merkulov powder rockets were to assist take-off and initial climb, and the I-302's armament was to consist of four ShVAK cannon — double that on the BI. Gliding tests with a Pe-2 tug were under way when the project ended, but official interest in rocket fighter development was rekindled briefly when captured German aircraft and engines were available for examination and testing in 1945.

In 1944 when aircraft production reached 40,300 machines, the industry's workforce had almost doubled in size although the supply of machine-tools under Lend-Lease and the improvement in production methods had already enabled some reduction in the total workforce needed to be made. It was then estimated by the *Luftwaffe* that the USSR possessed nine major aeroengine and twenty-one major airframe factories, an estimate supported by the number of NKAP plants accorded decorations or commendations during the Great Patriotic War[28]. By mid-1944 the reserve of combat aircraft was such that the re-equipment of the Far Eastern and Trans-Baikal air forces had begun, and at the end of the war the Soviet aircraft industry had attained a productive capacity of over 42,000 machines a year. The evacuations of 1941 had, however, made a permanent impact on the siting of production centres, and while aircraft production in the Moscow area resumed its pre-war level[29], in the Gorky — Kuibyshev — Kazan' — Saratov area it had increased fivefold, in the Urals elevenfold and in Eastern Siberia thirtyfold with corresponding decreases in western Russia[30].

---

[28] Schwabedissen *The Russian Air Force in the Eyes of German Commanders* and *SSSRvVOV: kratkaya khronika.*

[29] Over 16,000 aircraft were built in the Moscow area during the war — *Sovetski tyl v Velikoi Otechestvennoi Voine.*

[30] Kravchenko. *Ekonomika SSR v gody Velikoi Otechestennoi Voiny.*

203

Soviet Air Force

Between July 1941 and September 1945 the Soviet aircraft industry had produced 136,838 aircraft, 108,028 of these combat machines — representing 79% of the total. But without denying its heroic and impressive achievements over the war years and the great difficulties it had to overcome, it remained backward and inexperienced in several crucial areas at their close. The mass of the machines it had produced had been single-engined aircraft with predominantly timber airframes and powered by efficient if undistinguished engines, and it lacked any real background of experience in metal airframe construction, in the manufacture of multi-engined aircraft, in electronics and in the development of gas-turbine engines. Its next battle, which had begun even before the Third Reich was defeated, was to be for technical parity with the United States and Western Europe.

13 The Day of the MiG-15

As the Third Reich toppled in the spring of 1945, Stalin was well aware of his opportunities to exploit German technical expertise in the interests of post-war Soviet military potential. Two thirds of the German aircraft industry with its research and production facilities in Austria and Czechoslovakia fell into Soviet hands as the Red Army battled westwards and technical plunder had first priority. In the field of airframe and aeroengine engineering alone the Soviets were presented with prototypes and production examples of new aircraft, rocket and gas-turbine engines, missiles, and top secret optical and electronic equipment. For the Soviet aircraft industry, conscious of its technological deficiencies, it was the chance not merely to catch up with its British and American counterparts but to overtake them at a stroke.

Most of the aircraft factories in Soviet-occupied areas — the Junkers plant at Dessau, the Siebel plant at Halle, the Heinkel works at Rostock-Warnemünde and Oranienburg, the Messerschmitt factory at Wiener Neustadt, the Arado plant at Babelsberg, the Henschel works at Erfurt and Berlin and the Dornier plant at Wismar, were stripped of their presses — including two of the world's largest hydraulic die-forging presses which had been used to produce spars for the Ju 88 — and their machine-tools as well as drawings, models and equipment. The dismantling and transportation of the captured factories were supervised by special squads of engineers sent out from Soviet aircraft plants[1] and train loads of machinery were sent east, many destined for the 1st Experimental Factory at Podberez'e-Ivankovo 100 kilometres northwest of Moscow, while engines, parts and plans from Junkers Motorenwerke at Bernburg and the BMW Eisenbach plant arrived at

---
[1] Shakhurin *Aviatsionnaya promyshlennost' nakanune i v gody Velikoi Otechestvennoi Voiny* in *Sovetski tyl*.

Soviet Air Force

Krasnaya Glinka, just outside Kuibyshev, the site of the 2nd Experimental Factory. Both factories were carefully established and equipped to serve as key centres for the exploitation of German engineers and specialists who would work in close collaboration with experts from TsAGI, TsIAM and the Ministry for Aircraft Production.

With promises of security, food and employment, the Soviets had little difficulty in persuading many German technicians and designers previously employed by the German armaments industry to continue their former work for new masters. In the spring of 1946 the recruits were housed in selected residential areas around Berlin where, although segregated and guarded, they enjoyed a standard of living they would not have believed possible six months before. The honeymoon ended on the night of 21-22 October when at least three and perhaps as many as six thousand German specialists[2] were awoken, courteously but firmly told to dress at once and driven in army trucks to the railway station. Packed into ninety-two special trains with a few personal effects and their nearest relatives and dependents to serve for a guaranteed five years in the USSR, the German experts discussed their possible fate with a mixture of apprehension and indignation as they watched the kilometres separating them from their homeland fly past. At the same time the German POW camps in the Soviet Union were being sifted for scientists, engineers and technicians — prospective additions to the new military-scientific colonies.

From the German aircraft industry the Soviets netted a number of outstanding experts — Prof. Günther Bock, chief of research for the *Deutsche Versuchsansalt für Luftfahrt* or Experimental Aeronautics Institute at Berlin-Aldershof, Rudolph Rental, project engineer for the Me 163 and Me 262 fighters, Dr. Adolph Betz, a specialist in swept-wing research, Dr. Brunolf Baade, formerly chief designer for Junkers and Siegfried Günther, designer of the Heinkel He 162[3]. On their arrival at Podberez'e, the Germans were amazed at the

---

[2] See Stockwell and Michel Bar-Zohar *La Chasse aux Savants Allemands* (Librairie Artheme Fayard 1965).

[3] Günther, who agreed to go over to the Russians while working in a garage in the French Zone, was later to be linked with the alleged development of Kurt Tank's projected Ta 183 jet fighter in the USSR and with preliminary design drafts for the MiG 15. There were unsubstantiated reports that the Ta 183 or an aircraft of very similar configuration had been sighted in the USSR in 1951. See *Ta flog in Russland* in *Flugwelt*, March-April 1961.

thoroughness with which their drawing offices and workshops had been reconstructed; even the ashtrays and calendars had been brought from Germany.

For NII-VVS the first task was to carry out as complete an evaluation of the newer German aircraft as possible. Andrei Kochetkov, Head of NII-VVS Fighter Test Section, headed the team working on the Me 262 — becoming the first Soviet pilot to fly a gas-turbine engined aircraft when he flew the jet fighter from the Shcholkovo runway on 15 August 1945 — and following the discovery of an Arado Ar 234 twin-jet bomber at Damgarten a NII-VVS team under Aleksei Kubyshkin went out in the sole Lend-Lease C-46 transport in March 1946 to inspect the aircraft and report on its suitability for flight tests. The Arado was then flown to Rechlin where a brief evaluation programme was carried out despite a series of engine and undercarriage failures. Tests of the latest Fw 190 fighter series, probably on behalf of the Lavochkin KB, were made by Viktor Rastorguev and several other leading NII-VVS pilots, notably Shiyanov and Demid, were temporarily diverted to concentrate on the tests of German aircraft. The Me 163 was a particular source of interest, but the lack of hydrogen peroxide in quantity for the fighter's HWK 109-509 rocket engine limited exploration to a series of airframe gliding tests using ballasted examples towed aloft by a Tu-2. Four NII-VVS pilots, including Gallai, were involved in these unpopular flights which sometimes culminated in 'heavy' landings[4].

Nonetheless, the measures taken by the *Luftwaffe* to develop target-defence rocket fighters for use against high-altitude day bombers were not lost on the Soviets. Over the winter of 1945-46 Valentin Glushko as head of the rocket-engine research team at Kazan' toured German rocket-engine production and test sites with members of his staff while his former deputy, Sergei Korolyov, was promoted to head the V 1 development project at Kapustin Yar. Glushko and Dushkin modified the German Walter HWK 509C-4 bi-fuel rocket motor for installation in the I-270 (Zh) rocket-fighter, credited to the MiG KB but representing essentially a redesign of the Me 263 (originally the Ju 248). Tested in 1946, the I-270 (Zh) displayed a satisfactory climb-rate and horizontal speed but was handicapped by very limited endurance and poor manoeuvrability. Moreover, the new atomic age indicated that large formations of

---

[4]Gallai *Ispytano v nebe*.

heavy bombers would give way to faster, smaller formations or single intruders as the delivery vehicles for nuclear weapons. Equipped with airborne radars, these would undoubtedly be less vulnerable to the unexpected, high-speed surprise attack of fighters like the Me 163, and development of the I-270 (Zh) is thought to have been abandoned by 1947[5]. In that year, however, Captain Wolfgang Zeisse, formerly chief test-pilot for Siebel, is reported as having made the first powered flight on the DFS 346 rocket-powered research aircraft, completed in the USSR and air-launched from one of the impounded US B-29 bombers after preliminary pilot training in prone position control on modified Grunau and Kranich sailplanes had been undertaken[6]. Two later test-flights on the Soviet DFS 346 were allegedly unsuccessful due to malfunctions in the Soviet in-flight detachment mechanisms.

The decision not to place any of the advanced German combat aircraft in production for the Soviet Air Force had already been taken in December 1945 at a Kremlin conference attended by representatives from the Soviet Air Force and the Ministry of Aircraft Production when Shakhurin raised the question of manufacturing the Me 262 fighter. Yakovlev as Shakhurin's deputy for Research and Development argued strongly against the idea on the grounds that the impressive German fighter was too complex a design to be confidently undertaken by the Soviet aircraft industry and that its demands in piloting and field maintenance would be excessive. He was also apprehensive about the effects such plagiarism might have on the morale of Soviet designers just starting to grapple with the basics of jet aircraft design[7], although there was to be clear evidence of the sources of inspiration in several early Soviet prototypes. Sukhoi's Su-9 tested in 1946 bore a remarkable resemblance to a straight-wing version of the Me 262 and Il'yushin's Il-22 developed at the same time had many features in common with the projected He 343, a four-engined development of the Arado Ar 234 twin-jet bomber[8]. Particular attention was given to the Junkers

---

[5]This aircraft was observed at Ramenskoe in 1947, described as a straight-wing rocket research aircraft, and allocated the Type number 11.

[6]This flight, possibly made in May 1947, may have been associated with the Soviet claim to have broken the sound barrier that month. See Smith & Kay *German Aircraft of the Second World War* (Putnam 1972).

[7]Yakovlev *Tsel' Zhizni*.

[8]Both prototypes were demonstrated at the Tushino Air Day Flypast in August 1947 and allocated the Type numbers 8 and 10 respectively.

Ju 287V2 bomber prototype with swept-forward wings which was discovered at Dessau and transported to Podberez'e together with its designer, Hans Wocke, components for the uncompleted Ju 287V3 and possibly also the bomb-damaged original prototype, the Ju 287V1. A series of experiments with swept-forward winged gliders designed by Tsybin in 1947-48 were probably associated with investigations inspired by the unusual Junkers wing planform, and after the Ju 287V2 had been successfully flight-tested at Ramenskoe in 1947 a number of developments were contemplated including the EF 140, a reconnaissance variant probably tested in prototype form, and the EF 131 six-engined bomber which remained uncompleted. Work on the EF 132 with engines housed in the roots of its swept-back wings and on the EF 150, a four-jet bomber also with swept-back wings, was also rumoured before further research on Junkers designs was transferred to the German Democratic Republic and Brunolf Baade given charge of developing a four-engined commercial transport under the designation Type 152.

If the Soviets were dubious of the benefits to be derived from copying German airframes, they showed no such hesitation regarding the axial-flow gas-turbine engines they had acquired. While later claiming some pre-war commitment to gas-turbine engine research[9], the Soviets continued the production of the BMW 003A and Junkers Jumo 004B axial-flow engines, making them available for installation in Soviet prototypes and giving them the new designations RD-20 and RD-10. Subsequent development of the BMW 003 was undertaken by increasing the fuel feed, the temperature of the gases at the post-turbine stage and the rpm of the turbine to give a thrust of 1,000 kg under the designation RD-21, and versions of the Jumo 004B with increased power output and afterburning to yield 1,000 kg and 1,100 kg thrust were evolved as the RD-10A and RD-10F engines. An order for Soviet fighter airframes to house the German engines was issued as early as February 1945, and in the late autumn the Yakovlev, Mikoyan, Lavochkin and Sukhoi design bureaux had already presented projects for consideration by Stalin, Novikov and Shakhurin.

The first two prototypes to be completed — the Yak-15 adapted

---

[9]The Soviets claim that development of the VRD-1, a 600 kg axial-flow gas-turbine designed by A. Lyul'ka, I.F. Kozlov and P.S. Shevchenko in Leningrad, was interrupted by the outbreak of war in 1941. A development, the 700 kg VRD-2 was built during the war followed by the 1,300 kg VRD-3 which, developed under the designation TR-1, was installed in the Il-22 and Su-11 prototypes of 1947 and 1948.

Soviet Air Force

from the Yak-3 by the simple expedient of exchanging the VK-107 piston engine for a 900 kg thrust Jumo 004B exhausting under the fuselage, and the specially designed MiG-9 powered by two BMW 003 units mounted side by side in the nose — were first flown on the same day, 24 April 1946, by the design bureaux test pilots Mikhail Ivanov and Aleksei Grinchik, who was to lose his life testing one of the MiG-9 prototypes three months later. In August and September they were followed by their ultimately unsuccessful competitors, Sukhoi's twin-engined Su-9 fighter-bomber and the first of Lavochkin's La-150 prototype variants. The Yak-15 and the MiG-9, each built in three prototype examples, were first exhibited to the Soviet public over Tushino on 18 August 1946[10], and Stalin ordered that a further fifteen of each type were to be built in time to take part in the flypast marking the anniversary of the Bolshevik Revolution, the first pre-production machines leaving their factories after a crash production programme by the end of September.

Lieutenant-General Sbytov, soon afterwards replaced by Vasili Stalin as Air Commander of the Moscow Military District, was put in charge of a special jet-fighter pilot training programme [11] and thirty-two pilots trained on the Yak-15 and the MiG-9 were standing by on 7 November when fog and severe icing led to the flypast's cancellation. Stalin immediately ordered that two groups of fifty Yak-15 and MiG-9 fighters were to be prepared for a formation flypast over Moscow the following May Day with rehearsals and preparations commencing in December 1946. The problems posed by co-ordinating the groups of jet fighters with their limited endurance flying from different airfields had not been entirely solved by the end of April and a number of forced landings and accidents took place after this impressive display of Soviet jet-fighter power *en masse* had been held[12]. For Stalin these were minor details and a hundred and ten pilots were decorated for taking part in the flypast, four of them with the Order of Lenin.

---

[10] In this first post-war exhibition of new Soviet aircraft the Bratukhin 'Omega' and G-3 helicopters, the Il-12 transport, the experimental tail-first MiG-8 'Utka' and Lavochkin fighters boosted by auxiliary rocket and pulse-jet engines were shown for the first time.

[11] Four groups were formed consisting of nineteen pilots on the Yak-15, fourteen on the MiG-9, twelve on the I-250 and seven on the La-150 series. See Sbytov *Yeshcho o reaktivnom starte* in *Aviatsiya i Kosmonavtika*, February 1973.

[12] See the account of this flypast in Pyotr Pirogov's *Why I Escaped: The Story of Peter Pirogov* (Duell, Sloan & Pearce, Inc., New York, 1950).

The Day of the MiG-15

The development of jet bombers proceeded more slowly and although the experimental Il-22 four-jet and the Tu-12 twin-jet bombers — the latter adapted from the Tu-2 — both began flight tests in July 1947, neither was accepted for series production and the Red Air Force continued to rely on its piston-engined tactical bombers throughout the nineteen-forties. Over 3,000 examples of the Tu-2 and its later refinements were supplied in the post-war years and these represented the most modern types to augment the stocks of wartime Pe-2, Il-4 and Lend-Lease bombers. The first tactical jet bomber to be built was Il'yushin's Il-28 which was first flown in August 1948 with production for Soviet Air Force bomber regiments commencing shortly afterwards. The twenty-five examples first exhibited at the 1950 May Day flypast were the forerunners of some 5,000 Il-28s manufactured until production was terminated in the spring of 1957. Tupolev also evolved a series of jet-bomber prototypes at this time, the final model being placed in production in 1950 for the Soviet Naval Air Forces (A-VMF) as the Tu-14. Manufacture was, however, limited and only 400 had been delivered before production was phased out in the autumn of 1953. Endeavours to provide an up-dated *shturmovik* were also made but without successfully replacing the Il-10 conceived in 1943. Almost 5,000 Il-10 *shturmoviks* had been supplied to Frontal Aviation's ground-attack regiments before production was terminated in the USSR and transferred to Czechoslovakia for a further four years until 1954. The Il-10 was still in frontline service with the Red Air Force until at least 1956.

Full aerobatic trials on the Yak-15 were made early in 1947 but only 280 examples of the Yak-15 and the modified Yak-15U with a tricycle undercarriage had been built before they were superceded by the improved Yak-17 featuring aerodynamic refinements and the RD-10A engine with uprated thrust. A total of 430 Yak-17 fighters and Yak-17UTI two-seat fighter conversion trainers were built between March 1948 and August 1949, with the first fighter regiments becoming operational on the new Yak-17s by late 1948. In comparison with fighter production during the war years, the first Yak jets were supplied on a small scale as were the MiG-9s of which 550 were built between early 1947 and July 1948. Numerically, the Soviet fighter force relied on its extensive reserve of piston-engined fighters of which the latest types were the Yak-9U and Yak-9P, the Yak-3U fitted with the VK-107 inline engine, and the La-9 and its development the La-11 built for the Soviet Air Force from 1946 and 1947 respectively[13]. The La-9 with four 23mm cannon was the most heavily armed Soviet fighter yet built and was intended for close-support while its 1947 development, the La-11, was modified as a long-range escort fighter with a range of 2,550 km; both were powered by late production versions of Shvetsov's ASh-82 radial. Behind such modern fighters stood a vast reserve of older models inherited from the Great Patriotic War.

The Yak-17 and MiG-9 were seen essentially as interim measures pending the introduction of a more advanced day fighter for the Soviet Air Force with high-altitude intercept capabilities, for which a specification had been issued early in 1946 with the wealth of German research on swept-wing and high-speed aircraft design to draw upon. Its fundamental purpose would be to counter the high-altitude strategic bomber, and for this the new fighter was to be provided with a substantial cannon armament, a high rate of climb, good manoeuvrability at altitudes over 11,000 metres and an endurance of at least one hour. Designs were submitted by the Yakovlev, Lavochkin and Mikoyan design bureaux with the latter's 'Type S' emerging victorious to enter widescale production as the legendary MiG-15. All three competing design bureaux, in common with the Il'yushin, Tupolev and Sukhoi KBs engaged on bomber projects, availed themselves of the generously supplied British Nene 2 and Derwent 5 centrifugal-flow gas-turbines[14] which were copied and placed in production at top speed as the RD-45 and RD-500 at GAZ No. 45 and GAZ No. 500, Moscow, manufacture being subsequently extended to larger aeroengine plants as soon as the pilot series had been satisfactorily completed. The officially declared first flight by the MiG-15 took place on 30 December 1947[15], and it had already

---

[13] When discussing the production of the La-11 with Lavochkin, Stalin displayed a distinct preference to the proven piston-engined fighter as opposed to the unknown factor of Mikoyan's MiG-9. When Lavochkin recommended the production of his competitor, Stalin is reported to have said, 'The La-11 is an aircraft in which all the defects have been eliminated, there is a pilot who can fly it and a mechanic to look after it. But what is the MiG? A heap of metal......' Arlazorov *Front idyot cherez KB*.

[14] The British government gave permission in September 1946 for ten Nene engines to be exported to the USSR followed by fifteen more in March 1947. In all twenty five Rolls-Royce Nene 2 and thirty Derwent 5 jet engines were supplied in 1947.

[15] A first flight by an earlier prototype which later crashed is rumoured to have taken place the previous July. Up to now the Soviets have been more reticent about the development of the MiG-15 than about their other early jets.

been decided to place the fighter in production at GAZ No. 1, Kuibyshev, before the contending Lavochkin and Yakovlev prototypes had been handed over to NII-VVS for flight tests in the summer of 1948[16]. Armed with two 23 mm cannon, soon supplemented by a 37mm N cannon on the port side of the nose, the first pre-production examples of the MiG-15 were delivered to NII-VVS for State tests in the autumn of 1948 powered by a 2,200 kg thrust RD-45 engine. First deliveries to IA-PVO began shortly afterwards and at an early stage in manufacture the RD-45 was replaced by the revised and more powerful RD-45F to give the new MiG a top speed of 1,050 kph at sea-level and 983 kph at 10,000 metres with a normal loaded weight of 4,806 kgs, making it the world's lightest as well as one of its fastest jet fighters at that time.

While successful in meeting the 1946 specification requirements, the new fighter was not without its drawbacks. It had a tendency to flick over into a spin if turned too tightly and was to prove an unstable gun-platform at high speeds with a sub-sonic airframe prone to snaking if driven over Mach 0.86. Its instrumentation was sparse by Western standards and its cockpit cramped. Combat experience was to show that its slow firing cannon placed it at a decided disadvantage when confronted by fighters with faster firing, smaller-calibre armament. Even so, the MiG-15 signified a dramatic advance in Soviet day fighter capability and alerted the West to the realisation that the makeshift era of the Yak-17 and MiG-9 had passed. Production of the MiG-15 was soon extended from Kuibyshev to include the fighter plants at Gorky and Tbilisi; in all between 15,000 and 16,000 MiG-15 fighters were built between 1948 and 1956 when residual production was finally ended[17].

The MiG-15 was first encountered in combat by USAF F-51

---

[16]Lavochkin produced three very similar fighter prototypes with swept-back, shoulder-mounted wings. The La-168 with a Derwent engine and its development, the La-174, with a RD-500, were both tested in 1948 with the latter accepted for limited series production comprising about a hunded and fifty examples as the La-15 in 1948-49. The La-176 developed in parallel but with the more powerful RD-45F engine was the first Soviet jet aircraft to dive through the sound barrier in January 1949 but it was not manufactured. Yakovlev's swept-wing Yak-30 with a RD-500 engine was evolved from the straight-winged Yak-19 and Yak-25 fighters prototypes developed in parallel with the Yak-15 and Yak-17 whose ultimate refinement, the Yak-23 with a RD-500 engine, emerged as a back-up design in case of failure by the more adventurous swept-wing fighters.

[17]US Intelligence estimated that between 5,500 and 6,200 MiG-15s had been produced by 1951. Rees *The Limited War*.

Soviet Air Force

fighters over Korea on 1 November 1950 and the new Soviet fighter was soon recognised as the most potent element in the opposing communist air forces. Generally vulnerable to the F-86 Sabre with its machine-gun armament, better gunsight and superior piloting, the MiG-15 showed a disconcertingly better climb, better operating ceiling and better turning ability than its US adversary at altitude while its cannon exacted a heavy toll for daylight bombing by B-29 formations unless effective escort was provided. Against the F-86 the Chinese communist trainees and their Soviet instructors operating from airfields in Manchuria north of the Yalu river preferred stern dive attacks, breaking away after one pass and using the MiG's superior climb-rate to disengage. Protracted dogfights were avoided and when pursued and overtaken novice MiG-15 pilots showed a decided preference for absorbing hits in the tail and engine and ejecting rather than attempting evasive manoeuvres which would leave them exposed to hits nearer the cockpit. More sophisticated tactics including the use of decoy groups and staggered formations were used against the F-86 in 1952 when blocks of up to a hundred and eighty MiG-15s ventured south of the Yalu. At the end of the Korean War the Chinese Communist Air Force was estimated to possess up to 2,000 MiG-15 fighters out of an overall total of 4,000 supplied by the USSR. Eight hundred and fifty MiG-15 fighters were claimed as destroyed and it was calculated that in excess of a thousand more had been lost as a result of battle damage, accidents or mechanical failure.

Work on four developments of the basic MiG-15 was begun shortly after the fighter had entered production. The SD, later the MiG-15*bis*, was an improved version of the standard day fighter with more comprehensive radio and electronic equipment and powered by a 2,700 kg thrust VK-1 engine, which was developed by Klimov from the basic Nene, tested late in 1949 and replacing the earlier MiG-15 on the production lines the year following. The ST or MiG-15UTI two-seat conversion trainer of which over 1,700 were built was placed in production in 1949 to ease the problems of pilot training and replace the only extant jet fighter trainer, the superannuated Yak-17UTI. Later models of the MiG-15UTI shared the same powerplant and basic airframe as the MiG-15bis. The SP, a modified MiG-15UTI with an early *Izumrud* (Emerald) S-band radar mounted in a lip fairing over the air intake was an endeavour to provide an all-weather version of the MiG-15 and was probably

The Day of the MiG-15

dictated by the failure of Sukhoi's cumbersome Su-15 all-weather fighter prototype which was lost during tests in 1948. The *Izumrud* was subsequently installed in the single-seat MiG-15*bis* and supplied as the MiG-15P interceptor. The SI was a more radical approach to remedying the MiG-15's aerodynamic shortcomings, and after completing satisfactorily its test programme begun in January 1950 it was placed in production as the MiG-17. From now on the abbreviation MiG was to be synonymous with the words Soviet fighter.

German technology was not the only impetus behind the post-war Soviet Air Force. In August and November 1944 three USAF B-29 Superfortresses force-landed on Soviet territory in the Far East after carrying out raids over Japan, presenting Stalin with examples of the world's most sophisticated strategic bomber. Two of the B-29s were dismantled and their components reproduced by the Tupolev KB to create its own copy of the United States machine under the designation Tu-4. A crash programme to produce a series of pre-production examples was then mounted at GAZ No. 22, Kazan', each aircraft being immediately collected by NII-VVS pilots on its completion and flown to Shcholkovo for exhaustive flight tests. Modifications proposed as the tests proceeded, including improved vision from the cockpit, lighter controls and an effective de-icing system, were incorporated in later examples of the pre-production batch and difficulties encountered with the eighteen-cylinder ASh-75TK radial, Shvetsov's adaption of the Wright Cyclone R-3350 installed on the B-29, were overcome. The acquisition of the B-29 and its unlicenced production in the USSR enabled the Long-Range Air Force or *Dal'nyaya aviatsiya* (DA) to be reconstituted in April 1946 under Chief Air Marshal Golovanov, one of the few Soviet Air Force Command veterans of the Great Patriotic War to survive the year.

The appearance of the first three Tu-4 pre-production machines at the 1947 Air Day flown by NII-VVS pilots Rybko, Gallai and Vasil'chenko with Marshal Golovanov in the lead bomber came as stunning confirmation that the USSR was producing its own 'Superfortresses', although there had already been intimations that the Soviets were at work copying the impounded USAF bombers, and agents acting for the Soviet government had tried to purchase tyres, wheels and brake assemblies for the B-29 the year before. Confusion in the aircraft control over Tushino on this occasion forced the four-engined bombers to pass only 200 metres over the heads of the spectators who applauded wildly, believing this to be a planned thrill. The flight test programme took almost two years with the first deliveries of the Tu-4 to DA regiments taking place in 1949, by which time the B-29 was already obsolete. Over 1,500 Tu-4 bombers were built, mainly in Kazan', before production ended in 1954.

Although the Tu-4 provided a standard modern bomber for the DA, it was by no means fully intercontinental or a match for the mightly USAF B-36, and Tupolev was directed to prepare a larger development of the Tu-4 with the range necessary for return strikes over North America. Work on the resulting Tu-85 was undertaken in 1949, and the huge aircraft powered by four VD-4K 28-cylinder engines and with an ultimate range of 12,000-13,000 kms was ready for flight testing in 1951 when it was first publically displayed over Tushino. By this time, however, the emergence of the United States B-52 four-engined turbojet bomber had already relegated piston-engined strategic bombers to the realms of obsolescence and development of the imposing Tu-85 was abandoned in favour of new turbojet and turboprop projects prepared by the Tupolev, Myasishchev and Il'yushin design bureaux[18]. The Tu-85 was certainly successful indirectly in inducing the Soviet long-range bomber scare of the early fifties and in obliging the USA to divert considerable resources into strengthening its strategic air defences.

The Soviet Union ended the Second World War with a frontline strength of 16,000 to 18,000 aircraft but by 1946, as manufacture was cut back and obsolete types discarded, this total had been reduced by about 4,000 machines — rising again to an estimated 20,000 aircraft by the start of the fifties as the mass production of jet types got under way[19]. Changes were also made in the High Command of the Soviet Air Force as well as in its equipment. In March 1946 Chief Air Marshal Novikov, twice decorated as a Hero of the Soviet Union the year before, was dismissed as C-in-C Soviet Air Force (a title replacing that of Red Air Force) in favour of General Vershinin,

---

[18] A detailed history of the acquisition, copying and development of the B-29 in the USSR appeared under the title *Billion Dollar Bomber* in 'Air Enthusiast', July-October 1971. Gallai's account of the Tu-4 test programme in his book *Ispytano v nebe* is also of particular interest.

[19] USAF Intelligence assessed the Soviet Air Force's general distribution at this time as 7,000 aircraft in East Germany and the Eastern European Satellites, 5,000 in the Far East and 8,000 in the European, Central and Siberian USSR. Cain & Voaden *Military Aircraft of the USSR*.

former commander of the 4th Air Army. Allegedly libelled by Stalin's son, Vasili[20], Novikov was arrested and interned, to be released only after the death of the dictator he had served so faithfully. With Novikov went almost his entire wartime command; his Chief of Air Staff, Marshal Khudyakov, had already been replaced by General Sudets and relegated to the command of an air army in the Far East whence General Zhigarev was now recalled to take over as First Deputy C-in-C Soviet Air Force from General Vorozheikin, who was rusticated to head a faculty at the Zhukovski Air Force Engineering Academy. Marshal Falaleev was also dropped from his post as a Deputy C-in-C and put in charge of the Red Banner Air Force Academy at Monino, Marshal Zhavoronkov removed as Commander of Naval Air Forces (A-VMF) and General Aleksandr Repin, Head of the Air Force Engineering-Technical Service (ITS) replaced by General Ivan Markov who had served in a similar capacity for Golovanov's wartime ADD.

Earlier, in December 1945, Shakhurin had been dismissed and replaced as Minister for Aircraft Production by Khrunichev, one of his wartime deputies. Tried and later interned for alleged mismanagement of the aircraft industry during the evacuation of 1941, a commission to investigate charges against Shakhurin was assembled in early 1946 and 'evidence' exacted from factory directors, chief engineers and aircraft designers[21].

Late in 1947 further changes were made. Marshal Astakhov was replaced as Head of GU-GVF (retitled the Ministry of Civil Aviation in 1964) by General Baidukov, wartime commander of IV *Shturmovik* Corps, and Chief Air Marshal Golovanov who had hitherto had the special patronage of Stalin was removed from Command of the Long-Range Air Force. Golovanov was replaced by Zhigarev who retained his post as First Deputy C-in-C Soviet Air Force, bringing the DA back into the overall command structure of the Soviet Air Force. In 1949 Stalin turned the wheel of fortune once more, dismissing Vershinin and making Zhigarev the new C-in-C Soviet Air Force. For the next seven and a half years the hand at the helm of the Soviet Air Force was the same one that had presided over its destruction in 1941.

---

[20]Svetlana Alleluyeva *Twenty Letters*.
[21]Lavochkin incurred Stalin's displeasure by refusing to testify against Shakhurin. See Chesanov's article on Lavochkin in *Aviatsiya i Kosmonavtika*, September 1963.

14 Continuity & Change in the Soviet Air Forces

After the series of capricious command changes carried out by Stalin in the four years after the Great Patriotic War, the Soviet Air Forces were to enjoy a far greater degree of command continuity over the next two decades. Zhigarev surivived the change of political leadership on the death of Stalin and remained C-in-C Soviet Air Forces for a further four years until Khrushchov retired him honorably to head the Civil Air Fleet (GVF) Administration[1] and recalled Vershinin from the Baku PVO Zone for a second and longer term of office. The Tactical Air Force or *Frontovaya aviatsiya* (FA) comprising the air armies came under a deputy to the C-in-C Soviet Air Forces and until the end of the nineteen-fifties was the responsibility in turn of Generals Zhigarev, Agal'tsov and Rudenko. The FA remained the largest component of the Soviet Air Forces, although its strength declined from an estimated 12,000 aircraft in the early fifties to between 4,000 and 5,000 aircraft backed up by some 2,000 additional obsolescent types in service in the interior or utilised for training at the opening of the seventies. In the fifties the FA was composed of about fifteen air armies, a number of which had been reformed and redesignated. Rudenko's 16th Air Army which remained to support the Group of Soviet Forces in East Germany was subsequently redesignated the 24th Air Army, indicating that at least six new air armies had been formed while others, including the 3rd and 6th Air Armies, were disbanded either shortly before or soon after the end of the Second World War. Air armies were also deployed in support of the Northern, Central and Southern Groups of Soviet Forces based in the East European Satellites as well as in the

---

[1]GVF was headed by a series of former Soviet Air Force Command Staff in the twenty-five years following the Second World War. General Baidukov, former commander of IV *Shturmovik* Corps, was replaced as head of GU-GVF by Marshal Zhavoronkov, ex- C-in-C Naval Air Forces in 1949, followed by Marshal Zhigarev between 1957 and 1959 and Marshal Loginov until 1970.

military districts of the USSR itself. The current status of the Soviet air armies is uncertain and there have been reports that the air army as such no longer exists, the air division remaining as the highest echelon with attachment directly to the headquarters of army group or military district commands. It would, however, be more likely to be the corps echelon which has been discarded since its primary function of enabling the wartime GKO to mount concentrated air power in chosen sectors is no longer relevant to present-day Soviet air doctrines. During the fifties and early sixties corps attachment to air army headquarters was, in any case, on a far more permanent basis than in wartime and the usual air army complement comprised two fighter, a bomber and a *shturmovik* corps, the last being phased out with the disappearance of the Il-10 and the transfer of its ground-attack function to fighter-bombers. Tactical bomber strength was also reduced with the transfer of bomber regiments from the ageing Pe-2 and Tu-2 piston-engined bombers to the twin-jet Il-28 from 1950 when the largest tactical bomber echelon in the air army was usually a division.

The phasing out of the Il-10 deprived the FA temporarily of a specific ground-attack aircraft and attempts to update the concept in the form of the turboprop Tu-91, shown to a Western air delegation at Kubinka in 1956, and Il'yushin's Il-40 powered by two turbojets were eventually cut short by Khrushchov's decision to terminate development of this line of combat aircraft. For a decade the FA had to rely on its MiG fighters and Il-28 bombers for close-support until the introduction in 1959 of Sukhoi's Su-7 fighter-bomber which, despite a restricted combat radius and limited capacity to carry external ordnance, has served faithfully alongside the multi-role MiG-21 in a series of versions incorporating uprated engines, more sophisticated electronic equipment and an improved capability to operate from short tactical air strips.

A suitable replacement for the Il-28, obsolescent by the mid-fifties, took longer to arrive and was only fully achieved with the introduction of the twin-engined, two-seat multi-purpose Yak-28 in 1963-64 preceded by an earlier version, the Yak-27R, which was built in small numbers and primarily for tactical reconnaissance at the close of the fifties.

The Soviet Air Defence (PVO) organisation emerged from the Great Patriotic War with four fronts — the Western, South-Western, Central and Transcaucasian — and the Maritime, Amur and

Transbaikal PVO Armies in the Far East, but still under the Commander of Red Army Artillery who co-ordinated PVO resources through the *Tsentral'ny shtab PVO strany* or Central Homeland Defence Staff and the *Tsentral'ny shtab istrebitel'noi aviatsii* — the Central PVO Fighter Staff under General Savitski, former commander of III Guards Fighter Corps, who was attached to the Command Staff of the Soviet Air Forces. In 1948 the PVO Troops (*voiska PVO*) were detached from the Red Army Artillery Command and placed under Marshal Leonid Govorov who had served since the war as Commander of the Leningrad Military District and Chief Inspector of Soviet Land Forces. In May 1954 Govorov received the official title of C-in-C PVO Troops (*Glavnokomanduyushchi voiskami PVO*) and was made a Deputy Minister for Defence, reflecting the enhanced importance attached to an autonomous strategic air defence command since Stalin's death.

When Govorov died in 1955, the PVO Command passed to his deputy, General Biryuzov, formerly in command of the Maritime PVO Army in the Far East, who was later appointed C-in-C Strategic Rocket Forces by Khrushchev in April 1962 when his place was taken by General Sudets, moved from the Command of the Long-Range Air Force. General Pavel Batitski who assumed the Command of PVO in July 1966 and was made a Marshal two years later, was at that time First Deputy Chief of the General Staff with a variegated but extensive Air Force and PVO career behind him. The command upheavals at the end of the nineteen-forties had raised Batitski from chief of staff in a PVO region to the combined posts of First Deputy to the C-in-C Soviet Air Forces and Chief of Air Staff under Zhigarev until, with Stalin's demise, he was relegated to serve as deputy and ultimately PVO commander in the Moscow Military District for the next ten years.

During the period between 1945 and 1950 the *Istrebitel'naya aviatsiya-PVO* or Air Defence Fighter Command had a strictly limited night and all-weather capability and, for the first half of the fifties, was reliant on all-weather versions of the MiG-15 and MiG-17 day fighters. The provision of a truly all-weather strategic air defence fighter presented considerable problems to the aircraft industry with its lack of technological experience in this field, and neither the Mikoyan I-320 or the Lavochkin La-200 twin-engined two-seat purpose-designed all-weather interceptors built and tested in 1949-51 were accepted for production. The deadlock was resolved

Continuity & Change in the Soviet Air Forces

in the summer of 1951 when Stalin decreed that other projects were to be dropped in favour of the twin-engined two-seat Yak-25, powered initially by two AM-5 axial-flow engines, which was tested in 1953 and first publically displayed over Tushino during the 1955 Air Day display. Production of the Yak-25 for PVO Fighter Command began in 1953 with some 600 examples supplied over the next four years and the basic design utilised for the evolution of an associated series of tactical bomber and reconnaissance aircraft, all-weather fighter developments, and a high-altitude strategic reconnaissance machine employed in a similar manner to Gary Powers Lockheed U-2 brought down by Biryuzov's PVO missile batteries near Sverdlovsk in May 1960.

While deliveries of the Yak-25 were being made, a new single-seat delta-wing missile-armed all-weather interceptor was being developed by the Sukhoi design bureau, first shown at the Tushino Air Day in 1956 but not entering operational service with IA-PVO until about five years later as the Su-11. In the latter half of the sixties a revised version of the Su-11 with an uprated AL-7F engine, improved radar and more advanced air-to-air missiles was supplied to IA-PVO which then consisted of an estimated 3,500 fighters and accounted for approximately half the total manpower of the *voiska PVO*, the other half comprising the *Zenitnaya artilleriya PVO* (ZA-PVO) or Anti-Aircraft Artillery Command armed with a growing proportion of surface-to-air missiles.

At the 1961 Air Day display twelve examples of a new, heavy fighter of bomber dimensions passed over Tushino — apparently designed for long-range reconnaissance and strike roles — but in 1967 their revised versions were accompanied by another variant, the Tu-28P, armed with air-to-air missiles and clearly equipped and intended for long-endurance peripheral patrols over areas unprotected or inadequately covered by the ZA-PVO missile defences. At this time too a special version of the Tu-114 turboprop transport revised to act as an airborne warning and control aircraft by mounting a 'saucer' type early warning radar scanner over the fuselage was noted entering service with PVO. With its 'look-down' radar capability, this aircraft can mount long-endurance surveillance patrols over remote border regions unprotected by surface-to-air missile screens and direct interceptors or patrolling Tu-28P fighters on to low-flying intruders indiscernible by ground radar defences.

By 1970 the IA-PVO was estimated as possessing some 3,000

Soviet Air Force

fighters, primarily all-weather MiG-21, Su-11 and Yak-28P fighters — the last representing the latest derivitive of the original Yak-25 — with a number of the larger Tu-28P fighters deployed in Northern and Eastern Siberia and a remaining fund of obsolescent MiG-17PF and MiG-19PM fighters still in service in the interior military districts of the USSR.

After the dismissal of Chief Air Marshal Golovanov in 1947 as C-in-C Long-Range Air Force or *Dal'nyaya aviatsiya* (DA), the command passed to a series of men well versed in tactical air warfare but lacking any real experience in the new strategic air power Stalin wished to create. Zhigarev was replaced as C-in-C Long-Range Air Force in 1949 by Rudenko, recalled from the air forces supporting the Soviet army group in East Germany, and in 1953 the Long-Range Air Force came under Chief Air Marshal Novikov, released and re-established after Stalin's death, until he in turn was replaced by General Sudents in 1955.

The main technological task lay in providing the Long-Range Air Force with a strategic bomber capable of raiding North America yet with the performance necessary for its survival in penetrating the US air defences. In the post-war period the requisite range seemed to demand the use of turboprop engines in such a bomber and work on the development of a high-power turboprop engine was centred on the 2nd Experimental Factory, Kuibyshev, where a team of German and Austrian engineers under Ferdinand Brandner attempted to couple two 6,040 eshp Jumo 022 units through a common gearbox. When the frontal area of the composite engine turned out to be too great, the project was taken over by Nikolai Kuznetsov, formerly deputy chief designer at GAZ No. 26, Ufa, who eventually produced the NK-12 turboprop driving contra-rotating airscrews initially capable of providing some 9,000 eshp but later improved to give 14,000 eshp as the NK-12MV. Work on Kuznetsov's preceding TV-4 turboprop designed to produce 4,000-4,500 eshp and then envisaged as a means of updating the Tu-4 was suspended, as was the development of the TV-02 turboprop of similar output and for the same purpose under Aleksandr Ivchenko at the rebuilt Zaporozh'e aeroengine plant. Both engines were, however, used subsequently to develop turboprop units for Antonov transports and Il'yushin's Il-18 airliner.

Four Kuznetsov NK-12 turboprops were installed in Tupolev's Tu-20 (Tu-95) swept-wing strategic bomber which showed unmistakable evidence of its derivation from the original B-29/Tu-4 and was developed in parallel with Myasishchev's M-4 four-turbojet strategic bomber and probably intended as a backup for it. Myasishchev had been granted considerable financial and technical resources at the newly established GAZ No. 23, Fili, but his M-4 bomber reported in 1953 and first publically shown during the 1954 May Day flypast in company with Tupolev's Tu-16 (Tu-88) twin-jet medium bomber and powered by the same AM-3 axial-flow engines, proved to be a disappointment. Its range of 9,000 kms fell a long way short of the 16,000 kms specified and while the design was not scrapped as Khrushchov later claimed in his memoirs[2], it seems probable that no more than 160 to 180 examples were built. Although later models were fitted with more powerful and economical Solovy'ev turbofan engines and its effective range extended with the introduction of in-flight refuelling, its importance as a strategic bomber had been eclipsed by Khrushchov's decision to concentrate resources on Marshal Nedelin's Strategic Rocket Forces. A number of M-4 bombers were handed over to the Naval Air Forces and adapted to serve in long-range maritime reconnaissance and tanker roles, in which form the last variant of the M-4 was exhibited during the 1967 Air Display. Myasishchev's second essay in strategic bomber design was no more successful. His striking delta-wing M-50 powered by four Solvy'ev turbofans developed in the late fifties is thought to have had a limited supersonic dash capability but, in common with the M-4, it lacked the range needed for return raids over the USA. Western observers were far more impressed by the M-50 than was Khruschov who closed down the design bureau, terminated further work on strategic bombers, turned the Fili factory over to helicopter production and put Myasishchev out to grass as Head of TsAGI. When Myasishchev's mighty delta was first openly revealed at the 1961 Air Day, it had already been relegated to research and development projects.

The inadequate range envinced by the M-4 switched strategic emphasis to the Tu-20, first openly revealed at the 1955 Air Day display where the appearance of no less than five pre-series aircraft indicated that its service introduction would not be long delayed. By 1961 the Tu-20 had acquired a 'stand-off' attack capability in the form of a 650 km air-to-surface missile carried under the fuselage, but

---

[2]Khrushchov Remembers: *The Last Testament*.

Soviet Air Force

while some fifty bombers armed in this way are thought to have been delivered to the Long-Range Air Force its strictly subsonic performance rendered its chances of penetrating the US air defences extremely doubtful. Later variants of the Tu-20 have been used for the collection of electronic intelligence and for long-range maritime reconnaissance and have been frequent visitors at NATO naval exercises. Whatever its limitations in the role for which it was conceived, the Tu-20 was undoubtedly successful in maintaining the spectre of Soviet strategic bomber potential and thus diverting US technical and financial resources into the construction of interceptor fighter bases and early-warning radar sites.

Production of both the M-4 and the Tu-20 had probably ceased before command of the Long-Range Air Force passed in 1962 to General Agal'tsov — 'Comrade Martin' of the Soviet Volunteer Air Group in Spain, interned and then 'rehabilitated' during the Great Patriotic War. Agal'tsov had shown an amazing talent for survival and for reclimbing the command ladder, his post-war career having already included serving as First Deputy C-in-C Soviet Air Forces under Zhigarev, two years as Inspector-General to the Air Forces, and a term in an unspecified Command Staff post as a deputy under Vershinin.

Most of Agal'tsov's machines were medium-range Tu-16 twin-jet bombers of which some 1,800 were produced for the Long-Range and Naval Air Forces between 1952 and 1958. With a range of around 7,000 kms, the usefulness of the Tu-16 was increased with the introduction of wingtip-to-wingtip in-flight refuelling techniques and the conversion of many Tu-16s in the early 1960s to carry either two 100 km RD-500 powered air-to-surface missiles under its wings or a single RD-9 powered missile housed under the fuselage and with a range of over 200 kms. The second half of the sixties saw the Tu-16 being replaced by its successor, the sleek Tu-22 twin-jet with an unfuelled range of about 2,300 kms and armed with a 750 km air-to-surface missile, although many Tu-16s remain in service as missile-carrying bombers, tankers, reconnaissance aircraft and electronic intelligence collectors. At the end of the sixties the Long-Range Air Force had about a hundred M-4 bombers, probably half of which had been modified to serve as tankers, and some fifty Tu-20s supported by about seven hundred Tu-22 and Tu-16 medium bombers armed with a variety of air-to-surface missiles. It had not attained the status of an inter-continental strategic force, however, and its future ability to do so remains in doubt.

The Naval Air Forces (A-VMF) were also expanded in the immediate post-war years, but General Preobrazhenski — the hero of the first Soviet retaliatory bomber raid over Berlin in August 1941 and C-in-C Naval Air Forces — was hit by the cut-back from 1953 onwards when the Soviet surface fleet was reduced and the emphasis shifted to submarine construction. Naval Air Force fighter units were absorbed into coastal PVO zones and although, during the early nineteen-fifties, the mine and torpedo regiments exchanged their obsolete Il-4 and Tu-2 torpedo bombers for their modern Tu-14 and Il-28T twin-jet equivalents and the new Be-6 flying boat came into maritime reconnaissance service, few new types of aircraft were evolved for A-VMF and its condition came to resemble that of the 1938-41 period when it had been enlarged with machines discarded by the Red Air Force. Its role seemed to have been limited to supporting maritime frontier defence, general reconnaissance and anti-shipping tasks with only an embrionic anti-submarine warfare capability in the form of sonar-equipped shore-based Mi-4 helicopters assisting ASW coastal defence vessels. By the end of the 1950s A-VMF had started to improve its strike capability against carriers and large warships with the introduction of the Tu-16 equipped for in-flight refuelling and armed with 100 km and 200 km air-to-surface missiles, both of which were in fact better suited to an anti-shipping strike function than for use as stand-off weapons with the Long-Range Air Force.

Further development of the A-VMF and a reshaping of its part in the new global Soviet defence strategy was undertaken by Colonel-General Borzov[3] who assumed command of the Naval Air Forces in 1962, and more serious attention was given to developing anti-submarine warfare capability, specifically against Polaris submarines able to launch their missiles while still far from Soviet coastal waters. New Kamov Ka-25 ASW helicopters were taken to sea on board the *Kresta*-class cruisers and in 1967 the first Soviet ASW helicopter-carrier, the 18,000 ton *Moskva* appeared followed by her sister ship, *Leningrad*, whose Ka-25s were equipped with search radars, dunking sonar, magnetic anomaly detectors and an internal weapons bay. An

---

[3] Borzov had commanded the 1st Guards Mine & Torpedo Bomber Regiment in the Baltic during the Great Patriotic War and was decorated as a Hero of the Soviet Union. From December 1951 Borzov served as a deputy Fleet Air Force commander and from 1960 as Preobrazhenski's deputy.

extended and more sophisticated visual and electronic reconnaissance potential and the ability to exercise in-flight control of cruise missiles launched from surface vessels and submarines came with special long-range maritime surveillance and electronic intelligence versions of the Tu-20, Tu-16 and M-4 — joined by the new Be-12 turboprop ASW flying boat in countering the threat presented by the longer-range Polaris A-2 and A-3 rockets. By 1970 A-VMF was credited with a force of about a thousand aircraft, including at least 350 Tu-16 and Tu-22 missile carriers, some sixty Be-6 and Be-12 flying boats and well over a hundred Mi-4 and Ka-25 ASW helicopters.

The fifth and newest element of the post-war Soviet Air Forces was Marshal Skripko's *Voenno-transportnaya aviatsiya* (VTA) formed shortly after the end of the Second World War as the *Desantno-transportnaya aviatsiya* (DTA) or Airborne Forces Transport Command. The later VTA's role was wider than conveying the paratroops of Colonel-General Margelov's *Vozdushno-desantnye voiska* (VDV) although this remains its most important function. Until the introduction of the Antonov turboprop transports in the mid-fifties, VTA had to rely on the wartime Li-2 (C-47) which was produced in the USSR until 1953 and on the post-war Il-12 and Il-14 twin piston-motor transports supplemented by converted Tu-4s[4] and discarded Tu-2 bombers adapted to carry loads slung under the fuselage. Towards the end of the nineteen-forties troop-carrying gliders were supplied in small numbers to offset the low delivery capability of the twin-engined transports then available, but by 1954 the Mi-4 helicopter was already in service with VTA as a delivery vehicle for troops and light equipment. At least half the total of VTA's 3,000 machines were helicopters by the end of the sixties, and the Mi-4 had been surplanted by the larger and more powerful Mi-6, Mi-8 and Mi-10 helicopters powered by turboshaft engines[5].

Antonov's first turboprop transport, the twin-engined An-8 first shown at the 1956 Tushino Air Day, proved too small for VTA's general requirements and less than two hundred were built before it

---

[4]Although the Tu-70 prototype military transport derived from the B-29 first flew in 1947 neither it or its later development with rear-fuselage ramp-loading, the Tu-75, were built for VTA.

[5]During the late 1940's Bratukhin developed a series of heavy twin-rotor helicopters based on his wartime 'Omega' design. None were successful and the Bratukhin design bureau was disbanded in 1951.

was replaced by the larger four-engined An-12 accommodating a hundred troops or carrying trucks, light tanks and armoured personnel carriers. Over six hundred An-12 transports have been delivered to VTA since 1959 and, together with the larger An-22 able to carry tanks and tracked missile-launchers which entered service in 1967, these provide the basic air transport for the USSR's seven airborne divisions. During the *Dvina* exercise of March 1970, the VTA was able to land an airborne division together with its supporting heavy equipment within the space of twenty-two minutes, and transport deliveries to the front line or landings in the rear of the 'enemy' have since played a prominent part in Soviet Army manoeuvres. However, as the impressive exercises involving the Red Army and the Special Purpose Air Arm in the 1930s later demonstrated, show-piece exercises are no real criteria for assessing actual performance under authentic battle conditions.

The post-war Ministers for Aircraft Production M.V. Khrunichev and P.V. Dement'ev, both of whom served as deputies under Shakhurin, have presided over an expanding industry as new factories producing electronic equipment and missiles were established. Of the four hundred or so MAP plants there are five fighter factories, nine producing bombers, transports and the larger civil aircraft, ten manufacturing helicopters, light and utility aircraft and ten aeroengine plants. These major factories have also been producing military and civil aircraft for export in increasing quantities as well as supplying the Soviet Air Forces and *Aeroflot*, with their 'fringe' productive capacity taken up by the manufacture of such items as buses, bicycles, radios and saucepans which are turned out for the consumer market under the same roof as MiG-21 fighters or An-12 transports. The residual production of older but still useful types of aircraft has frequently been transferred to factories in Poland and Czechoslovakia, the latter in turn successfully exporting to the USSR its light Aero and Zlin types and the 'Delfin' and L39 basic jet trainers.

Many of the manufacturing precepts applicable to military aircraft in the Great Patriotic War have been maintained over the past thirty years and the emphasis has remained on providing simple, sturdy machines with good handling qualities and presenting as few problems as possible to routine servicing and maintenance in the field. Despite the immense technological advances made in the industry, however, many western observers with the opportunity of

Soviet Air Force

studying Soviet aircraft at close quarters have commented on the relative crudity of their finish. Overall, aircraft types have been selected carefully for production and retained in manufacture for long periods with a distinct preference for extensive up-datings of the basic airframe rather than embarking on an entirely new design.

The classic example here has been the MiG-21 fighter which has been in service for over fifteen years and whose 'third generation' developments now being delivered will certainly still be in the frontline of the Soviet Air Forces' combat aircraft at the end of the seventies. Like the MiG-15, the MiG-21 was envisaged as an air superiority day fighter with project work commencing in late 1953 or 1954 when the new MiG-19 had barely entered service[6]. The project prototypes were built in 1954-55, two with swept-back wings — the first of which, the Ye-50, was flown in 1955 followed by the second, the Ye-2A — and the Ye-5 with a delta-wing planform in 1956. The Ye-2A and the Ye-5, both first exhibited at the 1956 Air Day display, were built in batches of twenty-five examples for evaluation by NII-VVS in 1957, the Ye-5 delta emerging as the victor with production of a hundred pre-series service fighter models, delivered to regiments in the Moscow Military District in the summer of 1959, being undertaken at GAZ No. 21, Gorky. Revisions were speedily incorporated into the series production day fighter, the first of which were noted over East Germany in 1961 when an all-weather development with a search and track radar housed in an air intake centrebody was flown over Tushino during the Air Day display, and manufacture was extended to other factories — including GAZ No. 31, Tbilisi. Since then a progressive series of up-dated developments of this standard Mach 2.0 fighter, including tactical reconnaissance and two-seat training conversion versions, have been built of which the most recent — with increased fuel tankage and the more powerful Tumanski R-13 engine to boost the MiG-21's limited range and speed — entered service with the Soviet Air Forces twenty years after its original design had been drafted in the drawing offices of the Mikoyan design bureau. Similarly, later variants of the Yak-18 basic trainer — itself derived from the pre-war UT-2 — and the An-2 biplane utility transport, both placed in production in the mid-forties, are still manufactured.

---

[6]The MiG-19 in fact bore all the hallmarks of a stop-gap fighter with only 2,500 built until production was terminated at the end of 1957. The last of the 8,800 MiG-17 fighters manufactured had been completed earlier the same year.

Continuity & Change in the Soviet Air Forces

In some instances, primarily with reference to the Yak-25/27/28 series, a basic airframe has been evolved to produce a number of aircraft related in general layout but with specific functions — a latterday extension of Trotski's original *'odnotipnost"*. In others an airframe has been utilised to fulfil a function quite different from that for which it was originally conceived, either to meet an immediate need or to obviate the time and expense involved in developing an entirely new purpose-designed aircraft. Here, the example of the Tu-28P long-endurance all-weather fighter based on the Tu-28 reconnaissance and strike aircraft is apparently being followed by its replacement, the Tu-22P, adapted from the Tu-22 medium-range bomber.

Obsolescent types have been 'revived' for non-combat roles, notably the tanker, reconnaissance and electronic warfare versions of the M-4, Tu-16 and Tu-20 bombers, or, as in the case of MiG-17UTI trainers or An-2 paratroop transports, handed down to DOSAAF, the new title for the former *Osoaviakhim*[7].

During the fifties, as in the thirties, a number of civil aircraft were developed from military types — the Tu-104 and Tu-114 airliners being evolved from the Tu-16 and Tu-20 bombers with production taking place at the same factory since both military and civil variants of the basic design had many components in common. Other types including the Antonov turboprop transports and the Mil' helicopters have fulfilled both civil and military functions. Lately, however, the current has begun to flow the other way with the adaption of the Tu-114 as an airborne warning and control aircraft and the appearance of the Il-38 long-range maritime patrol aircraft based on the Il-18 turboprop airliner.

There is as yet no reason to suppose that the Soviet aircraft industry will abandon any of these underlying principles, or lose any of its versatility and ingenuity in providing future aircraft for the Soviet Air Forces.

---

[7] *Osoaviakhim* was broken down into separate 'voluntary societies' for the support of the army, air force and navy in 1949 but reconstituted in 1951 as DOSAAF — the Voluntary Society for the Support of the Army, Aviation and Fleet.

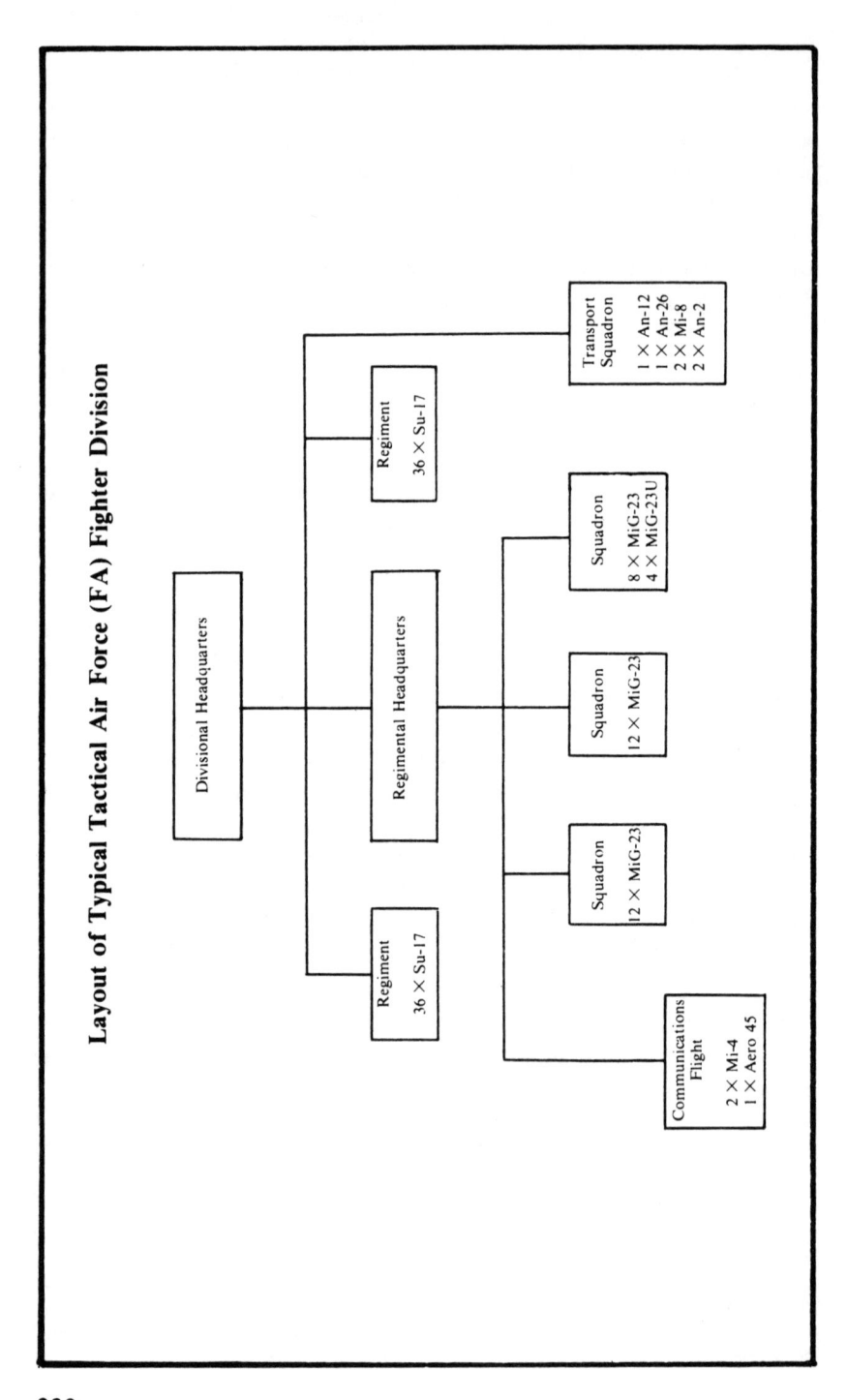

Layout of Typical Tactical Air Force (FA) Fighter Division

```
                    Divisional Headquarters
                              │
         ┌────────────────────┼────────────────────┐
         │                    │                    │
      Regiment          Regimental Headquarters  Regiment
      36 × Su-17                │                 36 × Su-17
                                │
                                │                              Transport
                                │                              Squadron
                                │                              1 × An-12
                                │                              1 × An-26
                                │                              2 × Mi-8
                                │                              2 × An-2
    ┌──────────┬────────────┬───┴────────┬──────────┐
    │          │            │            │
Communications Squadron   Squadron    Squadron
Flight         12 × MiG-23 12 × MiG-23 8 × MiG-23
2 × Mi-4                              4 × MiG-23U
1 × Aero 45
```

230

15 The Soviet Air Force in the Seventies

The present C-in-C Soviet Air Forces is Pavel Stepanovich Kutakhov, made Air Marshal in 1971 and Chief Air Marshal the following year, who replaced Chief Air Marshal Vershinin in March 1969[1] after serving as his First Deputy C-in-C since July 1967. Now in his early sixties, Chief Air Marshal Kutakhov joined the Red Air Force in 1935 and graduated as a pilot three years later. He first saw action in the Winter War with Finland of 1939-40, but his subsequent command career during the Great Patriotic War was not particularly distinguished. Unlike his predecessors he did not rise to command an air army nor did he fly in any of the great air battles against the *Luftwaffe*, ending the war as the commander of a fighter regiment in the 7th Air Army on the Karelian Front with fourteen personal 'kills' to his credit and as a Hero of the Soviet Union — a decoration conferred on him in May 1943 as a squadron leader in the 19th Guards Fighter Regiment.

His present Command Staff includes Air Marshal A.P. Silantyev as Chief of Air Staff and his Deputy Chief of Staff, Colonel-General S.F. Ushakov, both decorated as Heroes of the Soviet Union during the Great Patriotic War, Lieutenant-General I.M. Moroz as Political Deputy, a post he has probably occupied since the death of Colonel-General Rytov in 1967, Colonel-General Mishuk as Head of the Engineering-Technical Service, and his First Deputy C-in-C, Colonel-General Aleksandr Nikolaevich Yefimov, twice decorated as a Hero of the Soviet Union flying *shturmoviks* in Vershinin's 4th Air Army. Colonel-General Yefimov is probably the present Commander of Tactical Air Forces (FA) responsible for slightly over 5,000 first-line tactical combat aircraft with a further 3,000 second-line machines as reserve and training aircraft. The strength of the

---

[1] Chief Air Marshal Vershinin died early in 1974 at the age of seventy-three.

Soviet Air Force

Tactical Air Forces rose from over 4,000 first-line combat aircraft at the end of the sixties to nearly 5,500 by 1973 and the present reduction is no doubt a temporary one as older types are phased out and new ones introduced. The second half of the seventies should see the disappearance of the remaining MiG-17 and MiG-19 fighters and Il-28 bombers and their replacement by the three new short take-off and landing (STOL) types entering service which will endow the Tactical Air Forces with a far greater degree of deployment and strike mobility. These include the Su-17 derived from the Su-7 fighter-bomber but with outer wing panels pivoting between straight and swept-back positions to give a variable-geometry (VG-wing) planform, an uprated AL-21F engine and increased fuel capacity to improve the original Su-7's restricted combat radius. An early development model for the Su-17 was exhibited at the 1967 Air Display at Domodedovo airfield outside Moscow when the new Mikoyan MiG-23 and MiG-25 fighters were also shown to the public for the first time.

The MiG-23 is an entirely new VG-wing fighter-bomber with a Mach 2.3 capability which is thought to have been in production since 1971 and first delivered to FA regiments in 1973. Two-seat conversion trainer and interceptor versions of the MiG-23 have also been noted. The MiG-25 delta-wing fighter is essentially an air superiority interceptor with a combat radius of between 750 and 1,300 kms and a short dash speed of Mach 3.2 at high altitude. While probably intended primarily for IA-PVO regiments, a tactical reconnaissance version of the MiG-25, thought to be designated MiG-25R, is known to be in FA service.

The third VG-wing VTOL type has been identified as the two-seat Su-19 fighter-bomber whose prototype was first seen in 1970 and which was at first reported to be a development of the MiG-23. The new Su-19 was being delivered to FA regiments in 1974-75 together with the first of the 'third generation' MiG-21 fighters. In 1974 there were also tentative reports of a new single-seat, single-engined Mikoyan fighter-bomber of 'tailed-delta' configuration under tests, bearing a strong resemblance to a Mikoyan fighter prototype fitted with lift engines which was exhibited at the 1967 Air Day but which did not then appear to be going into production.

Over 2,000 helicopters are now thought to be in service with FA, including a military version of the Mi-8 and the new Mi-24 able to transport up to sixteen troops and armed with rocket pods and anti-tank missiles. Over fifty of these combat helicopters were already in service with the army helicopter regiments or *polka armeiskikh vertolyotov* attached to the Group of Soviet Forces in Germany in the spring of 1974 and their number has since significantly increased. The number of electronic counter-measures aircraft in FA service has also grown rapidly over recent years and now includes a version of the An-12 and an ECM-escort version of the twin-engined Yak-28 fighter-bomber.

The Air Defence Fighter Command (IA-PVO) under Colonel-General A.Ye.Borovykh is currently thought to possess some 2,600 fighters. In common with FA its numerical strength has declined by about four hundred machines since 1973 with the replacement of older types by more advanced aircraft. Over the 1973-75 period, IA-PVO was assessed at 1,100-1,200 Yak-28P, Tu-28P, Su-15 and MiG-25 fighters, 700-750 Su-11 fighters and 1,000-1,100 MiG-21 and obsolescent MiG-17, MiG-19 and Yak-25 'back-up' fighters. The next four years should see this 'back-up' reserve phased out and the Su-11 progressively replaced by the twin-engined Mach 2.5 Su-15 all-weather interceptor which was first revealed in 1967 with early production models reaching IA-PVO two years later. An interceptor version of the MiG-23 is thought to be entering service with IA-PVO and the first long-endurance Tu-22P interceptors should soon be replacing the Tu-28Ps on remote periphery fighter patrols. The next few years should also see the replacement of the Tu-114 derived airborne warning and control systems aircraft by an up-dated design to fulfil this crucial air defence role.

The Long-Range Air Force (DA) under the command of Colonel-General V.V. Reshetnikov[2] may now be endeavouring to attain the intercontinental strike capacity denied to it under Marshal Agal'tsov with the development of a Mach 2.0 VG-wing bomber with an anticipated range of 8,800-9,600 kms and a new stand-off missile. This aircraft — attributed to the Tupolev design bureau — was reported to be under test in 1969 with a possible pre-series batch of twelve under evaluation by 1972. Staging from Arctic bases and with in-flight refuelling, it has been estimated that this bomber could cover virtually all the United States on return missions at subsonic speeds and limited low-level penetration, although in-flight refuelling by M-4 tankers or a tanker version of the Il-76 transport

---

[2] Colonel-General Reshetnikov replaced Marshal Agal'tsov in this command in August 1969.

Soviet Air Force

would be needed for such missions where extended supersonic flight or extended low-level penetration were applied. While reports of this aircraft have given some anxiety to the United States Defence Staff, it would seem more probable that it represents a Tu-22 replacement and to be more suited for un-refuelled missions over Asia or Western Europe. It may well, like the M-4 and Tu-20, be successful in posing new problems to the United States whose air defence resources would have to be divided between early warning and intercept systems for missiles and manned aircraft if the threat is taken seriously. New rumours of a Soviet supersonic delta-wing strategic bomber developed in competition with the VG-wing bomber but abandoned after undergoing flight tests were circulating in 1972.

Perhaps the most dramatic strides have been made by Colonel-General Mironenko's[3] Naval Air Forces (A-VMF) with the launching in 1972 of the USSR's first aircraft carrier — the 35,000 ton *Kiev* — the largest warship yet built for the Soviet Navy which was undergoing trials in 1974 and which should be commissioned in 1976. The *Kiev* is due to be followed by her sister-ship *Minsk* in 1978. Both carriers could carry a mixed complement of ASW helicopters and reconnaissance and strike V/STOL fighters — the latter possibly derived from the Yakovlev development aircraft with lift engines shown at the 1967 Air Day. It has been estimated that the Soviet Navy could have six carriers of the *Kiev* class at sea by the early nineteen-eighties. Other new A-VMF developments likely to take place over the next four years may include the use of the Mi-24 operating from attack carriers in a coastal assault role and the introduction of the new VG-wing bomber as an anti-shipping replacement for the Tu-22.

Lieutenant-General Pakilev's Air Transport Command (VTA) is scheduled to take delivery of the new Il-76 four-jet transports, and even larger jet transports may be considered to airlift the Soviet Army's strategic missiles and tactical missile-launchers as the Antonov turboprops are phased out.

The Soviet aircraft industry is now estimated to be turning out some 1,800-2,000 aircraft each year for the Soviet Air Forces, of which at least 700 are frontline combat aircraft. The past six years have, however, taken their toll of the great aircraft designers who have provided machines for the Red Air Force — in some cases since

---

[3]Colonel-General A.A. Mironenko succeeded Marshal Borzov as C-in-C A-VMF in 1974.

its very inception. Artyom Mikoyan died in December 1970, in which year Sergei Il'yushin at the ripe old age of seventy-six finally turned his design bureau over to his first deputy, Genrikh Novozhilov, and in December 1972 the death of Andrei Tupolev brought to an end an era spanning his first all-metal ANT-2 of 1924 and the supersonic Tu-144 airliner of today. The leading helicopter designers Mikhail Mil' and Nikolai Kamov died in January 1970 and November 1973 respectively, bequeathing their bureaux to their first deputies Mikhail Kupfer and Marat Tishchenko. Both Pavel Sukhoi and Aleksandr Yakovlev celebrated their seventy-fifth birthdays in 1975 and have long since relegated the majority responsibility for new design work to their younger deputies, leaving Oleg Antonov who is seventy this year as the last active designer of their generation.

The latest Soviet aircraft may bear entirely different designations from the familiar MiG and Tu, unless their design bureaux honour their founding fathers by retaining the traditional initials. We may be given the opportunity to see them at the Soviet Air Day display in 1977 — a decade since the last flypast of new types over Domodedovo, and a likely year for new revelations since it marks the sixtieth anniversary of the Bolshevik Revolution which brought the modern Soviet Air Force into being.

SOVIET AIR FORCE PRODUCTION & TRAINING CENTRES

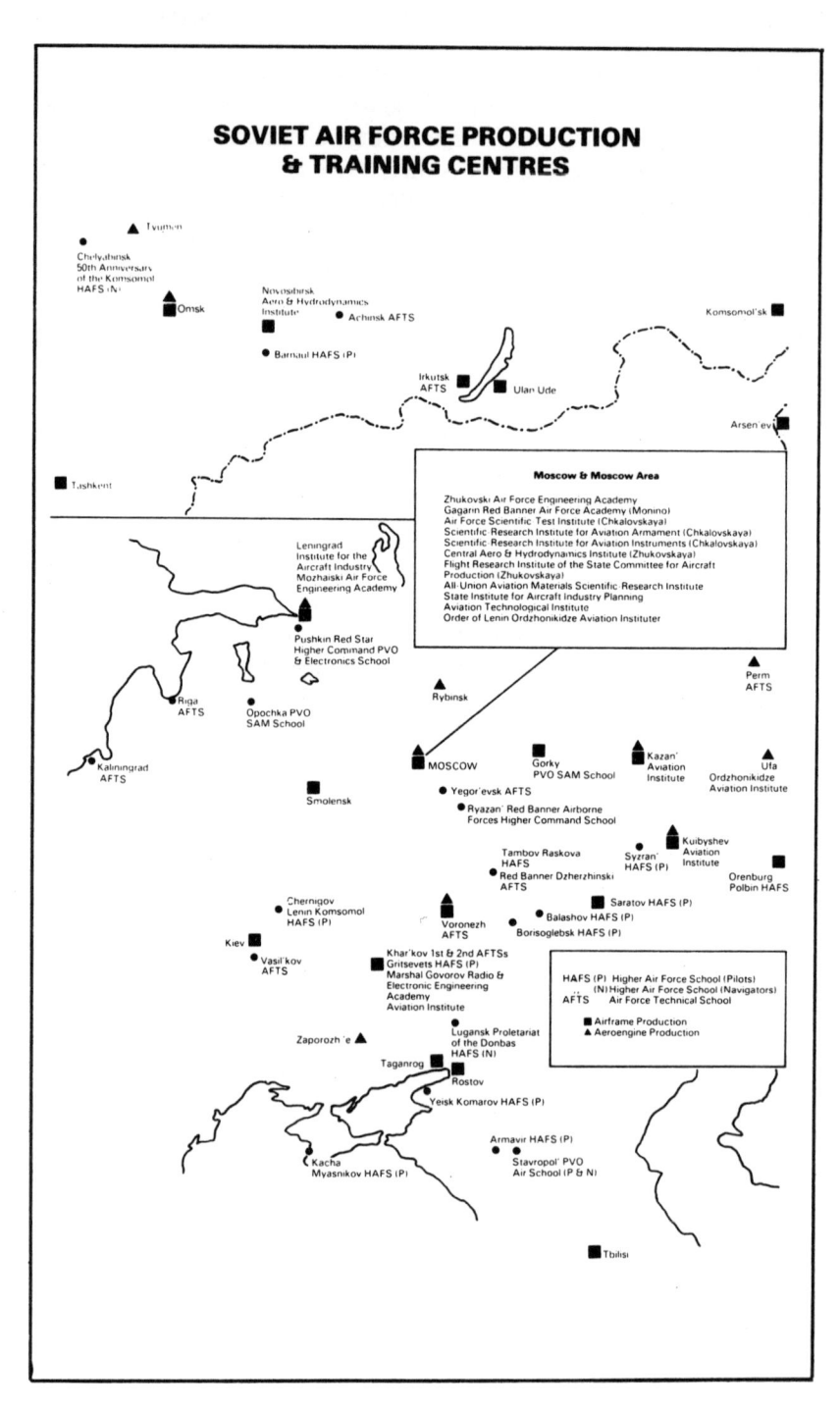

▲ Tyumen

● Chelyabinsk
50th Anniversary
of the Komsomol
HAFS (N)

■ Omsk

Novosibirsk
Aero & Hydrodynamics
Institute
● Achinsk AFTS

■ Komsomol'sk

● Barnaul HAFS (P)

Irkutsk
AFTS
Ulan Ude

Arsen'ev

■ Tashkent

Leningrad
Institute for the
Aircraft Industry
Mozhaiski Air Force
Engineering Academy

Moscow & Moscow Area
Zhukovski Air Force Engineering Academy
Gagarin Red Banner Air Force Academy (Monino)
Air Force Scientific Test Institute (Chkalovskaya)
Scientific Research Institute for Aviation Armament (Chkalovskaya)
Scientific Research Institute for Aviation Instruments (Chkalovskaya)
Central Aero & Hydrodynamics Institute (Zhukovskaya)
Flight Research Institute of the State Committee for Aircraft Production (Zhukovskaya)
All-Union Aviation Materials Scientific Research Institute
State Institute for Aircraft Industry Planning
Aviation Technological Institute
Order of Lenin Ordzhonikidze Aviation Instituter

● Pushkin Red Star
Higher Command PVO
& Electronics School

▲ Perm
AFTS

● Riga
AFTS

● Opochka PVO
SAM School

● Rybinsk

■ Kazan'
Aviation
Institute

▲ Ufa

■ Kaliningrad
AFTS

■ MOSCOW

Gorky
PVO SAM School

■ Ordzhonikidze
Aviation Institute

■ Smolensk

● Yegor'evsk AFTS

● Ryazan' Red Banner Airborne
Forces Higher Command School

Tambov Raskova
HAFS
● Red Banner Dzherzhinski
AFTS

Syzran'
HAFS (P)

■ Kuibyshev
Aviation
Institute

■ Orenburg
Polbin HAFS

● Chernigov
Lenin Komsomol
HAFS (P)

● Voronezh
AFTS

■ Saratov HAFS (P)
● Balashov HAFS (P)
● Borisoglebsk HAFS (P)

■ Kiev

● Vasil'kov
AFTS

Khar'kov 1st & 2nd AFTSs
Gritsevets HAFS (P)
Marshal Govorov Radio &
Electronic Engineering
Academy
Aviation Institute

HAFS (P) Higher Air Force School (Pilots)
       (N) Higher Air Force School (Navigators)
AFTS   Air Force Technical School

■ Airframe Production
▲ Aeroengine Production

▲ Zaporozh'e
● Taganrog
● Rostov

Lugansk Proletariat
of the Donbas
HAFS (N)

● Yeisk Komarov HAFS (P)

● Armavir HAFS (P)
● Kacha
Myasnikov HAFS (P)

Stavropol' PVO
Air School (P & N)

■ Tbilisi

236

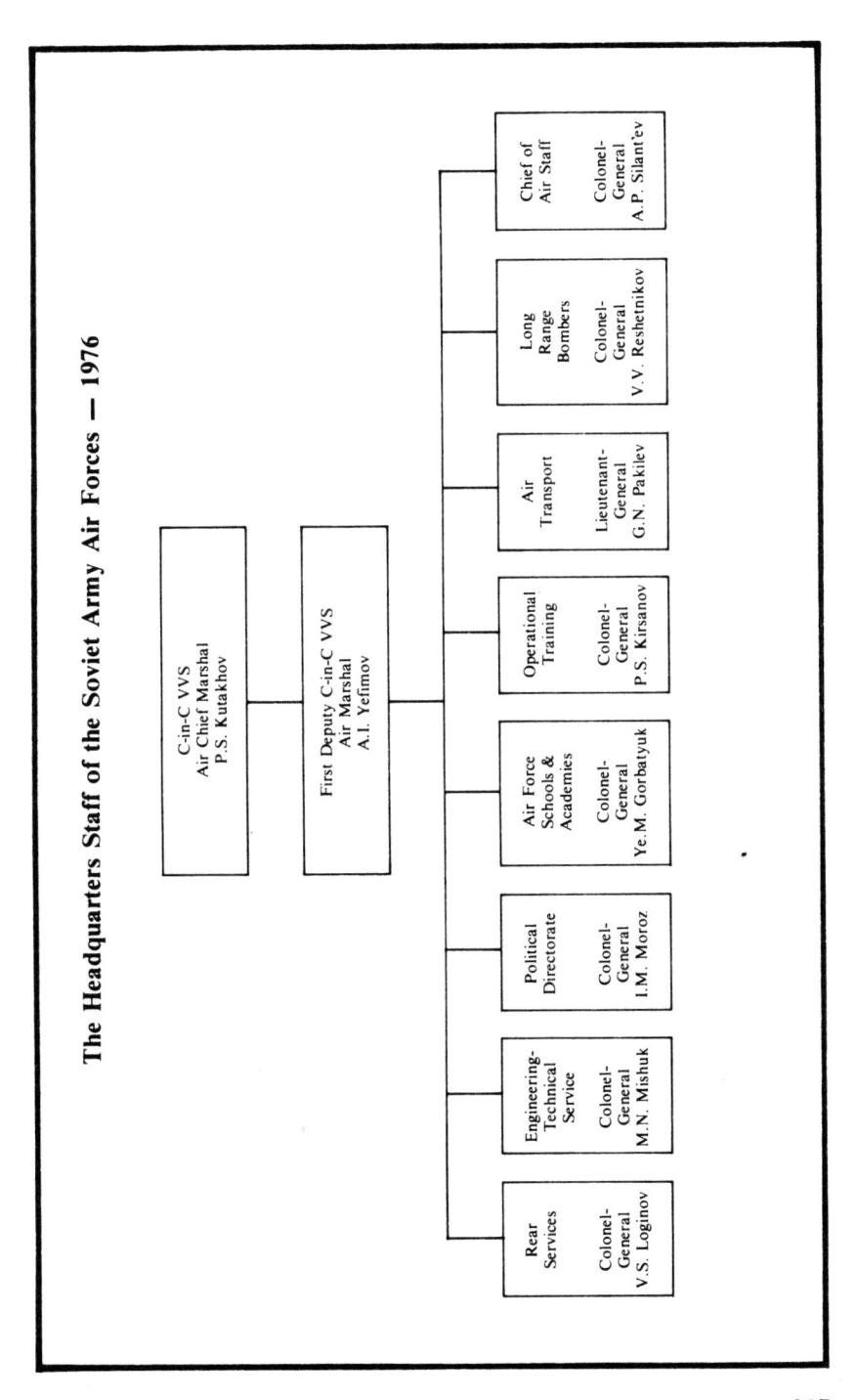

The Headquarters Staff of the Soviet Army Air Forces – 1976

- **C-in-C VVS**
  Air Chief Marshal
  P.S. Kutakhov
  - **First Deputy C-in-C VVS**
    Air Marshal
    A.I. Yefimov
    - **Rear Services**
      Colonel-General
      V.S. Loginov
    - **Engineering-Technical Service**
      Colonel-General
      M.N. Mishuk
    - **Political Directorate**
      Colonel-General
      I.M. Moroz
    - **Air Force Schools & Academies**
      Colonel-General
      Ye.M. Gorbatyuk
    - **Operational Training**
      Colonel-General
      P.S. Kirsanov
    - **Air Transport**
      Lieutenant-General
      G.N. Pakilev
    - **Long Range Bombers**
      Colonel-General
      V.V. Reshetnikov
    - **Chief of Air Staff**
      Colonel-General
      A.P. Silant'ev

Glossary of Abbreviations

A	*avtozhir* — autogyro
ACh	Aleksei Charomski (aeroengine designer)
ADD	*Aviatsiya dal'nevo deistviya* — Long-Range Air Arm
AGOS	*Aviatsiya, gidroviatsiya i opytnoe stroitel'stvo* — Aviation, Hydro-Aviation and Experimental Design
AI	Aleksandr Ivchenko (aeroengine designer)
AL	Arkhip Lyul'ka (aeroengine designer)
AM	Aleksandr Mikulin (aeroengine designer)
An	Antonov (aircraft designer)
ANT	Andrei Nikolaevich Tupolev (aircraft designer)
AON	*Aviatsiya osobovo naznacheniya* — Special Purpose Air Arm
Ar	Arkhangel'ski (aircraft designer)
ASh	Arkadi Shvetsov (aeroengine designer)
Aviadarm	*Aviatsiya deistvuyushchei armii* — Operational Army Air Arm
Avianito	*Aviatsionnoe nauchno-issledovatel'skoe tekhnicheskoe obshchestvo* — Aviation Scientific-Research Technical Society
A-VMF	*Aviatsiya voenno-morskovo flota* — Naval Air Force
BAO	*Batal'on aerodromnovo obsluzhivaniya* — Airfield Servicing Battalion
BB	*Blizhni bombardirovshchik* — Close-Support Bomber
Be	Beriev (aircraft designer)
BNK	*Byuro novykh konstruktsi* — New Design Bureau

Soviet Air Force

BOK	*Byuro osobykh konstruktsi* — Special Design Bureau
BSh	*Bronirovanny shturmovik* — Armoured Ground-Attack Bomber (lit. 'Assaulter')
DA	*Dal'nyaya aviatsiya* — Long-Range Air Force
DA	*Degtyarev aviatsionny* — Degtyarev aircraft machine-gun
DB	*Dal'ni bombardirovshchik* — Long-Range Bomber
DBA	*Dal'no-bombardirovochnaya aviatsiya* — Long-Range Bomber Force
DI	*Dvukhmestny istrebitel'* — Two-Seat Fighter
DIP	*Dvukhmestny istrebitel' pushechny* — Two-Seat Cannon-Armed Fighter
DIS	*Dvukhmotorny istrebitel' soprovozhdeniya* — Twin-Engined Escort Fighter
DOSAAF	*Dobrovol'noe obshchestvo sodeistviya Armii, Aviatsii i Flotu* — Voluntary Society for the Support of the Army, Aviation and Fleet
DVB	*Dal'ni vysotny bombardirovshchik* — Long-Range High-Altitude Bomber
FA	*Frontovaya aviatsiya* — Frontal Air Forces
G	*Grazhdanski* — Civil
GAZ	*Gosudarstvenny aviatsionny zavod* — State Aircraft Factory
GKAT	*Gosudarstvenny komitet aviatsionnoi tekhniki* — State Committee for Aviation Equipment
GKO	*Gosudarstvenny komitet oborony* — State Committee for Defence
Glavkoavia	*Glavnoe pravlenie ob"edinyonnykh aviatsionnykh zavodov* — Main Directorate for the Amalgamated Aircraft Factories
GST	*Gidrosamolyot transportny* — Seaplane Transport
GU	*Glavnoe upravlenie* — Chief Directorate
GUAP	*Glavnoe upravlenie aviatsionnoi promyshlennosti* — Chief Directorate of the Aircraft Industry
GVF	*Grazhdanski vozdushny flot* — Civil Air Fleet
I	*Istrebitel'* — Fighter

Soviet Air Force

IA - PVO	*Istrebitel'naya aviatsiya protivovozdushnoi oborony* — Air Defence Fighter Command
Il	Il'yushin (aircraft designer)
ITS	*Inzhenerno-tekhnicheskya sluzhba* — Engineering-Technical Service
K	Kalinin (aircraft designer)
Ka	Kamov (rotating-wing aircraft designer)
KAI	*Kazan'ski aviatsionny institut* — Kazan' Aviation Institute
KB	*Konstruktorskoe byuro* — Design Bureau
KhAI	*Khar'kovski aviatsionny institut* — Khar'kov Aviation Institute
Komsomol	*Kommunisticheski soyuz molodyozhi* — Communist Youth League
KOR	*Korabel'ny razvedchik* — Shipborne Reconnaissance
KOSOS	*Konstruktorski otdel opytnovo samolyotostroeniya* — Experimental Aircraft Design Section
La	Lavochkin (aircraft designer)
LaGG	Lavochkin, Gorbunov & Gudkov (aircraft designers)
Li	Lisunov (chief engineer of aircraft factory)
LII	*Lyotno-issledovatel'ski institut* — Flight Research Institute
LR	*Lyogki razvedchik* — Light Reconnaissance
LSh	*Lyogki shturmovik* — Light Ground-Attack Bomber
M	*Motor* — Engine
M	*Morskoi* — Naval; Maritime
M	Myasishchev (aircraft designer)
MAI	*Moskovski aviatsionny institut* — Moscow Aviation Institute
MAP	*Ministerstvo aviatsionnoi promyshlennosti* — Ministry for Aircraft Production
MBR	*Morskoi blizhni razvedchik* — Short-Range Reconnaissance Flying Boat
MDR	*Morskoi dal'ni razvedchik* — Long-Range Reconnaissance Flying Boat
Mi	Mil' (helicopter designer)

Soviet Air Force

MiG	Mikoyan and Gurevich (aircraft designers)
MR	*Morskoi razvedchik* — Reconnaissance Flying Boat
MTB	*Morskoi tyazhyoly bombardirovshchik* — Heavy Bomber Flying Boat
MU	*Morskoi uchebny* — Flying Boat Trainer
MVTU	*Moskovskoe vysshee tekhnicheskoe uchilishche* — Moscow Higher Technical College
N	Nudel'man (designer of aircraft armament)
NIAT	*Nauchny institut aviatsionnoi tekhniki* — Scientific Institute for Aviation Equipment
NII	*Nauchno-ispytatel'ny institut* — Scientific-Test Institute
NK	Nikolai Kuznetsov (aeroengine designer)
NKAP	*Narodny komissariat aviatsionnoi promyshlennosti* — People's Commissariat for the Aircraft Industry
NKTP	*Narodny komissariat tyazhyoloi promyshlennosti* — People's Commissariat for Heavy Industry
NKVD	*Narodny komissariat vnutrennykh del* — People's Commissariat for Internal Affairs
NR	Nudel'man and Rikhter (designers of aircraft armament)
NS	Nudel'man and Suranov (designers of aircraft armament)
ODVA	*Otdel'naya daln'no-vostochnaya armiya* — Independent Far-Eastern Army
ODVF	*Obshchestvo druzei vozdushnovo flota* — Society of Friends of the Air Fleet
OGPU	*Ob'edinyonnoe gosudarstvennoe politicheskoe upravlenie* — Amalgamated State Political Directorate
OMOS	*Otdel morskovo opytnovo samolyotostroeniya* — Experimental Floatplane and Flying Boat Design Section
OOK	*Otdel osobykh konstruktsi* — Section for Special Designs

Osoaviakhim	*Obshchestvo sodeistviya oborone, aviatsionnomu i khimicheskomu stroitel'stvu* — Society for the Support of Defence and of Aviation and Chemical Construction
OSS	*Otdel sukhoputnovo samolyotostreniya* — Landplane Design Section
PS	*Passazhirski samolyot* — Passenger Aircraft
PARM	*Podvizhnye aviatsionnye remontnye masterskie* — Mobile Air-Repair Workshops
PB	*Pikiruyushchi bombardirovshchik* — Dive-Bomber
Pe	Petlyakov (aircraft designer)
PI	*Pushechny istrebitel'* — Cannon-Armed Fighter
Po	Polikarpov (aircraft designer)
PTAB	*Protivotankovaya aviatsionnaya bomba* — Anti-Tank Bomb
PV	*Pulemyot vozdushny* — Aircraft Machine-Gun
PVO	*Protivovozdushnaya oborona* — Air Defence
R	*Razvedchik* — Reconnaissance
RAB	*Raion aviatsionnovo bazirovaniya* — Air Basing Region
RD	*Reaktivny dvigatel'* — Reaction Engine
Revvoensovet	*Revolyutsionno-voenny sovet* — Revolutionary Military Council
RIB	*Raschotno-ispytatal'noe byuro* — Evaluation & Test Bureau
RKKVVF	*Raboche-Krest'yanski Krasny vozdushny flot.* — Workers & Peasants Red Air Fleet
RNII	*Reaktivno-issledovatel'ski institut* — Reaction-Motor Research Institute
ROM	*Razvedchik otkrytovo morya* — Open Sea Reconnaissance
RS	*Raketny snaryad* — Rocket Missile
S	*Sanitarny* — Ambulance
SB	*Skorostnoi bombardirovshchik* — High-Speed Bomber
ShKAS	*Shpital'ny-Komaritski aviatsionny skorostrelny* — Shpital'ny—Komaritski Rapid-Firing (aircraft machine-gun)

Soviet Air Force

ShON	*Shturmovik osobovo naznacheniya* — Special Purpose Ground-Attack Bomber
ShVAK	*Shpital'ny-Vladimirov aviatsionnaya krupnokalibernaya* — Shpital'ny-Vladimirov Large-Calibre (aircraft cannon)
Sovnarkom	*Sovet narodnykh komissarov* — Council of People's Commissars
SS	*Samolyot svyazi* — Liaison Aircraft
Stavka	*Shtab glavnovo/verkhovnovo komandovaniya* — Chief/Supreme Command Staff
Su	Sukhoi (aircraft designer)
TB	*Tyazhyoly bombardirovshchik* — Heavy Bomber
TDA	*Transportno-desantnaya aviatsiya* — Airborne Forces Transport Command
TIS	*Tyazhyoly istrebitel' soprovozhyodeniya* — Heavy Escort Fighter
TR	*Turboreaktivny* — Gas-Turbine
TsAGI	*Tsentral'ny aerogidrodinamicheski institut* — Central Aero & Hydrodynamics Institute
TSh	*Tyazhyoly shturmovik* — Heavy Ground-Attack Bomber
TsKB	*Tsentral'noe konstruktorskoe byuro* — Central Design Bureau
Tu	Tupolev (aircraft designer)
TV	*Turbovintovy* — Turboprop
U	*Uchebny* — Training (Basic)
UT	*Uchebno-trenirovochny* — Training (Primary)
UTI	*Uchebno-trenirovochny istrebitel'* — Fighter Trainer
VB	*Vysotny bombardirovshchik* — High-Altitude Bomber
VD	Viktor Dobryin (Aeroengine designer)
VDV	*Vozdushno-desantnye voiska* — Parachute Troops
VI	*Vysotny istrebitel'* — High-Altitude Fighter
VIAM	*Vsesoyuzny institut aviatsionnykh materialov* — All-Union Institute for Aviation Materials
VIT	*Vozdushny istrebitel' tankov* — Anti-Tank Aircraft

VK	Vladimir Klimov (aeroengine designer)
VMF	*Voenno-morskoi flot* — Navy
VNOS	*(Sluzhba) vozdushnovo nablyudeniya, opoveshcheniya i svyazi* — Air Observation, Alert and Communications (Service)
VP	*Vysotny perekhvatchik* — High-Altitude Interceptor
VS	*Voiskovaya seriya* — Military series
VTA	*Voenno-transportnaya aviatsiya* — Military Transport Command
VVS	*Voenno-vozdushnye sili* — Air Forces
VYa	Volkov-Yartsev (designers of aircraft armament)
Yak	Yakovlev (aircraft designer)
Yer	Yermolaev (aircraft designer)
ZA	*Zenitnaya artilleriya* — Anti-Aircraft Artillery
ZOS	*(Sluzhba) zemnovo obespecheniya samolyotovozhdeniya* — Ground Assistance to Air Navigation (service)

Bibliography

The following select bibliography lists under Section A the primary Russian sources drawn upon in the preparation of this study, and under Section B the main body of non-Russian material consulted by the author. Section C lists the most notable Soviet works dealing with the theory of air power to appear between 1925 and 1940.

Much invaluable information has been gleaned from the Soviet Air Force's *Aviatsiya i Kosmonavtika* (formerly *Vestnik Vozdushnovo Flota*), the Civil Air Fleet's *Grazhdanskaya Aviatsiya* and DOSAAF's *Kryl'ya Rodiny* monthly magazines, from the Soviet Armed Forces' daily newspaper *Krasnaya Zvezda* and from the Czech fortnightly aviation review *Letectví + kosmonautika* (formerly *Kridla Vlasti*). The British aviation monthly 'Air International' (formerly 'Air Enthusiast') and the periodic 'Bulletin of the Russian Aviation Research Group of Air Britain' are recommended to readers with interests in both the historical and current aspects of Soviet air power.

Comprehensive descriptions of Soviet aircraft over the past thirty-five years can be found in two excellent and extensively illustrated works of reference — Jean Alexander's 'Russian Aircraft Since 1940' and 'The Observer's Soviet Aircraft Directory' by William Green and Gordon Swanborough. The development of Soviet aircraft design up to 1938 is covered in great detail by Vadim Shavrov's *Istoriya konstruktsii samolyotov v SSSR* which is not, alas, available in translation.

SECTION A: PRIMARY RUSSIAN SOURCE MATERIAL
Arlazorov, M.S. *Front idyot cherez KB* (The Frontline Goes Through the Design Bureau) Moscow: Znanie 1975 (1st edn 1969)
Arlazorov, M.S. *Konstruktory* (The Designers) Moscow: Sovetskaya Rossiya 1975

Astashenkov, P.T. *Konstruktor legendarnykh Ilov* (The Designer of the Legendary Ils) Moscow: Politizdat 1972

Astashenkov, P.T. *Orbity glavnovo konstruktora* (The Orbits of the Chief Designer) Moscow: DOSAAF 1973

Aviatsiya i Kosmonavtika SSR (Aviation & Cosmonautics of the USSR) Moscow: Ministry of Defence 1968

Bitva za Moskvu (The Battle for Moscow) Moscow: Moskovski Rabochi 1968 (1st edn 1966)

Chechel'nitski, G.A. *Lyotchiki na voine: voenno-istoricheski ocherk o boevom puti 15-i vozdushnoi armii 1942-45* (Airmen at War: A Military-Historical Survey of the Operational Career of the 15th Air Army 1942-45) Moscow: Ministry of Defence 1974

Chetvyortaya vozdushnaya armiya v Velikoi Otechestvennoi Voine (The Fourth Air Army in the Great Patriotic War) Monino: Red Banner Air Force Academy 1968

Den' pervy, den' posledni (First Day, Last Day) Moscow: Sovetskaya Rossiya 1966

Fyodorov, A.G. *Aviatsiya v bitve pod Moskvoi* (Aviation in the Battle of Moscow) Moscow: Nauka 1975

Gallai, M.L. *Ispytano v nebe* (Tested in the Sky) Moscow: Molodaya Gvardiya 1963

Glukhovski, S. *Kogda vyrastali kryl'ya* (When Wings Grew) Moscow: Ministry of Defence 1965

Golovanov, Ya. K. *Korolyov* Moscow: Molodaya Gvardiya 1973

Grazhdanskaya aviatsiya SSSR (Civil Aviation of the USSR) Moscow: Transport 1967

Gusev, A.I. *Gnevnoe nebo Ispanii* (The Angry Sky of Spain) Moscow: Ministry of Defence 1973

Istoriya Velikoi Otechestvennoi Voiny Sovetskovo Soyuza 1941-45 [IVOVSS] (The History of the Great Patriotic War of the Soviet Union 1941-45) six volumes Moscow: Voenizdat 1960

Ivanov, P.N. *Krylya nad morem* (Wings Over the Sea) Moscow: Ministry of Defence 1973

Izakson, A.M. *Sovetskoe vertolyotostroenie* (Soviet Rotating-Wing Aircraft Design) Moscow: Mashinostroenie 1964

Kerber, L.L. *TU — chelovek i samolyot* (TU — The Man and the Aircraft) Moscow: Sovetskaya Rossiya 1973

Komandarm Krylatykh (Commander of the Winged Armies) Riga: Liesma 1973

Soviet Air Force

Kostenko, F.A. *Korpus krylatoi gvardii* (Winged Guards Corps) Moscow: Ministry of Defence 1974

Kozhedub, I.N. *Vernost' otchizne* (Loyalty to the Native Country) Moscow: Voenizdat 1975

Krasovski, S.A. *Zhizn' v aviatsii* (A Life in Aviation) Moscow: Voenizdat 1960

Kravchenko, G.S. *Ekonomika SSSR v gody Velikoi Otechestvennoi Voiny* (The Economy of the USSR in the Great Patriotic War) Moscow: Ekonomika 1970

Magid, A.S. *Bol'shaya zhizn'* (A Big Life) Moscow: DOSAAF 1968

Maslennikov, M.M. & Rapiport, M.S. *Aviatsionnye porshnevye dvigateli* (Aircraft Piston Engines) Moscow: Ministry of Defence 1951

Novikov, A.A. *V nebe Leningrada: zapiski komanduyushchevo aviatsii* (In the Sky of Leningrad; Notes of the Air Commander) Moscow: Nauka 1970.

Pokryshkin, A.I. *Nebo voiny* (The War Sky) Moscow: Molodaya Gvardiya 1968

Ozerov, G.A. *Tupolevskaya sharaga* (The Internee Tupolev Design Bureau) Frankfurt/M: Possev-Verlag 1971

Polynin, F.P. *Boevye marshruty* (On Active Service) Moscow: Ministry of Defence 1972

Popov, V.A. *Osnovy aviatsionnoi tekhniki* (The Bases of Aviation Technology) Moscow: Oborongiz 1947

Pospelov, P.N. (ed) *Sovetski tyl v Velikoi Otechestvennoi Voine* (The Soviet Home Front in the Great Patriotic War) Moscow: Mysl' 1974

Rodimtsev, A.I. *Pod nebom Ispanii* (Under the Sky of Spain) Moscow: Sovetskaya Rossiya 1974

Rokossovski, K.K. (ed) *Velikaya bitva na Volge* (The Great Battle on the Volga) Moscow: Voenizdat 1965

Rudenko, S.I. *Shestnadtsataya vozdushnaya: voenno-istoricheski ocherk o boevom puti 16-i vozdushnoi armii 1943-45* (The Sixteenth Air Army: A Military-Historical Survey of the Operational Career of the 16th Air Army 1942-45) Moscow: Voenizdat 1973

Semyonov, G.K. *Parol'* — *'Ispaniya'* (Password — 'Spain') Khar'kov: Prapor 1974

Shavrov, V.B. *Istoriya konstruktsii samolyotov v SSSR do 1938* (A History of Aircraft Design in the USSR to 1938) Moscow: Mashinostroenie 1969

Shavrov, V.B. *Samolyoty strany sovetov* (Aircraft of the Land of the Soviets) Moscow: DOSAAF 1974
Shingarev, S. *Chatos idut v ataku* (The Chatos Attack) Moscow: Moskovski Rabochi 1971
Shtemenko, S.M. *General'ny shtab v gody voiny* (The Soviet General Staff at War) Moscow: Voenizdat 1973
Simakov, B.L. & Shipilov, I.F. *Vozdushny flot strany sovetov* (The Air Fleet of the Land of the Soviets) Moscow: Ministry of Defence 1958
Sovetskaya aviatsionnaya tekhnika (Soviet Aviation Technology) Moscow: Mashinostroenie 1970
Sovetskie voenno-vozdushnye sily v Velikoi Otechestvennoi Voine 1941-45 [SVVSVOV] (The Soviet Air Forces in the Great Patriotic War) Moscow: Ministry of Defence 1968
SSSR v Velikoi Otechestvennoi Voine 1941-45: kratkaya khronika (The USSR in the Great Patriotic War: A Short Chronicle) Moscow: Ministry of Defence 1964
Stefanovski, P.M. *Trista neizvestnykh* (Three Hundred Strangers) Moscow: Ministry of Defence 1973 (1st edn 1968)
Telegin, K.F. *Ne otdali Moskvy!* (They Did Not Surrender Moscow!) Moscow: Sovetskaya Rossiya 1975 (1st edn 1968)
Timokhovich, I.V. *Sovetskaya aviatsiya v bitve pod Kurskom* (Soviet Aviation in the Battle of Kursk) Moscow: Ministry of Defence 1959
Timokhovich, I.V. *Operativnoe iskusstvo Sovetskikh VVS v Velikoi Otechestvennoi voine* (The Operational Art of the Soviet Air Forces in the Great Patriotic War) Moscow: Ministry of Defence 1976
Tumanski, A.K. *Polyot skvoz' gody* (Flight through the Years) Moscow: Ministry of Defence 1962
Vershinin, K.A. *Chetvyortaya Vozdushnaya* (Fourth Air Army) Moscow: Ministry of Defence 1975
Vinogradov, R.I. & Minaev, A.V. *Kratki ocherk razvitiya samolyotov v SSSR* (A Short Survey of the Development of Aircraft in the USSR) Moscow: Ministry of Defence 1956
Vinogradov, R.I. & Minaev, A.V. *Samolyoty SSSR* (Aircraft of the USSR) Moscow: Ministry of Defence 1961
V nebe frontovom (In the Frontline Sky) Moscow: Molodaya Gvardiya 1962
Voiska protivozdushnoi oborony strany (The National Air defence Force) Moscow: Ministry of Defence 1968

Soviet Air Force

Vodop'yanov, M.V. *Druz'ya v nebe* (Friends in the Sky) Moscow: Sovetskaya Rossiya 1967
Voennye samolyoty SSSR (Military Aircraft of the USSR) Moscow: Voenizdat 1941
Vorozheikin, A.V. *Istrebiteli* (Fighters) Moscow: Ministry of Defence 1961
Yakovlev, A.S. *Pyatdesyat let sovetskovo samolyotostroeniya* (Fifty Years of Soviet Aircraft Design) Moscow: Nauka 1968
Yakovlev, A.S. *Tsel' Zhizni* The Aim of Life) Moscow: Politizdat 1972 (1st edn 1967)
Zil'manovich, D.Ya. *Teodor Kalep* Moscow: Nauka 1970

SECTION B: NON-RUSSIAN REFERENCES

Alexander, J.P. Russian Aircraft Since 1940 London: Putnam 1975
Baumbach, W. Broken Swastika: The Defeat of the Luftwaffe London: Robert Hale 1960 (originally as *Zu Spät? Aufstieg und Untergang der Deutschen Luftwaffe* München: Richard Pflaum Verlag 1949)
Bekker, C. The Luftwaffe War Diaries London: Macdonald 1967 (originally as *Angriffshöhe 4000* Hamburg: Gerhard Stalling Verlag 1964)
Cain, C.W. & Voaden, D.J. Military Aircraft of the USSR London: Herbert Jenkins 1952
Carell, P. Hitler's War on Russia London: Harrap 1964 & 1970 (originally as *Unternehmen Barbarossa: Der Marsch nach Russland* Frankfurt/M & Berlin: Verlag Ullstein GmbH 1963 & 1966)
Condon, R.W. The Winter War: Russia versus Finland London: Pan/Ballantine 1972
Craven, W.F. & Cate, J.L. (eds) The Army Air Forces in World War II Chicago: University of Chicago Press 1955 (six volumes)
Cynk, J.B. History of the Polish Air Force, 1918-1968 Reading U.K.: Osprey Publishing Ltd 1972
Erickson, J. The Road to Stalingrad London: Weidenfeld & Nicolson 1975
Erickson, J. The Soviet High Command, 1918-1941 London: Macmillan 1962
Futrell, R.F. The United States Air Force in Korea, 1950-53 New York: Durell, Sloan & Pearce 1961
Garthoff, R.L. Soviet Military Doctrine Glencoe, Illinois, USA: The Free Press 1953

Green, W. & Fricker, J. The Air Forces of the World London: Macdonald 1958

Green, W. & Swanborough, G. The Observer's Soviet Aircraft Directory London & New York: Warne 1975

Griffith, H. R.A.F. in Russia London: Hammond, Hammond & Co. Ltd. 1942

Irving, D. The Rise and Fall of the Luftwaffe: The Life of Erhard Milch London: Weidenfeld & Nicolson 1973

Jackson, R. The Red Falcons: the Soviet Air Force in Action, 1919-1969 London: Clifton Books 1970

Jukes, G. The Defence of Moscow London: Macdonald 1971

Jukes, G. Stalingrad: The Turning Point London: Macdonald 1968

Keegan, J. Barbarossa: Invasion of Russia 1941 London: Macdonald 1971

Kilmarx, R.A. A History of Soviet Air Power London: Faber & Faber 1962

Leach, B.A. German Strategy Against Russia, 1939-1941 Oxford: Clarendon Press 1973

Lee, A. The Soviet Air Force London: Duckworth 1952 (1st edn 1950)

Lee, A. (ed) The Soviet Air & Rocket Forces London: Weidenfeld & Nicolson 1959

Liddell Hart, B.H. (ed) The Soviet Army London: Weidenfeld & Nicolson 1956

Morzik, Generalmajor a.D. **F.** German Air Force Airlift Operations New York: Arno Press 1968 (prepared by the USAF Historical Divsion as GAF 167)

Němeček, V. Ceskoslovenská Letadla Prague: Nase Vojsko 1968

Nemecek, V. Sovetská Letadla Prague: Naše Vojsko 1969

Odom, W.E. The Soviet Volunteers: Modernization & Bureaucracy in a Public Mass Organization Princeton U.S.A.: Princeton University Press 1973

Pirogov, Pyotr Why I escaped: The Story of Peter Pirogov Duell, Sloan & Pearce, Inc., New York, 1950

Plocher, Generalleutnant **H.** The German Air Force versus Russia, 1941 New York: Arno Press 1966 (prepared by the USAF Historical Division as GAF 153)

Plocher, Generalleutnant **H.** The German Air Force versus Russia, 1942 New York: Arno Press 1966 (prepared by the USAF Historical Division as GAF 154)

Plocher, Generalleutnant **H.** The German Air Force versus Russia, 1943 New York: Arno Press 1967 (prepared by the USAF Historical Division as GAF 155)

Salas Larrazabál, J. *La Guerra de España desde el Aire* Barcelona: Ediciones Ariel 1972 (1st edn 1970)

Sanchís, M. *Alas Rojas sobre España* Madrid 1956-57

Schliephake, H. The Birth of the Luftwaffe London: Ian Allan 1971

Schwabedissen, Generalleutnant a.**D.W.** The Russian Air Force in the Eyes of German Commanders New York: Arno Press 1968 (prepared by the USAF Historical Division as GAF 175)

Shores, C. & Ward, R. The Finnish Air Force, 1918-1968 Canterbury U.K.: Osprey Publications Ltd. undated

Stewart, Col. **J.F.** Airpower, the Decisive Force in Korea Princeton U.S.A.: Van Nostrand 1957

Stockwell, R.E. Soviet Air Power New York: Pageant Press 1956

Stroud, J. The Red Air Force London: The Pilot Press 1943

Taylor, J.W.R. ABC Russian Aircraft London: Ian Allan 1960 (1st edn 1958)

Titz, Z. The Czechoslovakian Air Force, 1918-1970 Canterbury U.K.: Osprey Publications Ltd. 1971

Trevor-Roper, H.R. (ed) Hitler's War Directives, 1939-1945 London: Sidgwick & Jackson 1964 (originally as *Hitlers Weisungen für die Kriegführung 1939-45* Frankfurt/M: Bernard und Graefe Verlag)

Uebe, Generalleutnant a.D. **K.** Russian Reactions to German Airpower in World War II New York: Arno Press 1968 (prepared by the USAF Historical Division as GAF 176)

SECTION C: SOVIET WRITINGS ON THE THEORY OF AIR POWER 1925-1940

Algazin, A.S. *Obespechenie vozdushnykh operatsi* (The Support of Air Operations) Moscow: Gosizdat 1928

Algazin, A.S. *Taktika bombardirovochnoi aviatsii* (The Tactics of Bomber Aviation) Moscow 1934

Algazin, A.S. *Aviatsiya v sovremennoi voine* (Aviation in Modern Warfare) Moscow 1935

Khripin, V.V. *Voprosy strategii i taktiki Krasnovo vozdushnovo flota* (Questions of Red Air Fleet Strategy & Tactics) in 'Vestnik Vozdushnovo flota' Nos 8 & 10 Moscow 1925

Khripin, V.V. *O gospodstve v vozdukhe* (On Mastery in the Air) Moscow 1935

Khripin, V.V. & Tatarchenko, E.I. *Vozdushnaya voina* (Air Warfare) in 'Vestnik Vozdushnovo flota' No. 4 Moscow 1934

Lapchinski, A.N. *Taktika aviatsii* (Tactics of Aviation) Moscow 1926 (with revised editions in 1928 and 1931)

Lapchinski, A.N. *Krasny Vozdushny flot 1918-1928* (The Red Air Fleet 1918-1928) Moscow 1928

Lapchinski, A.N. *Tekhnika i taktika vozdushnovo flota* (Equipment & Tactics of the Air Fleet) Moscow: Gosvoenizdat 1930

Lapchinski, A.N. *Vozdushnye sily v boyu i operatsii* (Air Forces in Combat & Operations) Moscow: Gosvoenizdat 1932

Lapchinski, A.N. *Vozdushny boi* (Air Combat) Moscow 1934

Lapchinski, A.N. *Bombardirovochnaya aviatsiya* (Bomber Aviation) Moscow 1937

Lapchinski, A.N. *Vozdushnaya razvedka* (Air Reconnaissance) Moscow 1938

Lapchinski, A.N. *Vozdushnaya armiya* (The Air Army) Moscow: Voenizdat 1939

Sergeev, A.K. *Strategiya i taktika Krasnovo Vozdushnovo flota* (Strategy & Tactics of the Red Air Fleet) Moscow 1925

Tatarchenko, E.I. *Vozdushny flot Ameriki (SShA)* (The Air Fleet of America (USA)) Moscow 1923

Tatarchenko, E.I. *Vozdushny flot Britanskoi imperii* (The Air Fleet of the British Empire) Moscow 1923

Tatarchenko, E.I. *Vozdushnaya voina v osveshchenii inostrannoi literatury* (Foreign Literature Devoted to Air Warfare) Moscow 1933

Teplinski, B.L. *Vozdushnoe nablyudenie* (Air Observation) Moscow 1931

Teplinski, B.L. *Osnovy obshchei taktiki voenno-vozdushnykh sil* (Bases of General Air Force Tactics) Moscow: Gosvoenizdat 1940

Teplinski, B.L. *Aviatsiya v boyu nazemnykh voisk* (Aviation in Ground Warfare) Moscow: Voenizdat 1940

Index of Names

N.B. n after page number indicates footnote reference only

Agal'tsov, Air Marshal, F.A., 76n, 78, 80-81, 182, 218, 224, 233n
Alksnis, General Ya. I., 12, 20, 23, 25, 34-37, 56n, 57-58, 63, 68, 75, 81, 88, 141
Akashev, K.V., 2, 5
Andreev, N.P., 80
Anisimov, A.F., 63
Antonov, O.K., 15-16, 197n, 222, 226, 229, 235
Antoshkin, General I.D. 173, 180
Arkhangel'ski, A.A. (aircraft designer), 5, 40, 45, 51, 53n, 62, 103
Arkhangel'ski, General P.P. (Commander 1V Bomber Corps), 81
Artseulov, K.K., 15
Arzhenukhin, F.K., 76n, 78, 80
Aschenbrenner, Colonel Heinrich, 104 etc
Astakhov, Air Marshal F.A., 72n, 89n, 122, 136, 157, 217

Baade, Brunolf, 206, 209
Baidukov, General G.F., 65n, 67, 217, 218n
Bakhchivandzhi, G. Ya., 87n, 202
Baranov, P.I., 12, 19, 23, 28, 35-37, 41, 58
Bartini, Roberto, 29n, 41, 49n, 53, 99
Barzhanov, N.N., 100
Bashko, Colonel I.S., 4n
Batitski, Marshal P.F., 220
Baumbach, Werner, 104
Belaikin, 101
Beletski, General Ye. M., 142, 143, 156, 162n
Belyakov, General A.V., 65n
Bergol'ts, A.I., 76
Bergstrem, V.K., *See* Plates

Beria, L.P., 103, 105, 133
Beriev, G.M., 29, 40
Beryozkin, M.F., 89n
Betz, Adolph, 206
Biryuzov, Marshal S.S., 220-221
Blagoveshchenski, General A.S., 142, 176
Blukher, Marshal V.K., 37n, 80, 83
Bock, Günther, 206
Bolkhovitinov, V.F., 67
Borman, General A.V., 89n, 165
Borovkov, A.A., 50n
Borovykh, General A.Ye., 233
Borzov, Air Marshal I.I., 225, 234n
Brandner, Ferdinand, 222
Bratukhin, I.P., 42, 100, 210, 226n
Budyonny, Marshal S.M., 37n, 119
Bukharin, N.I., 19n
Buob, I.A., 4
Butelin, Lt L.D., 117

Charomski, A.D., 66n
Cheranovski, B.I., 15-16, 45
Cheremukhin, A.M., 42n, 99-100
Chernobrovkin, S.A., 89n
Chernykh, General S., 77
Chernyshev, V.N., 40, 45
Chetverikov, I.V., 29, 40
Chizhevski, V.A., 66, 100
Chkalov, V.P., 45-48, 63, 65, 67, 100, 101n
Churchill, Sir Winston, 167

Danilin, General S.A., 65n, 121, 143
Danilov, General S.P., 176
Deich, Max, 94
Dement'ev, P.V., 104, 187n, 196n, 227
Demid, F.F., 207
Demidov, General A.A., 132

254

Denikin, General A.I., 4
Denisov, General S.P. (fighter commander), 83
Denisov, V.S. (aircraft engineer), 33
Dessloch, General Otto, 24, 173
Douhet, General Giulio, 57
Doronin, I.V., 61n
Dushkin, L.S., 201, 207

Eideman, R.P., 88, 94

Falaleev, Air Marshal F.Ya., 72n, 120, 122, 141, 182, 217
Fiebig, General Martin, 24, 161n
Filin, A.I., 68, 100, 102
Florov, I.F., 50n
Förster, General Helmut, 113
Franco, General Francisco, 74
Frunze, M.V., 3n, 18-20

Gallai, M.L., 207, 215, 216n
Galunov, General D.P., 175
Gamarnik, Ya.B., 83n
Gastello, Capt N.F., 118
Georgiev, Colonel I.V., 136
Giral y Pereira, José, 74
Glazunov, General V.A., 136-137
Glushko, V.P., 201, 207
Golovanov, Chief Air Marshal A.Ye., 70-73, 159, 164, 182, 215, 217, 222
Golovnya, General M.M., 89n
Gol'tsman, A.A., 37n, 52
Gorbatsevich, General L.A., 71
Gorbatyuk, General Ye.M., *See* Diagrams
Gorbunov, S.P., 25, 27, 37n
Göring, Reichsmarshall Hermann, 77, 104, 110, 161
Gorlachenko, General M.I., 81
Goryunov, General S.K., 164, 173, 179
Govorov, Marshal L.A., 220
Gribovski, V.K., 15-16
Greim, Field-Marshal Robert von, 113, 171, 177
Grendal, General D.D., *See* Diagrams
Grigorovich, D.P., 28-31, 33, 34n, 40, 44, 56n
Grinchik, A.N., 210
Gritsevets, S.I., 13n, 77n, 87
Grizodubova, V.S., 66n
Grokhovski, P.I., 60
Gromadin, General M.S., 128, 171n
Gromov, General M.M., 14, 26, 45n, 51, 55-56, 60-61, 64-65, 67-68

Grushin, P.D., 45
Guderian, General Heinz, 124, 127
Gudkov, M.I., 197
Günther, Siegfried, 206
Gurevich, M.I., 29, 43
Gusev, General A.I., 77n, 86, 103
Gvozdkov, General G.K., *See* Diagrams

Hartmann, Maj Erich, 123
Heinkel, Ernst, 20, 29, 34, 49n
Hidalgo de Cisneros, General, 76
Hitler, Adolf, 24-25, 74-75, 104-105, 108, 122, 127, 155, 166, 170, 177, 183
Hoth, General Hermann, 170

Il'yushin, S.V., 8, 10-11, 15, 34, 39, 40, 43, 49n, 66-67, 102-103, 191, 193-194, 196, 199, 208, 211, 215, 219, 222, 235
Ingaunis, F.A., 23, 89
Ionov, General A.P., 114
Itskovich, Z.I., 53
Ivanov, Lt I.I. (fighter pilot, Hero of the Soviet Union), 117
Ivanov, M.I. (test-pilot), 210
Ivchenko, A.G., 222
Isacco, Vittorio, 29n
Izakson, A.M., 42, 100

Jeschonnek, General Hans, 161n, 171
Junkers, Prof Hugo, 9-10, 18, 25-26, 55

Kaganovich, Lazar M. (Politburo Member), 103n
Kaganovich, Mikhail M. (Commisar for Aircraft Production), 41, 83, 101, 103
Kalinin, K.A. (aircraft designer), 15, 53n, 62
Kalinin, M.I. (Chairman, Central Executive Committee of the USSR), 14
Kamanin, General N.P., 11, 61n
Kamenev, S.S., 14
Kamov, N.I., 16, 29, 42, 100, 225, 235
Karavitski, General A.Z., 173
Karmanov, A.G., 113n
Keller, General Alfred, 109
Kempf, General, 170
Kesselring, Field-Marshal Albert, 109
Khalshchevnikov, 201
Kharitonov, S.N., 117
Kharlamov, N.M., 99
Khlobystov, A.S., 117
Khol'zunov, S.G., 77n

255

Khorkov, S.G., 11
Khripin, V.V., 57-58, 89
Khrunichev, M.V., 187n, 217, 227
Khrushchov, N.S., 103n, 218-220, 223
Khrustalev, P.A., 23
Khryukin, General T.T., 81, 121, 157, 176, 179, 181-182
Khudyakov, Air Marshal S.A., 11, 72n, 140-141, 173, 175-176, 183, 217
Kirsanov, General P.S., *See* Diagrams
Kleimenov, I.T., 100
Kleist, Field-Marshal Ewald von, 158
Klimov, General I.D. (PVO fighter commander), 128-129, 171n, 175
Klimov, V. Ya. (aeroengine designer), 39, 151, 192, 199-201, 214
Klimovskikh, General V. Ye., 114
Kluge, Field-Marshal Günther von, 169
Kobzan, B.I., 117
Kocherigin, S.A., 40-41, 43
Kochetkov, A.G., 167, 207
Kokkinaki, V.K., 67
Kokorev, D.V., 117
Kolchak, Admiral A.V., 4
Kol'tsov, M. Ye., 61n
Kondratyuk, General D.F., *See* Diagrams
Konev, Marshal I.S., 131, 173
Kopets, General I.I., 76, 79-80, 114
Korf, S.Ya., 23
Kork, General A.I., 88
Korolyov, S.P. (aircraft and rocket engine designer), 15, 29, 100, 201-202, 207
Korolyov (Commisar for Aircraft Production), 41
Korvin, V.L., 31
Kosarev, A.V., 16-17
Kostkin, I.M., 31, 34, 100
Kosygin, A.N., 187
Kosykh, General M.M., 174
Kozlov, I.F., (aeroengine designer), 209n
Kozlov, S.G., (aircraft designer), 62
Krasovski, Air Marshal S.A., 158, 172-173, 179, 181-182
Kravchenko, General G.P., 85, 87, 91, 134
Kubyshkin, A.G., 207
Kudrin, B.N., 202
Kupfer, M.A., 235
Kulev, 53n

Kurchevski, L.V., 43
Kushakov, V.A., 89
Kutakhov, Chief Air Marshal P.S., 231
Kuznetsov, A.I. (Deputy Commissar for Aircraft Production), 187n
Kuznetsov, N.D. (aeroengine designer), 222
Kuznetsov, V.A. (rotating-wing aircraft designer), 42
Kuznetsov, V.P. (Deputy Commissar for Aircraft Production), 104, 187n

Langemak, G.Ye., 100
Lapchinski, A.N., 57n
Lapin', A.Ya., 56, 83-84, 89n
Laville, André, 29n
Lavochkin, S.A., 29, 45, 135n, 192-193, 196-198, 200-201, 207, 209-210, 212-213, 217n, 220
Lavrov, V.K., 89n
Leeb, Field-Marshal Wilhelm von, 112
Lelyushenko, General D.D., 132
Lemeshko, General P.N., 183
Lenin, V.I., 2, 6, 18
Levanevski, S.A., 61n, 65, 67
Levashov, General A.F., 136-137
Litvyak, Lidiya, 165n
Loginov, General V.S. (Chief Rear Services, Main Air Staff), *See* Diagrams
Loginov, Air Marshal Ye.F., 218n
Löhr, General Alexander, 110
Loktionov, General A.D., 58n, 80, 82, 89, 90n, 97, 101
Lopatin, V.N., 89
Lörzer, General Bruno, 112
Lyapidevski, General A.V., 61n
Lyul'ka, A.M., 209n
Lyushin, S.N., 45

Mamontov, General K.K., 12
Manstein, Field-Marshal Erich von, 161, 169, 173
Margelov, General V.F., 226
Markov, General I.V., 71n, 217
Mayakovski, Vladimir, 14
Meister, General Rudolf, 178
Mekhonshin, K.A., 15
Menzhinski, V.R., 33
Merkulov, I.A., 201
Mezhenikov, S.A., 23, 58
Mezheraup, P. Kh., 14, 23

Michugin, General F.G., 114, 123n
Mikheev, I.V., 62
Mikoyan, Artyom I. (aircraft designer), 11, 199, 207, 220, 228, 232, 235
Mikoyan, Anastas I. (Politburo member & Head Industrial Evacuation Resettlement Council), 190, 200, 209, 212
Mikulin, A.A., 10, 39, 191, 199-201
Mil', M.L., 229, 235
Milch, Field-Marshal Erhard, 104, 110, 163
Minder, K., 51
Mironenko, General A.A., 234
Mishuk, General M.N., 231
Mitenkov, General A.I., 130
Model, Field-Marshal Walther, 170, 176
Moiseev, Ya.N., 14
Molokov, General V.S., 61n, 122, 136
Molotov, V.M., 101
Moroz, General I.M., 231
Mosolov, G.K., 156
Mussolini, Benito, 29n, 74-75
Myasishchev, V.M., 71n, 99, 196, 199, 215, 223

Nadashkevich, A.V., 33-34
Naumenko, General N.F., 120, 123, 140, 157n, 164, 176
Nedelin, Marshal M.I., 223
Neman, I.G., 53, 99
Nikashin, A.I., 197
Nikitin, General A.V. (Chief Formations Directorate, Main Air Staff), 141-142
Nikitin, V.V. (aircraft designer), 50n
Nikolaenko, General Ye. M., 123
Nobile, General Umberto, 29n
Novikov, Chief Air Marshal A.A., 72, 116, 120, 140-141, 159, 161-162, 165, 173, 175, 209, 216-217, 222
Novozhilov, G.V., 235
Nyukhtikov, M.A., 56, 67

Okromeshko, N.V., 31
Opadchi, F.F., 150n
Ordzhonikidze, G.K. (Sergo), 34-35, 41n, 44, 51
Osipenko, Polina, 66n, 80n
Ostryakov, General N.A., 156n
Ozerov, G.A., 99, 188
Pakilev, General N.F., 181-182

Paufler, 33
Paulus, Field-Marshal Friedrich von, 164
Pavlov, General D.G. (Commander, Western Military District), 114
Pavlov, I.U. (Military District Air Commander), 23
Perminov, General N.V., 71n
Pervukhin, M.G., 187
Petlyakov, V.M., 40, 60, 68, 71n, 99, 103, 196
Petrov, 37n
Petrov, General I.F., 83, 99, 103, 119, 124, 140
Pflugbeil, General Kurt, 24, 122, 157
Piontkovski, Yu. I., 41, 67
Pirogov, P., 210n
Plocher, General Hermann, 24
Podgorny, General I.D., 173
Pogosski, I.I., 40
Pogrebov, General B.A., 123
Pokryshkin, Air Marshal A.I., 113, 167
Polbin, General I.S., 13n, 143, 151, 158, 173
Polikarpov, N.N., 8, 15, 21, 27-33, 34n, 40-42, 45-50, 56n, 67, 101, 103, 196-197, 199-200, 203
Polynin, General F.P., 124, 132, 181-182, 195n
Pomerantsev, General Z.M., 12, 89n
Potez, Henri, 36
Powers, Gary, 221
Preobrazhenski, General Ye. N., 70, 225
Primakov, General V.M., 88
Proskurov, General I.I., 77n
Ptukhin, General Ye. S., 76n, 78-81, 114, 120
Pukhov, General P.I., 174
Pumpur, General P.I., 76n, 77, 85n, 91
Putilov, A.I., 53, 99
Putna, General V.K., 88

Rafaelyants, A.N., 53n
Raskova, Marina, 13n, 66n, 165n
Rastorguev, V.L., 207
Rental, Rudolph, 206
Repin, General A.K., 141, 217
Reshetnikov, General V.V., 233
Richard, Paul Aimé, 29
Richthofen, Field-Marshal Wolfram Freiherr von, 24, 155-156, 159, 161, 163, 173, 178

Rohrbach, Adolf, 29n
Rokossovski, Marshal K.K., 170
Roosevelt, President Franklin, 167
Rössler, Rudolph, 170n
Rotenburg, A.G., 101
Rowehl, Colonel Theodor, 104-105
Rozengol'ts, A.P., 6, 18-19
Rudel, Colonel Hans-Ulrich, 177
Rudenko, Air Marshal S.I., 11-12, 89n, 140, 143, 158, 160, 172-174, 176, 181-182, 218, 222
Ryabushinski, 5
Ryazanov, General V.G., 142, 173
Rybal'chenko, General S.D., 179
Rybkin, General L.G., 81
Rybko, N.S., 215
Rytov, General A.G., 231

Safonov, B.F., 116
Samokhin, General M.I., 180
Saukke, B.A., 62n
Savitski, Air Marshal Ye. Ya., 143, 164, 220
Sbytov, General N.A., 132-133, 210
Semyonov, General I.S., 169n
Senatorov, General A.S., 77n, 79, 81, 183
Sergeev, A.V., 3-5, 6n
Serov, A.K., 77n, 79, 80, 82
Shakht, Ye. G., 77
Shakhurin, A.I., 103-104, 187-188, 190-191, 194, 197, 200, 208-209, 217, 227
Shavrov, V.B., 16, 29
Shcherbakov, A.S., 111
Shelukhin, General P.S., 114, 122
Shenkman, B., 190
Shestakov, S.A., 14, 26-27
Shevchenko, P.S. (aeroengine designer), 209n
Shevchenko, General V.I. (Commander I Composite Air Corps), 143
Shevchenko, V.V. (aircraft designer), 50, 82
Shevelev, General M.I., 71n, 169n
Shimanov, General N.S., 41
Shiyanov, G.M., 207
Shpanov, N., 111n
Shtern, General G.M., 76, 85
Shul'zhenko, M.N., 99, 102
Shvernik, N.M., 190
Shvetsov, A.D., 10, 31, 39, 101, 198-201, 212

Sikorski, I.I., 3-4, 27
Silant'ev, Air Marshal A.P., 231
Sinyakov, General S.P., 89n
Skripko, Air Marshal N.S., 12, 72n, 164, 226
Skrzhinski, N.K., 29, 42
Slepnev, M.T., 61n
Slyusarev, General S.V., 179
Smirnov, General K.N., 172
Smushkevich, General Ya. V., 12, 76n, 77, 79-80, 82, 86-87, 89-90, 99, 102
Sobolevski, O., 79
Sokolov, General I.M., 180, 183
Solov'yov, P.A., 223
Stahr, Major, 24
Stalin, I.V., 17-18, 23, 31, 33-34, 41, 43-44, 46, 49, 51, 55-57, 65, 67-70, 73-74, 81, 83, 89, 91, 94, 99, 101, 103, 105, 109, 119, 124, 129, 131-132, 134-135, 137, 140, 142, 157, 170-171, 177, 183, 187, 190, 194, 196n, 197, 200, 202n, 205, 209-210, 212n, 215, 217-218, 220-222
Stalin, General V.I., 13n, 210, 217
Stechkin, B.S., 38, 99
Stefanovski, P.M., 47, 56, 83, 118n, 130
Stepanchonok, V.A., 15
Stepanov, General P.S., 119, 133n, 140, 158
Sterligov, General B.V., 23, 141
Sudets, Air Marshal V.A., 12, 142, 172, 179, 217, 220, 222
Sukhoi, P.O., 21, 30, 40-41, 44, 47, 64, 66-67, 99, 196-197, 199, 201-202, 208-210, 212, 215, 219, 221, 235
Suprun, S.P., 47, 83, 85, 89n, 118n
Suzi, T., 44
Sveshnikov, General B.F., 78, 81

Talalikhin, Lt V.V., 130
Tank, Prof Kurt, 206n
Tarkhov, S.F., 76
Tayurski, General A.I., 123n
Tevosyan, I.F., 103-104
Tikhonravov, M.K., 203
Timoshenko, Marshal S.K., 91, 111, 115, 119, 131, 157
Tishchenko, M.N., 235
Todorski, General A.I., 89
Tokarev, General B.K., 183
Tomashevich, D.L., 101, 195
Tret'yakov, A.T., 190

Trifonov, Colonel D.M. (Commander 1st GKO Air Reserve Group), 133, 140
Trifonov, Colonel K.N. (Commander Southern Sector Moscow Air Defence Zone), 130
Trotski, Leon D., 3, 13-14, 18-19, 25, 229
Troyanker, B.U., 23, 89
Tsander, F.A., 16
Tsybin, P.V., 209
Tukhachevski, Marshal M.N., 4, 19n, 20, 25, 36-37, 43-44, 57-58, 88, 100
Tumanski, S.K., 39, 101, 192, 228
Tupolev, A.N., 5, 15, 26, 28, 30, 33-34, 38, 40-44, 51, 53n, 55, 60, 62, 64, 67-68, 71n, 99, 103, 192, 196-197, 199, 211, 215-216, 222-223, 233, 235
Turkel', General I.L., 141
Turzhanski, General A.A., 78, 89n

Uborevich, General I.P., 88
Udet, General Ernst, 104
Unshlikht, I.S., 16, 20, 52
Ushakov, General S.F. (Deputy Chief of Air Staff), 231
Ushakov, General V.A. (Commander II Bomber Corps), 164
Uvarov, 89

Vakhmistrov, V.S., 45n, 62-64
Vasil'chenko, A.G., 215
Vatutin, General N.F., 170
Velling, B.K., 14
Vershinin, Chief Air Marshal K.A., 11-12, 122, 157, 164, 173, 179, 181, 216-218, 224, 231n
Vetchinkin, V.P., 5
Vitruk, Colonel A.N., 134
Vodop'yanov, M.V., 61n, 70n
Voronin, P.A., 187n
Voroshilov, Marshal K. Ye., 3n, 37, 44, 57, 64, 82, 88, 91, 98, 101, 119
Vorozheikin, Air Marshal G.A., 72n, 124, 140-141, 173
Vrangel, General P.N., 4

Wocke, Hans, 209

Yakir, General I. Ye., 58, 88
Yakovlev, A.S., 11, 15-16, 21, 41, 99, 103, 119, 135n, 187n, 189, 193, 195-198, 201, 208-209, 212-213, 234-235
Yakushin, General M.N., 79, 80n, 81, 130
Yefimov, Air Marshal A.N., 231
Yegorov, Marshal A.I., 37n, 56n
Yeremenko, General A.I. (Commander Bryansk Front), 124
Yeremenko, I.T. (Commander of Soviet fighter group in Spain), 77n, 79
Yeremenko, General N.T. (Commander II Composite Air Corps), 165
Yerlykin, General Ye. Ye., 175
Yermachenkov, General V.V., 156
Yermolaev, V.G., 53, 67n
Yevseev, 79
Yudenich, General N.E., 4
Yumashev, General A.B., 15, 55-56, 65n, 128, 173, 175
Yur'ev, B.N., 5

Zashikhin, General G.S., 171n
Zarzar, V.A., 37n
Zavitaev, A.A., 187n, 199
Zdorovtsev, Lt S.I., 117
Zeisse, Wolfgang, 208
Zharov, General F.I., 141
Zhavoronkov, Air Marshal S.F., 70, 72n, 91, 93, 217, 218n
Zhdanov, General V.N., 159, 181
Zhemchuzhin, N.A., 101
Zhigarev, Chief Air Marshal P.F., 11, 85, 89n, 90, 119-120, 124, 132, 134, 140, 183, 217-218, 220, 222, 224
Zhukov, Marshal G.K., 86, 140, 173, 176, 196
Zhukov, Lt M.P., 117
Zhukovski, N. Ye., 5, 9, 11
Zhuravlev, General I.P. (Commander 14th Air Army), 179
Zhuravlev, General N.A. (Chief Operations Section, Main Air Staff), 141, 146
Zlatotsvetov, General A. Ye., 81